NEWCOMER'S
HANDBOOK®

FOR MOVING TO AND LIVING IN

Atlanta

Including Fulton, DeKalb, Cobb,
Gwinnett, and Cherokee Counties

3rd Edition

6750 SW Franklin
Portland, OR 97223
503-968-6777
www.firstbooks.com

Author: Shawne Taylor
Contributor: Wendy Dunham
Series Editor: Bernadette Duperron
Proofreader: Linda Weinerman
Publisher: Jeremy Solomon
Cover and Interior design, composition: Erin Johnson Design
Maps Jim Miller/fennana design
MARTA transit map reproduced with the permission of the Metropolitan Atlanta Rapid Transit Authority.

Published by Firstbooks.com, Inc., 6750 SW Franklin Street, Portland, OR 97223-2542, 503-968-6777, www.firstbooks.com.

ISBN-13: 978-0-912301-61-7
ISBN-10: 0-912301-61-9

Printed in the USA on recycled paper.

What readers are saying about Newcomer's Handbooks:

I recently got a copy of your Newcomer's Handbook for Chicago, and wanted to let you know how invaluable it was for my move. I must have consulted it a dozen times a day preparing for my move. It helped me find my way around town, find a place to live, and so many other things. Thanks.
—Mike L.
Chicago, Illinois

Excellent reading (Newcomer's Handbook for San Francisco and the Bay Area) ... balanced and trustworthy. One of the very best guides if you are considering moving/relocation. Way above the usual tourist crap.
—Gunnar E.
Stockholm, Sweden

I was very impressed with the latest edition of the Newcomer's Handbook for Los Angeles. It is well organized, concise and up-to-date. I would recommend this book to anyone considering a move to Los Angeles.
—Jannette L.
Attorney Recruiting Administrator for a large Los Angeles law firm

I recently moved to Atlanta from San Francisco, and LOVE the Newcomer's Handbook for Atlanta. It has been an invaluable resource — it's helped me find everything from a neighborhood in which to live to the local hardware store. I look something up in it everyday, and know I will continue to use it to find things long after I'm no longer a newcomer. And if I ever decide to move again, your book will be the first thing I buy for my next destination.
—Courtney R.
Atlanta, Georgia

In looking to move to the Boston area, a potential employer in that area gave me a copy of the Newcomer's Handbook for Boston. It's a great book that's very comprehensive, outlining good and bad points about each neighborhood in the Boston area. Very helpful in helping me decide where to move.
—no name given (online submit form)

TABLE OF CONTENTS

CONTENTS

CONTENTS

WELCOME TO ATLANTA, A CITY THAT COMBINES DOWNHOME southern charm and cosmopolitan ambiance. A city proud of its past even as it looks to the future. It's the birthplace of the Reverend Martin Luther King, Jr., Coca-Cola, and CNN. It's home to championship sports teams, four-star restaurants, and one of the world's busiest airports. It's also home to over a dozen Fortune 500 companies, including Home Depot, Delta Airlines, and United Parcel Service. In business circles, Atlanta has long been recognized as the commercial capital of the South, and today is considered an entrepreneurial hot spot, perhaps due in part to a large and diverse labor pool, numerous colleges and universities, and business-friendly local and state governments. In the booming economy of the 1990s, Atlanta was a job magnet, and an average of almost 55,000 new jobs was added each year according to the Atlanta Regional Commission. Today, job growth has slowed in Atlanta, as it has throughout the rest of the country, but the local economy continues to hold steady.

Because of the city's rapid development and its commercial appeal, Atlanta attracts a multitude of newcomers. There's a running joke here that no one in Atlanta is actually from Atlanta—they've all moved here from other parts of the country. Of course this is not true, but it can feel that way. Maybe that's why you will find that Atlanta is a city friendly to fresh inhabitants.

Culturally, Atlanta boasts a flourishing arts scene, with a world-renowned symphony orchestra, a diverse and ever-growing local music industry, scores of museums and art galleries, and a wide array of theatrical productions. Among its other attributes: climate—temperate winters and sultry summers that allow residents to play outside year-round—and beauty. Both intown and suburban neighborhoods throughout metro Atlanta are covered in rolling hills and so many trees that, from overhead, the city seems to be cloaked in a dense forest. In the spring, as the dogwoods blossom and magnolias bloom, it's sometimes easy to forget you're in the middle of a bustling metropolis.

For all these reasons and more, Atlanta is a city bursting with growth and promise . . . that's probably why you moved here. And, if you're like most newcomers to the city, you will soon find yourself charmed by the easygoing lifestyle, that southern amiability mixed with a thriving international sensibility. You'll find big city culture and small town congeniality here.

This book is designed to guide you through your first exciting and perhaps disquieting weeks as a newcomer to Atlanta. It offers you a survey of neighborhoods, tips on how to settle in, suggestions for rest and relaxation as well as cultural outings, and other hints to help you acclimate to your new surroundings. The book covers not only Atlanta proper, but also nearby communities frequently populated by newcomers. According to the latest census estimates, the City of Atlanta is home to some 425,000 people, while the population of the entire metro Atlanta area is a whopping 4.7 million. Recent growth has centered primarily in northern counties of the metro area, though there has also been a resurgence of families and young professionals moving into and revitalizing the more urban, intown neighborhoods surrounding downtown.

Today's Atlanta metropolitan area encompasses over six thousand square miles, and even if you live right in the center of things, you will almost certainly need a car to get to where you want to go. The city streets are not especially friendly to bicycle or pedestrian traffic. And though it is becoming easier to get around the metro area using public transportation, the buses and trains still only service Fulton and DeKalb counties, so you will most likely find yourself longing for a car sooner or later. Unfortunately, even if you have a car, you'll find there's really no handy system for navigating Atlanta's city streets. If there is any logic to the arrangement of the city's roads, it has escaped even the most brilliant of minds! Due to the area's irregular terrain, many roads are winding, and some have two or more names. Piedmont Park blocks out a large portion of the Midtown area; therefore, few roads go east-west straight through the city. And then there is the "Peachtree" problem (see below). There is no doubt that you will get lost at least a few times, but don't despair. Keep a good map in your car, don't be afraid to stop for directions, and perhaps most importantly, ask friends to share their secret shortcuts; they can save you time and traffic headaches.

Here are a few additional **tips for finding your way around**:
- I-285 makes a loop around the perimeter of the city. If someone says that a place is located "outside the perimeter," what they mean is that you must travel beyond I-285 to find it.

- Although over fifty streets contain the word "Peachtree," only one of them is the main thoroughfare. It begins downtown as Peachtree Street and changes to Peachtree Road in the Midtown area. In the heart of Buckhead, Peachtree Road forks: The east side of the fork is Peachtree Road, which travels northeast towards Gwinnett County and eventually becomes Peachtree Industrial Boulevard north of the perimeter, and the west side of the fork is Roswell Road, which goes mostly north toward Sandy Springs and Roswell.
- Atlanta is divided roughly into four quadrants. Peachtree Street is the east-west dividing line and the north-south dividing line is Martin Luther King Jr. Drive, on the southern edge of downtown. Therefore, if NW follows an address, this means that your destination is somewhere downtown or north of the downtown area and west of Peachtree.
- Get to know the highways. These are the only major roads that connect county to county. Often, a merchant will name a highway exit number when giving you directions. For details about Atlanta area highways, see the **Transportation** chapter of this book.
- Remember the locations of malls. These are major landmarks in the city, and often people give directions based on a locale's proximity to the nearest mall.
- Don't assume that just because two streets run parallel to each other, they will stay that way. For example, Peachtree Street and Piedmont Road, the two major north-south routes, intersect in north Buckhead. Oxford Road crosses Briarcliff twice, effectively paralleling itself.
- Remember that Atlanta streets wind unpredictably. Even if you are convinced that the route you are taking leads you in a straight line, you may not end up where you think you should. Keep your sense of humor. Atlanta is a lovely city to get lost in.
- A detailed Atlanta street map is a must. Both **A Map & Graphics Company**, 2789 Veterans Memorial Hwy., Austell, 678-213-1134, www.amaps.com, and **Bradford Map Company**, 300 Hammond Drive, Sandy Springs, 404-843-9610 or 1873 Lawrenceville Highway, Decatur, 404-633-7562, www.bradfordmap.com, sell a full line of city, state, and regional map books. You can also pick up Atlanta maps at local bookstores like Barnes & Noble or Borders, or at any of the Office Max, Staples, or Office Depot locations, though they may not offer as wide a selection as the specialty map stores. You can also log onto the web and order an Atlanta street map from **First Books**, www.firstbooks.com.

LOCAL LINGO

In addition to traffic tips, you may also want to investigate, and perhaps memorize, some of the local slang to help you make your way around the city. While Atlanta's local lingo isn't terribly colorful, it is laced with highway and traffic nicknames, area landmarks and, yes, the occasional slow southern drawl. Though deep southern accents are less common, and often less noticeable, inside the perimeter, it's certain that you will run into them from time to time. You may find this drawl quaint, amusing, or just plain difficult to understand at times. Whatever the case, Atlanta's local lingo can definitely sound like a language of its own.

A complete listing is near impossible, but here are a few landmarks, roadways, and pronunciations to get you started:

Agnes Scott: a liberal arts college for women, located in Decatur

The AJC: *Atlanta Journal-Constitution*, Atlanta's daily newspaper

Atlanta: usually pronounced "at-LAN-ah," dropping the last "t"

The Big Chicken: 50-foot tall steel chicken sign advertising a local Kentucky Fried Chicken; the most recognizable landmark in Cobb County

The Bravos: nickname of the Atlanta Braves

Brookwood Interchange: where I-75 and I-85 southbound join and, when going northbound on the Downtown Connector (see below), where the two highways split

Buckhead Loop: the road that arcs from Piedmont Road across GA 400 to Peachtree Road

CDC: Centers for Disease Control, located near Emory

Chamblee: pronounced "SHAM-blee"

Cobb Cloverleaf: I-75 and I-285 on the northwest side of the perimeter, in Cobb County

The Concrete Campus: Georgia State University

The Connector: same as the Downtown Connector

DeKalb: usually pronounced "Dee-CAB" or "Duh-CAB"

Downtown Connector: the stretch of highway at which I-75 and I-85 are combined, located between 10th Street/14th Street to the north and Langford Parkway to the south

The Dunwoody Family: Chamblee-Dunwoody, Peachtree-Dunwoody and Ashford-Dunwoody roads, collectively

East Expressway: I-20 from downtown through the east side of metro Atlanta

East-West Connector: connects Town Center Mall near Kennesaw to the Cumberland Mall area in southeast Cobb (not to be confused with The Connector or the East and West expressways)

Emory: usually pronounced "EM-ree;" can refer to the university or the hospital

Fayetteville: often pronounced "FATE-vul"

Forsyth: pronounced "Fer-SYTH," though you may also hear it pronounced "FER-syth"

Freedom Parkway: parkway running from the Downtown Connector to Ponce de Leon Avenue

Glenridge Connector: a short, highly traveled road that runs from Peachtree-Dunwoody to I-285 and then becomes Glenridge Drive

Grady Curve: the curve of the Downtown Connector as it circumvents downtown's central business district near Grady Hospital

GSU: Georgia State University

The Highlands: nickname for the Virginia Highland neighborhood

The Hooch: nickname of the Chattahoochee River, most often used in the phrase, "shooting the hooch," which means spending the day rafting down the Chattahoochee

Inner Loop: the inside lanes of I-285

The ITC: the International Theological Center

Jesus Junction: the intersection of Peachtree, East Wesley, and West Wesley roads in Buckhead, so named because of the four large churches located there

L5P: Little Five Points (see **Neighborhoods** chapter)

Lawrenceville: often pronounced "LORNTZ-vul"

The Loaf—*Creative Loafing*, Atlanta's weekly alternative newspaper

Marietta: though usually pronounced "Mary-ETTA," you may occasionally run into someone who likes to call it "MAY-retta"; home of the Big Chicken

Marietta Loop: unofficial name of the 120 Loop, the North Marietta and South Marietta Parkways that encircle the center of Marietta

McMansions: the oversized homes that seem to pop up overnight in some of the more affluent neighborhoods in metro Atlanta

Morehouse: refers to both Morehouse College and Morehouse School of Medicine

Northeast Expressway: I-85 from downtown through the northeast side of metro Atlanta

Outer Loop: the outside lanes of I-285

The Perimeter: the more commonly used name for I-285, the interstate that circles Atlanta

Pill Hill: the intersection of Johnson Ferry Road and the Glenridge Connector in Sandy Springs, so named for the sprawling medical complex located there

Roswell: often pronounced "RAHZ-wul"

SoBu: South Buckhead, an area of trendy clubs and restaurants (see **Neighborhoods** chapter)

Southern Crescent: the southern region of metro Atlanta, including Butts, Clayton, Coweta, Fayette, and Henry counties

SoVo: *Southern Voice*, Atlanta's gay/lesbian newspaper

Spaghetti Junction: the soaring tangle of over- and underpasses, on-ramps and exits of I-85 at I-285; one of Atlanta's best known and appropriately nicknamed landmarks

Spelman: liberal arts college for women, located in Atlanta

Stone Mountain Freeway: unofficial term for US 78

Sunshine Slowdown: the effect of sunlight in motorists' eyes as they travel east on I-20 in the morning and west on I-20 in the evening

Tech: more common nickname of the Georgia Institute of Technology

Top End: the northern segment of I-285 from I-75 to I-85, generally the most congested part of the Perimeter

UGA: University of Georgia at Athens

Uga: pronounced "UGH-ah"; the bulldog mascot of the University of Georgia

West Expressway: I-20 from downtown through the west side of metro Atlanta

Y'all: not limited to Atlanta, but used frequently here nonetheless; a more easygoing and southern way of saying "you" or "you all"

ATLANTA HISTORY

The land that is now Atlanta originally was the site of a Creek Indian settlement named "Standing Peachtree." The first white settlement in the area was established in 1813, when Lt. George Gilmer erected a fort here, on the banks of the Chattahoochee River, to control growing disagreements between the Creek and their Cherokee neighbors. At the time the fort was built, the area was nothing more than a small outpost on the western edge of America's frontier. It didn't actually become part of Georgia until the Creek ceded their land to the state in 1821, to avoid going to war with the white settlers. But even after the Creek nation left to resettle on lands west of the Mississippi, the Cherokees continued to live in the area alongside white settlers well into the 1830s. The relationship was tenuous, though, and in 1832, the State of Georgia began to take away Cherokee farms and distribute them to white settlers in a land lottery. Many of the settlers took control of the land at gunpoint, resulting in much bloodshed and death. The issue culminated in 1835, when a handful of Cherokee leaders, realizing the futility of further resistance, signed over the rest of their land under the Treaty of New Echota, an act that led to the infamous Trail of Tears. With treaty in hand, and President Andrew Jackson's Indian Removal Act signed into law, over 17,000 Cherokee were rounded up by federal soldiers, herded into camps, and then forced to march westward, 800 miles to Oklahoma, where they were resettled. At least 4,000 died on the journey, and those that survived suffered terribly from hunger, cold, and disease.

Throughout the 1830s, Fort Peachtree, as it had come to be called, became a thriving trading post. In fact, when the Georgia Legislature voted to establish a state-sponsored railroad system linking Georgia to the North and Midwest, this locale was considered as a possible location where the railroads could come together, though the numerous creeks and unsuitable gradients proved to be insurmountable. In 1837, after surveying half-a-dozen possible routes, railroad engineer Stephen Long chose the perfect location for the southern end of the new rail line. He staked out a point approximately eight miles south of the river, and marked it with a "zero-mile" marker on land that is now Five Points in Downtown Atlanta. A plaque in Underground Atlanta commemorates the location today, not far from the actual spot that Long chose.

Soon after the location was approved, railroad workers began settling into the area and a new town, Terminus, was established, which grew quickly to include banks, warehouses, sawmills, and more. The settlement attracted merchants, farmers, and craftsmen from as far away as Virginia and the Carolinas. Textile and ironworks industries soon followed.

In 1843 the name of the town was changed to Marthasville, in honor of Martha Lumpkin, daughter of former governor Wilson Lumpkin, a man who was instrumental in bringing the railroad to the area. Two years later, the town's name changed once more, this time to Atlanta. There are several theories of how this name came to be. One claims that Atlanta was chosen because it is the feminine version of the word Atlantic; the other is that it's a shortened version of the name Atlantica-Pacifica Railroad. Governor Lumpkin, however, maintained that it was yet another tribute to his daughter Martha, whose middle name happened to be Atalanta. Whatever the case, the town continued to grow and prosper, becoming incorporated as a city in 1847.

By 1860 Atlanta was the fourth largest city in the state and was home to nearly 10,000 people—a mix of white settlers and landowners, black slaves, and freed slaves. Additionally, the city boasted four rail lines, close to 3,000 homes, and numerous manufacturing and retail shops. At this time, the city was led primarily by merchants and railroad men who, for economic reasons, tended to oppose the idea of secession from the Union. In fact, in the election of 1860, most of Atlanta's voters cast their ballots for Union candidates. However, when Georgia finally seceded from the United States in January 1861, Atlanta joined with the Confederacy and quickly became a major manufacturing and transportation center for Confederate forces during the Civil War. Many industries in the city were converted to wartime production, and new industries were established to produce much-needed munitions and supplies for Confederate soldiers. The two largest were the Quartermasters Depot and the Confederate Government Arsenal, which employed nearly 8,000 men and women. Because of these wartime industries and the employment opportunities associated with them, Atlanta's population swelled to 22,000 in just three short years. Unfortunately, the same productivity and rail lines that made Atlanta a crucial part of the Confederacy also made the city the prime target of Union General William T. Sherman.

In the summer of 1864, Sherman and his troops began their drive to Atlanta. A series of bloody battles ensued, and the city faced nearly daily bombardment from Union cannons. Many civilians were killed, and many homes and businesses were destroyed. On September 1, 1864, after a 117-day siege, General Hood ordered the evacuation of Atlanta, and the mayor surrendered the city to Sherman the next day.

While the terms of the surrender promised the protection of Atlanta, Sherman had a change of heart, ordering all Confederate-related buildings destroyed. And though his instructions called for the buildings to first be leveled and then torched, eager Union soldiers failed to wait for the structures to come down before setting them ablaze. Subsequently, many Atlanta homes and businesses not marked for destruction were also consumed in the fire that swept through the city. As Sherman and his troops continued their march to the sea, Atlanta was left engulfed in flames. Of the 3,600 homes and commercial buildings in Atlanta, all but 400 were destroyed in the burning. The city was left broken and bankrupt.

By 1865, despite the widespread destruction and lack of funds in the city treasury, many of the citizens who had fled the city began to return and rebuild. A plan was developed to repair damaged railroad facilities, and by the fall of that year, all five of the city's rail lines were again operational. In 1866 Atlanta was made the headquarters for area reconstruction. But it was during the Reconstruction Convention of 1867-1868 that Atlanta truly began its climb to become the city it is today. During the convention, city officials offered to provide facilities for the state government if Atlanta should be chosen as state capital. The convention accepted the proposal and Atlanta became the capital of Georgia on April 20, 1868.

At the turn of the 20th century, Georgia's new capital was the largest city in the state and the third largest in the Southeast. It was also a clear leader of commercial development in the region. Both wholesale and retail trade were prospering, the city limits were expanded, and the skyline was altered by the addition of Atlanta's earliest skyscrapers—the Equitable, Flatiron, Empire, and Candler buildings. Additionally, the city's population had tripled in just three decades to 90,000, a number that included 35,000 African Americans who were drawn to the city for its numerous educational and employment opportunities.

Though many of Atlanta's new African-American residents were shuffled into undesirable, even flood-prone sections of the city, it was these segregated neighborhoods that became home to renowned African-

American colleges and universities, including the old Fourth Ward (where Morris Brown College was originally located), the south side of town (where Clark University was established), and the west side (where Atlanta University and, later, Morehouse and Spelman colleges were located). In spite of the city's racial barriers, the presence of these strong African-American colleges and accompanying communities, along with increasing economic opportunity, laid the groundwork for Atlanta's prosperous and influential African-American middle class.

Atlanta's early 20th century growth and expansion marked a turning point in how the city was viewed, both from within and without. Local leaders began to encourage not only commercial growth but cultural growth as well, in a bid to transform Atlanta into a city of national prominence. As a result, the High Museum of Art and the Atlanta Historical Society were founded. The Chamber of Commerce also launched a national ad campaign titled "Forward Atlanta," designed to lure new businesses to the city. By all accounts, the campaign was a huge success, bringing companies such as Sears-Roebuck and General Motors to the area, and creating thousands of new jobs.

At the same time, Atlanta's African American-owned businesses, operating along Auburn Avenue, were prospering as well. Banks, hotels, restaurants, beauty schools, retail shops, and more were thriving along the thoroughfare that had been dubbed "Sweet Auburn." And the success of these local businesses had far-reaching repercussions. As the African American-owned and -operated newspaper, *Atlanta Independent,* observed, "Auburn Avenue is an institution with influence and power not only among Georgians, but American Negroes everywhere. It is the heart of Negro big business, a result of Negro cooperation and evidence of Negro possibility." While Auburn Avenue was a point of pride for Atlanta's growing African-American community, it was also still a symbol of segregation, an issue that would plague and even define the city for many years to come.

In the early 1920s, downtown Atlanta, as well as the city's pattern of residential development, was affected by a new mode of transportation—the automobile. Viaducts were built to raise the city's streets above the railroad lines located in the heart of downtown. These viaducts moved the business district up, literally, creating the area now known as Underground Atlanta. The growing use of the automobile also led to the creation of new suburbs outside the city limits and a ring of middle-class communities located just two to five miles from downtown. These communities included Virginia Highland to the north, Candler Park to the east, West End to the south, and Washington Park—an African-American suburban development—to the west.

Another major development in transportation, the airplane, helped shape Atlanta at that time as well. The airplane first made its appearance here in the early part of the decade, but by 1930, thanks in large part to William B. Hartsfield, a man who would later become mayor of the city, Atlanta had established its own airfield and passenger terminal, as well as its own mail and passenger routes. This early connection to the growing airline industry is a key component in Atlanta's rise to the metropolitan city it is today.

The growth and prosperity that defined the city for decades came to a halt in the 1930s, during the Great Depression. Atlanta was poorly prepared to meet this financial emergency, and there were few agencies or programs in place to assist the rising number of unemployed. Relief for the city's poor and newly unemployed residents didn't come until after the inauguration of President Franklin D. Roosevelt, whose "New Deal" legislation provided much needed funds and resources to hard-hit areas throughout the country. Atlanta took full advantage of the opportunities offered through the "New Deal," and was, in fact, one of the first cities in the nation to have a federally operated relief program. Millions of dollars were pumped into the local economy through agencies such as the Civil Works Administration, the Public Works Administration, and the Works Progress Administration, money that went toward building and repairing local schools and hospitals, the grading of runways at the city's airport, the organization of a 45-member symphony orchestra, and the construction of a new city-wide sewer system. It was also "New Deal" funds that paid for the development and construction of the nation's first public housing projects, Techwood Homes, then a community for low-income white residents, which opened in 1936. University Homes, for African-American residents, opened in 1938. Both projects were the idea of Atlanta real estate developer, Charles F. Palmer, who wanted to rid the city of its slums and replace them with federally funded public housing.

As the 1930s came to a close, Atlanta's economy picked up. Banks were back in operation, the local aviation industry continued to grow, and there was an increase in private business. The beginning of World War II helped Atlanta's economic recovery. Between 1941 and 1945 over $10 million of federal funds were invested in war industries and military bases located in the South. Atlanta, in particular, benefited from the investment, as new federal installations were established throughout the metro area and war-related industries provided thousands of new jobs. Many local men and women enlisted in the armed forces or signed on to help with the war effort. Thousands more soldiers and military support personnel either passed through the city or were stationed nearby during that time. Local businesses did their part as well. Bell Bomber (later, Bell Aircraft, and then Lockheed-Georgia) in Marietta devoted its entire production output to the war effort. And Coca-Cola, which was created here in 1886, began distributing bottles of Coke to servicemen around the world, establishing itself as a truly international company.

The growth and progress that occurred during the war years continued well into the 1950s; by 1954, there were over 800 industries in the city and almost 1,200 national corporations with offices in the metro area. Atlanta city limits were expanded to include an additional 82 square miles and 100,000 new residents. And highway construction was already well under way. Unfortunately, even as the new highway system improved Atlanta's connection to the rest of the country, and fed the city's suburban growth, it did little to improve the lives of its local black population. Atlanta's highway construction displaced almost 67,000 black residents between 1956 and 1966, creating a severe housing shortage within the community. This racial disparity, combined with years of segregation, finally came to a head in the 1960s. The local civil rights movement, led by the young Atlanta minister, Martin Luther King, Jr., turned its attention to overthrowing the Jim Crow law. Local African-American college students staged sit-ins around the city in the hopes of desegregating downtown restaurants and other public facilities. In the fall of 1961, the city itself began the court-ordered desegregation of its public school system, as nine African-American students peacefully enrolled and began classes at four Atlanta area high schools: Brown, Henry Grady, Murphy, and Northside. These important events led to even more dramatic changes for the city, as the courts ordered the removal of city barricades in southwest Atlanta (originally erected to separate black and white neighborhoods), allowing for black residential expansion into what had formerly been all-white communities. This, in turn, led to the quick exodus of white residents to the suburbs. In the late 1960s, Atlanta's African-American population increased by 68,587, while the white population declined by 60,132. And by 1970, Atlanta had a majority African-American population, which still holds today.

Interestingly, as African-American Atlantans worked for civil rights, they met little resistance from the city's white business leaders. In fact, most influential businessmen in Atlanta, including Coca-Cola CEO Robert Woodruff, were concerned about the city's image in national business circles, and wanted to spare residents the acts of racial violence that had occurred in other southern cities such as Little Rock and Birmingham. Rather than wage an ugly battle against the civil rights movement, white leaders instead nicknamed Atlanta "The City Too Busy to Hate," to differentiate it from its southern neighbors, and focused on urban renewal projects, construction of a new sports stadium, and the creation of a mass transit system that would benefit all residents, African-American and white.

Atlanta's mayor during this time was Ivan Allen, Jr., son of a prominent businessman and former president of the Atlanta Chamber of Commerce. Though Allen had originally been against African-American residential expansion, he soon became an advocate of the civil rights movement and a strong supporter of Martin Luther King, Jr. Mayor Allen even testified before the US Senate Commerce Committee in 1963 in favor of a national civil rights bill. He was the only southern elected official to do so.

By the early 1970s, Atlanta was settling into its role as a progressive and influential city. Three new sports teams—the Atlanta Braves, the Atlanta Falcons, and the Atlanta Hawks—called the city home; business continued to boom in the metro area; and the local political landscape was growing to reflect the diversity in Atlanta's population.

In 1972 Andrew Young, a colleague and former aide of Martin Luther King, Jr., became Georgia's first African-American congressman. African-American representation on the city council and in the state legislature had increased significantly. And, perhaps most significantly, in 1973 Maynard Jackson was elected Atlanta's first African-American mayor. He would go on to serve three terms—two consecutive, with a third in 1990.

Throughout the next two decades, transportation continued to be a crucial factor in Atlanta's growth and development. City voters approved the creation and funding of the Metropolitan Atlanta Rapid Transit Authority (MARTA), a citywide public transportation system combining bus routes and rapid rail service. Hartsfield International Airport (later renamed Hartsfield-Jackson International Airport) opened a new $450 million air terminal, and is now one of the busiest hubs in the world. And Atlanta's connection to interstate highways I-85, I-75, and I-20 continued to bring new residents into the area and facilitate suburban growth. By 1980, the population of metro Atlanta had reached two million.

The advances in Atlanta's transportation industries, particularly at Hartsfield, helped the city increase its convention and tourism business in the 1990s. The renovation and expansion of the World Congress Center, the revitalization of Underground Atlanta, and the construction of shiny, new sports facilities—Turner Field for the Braves, the Georgia Dome for the Falcons, and Philips Arena for the Hawks and the Thrashers—didn't hurt either. These new facilities not only provided increased entertainment options for residents and visitors, they also helped combat the movement of retail businesses and developments to the outlying suburbs. This intown revitalization movement reached its peak in the mid-1990s as the city proudly prepared to host the 1996 Summer Olympic Games. New facilities were built, including the 21-acre Centennial Olympic Park, and the Olympic Village (which was converted to student housing for Georgia Tech and Georgia State University once the games were over). And older, existing buildings were given much needed and long overdue face-lifts.

During this first decade of the 21st century, metro Atlanta has expanded to include 28 counties, and boasts the largest and most diverse population in its history. According to the 2000 Census, over 4 million residents now live in the metro area; 400,000 within the city limits itself. And of that 4 million, at least 10% are foreign born, with 76% of that group coming from countries in Latin America and Asia. There are now more than 1,000 foreign companies doing business in Atlanta, as well as over 30 foreign consulates and 20 trade and tourism offices.

With the city's continuing growth and the expansion of Atlanta's boundaries come new problems; namely, out-of-control sprawl and increased traffic congestion. Despite a small resurgence of families and young professionals settling back into Atlanta's intown neighborhoods, less expensive homes in the outer suburbs are still a powerful draw for many. Heavy traffic and excessively long commute times are the result, as more and more residents move away from the city and into the many communities outside the I-285 perimeter.

Over the last 15 years, the Georgia Department of Transportation has tried to ease the city's growing traffic problems by increasing the number of passenger lanes on Atlanta's interstates and highways, and by constructing a new toll road, Georgia 400, to directly connect Atlanta to the north suburbs. But, as of yet, none of the highway expansions or additions has done much to relieve Atlanta's traffic headache. And it's too soon to tell if additional plans, scheduled to be implemented over the next ten years, will have much of an effect either. What is known is that there are over 2.5 million vehicles registered in metro Atlanta, and the average daily commute is approximately 18 miles each way, with commute times ranging between two and four hours per day . . . something to keep in mind when deciding where to live and work.

TODAY'S GREATER ATLANTA AREA COMPRISES TWENTY-EIGHT counties, spanning over six thousand square miles. The epicenter, of course, is Atlanta itself, which includes parts of Fulton and DeKalb counties—both are profiled here, as are Atlanta's other two "inner-ring" counties, Cobb and Gwinnett. Additionally, for this third edition, we've chosen to describe a fifth metro Atlanta county, Cherokee, which is one of the region's most outlying, yet fastest growing areas. All of these counties, along with community profiles, contact information, and county resource listings, can be found below. The remaining metro Atlanta counties each possess a number of municipalities that might be appealing to newcomers, as long as the commute to the city, which can be an hour plus, with no public transportation alternatives, is not an issue. A listing of each outer-ring county, including contact information, has been provided in the **Additional Counties** section at the end of this chapter.

CITY OF ATLANTA—FULTON COUNTY

The City of Atlanta covers 132 square miles, and, according to the most recent census, is now home to over 400,000 residents. It's also host to a thriving arts scene and a wide variety of sports, entertainment, and dining options. The area's largest greenspace, Piedmont Park, is in the city as well.

In the not so distant past, Atlanta was shifting toward being a depressed city center with residents moving away from its intown core out to the suburbs to set up house. But the last 10 to 15 years have brought a dramatic turnaround to the city. Spurred by the city's bid to host the 1996 Summer Olympics, the 1990s ushered in a new wave of intown revitalization. City officials and local business leaders worked to rebuild Atlanta's historic communities and industrial areas, and that work paid off. Today the city is energized, and filled with families and young professionals who've chosen to make their homes here.

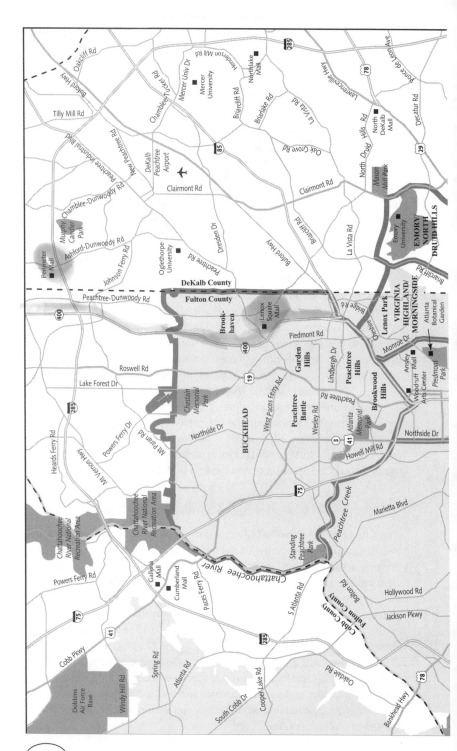

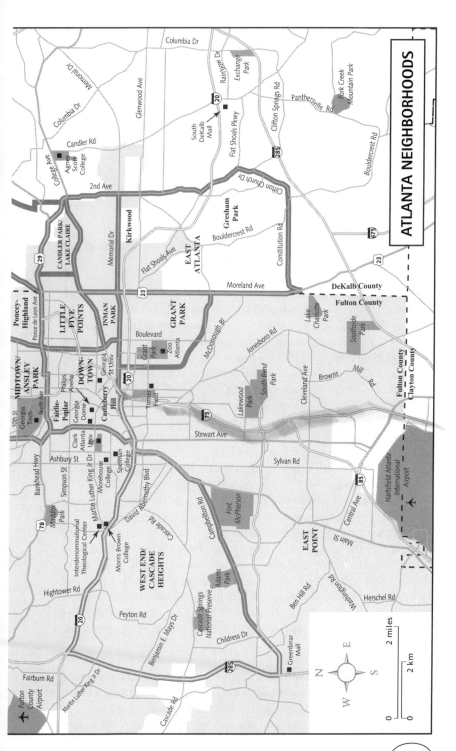

ATLANTA NEIGHBORHOODS

Most of Atlanta proper is located in Fulton County. And, in fact, that's where Downtown, with its many local and state government offices, is located. Along the east side of town, however, a few Atlanta neighborhoods overlap into DeKalb County.

DOWNTOWN

CASTLEBERRY HILL
FAIRLIE-POPLAR

Boundaries: North: North Avenue; **East**: Boulevard; **South**: I-20; **West**: Northside Drive

The Atlanta skyline is a beautiful sight, with buildings rising up to meet the sky and towering over the bustling sidewalks and streets that teem with pedestrians and cars. On a clear day, you can catch sight of Stone Mountain in the distance, looming above the horizon as if standing watch over the city. And in all directions there is green, the lush green of the inviting Centennial Olympic Park and of the hefty shade trees that crowd over Downtown's surrounding neighborhoods.

By day, the Downtown area is a crowded commercial district, home to city and state government, financial institutions, CNN Center, Philips Arena, and Underground Atlanta. But at night, the workaday population is replaced by residents who call this area home, and by visitors heading into Downtown to take advantage of its many sports, dining, and entertainment opportunities.

Thanks to an organized revitalization effort in recent years, Downtown Atlanta has undergone a massive face-lift. New retail establishments and entertainment and residential developments have been constructed and more are on the way. Centennial Olympic Park, located at Techwood Drive, Marietta Street, and International Boulevard, now fills a once-blighted area next to the CNN Center, and serves as a favorite lunch spot for downtown workers. It also plays host to a variety of concerts throughout the year and, with its grassy areas and beautiful Olympic Ring Fountain, has become an attractive and popular place for Downtown residents and visitors to hang out.

Other Downtown destinations, such as Imagine It! The Children's Museum of Atlanta on Centennial Olympic Park Drive, and the World of Coca-Cola Museum on Martin Luther King Drive, continue to attract families from all over metro Atlanta, and visitors from around the world.

With the surge in demand for housing, many of the city's older buildings were turned into lofts and condos. And new complexes are continuing to be built. Even the loft apartments along Trinity, Castleberry, and Marietta Street that once housed Olympic visitors are now being leased or sold to businesspeople, young hipsters, and families who've decided to make their home in the heart of the city. And, as the residents settle in, numerous retail establishments, including Kroger and Publix supermarkets, have followed suit, creating mini-communities throughout Downtown.

Probably the most popular Downtown community is **Fairlie-Poplar**. Coined for the cross streets, this National Historic District in the heart of the city has long been revered for its detailed architecture and charming narrow streets. But today it's also known for its interesting mix of retail, entertainment, and loft spaces as well. It was back in the late 1990s when Georgia State University led the way for the redevelopment of Fairlie-Poplar by renovating an old movie theater into the Rialto Center for the Performing Arts. The school also moved its College of Business and its schools of Music and Public Policy into the district, and eventually constructed a student dormitory on Techwood Drive. The goal of attracting merchants to the area by providing a steady flux of students worked. Area businesses include The Trinity Gallery, Starbucks, Gateway News, and two hip nightclubs, the Tabernacle and the Cotton Club. The Fairlie-Poplar Café and Grill, located at 85 Poplar Street, is *the* place for lunch.

Another bright spot among Downtown neighborhoods is **Castleberry Hill**. This historic warehouse district, located in southwest Atlanta, has undergone an amazing renaissance in recent years, thanks in part to a dedicated neighborhood association. What once was an overlooked, rundown industrial district is now a comfortable, cosmopolitan community, filled with artists, restaurants, and dramatic loft apartments. Residents here tend to be young, hip, and artsy. Today you'll find at least five art galleries in the neighborhood, including the renowned Marcia Wood Gallery on Walker Street, all within walking distance of the dozen or so warehouse-turned-loft buildings. You'll also find Slice, a chic and imaginative pizza and martini bar, serving up free wireless internet access alongside gourmet pizza slices and mixed drinks.

StudioPlex, a mixed-use development in the Auburn Avenue Warehouse district, is attractive to urban dwellers. This all-in-one site offers residential loft space as well as commercial, gallery, and live-work spaces for artists. Plans are also in the works to include an arts center, public park, and restaurant.

While Downtown Atlanta has experienced tremendous growth in recent years, developers are just getting started. According to Central Atlanta Progress, a private, nonprofit organization committed to economic growth in the city, more than $3 billion in development is currently underway in Downtown. Plans are to attract even more retail establishments and residents to the area, and create a true, 24-hour community in the heart of Atlanta.

Web Site: www.atlantaga.gov

Area Code: 404

Zip Codes: 30303, 30312, 30313, 30314, 30301, 30370, 30379, 30371, 30365, 30308

Post Offices: Central City Carrier (where downtown residents go to pick up packages), 400 Pryor Street, 404-222-0765; Phoenix Station, 41 Marietta Street, 404-534-2963; Civic Center, 570 Piedmont Avenue, NE; Gate City Station, 486 Decatur Street; Morris Brown, 50 Sunset Avenue, NW; CNN Center, One CNN Center; 800-275-8777, www.usps.com

Police Precincts: 398 Centennial Olympic Park Drive NW, 404-658-7054; 247 Auburn Avenue, 404-658-6452; 94 Pryor Street, 404-658-6364; www.atlantapd.org

Emergency Hospital: Grady Memorial Hospital, 80 Jesse Hill Jr. Drive, 404-616-4307; www.gradyhealthsystem.org

Libraries: Central Library, One Margaret Mitchell Square, NW, 404-730-1700; Auburn Avenue Research Library of African American Culture and History, 101 Auburn Avenue NE, 404-730-4001; Martin Luther King, Jr., 409 John Wesley Dobbs Avenue, 404-730-1185; www.af.public.lib.ga.us

Public School Education: Atlanta Public Schools, 404-802-3500; Homework Hotline, 404-827-8620; www.atlanta.k12.ga.us

Community Publications: *Atlanta Intown*, 404-586-0002, www.atlantanewsgroup.com

Community Resources: Atlanta Downtown Neighborhood Association, www.atlantadna.org; Central Atlanta Progress, Atlanta Downtown Improvement District, 404-658-1877, www.centralatlantaprogress.org; Downtown Atlanta Ambassador Force, 404-215-9600, www.central atlantaprogress.org; Metro Atlanta Chamber of Commerce, 404-880-9000, www.metroatlantachamber.com; Castleberry Hill Neighborhood Association, 404-228-2078, www.castleberryhill.org; StudioPlex, 404-523-4467, http://studioplex.net; Centennial Olympic Park, 404-223-4412, www.centennialpark.com; Rialto Center for the Performing Arts, 404-651-4727, www.rialtocenter.org; CNN Center, 404-827-4000, www.cnn.com; Underground Atlanta, 404-523-2311, www.under ground-atlanta.com; World of Coca-Cola, 404-676-5151, www.wocc atlanta.com; Imagine It! The Children's Museum of Atlanta, 404-659-5437, www.imagineit-cma.org; The Marcia Wood Gallery, 404-827-0030, www.marciawoodgallery.com

Public Transportation: **MARTA**, 404-848-4711, www.itsmarta.com; **East-West Line stations**: Dome/GA World Congress Center/Philips Arena, Five Points, Georgia State, and King Memorial; **North-South**

Line stations: North Avenue, Civic Center, Peachtree Center, Five Points, and Garnett; **Bus**: 1-C Coronet Way, 1-H Howell Mill/Marietta Street, 2 Ponce de Leon, 3 Auburn Avenue/MLK Jr., Drive, 4 Federal Prison/Grady Hospital, 10 Peachtree Street, 13 Fair Street/Techwood, 21 Memorial Drive, 26 Perry Homes, 46 Boulevard/St. Charles, 97 Atlanta Avenue/Georgia, 99 King Memorial/North Avenue

WEST END/CASCADE HEIGHTS

Boundaries: North: I-20; **East**: I-29; **South**: Campbellton Road; **West**: I-285

The southwestern edge of downtown Atlanta boasts one of the largest and most prominent bastions of historically African-American education, the Atlanta University Center. This renowned educational complex consists of six separate institutions: Clark Atlanta University, Interdenominational Theological Center, Morehouse College, Morehouse School of Medicine, Morris Brown College, and Spelman College. There aren't many new retail establishments in the heart of one of Atlanta's oldest neighborhoods; most businesses have been around for years. But don't let the lack of new development fool you. Local residents and business owners are proud of their community and do what they can to make their neighborhood inviting. Many area homes, apartments, and commercial buildings have been freshly painted, refurbished, or remodeled in recent years, and the once-blighted downtown neighborhood surrounding the Atlanta University Center has gone through a significant transformation, with local restaurants and boutiques displaying a much-needed face-lift.

Minutes away from the commercial district, heading southwest on Ralph D. Abernathy Boulevard, is the small-town community atmosphere of the historic **West End**. Once the center of Atlanta, this neighborhood of classic Victorians and charming bungalows dates back to 1835. Journalist Joel Chandler Harris, author of the beloved Uncle Remus stories, made his home here. His house, the Wren's Nest, is one of the area's prime tourist attractions. Its restoration is just part of a widespread effort by local residents and businesses to rejuvenate the neighborhood. Although the expansion of I-20 in the mid-sixties drove some residents away, the West End was able to maintain much of its original charm. Today, some new retail areas nicely coexist with old Victorian houses, offering residents middle-class comfort and suburban shopping convenience.

The West End also features a thriving exchange of African-American history and culture. The Hammonds House Galleries and Resource Center of African-American Art contains an outstanding permanent collection of African-American and Haitian art. This antebellum home also hosts various educational programs and cultural events. The Shrine of the Madonna Bookstore and Cultural Arts Center is the South's largest African-American bookstore and is another vibrant center of community life.

If you continue west on Cascade Road, the terrain becomes more wooded and rolling, and the pace of retail and housing developments much more hurried than in the West End. **Cascade Heights**, a small community bordered by Venetian Drive to the south and Centra Villa Drive to the east, begins as a series of quiet, tree-lined streets and comfortable houses set on nice, mid-sized lots. Most of the homes here represent the bungalow and brick ranch styles similar to the ones found in other old, middle-class Atlanta neighborhoods. In recent years, though, the area has seen a massive wave of development, resulting in the construction of numerous impressive single-family homes built around culs-de-sac and small man-made lakes. Newly developed subdivisions in the Cascade Heights area, such as Cascade Manor, Cascade Glen, and Cascade Knolls, provide middle- and upper-income residents with a peaceful suburban retreat within a short drive of downtown. The area's influx of new residents has encouraged the growth of sprawling new retail outlets that cater to expanding consumer needs. The development spreads beyond I-285, where exclusive communities are springing up alongside office parks.

Just west of Cascade Heights you'll find a pocket of land called the Cascade Springs Nature Preserve, which provides a peaceful recreation area; perfect for quiet walks. The preserve includes a quarry, nursery, hiking trails that lead past a creek, and a handicapped accessible trail.

Although technically not part of the city of Atlanta, another community in the area worth mentioning is the City of East Point, www.eastpointcity.org. Located just south of West End and Cascade Heights and a mere seven miles from downtown Atlanta, **East Point** is poised to become one of the next hot communities in metro Atlanta. Houses here are affordable and range from 1920s bungalows and 1950s ranch homes to recently built subdivisions. Young urbanites, drawn by East Point's lower home prices and friendly neighbors, as well as its proximity to Atlanta, have been coming in droves, breathing new life into the community. East Point's historic downtown, which boasts a handful of restaurants and blues bars, art galleries, and antique shops, is in the process of being revitalized. Growth in the city's commercial district is expected to continue as businesses and retail establishments position themselves accordingly to take advantage of the incoming young, hip, and culturally diverse population.

Web Site: www.atlantaga.gov
Area Code: 404

Zip Codes: 30310, 30311

Post Offices: Cascade Heights, 2414 Herring Road SW; West End, 848 Oglethorpe Avenue SW; 800-275-8777, www.usps.com

Police Precincts: 676 Fair Street, 404-658-6274; 1125 Cascade Circle SW, 404-756-1903; 2000 Campbellton Road, 404-755-1499; 3565 Martin Luther King Jr. Drive, 404-505-3131; www.atlantapd.org

Emergency Hospitals: Grady Memorial Hospital, 80 Jesse Hill Jr. Drive, 404-616-4307, www.gradyhealthsystem.org; South Fulton Medical Center, 1170 Cleveland Avenue, East Point, 404-305-3500, www.southfultonmedicalcenter.com

Libraries: Southwest Regional, 3665 Cascade Road SW, 404-699-6363; West End, 525 Peeples Street SW, 404-752-8740; www.af.public.lib.ga.us

Public School Education: Atlanta Public Schools, 404-802-3500; Homework Hotline, 404-827-8620; www.atlanta.k12.ga.us

Community Publications: *Atlanta Intown*, 404-586-0002, www.atlantanewsgroup.com

Community Resources: Atlanta University Center, 404-523-5148, www.aucenter.edu; West End Kiwanis Club, 2343 Campbellton Road SW, 404-344-3022; The Wren's Nest House Museum, 1050 Ralph David Abernathy Boulevard SW, 404-753-7735; Hammonds House Galleries, 503 Peeples Street SW, 404-752-8730, www.hammondshouse.org; The Shrine of the Madonna Bookstore and Cultural Arts Center, 404-752-6125, www.shrinebookstore.com; Cascade Youth Organization, 1620 Delowe Street SW, 404-753-8804; Cascade Springs Nature Preserve, 404-752-5385; Metro Atlanta Chamber of Commerce, 404-880-9000, www.metroatlantachamber.com

Public Transportation: **MARTA,** 404-848-4711, www.itsmarta.com; **North-South Line station**: West End Station; **Bus**: 20 College Park, 67 Westview, 68 Donnelly, 63 Atlanta University/Kennedy Center, 71 Cascade/Richland, 79 Friendly, 81 Venetian, 93 Sylvan Hills, 95 Stewart Avenue/Hapeville, 98 West End/Arts Center

BUCKHEAD

BROOKWOOD HILLS
PEACHTREE HILLS
PEACHTREE BATTLE
GARDEN HILLS
BROOKHAVEN

Boundaries: North: Atlanta city limits; **East**: Atlanta city limits; **South**: Downtown connector; **West**: Cobb County line

Before European settlers inhabited the Atlanta area, Cherokee and Creek Indian tribes inhabited what is now known as Buckhead. In 1838 South Carolina native Henry Irby bought 203 acres of land here, built a grocery store and tavern on the site, and named it "Irbyville." Soon after, the area became known as Buckhead, after the head of a buck that was mounted on a post outside the tavern. It was not until 1952 that Buckhead was annexed by the city of Atlanta.

Buckhead, which likes to think of itself as "The Beverly Hills of the East" because of the shopping, dining, and entertainment amenities it offers, is home to Atlanta's old money, and the beautiful mansions here (including the governor's) reflect the affluence of its residents. The heavily wooded, rolling terrain is broken into a number of neighborhoods that are perfect for well-to-do professionals with families seeking large homes and fine yards within the city and close to some of Atlanta's best public and private schools.

Five miles north of downtown in Buckhead is the **Brookwood Hills** district, recognized by the National Register of Historic Places. This neighborhood stands on the site of important Civil War clashes between Union and Confederate troops. After the war ended, the land remained primarily a rural tract until the early 1900s, when a resourceful developer, B. F. Burnette, envisioned the neighborhood as a self-contained community, complete with recreation facilities and a commercial district, and set out to bring his vision to life. The development boomed after World War I and continues to be an excellent and stately neighborhood with numerous finely crafted neo-Victorian style homes. Area amenities, besides Civil War sites, include the Brookwood Hills Community Club and a small commercial district located from Brighton to Collier Road. Here you'll find popular eateries and a number of art galleries. In addition, one of Atlanta's best emergency hospitals, Piedmont Hospital, is located nearby.

Just north of Brookwood Hills is the **Peachtree Hills/Peachtree Battle** neighborhood. Like its neighbor, this area was the site of fierce Civil War fighting during the Atlanta campaign known as "The Battle of Peachtree Creek." Those interested in the Civil War can learn about the battle by reading historical markers located throughout the neighborhood. The houses and estates along lovely Peachtree Battle Avenue and the surrounding streets are part of a planned community originally called Peachtree Heights, designed at the turn of the 20th century by architect and future Georgia governor Eurith D. Rivers. Unlike much of Atlanta, this neighborhood features wide boulevards, conceived for upper-class residents who owned automobiles. A tour of neighborhood homes reveals a variety of architectural styles, including art deco, Romanesque Revival, and the international style.

At the intersection of Peachtree Battle and Peachtree Road stands the Peachtree Battle shopping center, the commercial hub of the area. This strip contains a Chapter 11 Bookstore, Baskin Robbins, several restaurants, and a number of specialty stores. Behind the shopping center, the Peachtree Hills community continues east toward Piedmont Road. This section of the neighborhood features smaller wood-frame houses, brick bungalows, and quite a few apartment complexes, and is a wonderful place for younger families and singles. The neighborhood is also a dream come true for sports enthusiasts. Atlanta's largest tennis facility, the Bitsy Grant Tennis Center, is located here, as is the Bobby Jones Golf Course. Both facilities are open to the public.

Further north along Peachtree is **Garden Hills**, which sits like an oasis in the middle of Buckhead's busy commercial district. The northern portion of the neighborhood was developed in the 1920s and '30s and features a mixture of large as well as more modest, traditional style homes that were built after the Depression. Eurith D. Rivers originally designed the southern portion of Garden Hills as a counterpart to Peachtree Heights, calling it "Peachtree Heights East." Today, the neighborhood's many apartment complexes attract a large number of young singles.

The Garden Hills district is home to the "duck pond," a scenic picnicking spot for people and home to a variety of ducks and geese. In addition, the area boasts Atlanta's first Fellini's Pizza, now expanded with a goldfish fountain and spacious outdoor patio. Foreign film aficionados flock to the Garden Hills Cinema, purveyor of art and foreign films. In addition, the neighborhood contains its own public swimming pool, park, and community clubhouse at the intersection of East Wesley and Rumson roads.

Just to the north of Garden Hills, at the intersection of Peachtree and West Paces Ferry, is the heart of the **Buckhead** commercial district. In the two and a half blocks dubbed the "Village" area, there are over 100 restaurants and nightspots, including a piano bar, British pub, and bars ranging from trendy posh to sand-floor dives. Some of Atlanta's hottest clubs are located in this part of town, though many residents still head to Little Five Points or Midtown on Friday and Saturday nights. From Tongue and Groove to the Havana Club, this is the place to see and be seen. On the weekends the area attracts huge crowds of locals and "weathermappers" (people driving in from the outlying regions of the city featured on the weather map). Weekend nightlife in Buckhead is notorious for its rowdiness and its lack of parking, so be prepared to walk. In fact, pedestrians rule here on weekend nights, and walking from bar to bar is just part of the fun.

Buckhead's commercial district extends on Peachtree Road past Piedmont Road to what locals call "shoppers' paradise." Lenox Square and Phipps Plaza, two of Atlanta's largest and most luxurious malls, are located here at the intersection of Peachtree Street and Lenox Road. Shoppers come in droves to purchase goods at Neiman Marcus, J. Crew, Parisian, and Saks. While both malls are upscale enough to provide valet parking, Lenox

Square is the less fancy of the two. In addition to boutique shopping, Lenox also offers the requisite mid-priced stores like the Gap, Structure, and Rich's. Phipps Plaza, on the other hand, is about as opulent as a mall can get. Crystal chandeliers, elegant white columns, and a domed skylight grace the mall's lobby and walkways, and classical music is piped over the sound system, but quietly so as not to be intrusive. The mall also provides concierge, babysitting, and personal shopper services. And stores such as Lord & Taylor, Saks Fifth Avenue, Gucci, Dolce & Gabbana, Versace, and Tiffany & Co. set the tone. But Phipps Plaza is also home to shoe-store-extraordinaire Nike Town, as well as a 14-theater movie-plex, so don't be surprised at the hordes of teenagers roaming this mall alongside Atlanta's elite.

Across the street from Phipps, on Peachtree, is the recently developed Lenox Plaza. This architectural beauty houses a two-story Target Superstore, a Publix supermarket and Dick's Sporting Goods, which sells athletic clothes, shoes, equipment, and outdoor gear. Also nearby is a gorgeous, two-story Borders Books and Music store anchoring yet another shopping center.

North of the mall area, and spilling over into DeKalb County, is the **Brookhaven** district, Atlanta's first country club community. The beautiful residences along these narrow, winding streets were constructed as companions to the Capital City Club, an exclusive private country club in operation since the end of the nineteenth century. These larger country club style homes still stand, but are no longer the only type of housing found in the neighborhood. Travel a little further north on Peachtree Road and you'll find that Brookhaven now boasts several high-end apartment complexes, housing many of the students from nearby Oglethorpe University. There are also a large number of small, single-family homes in the bungalow and brick ranch styles that are so prevalent in Atlanta. There is no real commercial district in Brookhaven to speak of, though you will find a few good restaurants nearby, as well as a Kroger supermarket. If you want to be inside the perimeter and close to the center of Buckhead without the noise and traffic that other Buckhead neighborhoods must contend with, then Brookhaven may just be the place for you.

Web Site: www.atlantaga.gov
Area Code: 404
Zip Codes: 30305, 30309, 30324, 30326, 30327, 30342, 30355, 31126
Post Offices: Broadview Station, 780 Morosgo Drive NE; Brookhaven, 3851 Peachtree Road; Buckhead Loop, One Buckhead Loop Road; Glenridge, 5400 Glenridge Drive; Northside Carrier Facility, 3840 Roswell Road NE; Pharr Road, 575 Pharr Road NE; 800-275-8777, www.usps.com
Police Precincts: 3120 Maple Drive NE, 404-848-7231; 3393 Peachtree Road, 404-467-8061; www.atlantapd.org

Emergency Hospital: Piedmont Hospital, 1968 Peachtree Road NE, 404-605-5000; www.piedmonthospital.org
Libraries: Buckhead/Ida Williams Branch, 269 Buckhead Avenue NE, 404-814-3500; Northside Branch, 3295 Northside Parkway NW, 404-814-3508; www.af.public.lib.ga.us
Public School Education: Atlanta Public Schools, 404-802-3500; Homework Hotline, 404-827-8620; www.atlanta.k12.ga.us
Community Publications: *Atlanta Buckhead*, 404-586-0002, www.atlantanewsgroup.com
Community Resources: Buckhead Business Association, 404-467-7607, www.buckheadbusiness.org; Buckhead Chamber of Commerce, 404-266-9867, www.buckhead.org; North Buckhead Civic Association, www.nbca.org; Brookwood Hills Community Club, 404-351-0327, www.brookwoodhills.com; Bitsy Grant Tennis Center, 2125 Northside Drive, 404-609-7193; Bobby Jones Golf Course, 384 Woodward Way NW, 404-355-1009; Garden Hills Pool and Clubhouse, 404-848-7220, www.gardenhillspool.homestead.com; Capital City Club, 404-233-2121, www.capitalcity.org; Oglethorpe University, 404-261-1441, www.oglethorpe.edu
Public Transportation: **MARTA**, 404-848-4711, www.itsmarta.com; **North/Northeast-South Line stations**: Lindbergh, Lenox, Brookhaven, and Buckhead; **Bus**: 1 Howell Mill, 23 Lenox/Arts Center, 25 Peachtree Industrial, 37 Loring Heights, 38 Chastain Park, 40 West Paces Ferry/Garden Hills, 44 West Wesley, 47 Frontage Road, 48 Thomasville/Lenox Station, 58 Boulton Road 60 Moores Mill, 85 Roswell/Alpharetta, 92 Perimeter Mall, 140 Holcomb Bridge, 141 North Point Mall

MIDTOWN/ANSLEY PARK

Boundaries: North: Ansley Mall; **East**: Monroe Drive; **South**: Ponce de Leon Avenue; **West**: Downtown Connector

South of Buckhead, the **Ansley Park** district was originally conceived as a residential community suitable for automobile travel, with broad, rolling streets curving around wooded parcels of land. The developer, Edwin Ansley, patterned the neighborhood after the nearby Druid Hills area, which was designed by Frederick Law Olmsted. Plans provided for ample greenspace and hundreds of lots for a mixture of housing, from smaller homes to mansions. This neighborhood survived the post–World War II flight to the suburbs with little deterioration, and it has since earned a place on the National Register of Historic Places.

Ansley Park streets, which wind a hopeless tangle around the area between Peachtree Street and Piedmont Road, are some of the most confusing in the city, and only the brave or the initiated should enter without a map. This area is one of Atlanta's oldest and most comfortable neighborhoods, offering gorgeous homes to those who want to live close to the downtown business district or the now numerous Midtown office towers. Ansley Park architecture ranges from elaborate Victorian to American Georgian to one residence that resembles a medieval fortress.

The Ansley Park/Midtown section of Atlanta is home to Piedmont Park, the city's largest park. At 180 acres, many find it the best place in the city for rollerblading, running, or walking their dogs. It's also a great place to meet people. On any given day you're likely to find families setting up for an afternoon picnic, friends playing a rousing game of touch football, or young couples out for an afternoon stroll. There is a playground, a pond, and tennis courts. Piedmont Park also plays host to many Atlanta festivals throughout the year, including the Atlanta Dogwood Festival in April and the Atlanta Lesbian and Gay Pride Festival in June.

The neighborhood that sits south of Piedmont Park, officially known as **Midtown**, was home to the counter-culture of the late 1960s. Considered to be the largest "hippie district" in the southeast, Midtown offered inexpensive dwellings to the free-love generation. However, as area residents matured and became more fiscal-minded, they began buying and renovating the neighborhood's rundown houses, and over the last few decades, this area has been completely transformed with a proliferation of office buildings and pricey high-rise apartments and condominiums. While property values have risen steadily, the persistent buyer can still find a good value. Houses range from modest 1930s bungalows to impressive turn-of-the-century mansions, quite a few of which have been broken up into apartments.

The Midtown neighborhood is home to much of Atlanta's gay and lesbian community, as evidenced by the number of rainbow flags fluttering from houses and retail establishments. The gay and lesbian population here is out, loud, and very proud—numerous nightclubs, shops, and organizations in the area are gay-owned or gay-friendly, making this area an interesting and lively place to live.

Both Midtown and Ansley Park are conveniently located near several shopping areas, including Ansley Park Mall, the Midtown Promenade, and Colony Square. Residents of this area have a variety of recreational and cultural offerings right at their doorstep, including Piedmont Park and the Atlanta Botanical Gardens. In addition, the Woodruff Arts Center, housing the High Museum of Art, Symphony Hall, the Atlanta College of Art, and the Alliance Theatre are located nearby. Also, Atlanta's historic movie palace, the Fox Theatre (dubbed the "Fabulous Fox" by residents), presents film series and hosts a variety of presentations, including the Atlanta Ballet's Christmas-time performance of the Nutcracker.

Web Site: www.atlantaga.gov
Area Code: 404
Zip Codes: 30309, 30357, 30361, 30367
Post Office: Midtown Station, 1072 West Peachtree Street, 800-275-8777, www.usps.com.
Police Precinct: 1320 Monroe Drive NE, 404-853-3300, www.atlantapd.org
Emergency Hospital: Piedmont Hospital, 1968 Peachtree Road NE, 404-605-5000; www.piedmonthospital.org
Library: Peachtree, 1315 Peachtree Street NE, 404-885-7830, www.af.public.lib.ga.us
Public School Education: Atlanta Public Schools, 404-802-3500; Homework Hotline, 404-827-8620; www.atlanta.k12.ga.us
Community Publications: *Atlanta Intown*, 404-586-0002, www.atlantanewsgroup.com
Community Resources: Midtown Alliance, 404-892-4782, www.mid townalliance.org; Midtown Atlanta Neighborhood Association, www.midtownatlanta.org; Piedmont Park Conservancy, 404-875-7275, www.piedmontpark.org; the Atlanta Botanical Garden, 404-876-5859, www.atlantabotanicalgarden.org; Woodruff Arts Center, www.woodruffcenter.org; the High Museum, 404-733-HIGH, www.high.org; Atlanta Symphony Orchestra, 404-733-4900, www.atlantasymphony.org; the Alliance Theatre, 404-733-4650, http://alliancetheatre.org; the Fox Theatre, 404-881-2100, www.foxtheatre.org
Public Transportation: MARTA, 404-848-4711, www.itsmarta.com; **North-South Line stations**: Midtown and Arts Center; **Bus**: 2 Ponce De Leon, 10 Peachtree, 23 Lenox/Arts Center, 27 Monroe Drive, 35 Ansley Park, 36 North Decatur, 45 Virginia/McLynn, 46 Boulevard/St. Charles, 98 West End/Arts Center, 148 Powers Ferry

VIRGINIA HIGHLAND/MORNINGSIDE

LENOX PARK
PONCEY-HIGHLAND

Boundaries: North: Clifton Road; **East**: Briarcliff Road; **South**: Ponce De Leon Avenue; **West**: Monroe Drive

Home to a dazzling variety of retail and residential districts, the **Virginia Highland/Morningside** neighborhood is rightfully known as one of Atlanta's most desirable places to live, and it is certainly one of the city's most artsy environs. This part of town, however, was at one time in danger of sliding into urban decay. Middle-class flight to the suburbs and a planned highway that was to bisect the neighborhood caused real estate values to plummet in the late 1950s.

Thankfully, community activists successfully prevented the highway from becoming a reality (although not before a number of houses were razed) and the neighborhood experienced a renaissance in the 1960s. Many of the homes in this neighborhood have been rescued from slow but perceptible decline by an infusion of young, urban professionals whose remodeled kitchens and carefully decorated bedrooms often appear in the pages of *Atlanta Magazine.*

This influx of well-heeled new families coincided with the emergence of restaurants, bars, antique shops, art galleries, and clothing boutiques on Highland Avenue. This retail strip stretches from University Avenue to Ponce de Leon Avenue and is frequently interrupted by lush, green blocks that have remained residential. People from all over the metro Atlanta area gravitate to area bars, blues clubs, restaurants, and art galleries. Parking becomes scarce (by Atlanta standards) near Highland on weekends, requiring would-be shoppers to walk a couple of blocks from their cars to their destinations. On the other hand, those lucky enough to live within walking distance of these businesses enjoy some of the finest dining and shopping in Atlanta just outside their doors.

On the northern edge of Morningside, around Lenox Road, is the **Lenox Park** community. Made up of grand old houses, newly developed condos and townhouses, and mid-rise luxury apartment homes, this community is one of the toniest in Atlanta. This is where you'll find many of the city's old-moneyed families living alongside the just-moved-in, two-income, upwardly mobiles. Houses in Lenox Park start at around $350,000 and range upward to well over $1 million, a worthwhile investment for those who can afford it. Not only are Lenox Park residents close to the Virginia Highland retail district, they're also right down the street from Lenox Mall and Phipps Plaza.

Notwithstanding the area's reputation as a well-to-do community, there are a fair number of apartment complexes that provide living space for those who lack the gold bullion required to purchase a Morningside or Highland house. If this is your lot and this is your spot, your best bet is simply to drive through this area searching for vacancy notices since the better apartment buildings seldom bother to place ads posting open apartments. Pay particular attention to the three-story buildings along St. Charles and Virginia Avenue, as these house attractive apartments with considerable character.

The northern and southern edges of Virginia Highland contain a number of less aesthetically pleasing (read 1960s architectural style) apartment complexes. But don't let the exteriors scare you off. Reasonably priced, some of these small brick complexes actually have well-maintained interiors with large rooms and beautiful hardwood floors.

The area of Virginia Highland that runs along Ponce de Leon Avenue (or "Ponce" as locals call it) was once a seedy and neglected part of town. But thanks to the 1996 Olympics, much of this **Poncey-Highland** area is now rebuilt and revitalized. Mid-rise condos and new retail establishments have replaced many of the hotels along this thoroughfare that once housed transients, prostitutes, and drug dealers. Bike paths running from Freedom Park to Stone Mountain and downtown are in place. And the popular Market One, a gourmet takeout shop, now sits beside the Majestic, Ponce's famous 24-hour diner. All of this development has paid off for Virginia Highland residents. As the Poncey-Highland community has become a safer place to live and work, more families and young professionals have moved into the area, fitting in easily with the artists, poets, and musicians who congregate here.

The western edge of the community is characterized by its easy access to Piedmont Park, Atlanta's largest greenspace. Here, too, parking can become a problem on weekends. Another local attraction, the Midtown Promenade, located on Monroe and Virginia, offers a multiplex cinema as well as restaurants and stores.

In general, the Highland/Morningside community is an attractive and convenient, but increasingly expensive place to live. Those newcomers who are committed to making their home in this area should prepare for a lengthy apartment hunt or else resign themselves to paying a premium for the neighborhood's many fine attributes.

Web Site: www.atlantaga.gov

Area Code: 404

Zip Codes: 30306, 31106, 30309

Post Office: 1190 North Highland Avenue NE, 800-275-8777, www.usps.com

Police Precinct: Police Headquarters, 675 Ponce de Leon Avenue NE, 404-817-6900, www.atlantapd.org

Emergency Hospitals: Emory University Hospital, 1440 Clifton Road NE, 404-778-7777, www.emoryhealthcare.org; Piedmont Hospital, 1968 Peachtree Road NE, 404-605-5000; www.piedmonthospital.org

Library: Ponce de Leon, 980 Ponce de Leon Avenue NE, 404-885-7820, www.af.public.lib.ga.us

Public School Education: Atlanta Public Schools, 404-802-3500; Homework Hotline, 404-827-8620; www.atlanta.k12.ga.us

Community Publications: *Atlanta Intown*, 404-586-0002, www. atlantanewsgroup.com

Community Resources: Morningside Lenox Park Association, 404-872-7714, http://mlpa.org; Virginia Highland Business Association, www.virginiahighland.com; Virginia Highland Civic Association, 404-222-8244, www.vahi.org; Market One Specialty Foods, 1061 Ponce de Leon Avenue NE, 404-439-1100, www.m1atlanta.com; The Majestic, 1031 Ponce de Leon Avenue NE, 404-875-0276; Piedmont Park Conservancy, 404-875-7275, www.piedmontpark.org; YWCA of Greater Atlanta, 957 North Highland Avenue, 404-892-3476, www.ywcaatlanta.org

Public Transportation: **MARTA**, 404-848-4711, www.itsmarta.com; **Bus**: 2 Ponce de Leon, 27 Monroe Drive, 31 Morningside, 33 Briarcliff, 45 Virginia/McLynn, 46 Boulevard/St. Charles

LITTLE FIVE POINTS

Boundaries: North: Ponce de Leon Avenue; **East**: Oakdale; **South**: DeKalb Avenue; **West**: North Highland Avenue

If Buckhead is the "Beverly Hills of the East," then **Little Five Points** (or **L5P** for short) would have to be the "Haight-Ashbury" of the South. Populated by sidewalk wordsmiths hawking their poetry to pedestrians, artists selling jewelry on the street, and teenagers piercing any and all body parts, this hip little enclave is where all the cool kids come to hang out. In fact, Little Five Points has become so trendy that in recent years, residents are often in the minority, with most of the hipsters who come here to shop, drink, or listen to music trekking in from the suburbs.

The heart of this community is the retail district located at the intersection of Euclid Avenue and Moreland Avenue (which is what Briarcliff is called once it crosses Ponce to the south)—a district increasingly populated by savvy stores marketing stylized wares. Shopping here is more "alternative" than in Virginia Highland, offering the best in vintage clothes, new age paraphernalia, feminist books, and retro home furnishings. Popular stores here include The Junkman's Daughter, which has evolved from a cramped second-hand store into a sizable retail operation, anchoring a thriving strip mall on Moreland; Sevananda is the neighborhood natural foods co-op; and The Vortex, with its giant screaming-skull-head entrance, is one of the area's most recognizable, and popular bars. Part of L5P's charm stems from its intimate size. Unlike stores on Highland, which stretch for block after block, the Little Five Points retail strip is actually very small: a few blocks on Euclid and a few blocks more on Moreland. But those few blocks pack a huge punch, offering a wide variety of ethnic restaurants, funky boutiques, and some of the best live music venues in the city.

The neighborhood has traditionally provided students and the irregularly employed with affordable (if occasionally seedy) housing. Gentrification of the retail district over the last decade, however, has noticeably escalated area rents. Still, with perseverance, the determined apartment- or house-hunter can find lodging at more favorable rates than in Morningside/Highland or Druid Hills. And the neighborhood's many restaurants and stores allow for close-to-home entertainment.

Apartment buildings can be found along Moreland, as well as on Highland, and many of the quieter back streets offer attractive housing options. Architectural styles here range from the ubiquitous ranch to the quirky Victorian. If this is where you want to live, your best bet is to drive through the area looking for "for sale" signs. And be sure to check out *Creative Loafing,* the free, weekly newspaper, as they run numerous ads for rentals in L5P.

Web Site: www.atlantaga.gov
Area Code: 404
Zip Codes: 30307, 31107
Post Office: Little Five Points, 1987 Euclid Avenue NE, 800-275-8777, www.usps.com
Police Precincts: Police Headquarters, 675 Ponce de Leon Avenue NE, 404-817-6900; Little Five Points Mini Precinct, 428 Seminole Avenue NE, 404-658-6782; www.atlantapd.org
Emergency Hospital: Grady Memorial Hospital, 80 Jesse Hill Jr. Drive, 404-616-4307, www.gradyhealthsystem.org
Library: Ponce de Leon, 980 Ponce de Leon Avenue NE, 404-885-7820; www.af.public.lib.ga.us
Public School Education: Atlanta Public Schools, 404-802-3500; Homework Hotline, 404-827-8620; www.atlanta.k12.ga.us
Community Publications: *Atlanta Intown,* 404-586-0002, www.atlantanewsgroup.com
Community Resources: Little Five Points Community Center, 1083 Austin Avenue NE, 404-522-2926, www.l5p.com; Sevananda Food Co-op, 467 Moreland Avenue NE, 404-681-2831, www.sevananda.com; Junkman's Daughter, 404-577-3188; Variety Playhouse, 1099 Euclid Avenue, 404-524-7354, www.variety-playhouse.com
Public Transportation: **MARTA**, 404-848-4711, www.itsmarta.com; **Bus**: 16 Noble

INMAN PARK

Boundaries: North: DeKalb Avenue; **East**: Boulevard; **South**: Memorial Drive; **West**: Moreland Avenue

Located just south of Little Five Points, **Inman Park**, Atlanta's first planned suburb, was developed in the 1880s as a home for the city's elite. Named after civic leader Samuel M. Inman, the neighborhood was connected to nearby downtown by Atlanta's first electric trolley car. Many of the city's most prominent business leaders resided in this illustrious enclave, including Asa Griggs Candler, the founder of the Coca-Cola Company. His celebrated estate, "Callan Castle," still remains on the corner of Euclid Avenue and Elizabeth Street.

At the turn of the century, wealthy residents, drawn to other prosperous neighborhoods such as Ansley Park, diminished Inman Park's elitism, and eventually middle-income families settled here, building more modest houses and dividing lots. Subsequently, during the mid-century flight to the new suburbs, the area fell on hard times. Numerous houses fell into disrepair, and many were condemned or destroyed. By the early 1960s, the neighborhood was considered little better than a slum until young professionals began to notice the potential of many of the older houses. Revitalization of the neighborhood continues to this day, with the help of Inman Park Restoration, a civic organization whose butterfly emblem symbolizes the area's rebirth.

Though some houses are divided up into apartments, most homes are single-family units. The neighborhood still possesses a few bungalows in need of motivated tenants and major repairs; these are interspersed with fully renovated bungalows, ranch houses, and Victorian mansions.

Residents of Inman Park enjoy its proximity to the bohemian pleasures of Little Five Points. Only two miles east of downtown, the neighborhood also offers a short commute for those who work in the city.

Each April, inhabitants welcome the public into their neighborhood with the Inman Park Festival and Tour of Homes. Historical markers around the district remind inhabitants that the fierce Civil War fighting depicted in Grant Park's Cyclorama occurred in the Inman Park area.

Web Site: www.atlantaga.gov
Area Code: 404
Zip Code: 30307
Post Office: Ralph McGill, 822 Ralph McGill Boulevard NE, 800-275-8777, www.usps.com

Police Precincts: Police Headquarters, 675 Ponce de Leon Avenue NE, 404-817-6900; Little Five Points Mini Precinct, 428 Seminole Avenue NE, 404-658-6782; www.atlantapd.org

Emergency Hospital: Grady Memorial Hospital, 80 Jesse Hill Jr. Drive, 404-616-4307; www.gradyhealthsystem.org

Library: Ponce de Leon, 980 Ponce de Leon Avenue NE, 404-885-7820, www.af.public.lib.ga.us

Public School Education: Atlanta Public Schools, 404-802-3500; Homework Hotline, 404-827-8620; www.atlanta.k12.ga.us

Community Publications: *Atlanta Intown*, 404-586-0002, www.atlantanewsgroup.com

Community Resources: Inman Park Neighborhood Association, www.inmanpark.org; Inman Park Restoration, www.inmanpark.org; Inman Park Cooperative Preschool, 760 Edgewood Avenue NE, 404-827-9796, http://ipcp.org

Public Transportation: **MARTA**, 404-848-4711, www.itsmarta.com; **East-West Line station**: Inman Park/Reynoldstown; **Bus**: 16 Noble

GRANT PARK

Boundaries: North: Memorial Drive; **East**: Moreland Avenue; **South**: Atlanta Avenue; **West**: Hill Street

As the gleaming emblem of the New South, Atlanta surrenders relatively few glimpses into its antebellum past. Of course, Union General William T. Sherman's decision to burn the city to the ground played a major role in obscuring Atlanta's early history. But **Grant Park** is one of the city's few neighborhoods in which the past remains clearly visible.

History buffs celebrate the neighborhood as the site of the Battle of Atlanta during the Civil War. This military action was captured in an amazingly detailed diorama known as the Cyclorama. Standing some 50 feet high and hundreds of feet long, the cylindrical Cyclorama was painted by eleven German and Polish artists in the late nineteenth century and has been on display in its current site (next to Zoo Atlanta) since 1921. Today, visitors from around the world come to this unique theater in the round to hear the story of the Battle of Atlanta, as the studio revolves around the massive painting.

Grant Park, stretching from Cherokee to Boulevard, is the core of this district. Once home to Cherokee Indians (who were forcibly removed from the state in the 1830s), this lush, green park now provides city dwellers with open space and numerous athletic facilities.

Adjacent to the park is Zoo Atlanta, which offers visitors the chance to view a wide variety of animals in natural environments. Don't expect to see animals behind bars here. The habitats consist of large, open spaces designed for the individual species. In addition to its impressive assortment of animals, Zoo Atlanta entertains the public with a rainforest exhibit, storytelling, puppet shows, a miniature train, and a petting zoo for children. They've also partnered with Egleston Children's Hospital to create a wonderful playground and an "endangered species" carousel.

Many of the homes in this neighborhood were constructed in the late-nineteenth and early-twentieth century, when city officials actively encouraged residential development in the region. Unfortunately, the urban flight following World War II exacted a heavy toll on Grant Park and many houses fell into a state of disrepair. Since the 1970s, however, the area has been on the upswing as families took advantage of the then soft real estate market to purchase homes that were subsequently renovated. Urban trailblazers once had to dodge bullets in this former haven for drug dealers, but today the neighborhood has settled into a gentrified revivification. In recent years, the value of homes and apartments here has begun to reflect this happy trend, making it more and more difficult to find rock-bottom rents. Still, Grant Park's many Victorian homes make this a neighborhood worth exploring.

Homebuyers and apartment hunters should take note of a dwelling's location in relation to the park. A federal prison and neighborhoods with lower-income housing to the south make southern sections of Grant Park less enticing. However, streets off Memorial Boulevard possess charming refurbished Victorian houses and eclectic local businesses, such as the Young Blood Gallery and the ever-cool Grant Central Pizza and Pasta restaurant.

Web Site: www.atlantaga.gov
Area Code: 404
Zip Code: 30312
Post Office: Central City, 400 Pryor Street SW, 800-275-8777, www.usps.com
Police Precinct: 880 Cherokee Avenue, 404-624-0674, www.atlantapd.org
Emergency Hospital: Grady Memorial Hospital, 80 Jesse Hill Jr. Drive, 404-616-4307, www.gradyhealthsystem.org
Library: Georgia-Hill Neighborhood Center, 250 Georgia Avenue, 404-730-5427, www.af.public.lib.ga.us
Public School Education: Atlanta Public Schools, 404-802-3500; Homework Hotline, 404-827-8620; www.atlanta.k12.ga.us
Community Publications: *The Porch Press*, 1340 Metropolitan Avenue, 404-373-3130; *Atlanta Intown*, 404-586-0002, www.atlantanewsgroup.com

Community Resources: Grant Park Online, http://grantpark.org; Grant
Park Neighborhood Association, http://gpna.org; Grant Park
Conservancy, 404-521-0938, www.gpconservancy.org; Grant Park
Security Patrol, 404-577-3722, http://gpna.org/gpna/security.htm; Zoo
Atlanta, 800 Cherokee Avenue SE, 404-624-5600, www.zooatlanta.org;
the Atlanta Cyclorama, 404-658-7625, www.bcaatlanta.com; Young
Blood Gallery, 404-627-0393, www.youngbloodgallery.com
Public Transportation: **MARTA,** 404-848-4711, www.itsmarta.com;
Bus: 21 Memorial Drive, 31 Lindbergh/Morningside/Grant Park, 97
Atlanta Avenue/Georgia

CITY OF ATLANTA—DEKALB COUNTY

As mentioned above, most of the City of Atlanta is located within Fulton
County. A handful of Atlanta communities, however, either spill over into
or are completely located in neighboring DeKalb County. Because of their
geographic location, residents in many of the following neighborhoods
have access to both City of Atlanta and DeKalb County libraries, schools,
and other public services. This overlap is sometimes confusing for new residents, particularly those who are unsure as to whether they'll be paying
City of Atlanta or DeKalb County property taxes, or which school system
they belong to. So, if you're considering a move to any of the following
communities, be sure to find out as much as you can up front. The contact
listings and community resources listed below each profile may help.

EAST ATLANTA

KIRKWOOD
GRESHAM PARK

Boundaries: North: College Avenue West; **East**: Second Avenue;
South: Constitution Road; **West**: Moreland Avenue

Located primarily in DeKalb County (with a few streets crossing over into
Fulton), **East Atlanta** is the latest intown neighborhood to experience
rebirth. Like many other intown communities, this area was all but forgotten a decade ago. But thanks in part to the growing popularity of urban living and the reasonable home prices here, East Atlanta is finally experiencing
a renaissance. The drug dealers are gone, and boutiques and restaurants
have replaced the crack houses that once did a brisk business here.
    Less trendy and more family-friendly than nearby Little Five Points,
East Atlanta Village (as the retail district is called) gives the impression of a

toddler taking its first steps. It's what Virginia Highland might have been twenty years ago. Anchoring the East Atlanta retail movement are the shops along Flat Shoals and Glenwood avenues, which include a Joe's Coffee, a cozy little café that not only serves delicious coffee but also showcases local artists and poets, and the funky Chances Gallery, which specializes in local art. Other popular East Atlanta attractions include various clothing boutiques, music stores, gift shops, and restaurants, as well as the Echo Lounge, a live music venue, and Heaping Bowl and Brew.

On the northern edge of East Atlanta lies the revitalized neighborhood of **Kirkwood**. Amazingly, this area has become one of the hottest home sales markets in metro Atlanta. Attracted by low prices for starter homes, a refreshing mix of residents, new families, young professionals, and artists has begun pouring in. Houses range from 1930s Craftsman-style homes desperately in need of repair to the rare, fully renovated Victorian. The majority of the lots are large enough to accommodate children at play, and the lawns, while not as lush as those found in more upscale communities, are well maintained. Kirkwood is also home to Bessie Branham Park, a neighborhood greenspace that features a baseball/softball field, basketball court, playground, picnic tables, and a newly renovated recreation center.

Two miles away, on the south side of East Atlanta, is **Gresham Park**, another neighborhood profiting from Atlanta's urban renewal movement. Like Kirkwood, there is a strong sense of community here. Neighbors know each other's names, people wave hello as you drive past, and children run and play along the quiet streets. Homes range from 1950s style brick ranches, to older Victorians, to semi-mansions on several acres of land; such architectural diversity reflects the fact that Gresham Park was not a planned community. For the moment, home prices here are significantly lower than in other intown communities. But don't expect that to last. Like Kirkwood, Gresham Park is poised to become the next "hot" real estate market.

As more and more people seek out the urban experience, neighborhoods like Kirkwood and Gresham Park will continue to grow. For those looking to make their home in quaint, quiet communities close to downtown, without breaking the bank, now may be the time to buy, and East Atlanta may be just the place.

Web Site: www.atlantaga.gov
Area Code: 404
Zip Codes: 30317, 30316
Post Offices: East Atlanta, 1273 Metropolitan Avenue SE; Eastwood, 1926 Hosea L. Williams Drive NE; 800-275-8777, www.usps.com.
Police Precinct: East Atlanta, 2025 Hosea L. Williams Drive SE, 404-371-5002, www.atlantapd.org

Emergency Hospital: Grady Memorial Hospital, 80 Jesse Hill Jr. Drive, 404-616-4307, www.gradyhealthsystem.org

Libraries: East Atlanta, 457 Flat Shoals Avenue, 404-730-5438; Kirkwood, 11 Kirkwood Road, 404-377-6471; www.af.public.lib.ga.us; Gresham, 2418 Gresham Road, 404-244-4374; Scott Candler, 2644 McAfee Road, 404-286-6986; Flat Shoals, 4022 Flat Shoals Parkway, 404-244-4370; www.dekalb.public.lib.ga.us

Public School Education: Atlanta Public Schools, 404-802-3500; Homework Hotline, 404-827-8620; www.atlanta.k12.ga.us; DeKalb County School System, 678-676-1200, www.dekalb.k12.ga.us

Community Publications: *The Porch Press*, 1340 Metropolitan Avenue, 404-373-3130; *Atlanta Intown*, 404-586-0002, www.atlantanews group.com

Community Resources: East Atlanta Community Association, http://eaca.net; East Atlanta Security Patrol, http://eaca.net; Chances Gallery, 465B Flat Shoals Avenue, 404-521-9500; Kirkwood Neighbors Association, www.historic-kirkwood.com; Bessie Branham Park, 2051 Delano Avenue, 404-371-5010

Public Transportation: **MARTA**, 404-848-4711, www.itsmarta.com; **East-West Line station**: East Lake Station; **Bus**: 18 South Decatur, 21 Memorial Drive, 22 Second Avenue, 28 Eastlake Meadows, 34 Gresham, 107 Glenwood

CANDLER PARK/LAKE CLAIRE

Boundaries: North: Ponce de Leon Avenue; **East**: East Lake Drive; **South**: DeKalb Avenue; **West**: Oakdale

Candler Park, one of Atlanta's oldest suburbs, was originally founded as the City of Edgewood in 1890. As Edgewood, this community had its own government, school system, and electric company until 1908 when residents petitioned to become part of Atlanta. The neighborhood was annexed the following year.

The Candler Park community developed rapidly in the early 1900s as a mostly white, middle-class suburb. However, in the 1920s, realty companies and large property owners began to subdivide the area and sell off a large number of the smaller lots, while many of the homes here were subdivided and then rented by the week. This decline continued through the 1950s as more residents moved away from the intown community into newly developed suburbs around the perimeter. Fortunately, this trend began to change in the late 1960s, as people rediscovered Candler Park's charm and home-buyers took advantage of the housing bargains in the area, and the community found itself on an upswing that has yet to subside. Today, the going rate for a house in Candler Park rivals any Virginia Highland property.

Situated around the public Candler Park Golf Course, this neighborhood is a down-to-earth, family-friendly enclave that has attracted many people looking for a conventional lifestyle. Far less commercial than nearby Little Five Points, this district is filled with a wide variety of two-story, Craftsman-style frame houses and late-period Victorians that draw a more ethnically and economically diverse population than some neighboring suburbs. Residents pride themselves on their sense of community and their rejection of the extensive commercial development of communities such as Buckhead and Virginia Highland.

Nevertheless, because of the recent flood of higher-income homebuyers and the renovation of many older houses in the area, merchants are chomping at the bit to set up shop in Candler Park. The tiny strip of stores at the corner of McLendon and Clifton has taken on a new life as a Fellini's Pizza and La Fonda restaurant have settled in, despite initial protest from locals fearing increased traffic. Other popular additions to this commercial zone include a piercing parlor, ice cream shop, the Donna Van Gogh Gallery, Salon Red, and Kashi Atlanta Center for Yoga, Service and Community. Regardless of the infusion of capital, this small area still retains much of its earnest charm. The Flying Biscuit Café, with its down-home southern vibe and adjoining bakery, is a wonderful eatery renowned for its sublime biscuits and friendly wait staff.

Continuing east on McLendon, one reaches the **Lake Claire** district, which, despite its name, does not possess a lake. Nor does it have a commercial district of its own. It does, however, contain a wide variety of large and small homes from 1950s bungalows to post-Victorian revivals, inhabited increasingly by members of Atlanta's artistic community. Like neighboring Candler Park, Lake Claire has recently undergone a process of revitalization that has increased property values as well as the area's popularity.

You won't find any apartment complexes in Lake Claire. Most of the properties are either single-family homes or renovated duplexes. There is, however, an occasional basement apartment for rent, but they go quickly. Be sure to check the real estate listings in *Creative Loafing* and the *Atlanta Journal-Constitution* regularly if you want to make your home here.

A tour of the neighborhood reveals its diversity and the creativity of its inhabitants. Every May, visitors enjoy the Lake Claire Tour of Funky Homes, which highlights the often-unusual restoration efforts of the area's occupants. Expect to find brightly painted houses in unusual colors that are matched only by the brilliance of the district's famous flowers.

Web Site: www.atlantaga.gov
Area Code: 404

Zip Code: 30033
Post Office: Main Office, 520 West Ponce de Leon Avenue, 800-275-8777, www.usps.com
Police Precinct: Police Headquarters, 675 Ponce de Leon Avenue NE, 404-817-6900, www.atlantapd.org
Emergency Hospitals: DeKalb Medical Center, 2701 North Decatur Road, 404-501-1000; www.dekalbmedicalcenter.org; Emory University Hospital, 1440 Clifton Road NE, 404-778-7777, www.emoryhealthcare.org
Libraries: Kirkwood, 11 Kirkwood Road, 404-377-6471, www.af.public.lib.ga.us; Decatur, 215 Sycamore Street, 404-370-3070; www.dekalb.public.lib.ga.us
Public School Education: Atlanta Public Schools, 404-802-3500; Homework Hotline, 404-827-8620; www.atlanta.k12.ga.us; DeKalb County School System, 678-676-1200, www.dekalb.k12.ga.us
Community Publications: *Candler Park Messenger*, www.candlerpark.org/mainmess.htm; *Lake Claire Newsletter*, www.lakeclaire.org/news/letter.htm; *Atlanta Intown*, 404-586-0002, www.atlantanewsgroup.com
Community Resources: Candler Park Neighborhood Organization, www.candlerpark.org; Lake Claire Neighborhood Association, www.lakeclaire.org; Candler Park Golf Course, 404-371-1260, www.candlerparkgolf.com; Donna Van Gogh Gallery, 1651 McLendon Avenue, 404-370-1003; Kashi Atlanta, 404-687-3353, www.kashiatlanta.org
Public Transportation: **MARTA**, 404-848-4711, www.itsmarta.com; **East-West Line station**: Edgewood/Candler Park; **Bus**: 2 Ponce de Leon, 3 Auburn Avenue/MLK

EMORY/NORTH DRUID HILLS

Boundaries: North: Mason Mill Road; **East**: City of Decatur; **South**: Ponce de Leon Avenue; **West**: Briarcliff Road

The university neighborhood of **Emory/Druid Hills** offers a combination of lovely historic family homes and no-frills student housing. The neighborhood's quiet, family-oriented ambiance is in marked contrast to the nearby commercial districts of Virginia Highland and Little Five Points, where many of the younger residents of Emory/Druid Hills commonly find their nightlife fun.

Each school year, roughly ten thousand students congregate at Emory University—one of the South's top universities. With a campus consisting of hundreds of buildings, Emory casts a long shadow across the Druid Hills area. Constantly renovating its existing spaces and building new ones, the university keeps a small army of contractors busy and, in the process, is constantly reshaping the landscape. To the dismay of neighborhood residents, greenspaces have a tendency to disappear overnight, replaced by impressive research facilities, offices, and classrooms along Clifton Road and its few side streets.

Nevertheless, nature-lovers can still delight in the university-owned Lullwater estate, a charming park stretching from Clifton Road to Clairmont Road. The nearby Fernbank Forest offers nature on an even more spectacular scale. One of the few remaining old-growth forests in an urban area, the Fernbank Forest contains a two-mile trail open to hikers from 2 p.m. to 5 p.m., Sunday-Friday, and from 10 a.m. to 5 p.m. on Saturday. The access path to the forest is at the Fernbank Science Center, on Heaton Park Drive, just north of Ponce de Leon Avenue.

South and west of the University are some of the most spectacular homes in Atlanta, particularly the ones on Lullwater, Springdale, and Oakdale roads. This area was developed in the first decades of the twentieth century according to a plan designed by noted landscape architect Frederick Law Olmsted. Because so much of Olmsted's original design remains intact here, the Druid Hills area has been placed on the National Register of Historic Places. When the producers of the movie *Driving Miss Daisy* wanted to evoke images of old southern wealth, this was the neighborhood they chose.

Not surprisingly, such splendor comes at a steep price. A few lucky (or especially determined) renters occupy carriage houses that rest behind many of the stately mansions, but such living space is hard to come by. Ads for local rentals can be found on the bulletin boards in Emory's student center, as well as in *Creative Loafing* and the *Atlanta Journal-Constitution*. There are several large apartment complexes near the intersection of Clairmont Road and North Decatur that have their own leasing offices. Some of these provide excellent living accommodations for a reasonable price and, therefore, often have a waiting list for vacancies.

Residents enjoy a wide variety of shopping, dining, and culture. Located on North Decatur just outside Emory's gates, the Emory Village shopping strip is home to several gourmet coffee shops, clothing stores, and pizza restaurants, and the Cedar Tree, Atlanta's finest Lebanese restaurant. To the west, on Briarcliff Road, there's a two-story Kroger supermarket right down the street from Whole Foods. And further east on Clairmont Road, shoppers can find numerous restaurants and retail stores, including Bicycle South and Athens Pizza House.

The Fernbank Museum of Natural History (located on Clifton Road just north of Ponce de Leon Avenue) is the largest such museum in the South. Among its many attractions is an IMAX movie theater with a thirty-foot screen. Just across the street from Fernbank is the private Druid Hills Country Club.

Web Site: www.atlantaga.gov

Area Code: 404

Zip Codes: 30307, 30322, 30329

Post Offices: Briarcliff, 3104 Briarcliff Road NE; Druid Hills, 1799-X Briarcliff Road NE; 800-275-8777, www.usps.com

Police Precincts: Police Headquarters, 675 Ponce de Leon Avenue NE, 404-817-6900; www.atlantapd.org; Emory Police Department (emergency), 404-727-6111; Emory Police Department (non-emergency), 404-727-8005

Emergency Hospitals: Emory University Hospital, 1440 Clifton Road NE, 404-778-7777, www.emoryhealthcare.org; DeKalb Medical Center, 2701 North Decatur Road, 404-501-1000, www.dekalbmedical center.org

Libraries: Briarcliff, 2775 Briarcliff Road NE, 404-679-4400; Toco Hills-Avis G. Williams, 1282 McConnell Drive, 404-679-4404; www.dekalb.public.lib.ga.us; Ponce de Leon, 980 Ponce de Leon Avenue NE, 404-885-7820, www.af.public.lib.ga.us

Public School Education: DeKalb County School System, 678-676-1200, www.dekalb.k12.ga.us

Community Publications: *Atlanta Intown,* 404-586-0002, www.atlantanewsgroup.com

Community Resources: Emory University, 404-727-6123, www.emory.edu; North Druid Hills Residents Association, www.ndhra.org; Druid Hills Golf Club, 404-377-1766, www.druidhillsgolfclub.com; Fernbank Museum of Natural History, 767 Clifton Road NE, 404-929-6300, www.fernbank.edu/museum; Fernbank Science Center, 156 Heaton Park Drive NE, 678-874-7102, www.fernbank.edu; Bicycle South, 404-636-4444, www.bicyclesouth.com

Public Transportation: **MARTA**, 404-848-4711, www.itsmarta.com; **Northeast Line station:** Lindbergh Center; **Bus:** 6 Emory, 8 North Druid Hills, 19 Clairmont/VA Hospital, 33 Briarcliff, 36 North Decatur

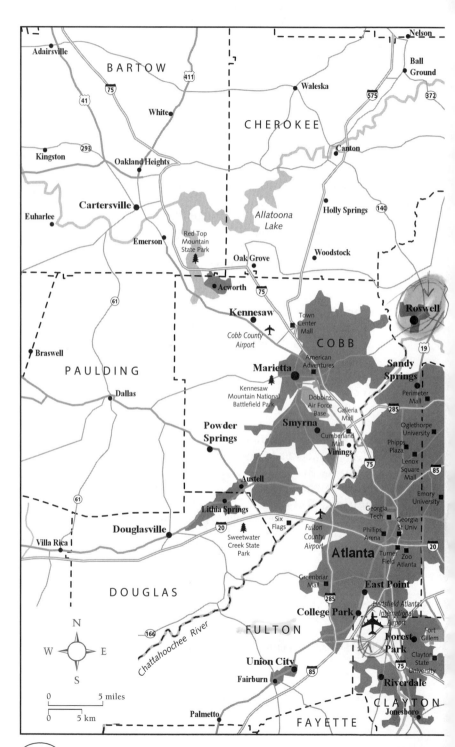

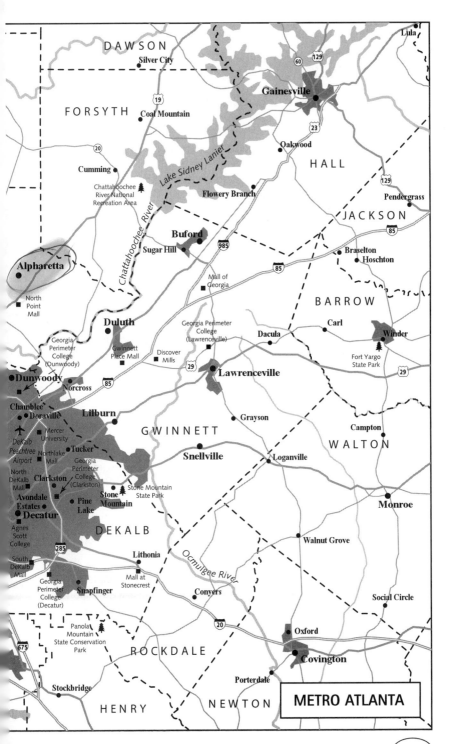

METRO ATLANTA

NEIGHBORING COMMUNITIES

NORTH FULTON COUNTY

North of Atlanta's city limits and further away from the inner-ring suburbs is the exurbia of North Fulton. One of the fastest growing areas in the country, North Fulton County boasts award-winning public schools and a "mediplex," along Johnson Ferry Road, in the Sandy Springs/Dunwoody area, featuring top-notch medical facilities. The county's growth, however, has created a traffic nightmare for residents in many neighborhoods. And, as of yet, there are no real solutions in sight. In some communities, rush-hour traffic is as bad on side streets as it is on the interstate. The freeway opening of the GA 400 extension in the early 1990s offers North Fulton residents a direct route into Atlanta proper, offering somewhat easier access to the city's many cultural and professional opportunities.

Despite the county's growth and development over the last decade, much of North Fulton still contains lush, forested, and hilly property that is the envy of many urban dwellers. For those seeking a suburban lifestyle, with good schools, and access to Buckhead, Midtown, and Downtown, North Fulton may be the perfect place.

SANDY SPRINGS

One of the area's busiest and most impressive retail business strips is in the North Fulton community of **Sandy Springs**. Once a Creek Indian settlement, this spot became a rest area of sorts for farmers and travelers due to the spring that was located at the intersection of two well-traveled trails. In 1842 Wilson Spruill purchased the land, and construction of a church and a few simple log cabins followed. Sandy Springs remained a quiet farm community well into the 20th century, until the City of Atlanta, its neighbor to the south, began encroaching.

Today, Sandy Springs boasts a population of over 85,000 people, with many of these residents working in the immediate area. Take a drive along busy Roswell Road (if you have an hour or so to spare) and you'll find dozens of strip malls, bars, office buildings, and fast-food restaurants. Cars sit bumper-to-bumper most of the day on this narrow street, and there are almost as many pedestrians here as there are in Buckhead. It's enough to make the faint of heart turn tail and head straight back to the quieter, intown neighborhoods. To many, it is this congestion along Roswell Road that comes to mind when they think of Sandy Springs. But, like most communities, if you look a little deeper you're sure to find pleasant and unexpected surprises. For instance, just blocks from the hustle and bustle of the commercial district, is the Peachtree Yoga Center; located on Sandy Springs Circle, which offers yoga classes for all levels, a nondenominational meditation room, and massage services. Just walking in the door and hearing the gurgling fountain can be enough to soothe someone who's spent two hours in traffic.

Another great contrast to the business hubbub of Sandy Springs is the design of the residential districts themselves. Just minutes away from traffic-clogged Roswell Road are tree-lined streets surrounding well-built, comfortable homes. In fact, Sandy Springs is full of beautifully maintained lawns supporting houses ranging from 1950s style bungalows to the predominant 1970s brick ranches.

The neighborhoods along Mt. Vernon Highway and Hammond Drive are older, with large shady lots and houses set back away from the street, while newer homes can be found along Glenridge Road and further south toward Buckhead in recently developed subdivisions. If you travel north along Roswell Road, away from the commercial district, there are lovely, ranch-style houses as well as larger contemporary homes lining the Chattahoochee River. These homes afford residents wonderful riverside views. This area's heavily wooded and rolling landscape attracts a large number of upwardly mobile young couples looking for the comfort of the suburbs for their growing children.

But Sandy Springs isn't just a suburb for growing families. It is also home to one of the largest populations of young singles in the metro Atlanta area and, therefore, offers a lot of newly built apartment complexes. From low-end, bare-bones studios to lushly landscaped, upscale gated communities, those looking for a particular type of apartment can surely find it here, most likely along Roswell Road.

Web Site: www.sandysprings.org

Area Codes: 404, 770

Zip Code: 30328, 30338, 30350, 30358, 31156

Post Offices: Glenridge Branch, 5400 Glenridge Drive; Sandy Springs Branch, 6094 Boylston Drive NE; Sandy Springs Postal Store, 227 Sandy Springs Place; North Springs, 7527 Roswell Road; Perimeter Station, 4707 Ashford-Dunwoody Road; 800-275-8777, www.usps.com

Police Precinct: North Fulton County Police Department, Patrol/Non-Emergency, 770-551-7600, www.fultonpolice.org

Emergency Hospitals: Northside Hospital, 1000 Johnson Ferry Road NE, 404-851-8000; St. Joseph's Hospital, 5665 Peachtree-Dunwoody Road, 404-851-7001, www.stjosephsatlanta.org

Library: Sandy Springs Regional, 395 Mount Vernon Highway, Atlanta, 404-303-6130; www.af.public.lib.ga.us

Public School Education: Fulton County School System, 404-763-6830, www.fulton.k12.ga.us

Community Publications: *Dunwoody Crier,* 770-451-4147, www.the crier.net

Community Resources: Sandy Springs Business Association, 404-255-5351, www.sandysprings.org/ssba; Sandy Springs Revitalization, Inc., 404-252-9352, www.sandysprings.org/ssri; Sandy Springs Community Action Center, 471 Mt. Vernon Highway NE, 404-256-4912; Heritage Sandy Springs, 404-851-9111, www.heritagesandy springs.org; Leadership Sandy Springs, 404-256-9091, www.leader-shipsandysprings.org; Greater North Fulton Chamber of Commerce, 1025 Old Roswell Road, Suite 101, 770-993-8806, www.gnfcc.com; North Fulton Education Force, 770-594-1055; North Fulton Optimist Club, www.nfoptimist.org; North Fulton Senior Services, 770-993-1906, www.seniorservicesnorthfulton.com; Peachtree Yoga Center, 404-847-9642

Public Transportation: **MARTA**, 404-848-4711, www.itsmarta.com; **North Line stations**: Medical Center, Sandy Springs, and North Springs; **Bus**: 5 Sandy Springs/Lindbergh Station, 25 Peachtree Industrial, 38 Chastain Park, 41 Windsor Parkway, 91 Henderson Mill, 92 Perimeter Mall

ROSWELL

North of Sandy Springs is the community of **Roswell**. Founded on the banks of the Chattahoochee River in 1839 by Georgia native Roswell King, this community's first claim to fame was as a small mill town. The King family's original Roswell Manufacturing Company was so successful they soon found themselves expanding by adding a second mill. King then began offering real estate and investment opportunities to his friends and associates, and soon there were homes, cottages, apartments, a general store, a church, and a school on the land surrounding the mills. The community grew and prospered until 1864 when Union troops led by General Sherman marched toward Atlanta. When Sherman discovered that clothes with the letters CSA (Confederate States of America) were being made at the mill, he ordered his troops to torch the community. Most residents were charged with treason and sent north. Amazingly, while the mill and local businesses burned, the homes and church were spared. After the war, many of the residents returned to their homes and rebuilt the mills. Textile manufacturing remained essential to Roswell's economy well into the 1970s.

Today, it's obvious that Roswell is a historic town. In fact, 640 acres of the area's 33.23 square miles are now listed with the National Register of

Historic Places. Many of the area's old homes, including Barrington Hal., Mimosa Hall, and Dolvin House, still stand and are currently used as private residences. However, Bulloch Hall, the childhood home of Mittie Bulloch (President Teddy Roosevelt's mother and Eleanor Roosevelt's grandmother), is open daily to the public and is a great place to visit. Even Roswell's town square has managed to retain the feel of an old-time rural community, despite an increase in population and local traffic. The historic square is beautifully laid out in a grid pattern similar to those found in New England. Today, unique stores, gift shops, and restaurants grace the square, and during the summer months it plays host to a concert series, along with numerous community-oriented festivals and events.

If you overlook the fact that 80,000 people now call Roswell home and that Holcomb Bridge Road, a busy four-lane street, is now the community's main thoroughfare, you may actually be convinced you're living in a small town rather than an ever-growing suburb of Atlanta. Roswell's neighborhoods contain a mixture of old Craftsman-style homes and newly developed subdivisions. Homes closest to the Chattahoochee Nature Center on and around Willeo Drive sit on large, tree-filled lots that offer residents a quiet, quasi-rural way of life. Houses closer to Holcomb Bridge Road are newer and often very similar in style. And, as in Sandy Springs, there are more than enough apartment communities to please all of the young couples and suburban singles moving to the area.

Web Site: www.roswellgov.com
Area Codes: 770, 678
Zip Codes: 30075, 30076, 30350
Post Offices: Roswell Main Office, 8920 Eves Road; Roswell Postal Store, 10719 Alpharetta Highway; Crosstown Carrier Annex, 225E Crossville Road; North Springs, 7527 Roswell Road NE; 800-275-8777, www.usps.com
Police Precincts: North Fulton County Police Department, Patrol/Non-Emergency, 770-551-7600; Fulton County Police Department, Northeast Precinct, 10205 Medlock Bridge Parkway, 770-495-8738, www.fultonpolice.org; Roswell Police Department, 39 Hill Street, 770-640-4100; www.roswellpd.org
Emergency Hospitals: North Fulton Regional Hospital, 3000 Hospital Boulevard, Roswell, 770-751-2500, www.northfultonregional.com; Northside Hospital, 1000 Johnson Ferry Road NE, 404-851-8000, www.northside.com
Library: Roswell Regional, 115 Norcross Street, Roswell, 770-640-3075, www.af.public.lib.ga.us
Public School Education: Fulton County School System, 404-763-6830, www.fulton.k12.ga.us

cations: *Alpharetta-Roswell Revue & News*, 770-442-
thfulton.com

ources: Historic Roswell Convention and Visitors
0-3253, www.cvb.roswell.ga.us; Roswell City Hall, 38
Hill Street, 641-3727, www.roswellgov.com; Roswell Cultural Arts
Center, 950 Forrest Street, 770-594-6232; Chattahoochee Nature
Center, 770-992-2055, www.chattnaturecenter.com; Greater North
Fulton Chamber of Commerce, 1025 Old Roswell Road, Suite 101, 770-
993-8806, www.gnfcc.com; North Fulton Education Force, 770-594-
1055; North Fulton Optimist Club, www.nfoptimist.org; North Fulton
Senior Services, 770-993-1906, www.seniorservicesnorthfulton.com

Public Transportation: **MARTA**, 404-848-4711, www.itsmarta.com;
North Line station: North Springs; **Bus**: 41 Windsor Parkway, 85
Roswell/Alpharetta, 140 Holcomb Bridge, 141 North Point Mall

ALPHARETTA

Further north is the community of **Alpharetta**. This North Fulton suburb
was originally a successful trading post village called New Prospect Camp
Ground, which was frequented by white settlers and local Indians alike. In
December 1857, the village was chartered and became the county seat of
Milton County and the village was renamed Alpharetta—from the Greek
word "Alpha" meaning "first" and "Retta" meaning "town." (In 1932,
Milton County was absorbed into Fulton County.)

Like Roswell, this fast-growing area remained rural until just three
decades ago. In fact, in 1980 Alpharetta's population was still a mere
3,000. But today, thanks to the sprawling growth of the metro area, the
population is nearing 35,000. This growth is significant, but has not yet
reached the levels of Sandy Springs and Roswell. Much of Alpharetta is still
lush, green, and undeveloped, but this is quickly changing as more and
more buildings replace greenspace. Driving through Alpharetta along
States Bridge Road or Abbots Bridge Road, for example, you could expect
to find a newly constructed apartment complex across the street from a
working farm . . . next door to a small subdivision . . . around the corner
from a strip mall. It's just this sort of ambiguity—greenspace next to homes
and shopping—along with the excellent schools and access to jobs that
makes Alpharetta one of the hottest markets in metro Atlanta for both residential and commercial real estate. You'll find the large colonial and ranch-
style homes in this community to be a bit higher priced than comparable
homes in other North Fulton suburbs. Many line the rugged bluffs over-
looking the Chattahoochee River, offering lovely views. Most homes are
built on nice-sized lots or in recently developed subdivisions. The newer

homes coexist easily with the older homes, as the overall architectural style is fairly traditional. Perhaps one of the most interesting things about Alpharetta is its equestrian theme. Wills Park, with entrances on Old Milton Parkway and Wills Road, features a world-class equestrian center complete with competition course and beautiful stables. Private ranches are also plentiful.

Web Site: www.alpharetta.ga.us
Area Codes: 770, 678
Zip Codes: 30004, 30005, 30022
Post Offices: Alpharetta Main Office, 2400 Old Milton Parkway; Webb Bridge Branch, 4575 Webb Bridge Road; 800-275-8777, www.usps.com
Police Precincts: North Fulton County Police Department, Patrol/Non-Emergency, 770-551-7600; Fulton County Police Department, Northeast Precinct, 10205 Medlock Bridge Parkway, 770-495-8738 www.fultonpolice.org; Alpharetta Police Department, 2565 Old Milton Parkway, 678-297-6300; Alpharetta Community Service Division, 678-297-6309; www.alpharetta.ga.us
Emergency Hospitals: North Fulton Regional Hospital, 3000 Hospital Boulevard, Roswell, 770-751-2500, www.northfultonregional.com; Northside/Alpharetta Medical, 3400 Old Milton Parkway, Alpharetta, 770-667-4000, www.northside.com
Libraries: Alpharetta, 238 Canton Street, Alpharetta, 770-740-2425; Northeast/Spruill Oaks Regional, 9560 Spruill Road, Alpharetta, 770-360-8820; Ocee, 5090 Abbotts Bridge Road, Alpharetta, 770-360-8897; www.af.public.lib.ga.us
Public School Education: Fulton County School System, 404-763-6830, www.fulton.k12.ga.us
Community Publications: *Alpharetta-Roswell Revue & News*, 770-442-3278, www.northfulton.com
Community Resources: Alpharetta City Hall, Two South Main Street, 678-297-6000, www.alpharetta.ga.us; Alpharetta Environmental Education Center, 770-410-5835; Alpharetta Wills Park Equestrian Center, 678-297-6120, http://alpharetta.ga.us; Greater North Fulton Chamber of Commerce, 1025 Old Roswell Road, Suite 101, 770-993-8806, www.gnfcc.com; North Fulton Education Force, 770-594-1055; North Fulton Optimist Club, www.nfoptimist.org; North Fulton Senior Services, 770-993-1906, www.seniorservicesnorthfulton.com
Public Transportation: **MARTA**, 404-848-4711, www.itsmarta.com; **Bus**: 41 Windsor Parkway, 85 Roswell/Alpharetta, 140 Holcomb Bridge, 141 North Point Mall

DEKALB COUNTY

DeKalb (pronounced "DeeCab") County is the most ethnically diverse county in the metro Atlanta area, is home to over 200 internationally owned businesses, and is also one of the largest refugee resettlement locations in the country. Parts of the City of Atlanta are governed by DeKalb, and the county is the region's most urban area.

DeKalb County identifies itself not only as the county with an international flavor, but also as the county with myriad biomedical facilities. The US Centers for Disease Control, the Yerkes Primate Center, Emory University's Rollins Research Center, and the American Cancer Society's national headquarters are all located here.

In addition to the handful of neighborhoods featured below, other DeKalb County communities worth looking into are **Doraville**, **Northlake**, **Tucker**, **Clarkston**, and **Pine Lake**.

DECATUR

The City of **Decatur**, the DeKalb County seat, was founded in 1823. The downtown area still conveys a small-town feeling with its Georgian-style courthouse and shops clustered around the town square. But recent development and congested one-way streets here are beginning to make downtown Decatur feel more like downtown Atlanta. On any given day, residents can expect to find streets blocked by construction equipment as new condos or office complexes are erected. Fortunately, people who work in Decatur's downtown area can take advantage of MARTA; the Decatur Station is located in the center of the community's commercial district, allowing easy access for pedestrians. Many opt to take the train in and out of downtown Decatur rather than fight traffic and scramble for parking.

Despite recent growth, Decatur's town square has preserved its small-town ambiance with wide sidewalks, wooden benches situated beneath curving light posts, and plenty of locally owned businesses. The square also plays host to a variety of events throughout the year, from family fun festivals to summertime concerts. Every July 4th, residents crowd the square to witness Decatur's famous fireworks display.

Because of its ethnic diversity, lower sales tax, and less expensive housing, Decatur attracts a mix of students, singles, young families, and retirees. West Ponce de Leon Avenue, Decatur's main street, is lined with eateries offering soul food, home cooking, Asian cuisine, and other fare. Near the downtown area is Eddie's Attic, a long-standing folk music haven frequented by the Grammy Award–winning Indigo Girls and up-and-coming local acts. Grammy-nominated performer Shawn Mullins got his start here and continues to play Eddie's whenever he's in town.

The area also tends to attract an open-minded, easygoing crowd, including many of Atlanta's nesting gay and lesbian inhabitants who prefer the laid-back Decatur atmosphere to the busy streets of Midtown. *The Decatur Focus,* the city's official newsletter, encourages recipients to "Help Decatur be a community where neighbors help neighbors."

Just a stone's throw away from the laid-back bustle of downtown is the pastoral campus of Agnes Scott, a women's college founded as the Decatur Female Seminary in 1888. The neighborhoods surrounding this beautiful campus are a wonderful balance to Decatur's commercial district, with shady sidewalks, quiet streets, and large Victorians and mid-sized bungalows.

On the quiet streets south of the downtown square, families reside in smaller homes ranging from the ever-present, one-story brick ranch to old, ornate Victorians. Students of metro Atlanta's many universities find Decatur the perfect place to put down temporary roots, and they quickly fill up the smaller apartment complexes and abundant rental houses. Rents in Decatur are less expensive than intown neighborhoods such as Virginia Highland and Buckhead, though it's located only six miles from downtown Atlanta.

Web Site: www.decatur-ga.com

Area Codes: 404, 770

Zip Codes: 30030, 30031, 30032, 30033, 30034, 30035

Post Offices: Main Office, 520 West Ponce de Leon Avenue; Decatur Carrier Annex, 3651 Memorial Drive; South Decatur, 2853 Candler Road; Scottdale, 3328 East Ponce de Leon Avenue; Avondale Estates, 15 Franklin Street; 800-275-8777, www.usps.com

Police Precincts: DeKalb County Police Department, 404-294-2519; Center Precinct, 3630 Camp Circle, 404-294-2580; South Precinct, 1816 Candler Road, 404-286-7900; www.dekalbpolice.com; DeKalb County Sheriff's Office, 404-298-8145, www.dekalbsheriff.org

Emergency Hospital: DeKalb Medical Center, 2701 North Decatur Road, 404-501-1000, www.dekalbmedicalcenter.org

Libraries: Main Library, 215 Sycamore Street, Decatur, 404-370-3070; Avis G. Williams, 1282 McConnell Drive, Decatur, 404-679-4404; Briarcliff, 2775 Briarcliff Road, Decatur, 404-679-4400; North Druid Hills, 1242 North Druid Hills Road, Decatur, 404-848-7140; Covington, 3500 Covington Highway, Decatur, 404-508-7180; Flat Shoals, 4022 Flat Shoals Parkway, Decatur, 404-244-4370; Scott Candler, 2644 McAfee Road, Decatur, 404-286-6986; Wesley Chapel, 2861 Wesley Chapel Road, Decatur, 404-286-6980; www.dekalb.public.lib.ga.us

Public School Education: Decatur City Schools, 404-370-4400, www.decatur-city.k12.ga.us; Decatur City Schools Hotline, 404-419-6055; DeKalb County Board of Education, 678-676-1200, www.dekalb.k12.ga.us

Community Publications: *The Decatur Focus*, 404-371-8386, www.decatur-ga.com; *Decatur DeKalb News Era*, 404-292-3536

Community Resources: Decatur Business Association, 404-371-8386; Decatur Arts Alliance, 404-371-9583, www.decaturartsalliance.org; Decatur Preservation Society, 404-371-4444, www.decaturpreservation alliance.org; Decatur Events Hotline, 404-371-8262; DeKalb County Chamber of Commerce, 404-378-8000, www.dekalbchamber.org; DeKalb County Convention & Visitors Bureau, 770-492-5000, www.atlantasdekalb.org; DeKalb History Center, 404-373-8287, www.dekalbhistory.org

Public Transportation: **MARTA**, 404-848-4711, www.itsmarta.com; **East/West Line station**: Decatur; **Bus**: 8 North Druid Hills, 12 Medlock, 17 Decatur/Lakewood, 18 South Decatur, 19 Clairmont Road, 22 Second Avenue, 24 Belvedere, 28 East Lake Meadows, 33 Briarcliff, 36 North Decatur, 96 Snapfinger/Wesley Chapel, 122 DeKalb College, 123 Decatur/Candler Park

AVONDALE ESTATES

East of Decatur lies **Avondale Estates**, a completely self-sustained residential development conceived and founded in the early 1920s by patent medicine millionaire George F. Willis. Willis envisioned a subdivision modeled after an old English village, and by 1930 he had converted 1000 acres of scenic farmland into his ideal community. Avondale Estates' public buildings and businesses were constructed in the Tudor style, gracing the commercial district with a small village ambiance that remains to this day. Homes here reflect numerous traditional styles including Tudor, English Cottage, Colonial Revival, and Craftsman.

The city, which was granted its own mayor, police department, and post office by the Georgia State government in 1926, is filled with curving, tree-lined streets. The area's small parks, its lake, pool, clubs, bird sanctuary, and tennis courts are accessible only to Avondale's residents and their guests, all of whom are identified by vehicle decals or temporary passes provided by city hall. Though this exclusivity is obviously an advantage to residents, it can be intimidating to outsiders. The community police department diligently patrols its every corner, and strangers to the neighborhood won't get very far without running across a friendly but inquiring officer.

Avondale Estates was placed on the National Register of Historic Places in 1986 for being the only documented example of an early twentieth century, planned town in the southeastern United States, as well as for the character of its architecture and landscape. Today, the Avondale city government is diligent in preserving the historic value of the community, strictly limiting the type of and amount of new construction and renovation allowed within the city. Historic preservation guidelines are available for anyone considering moving into the community.

Web Site: http://avondaleestates.org

Area Codes: 404, 770

Zip Code: 30002

Post Offices: Avondale Estates, 15 Franklin Street; Main Office, 520 West Ponce de Leon Avenue; Scottdale, 3328 East Ponce de Leon Avenue; 800-275-8777, www.usps.com

Police Precincts: Avondale Estates Police Department, 404-294-2000; DeKalb County Police Department, 404-294-2519; Center Precinct, 3630 Camp Circle, 404-294-2580; www.dekalbpolice.com; DeKalb County Sheriff's Office, 404-298-8145, www.dekalbsheriff.org

Emergency Hospital: DeKalb Medical Center, 2701 North Decatur Road, 404-501-1000, www.dekalbmedicalcenter.org

Libraries: Tobie Grant, 644 Parkdale, Drive, Scottdale, 404-508-7174; Main Library, 215 Sycamore Street, Decatur, 404-370-3070; www.dekalb.public.lib.ga.us

Public School Education: DeKalb County Board of Education, 678-676-1200, www.dekalb.k12.ga.us

Community Publications: *Atlanta Intown*, 404-586-0002, www.atlantanewsgroup.com

Community Resources: Avondale Estates City Hall, 21 North Avondale Plaza, 404-294-5400; Avondale Community Club, 59 Lakeshore Drive, 404-284-2934; DeKalb County Chamber of Commerce, 404-378-8000, www.dekalbchamber.org; DeKalb County Convention & Visitors Bureau, 770-492-5000, www.atlantasdekalb.org; DeKalb History Center, 404-373-8287, www.dekalbhistory.org

Public Transportation: MARTA, 404-848-4711, www.itsmarta.com; **East/West Line station**: Avondale; **Bus**: 36 North Decatur, 125 Brookhaven/Avondale

STONE MOUNTAIN

One of DeKalb County's places of pride is the **Stone Mountain** area, which includes the 3,200-acre Stone Mountain Park, Stone Mountain

Village, and neighborhoods radiating out along Memorial Drive. Of all the metro Atlanta communities, this one perhaps typifies what most Northerners might envision a small Georgia town to be like. Narrow streets and old frame houses with porches large enough for rocking chairs and swings dominate this community, giving it an old-world, rural feel not found in other Atlanta suburbs.

The community is named for the actual Stone Mountain, the world's largest monolith of exposed granite, rising over 800 feet above the ground and located in the heart of Stone Mountain Park. Local Native Americans once used the mountain for tribal rites and as a lookout point. By the time white settlers inhabited the area in the nineteenth century, the unusual rock formation was beginning to attract the attention of travelers and tourists. With the founding of the town of New Gibraltar (now the city of Stone Mountain), the area grew with the steady influx of tourist money.

Aside from its geological magnitude, Stone Mountain possesses an artistic magnitude of sorts, with the world's largest sculpture carved on its face. Originally conceived by noted sculptor Gutzon Borglum, who later carved the faces on Mt. Rushmore, the face of Stone Mountain depicts the three mounted figures of confederate heroes Robert E. Lee, Jefferson Davis, and Stonewall Jackson. Taking over 42 years to complete and utilizing the talents of three separate artists, the memorial was finally completed in 1972 and has been attracting onlookers ever since. Today, Stone Mountain Park offers nature trails, family activities, golf courses, swimming, fishing, boating, and a skylift to the top of the mountain. There is also a petting zoo, an antique car museum, and a number of shops and restaurants.

In the shadow of the great monolith, Stone Mountain Village contains turn-of-the-century commercial buildings, which house antique stores, gift shops, restaurants, and cafes. Now home to over 7,000 residents, the village is really a place where Old South meets New South. The history here is tricky, as Stone Mountain was, for many years, a predominantly white community and an annual Ku Klux Klan meeting site. But today the town is enjoying greater ethnic diversity than ever before, and residents are quick to point out that the community is more concerned with preserving its small-town character than its antiquated racist attitudes.

The homes in this area range from ornate Victorians to 1930s bungalows to newer, Craftsman-style houses, all at affordable prices. As in other suburbs, most of the older homes are on the largest lots and can be found closest to the Village, while the newer homes tend to be in planned subdivisions with smaller yards, many located on the side streets around Memorial Drive.

Web Site: www.stonemountaincity.org
Area Codes: 404, 770

Zip Codes: 30083, 30086, 30087, 30088

Post Offices: Stone Mountain Main Post Office, 5181 West Mountain Street; Stone Mountain Memorial Branch, 5152 Memorial Drive; Mountain Park Post Office, 1785 East Park Place Boulevard; 800-275-8777, www.usps.com

Police Precincts: City of Stone Mountain Police Department, 770-879-4980, www.stonemountaincity.org; DeKalb County Police Department, 404-294-2519; East Precinct, 2484 Bruce Street, 770-482-0300; www.dekalbpolice.com; DeKalb County Sheriff's Office, 404-298-8145, www.dekalbsheriff.org

Emergency Hospitals: Northlake Medical Center, 1455 Montreal Road, Atlanta, 770-270-3000, www.northlakemedical.com; DeKalb Medical Center, 2701 North Decatur Road, 404-501-1000, www.dekalbmedical center.org

Libraries: Sue Kellogg, 952 Leon Street, Stone Mountain, 770-413-2020; Hairston Crossing, 4911 Redan Road, Stone Mountain, 404-508-7170; www.dekalb.public.lib.ga.us

Public School Education: DeKalb County Board of Education, 678-676-1200, www.dekalb.k12.ga.us

Community Publications: *CrossRoadsNews*, 404-284-1888; www.crossroadsnews

Community Resources: City of Stone Mountain, 770-498-8984, www.stonemountaincity.org; Stone Mountain Village, www.stonemountainvillage.com; Stone Mountain Park, 770-498-5690, www.stonemountainpark.com; Main Street Stone Mountain, www.mainstreetstonemountain.com; Stone Mountain Woman's Club, 5513 East Mountain Street, 770-879-8771; DeKalb County Chamber of Commerce, 404-378-8000, www.dekalbchamber.org; DeKalb County Convention & Visitors Bureau, 770-492-5000, www.atlantas dekalb.org; DeKalb History Center, 404-373-8287, www.dekalb history.org

Public Transportation: **MARTA**, 404-848-4711, www.itsmarta.com; **East-West Line station**: Indian Creek; **Bus**: 120 Stone Mountain, 121 Mountain Industrial

LITHONIA

Further south in DeKalb County is the City of **Lithonia**, another of the area's ethnically mixed, yet still somewhat rural, communities. It's also home to the upscale, Lionshead subdivision, a predominantly African-American neighborhood boasting large, newly built, traditional-style homes.

Established in the mid-1800s, this community began as a small settlement known as Cross Roads. Shortly after, the name was changed to Lithonia, a Greek word meaning "Rock Place." In just ten years, Lithonia was home to about 250 residents. Today, Lithonia's population is just over 2,000.

Many choosing to live in Lithonia are looking to get away from the more crowded, intown neighborhoods and more heavily populated subdivisions. Here, residents get the best of all worlds—nice homes on large lots at reasonable prices, convenience to local highways and interstates for those who commute, well-respected schools and churches, and an interesting ethnic mix. Along with the residents who work in downtown Atlanta or Buckhead, Lithonia also attracts people who work all over the south side of the city, from Ford Motor Company's Hapeville plant to the Atlanta University Center.

Web Site: www.cityoflithonia.org
Area Codes: 770, 678
Zip Codes: 30038, 30058
Post Offices: Lithonia Post Office, 3035 Stone Mountain Street; Redan Post Office, 1544 Wellborn Road; 800-275-8777, www.usps.com
Police Precincts: City of Lithonia Police Department, 6980 Main Street, 770-482-4461; DeKalb County Police Department, 404-294-2519; East Precinct, 2484 Bruce Street, 770-482-0300; www.dekalb police.com; DeKalb County Sheriff's Office, 404-298-8145, www.dekalbsheriff.org
Emergency Hospitals: Northlake Medical Center, 1455 Montreal Road, Atlanta, 770-270-3000, www.northlakemedical.com; DeKalb Medical Center, 2701 North Decatur Road, 404-501-1000, www.dekalbmedical center.org
Libraries: Lithonia, 6821 Church Street, 770-482-3820; Bruce Street, 2484 Bruce Street, Lithonia, 770-482-0405; Salem-Panola, 5137 Salem Road, Lithonia, 770-987-6900; www.dekalb.public.lib.ga.us
Public School Education: DeKalb County Board of Education, 678-676-1200, www.dekalb.k12.ga.us
Community Publications: *CrossRoadsNews*, 404-284-1888, www.crossroadsnews.com
Community Resources: City of Lithonia, 770-482-8136, www.city oflithonia.org; DeKalb County Chamber of Commerce, 404-378-8000, www.dekalbchamber.org; DeKalb County Convention & Visitors Bureau, 770-492-5000, www.atlantasdekalb.org; DeKalb History Center, 404-373-8287, www.dekalbhistory.org
Public Transportation: **MARTA**, 404-848-4711, www.itsmarta.com; **Bus**: 18 South Decatur, 120 Stone Mountain, 121 Mountain Industrial

CHAMBLEE

Closer to the I-285 perimeter in DeKalb County is the community of **Chamblee** (pronounced SHAM-blee). As part of Atlanta's "International Corridor," this three-square-mile city, located northeast of Atlanta, has the most culturally diverse population in the State of Georgia. Families from Asia, India, Africa, Mexico, South America, Europe, and all parts of the United States now call Chamblee home.

Unlike the Chinatowns or a Little Italy in other US cities, in Chamblee you're likely to find a Mexican restaurant next to a Japanese grocery or Colombian bakery; a Chinese herb shop next to a Korean video store or an American fast food joint. And grocery stores like the popular International Farmers' Market or Atlanta Asian Foods operate in close proximity to American chain grocery stores such as Publix and Kroger.

But ethnic diversity is not the only thing Chamblee has to offer. In the heart of the historic business district is Chamblee's famous "Antique Row," the largest antique area in the South. Home to more than 150 dealers, the shops offer quality antiques and collectibles to fit any budget. Even if you don't want to buy anything, strolling along Antique Row is a great way to spend a Saturday afternoon. Parking is not usually a problem, but spaces are limited, so getting an early start is a good idea. And if you'd rather take advantage of Atlanta's transit system, you're in luck. The Chamblee MARTA station (on the Northeast rail line) is easily accessed.

Perhaps the biggest problem with Chamblee is that, at first glance, it appears to be too industrial to be a comfortable neighborhood. Traveling down either of its two main thoroughfares, Buford Highway and Peachtree Industrial Boulevard, it's hard to believe this community offers anything but restaurants, car dealerships, strip malls, and antique shops. But a closer look reveals delightfully quiet side streets leading into quaint old subdivisions like Huntley Hills and Sexton Woods where you'll find nice homes set on large, shaded lots, as well as neighborhood swimming pools and tennis clubs. Homes in this area are generally the split-level ranch style, and they sell quickly.

One great selling point for these neighborhoods, and for Chamblee as a whole, is the area's public school system. Several nearby elementary schools are well respected and conveniently located. But the feather in Chamblee's educational cap has to be Chamblee High School. Ninety-nine percent of Chamblee High's seniors take the SATs and average in the mid-500s in both math and verbal scores, and students here consistently rank among the top ten in test scores for the entire state.

For newcomers, especially those with young children, looking to live inside the perimeter, in a community close to I-285, the Perimeter Mall, and Buckhead, Chamblee is a good option.

Web Site: www.chambleega.com
Area Codes: 770, 678
Zip Codes: 30341, 30366
Post Offices: Chamblee Post Office, 3545 Broad Street; North Atlanta Carrier Facility, 1920 Dresden Drive NE; Embry Hills, 3579 Chamblee Tucker Road; 800-275-8777, www.usps.com
Police Precincts: Chamblee Police Department, 3518 Broad Street, 770-986-5005; DeKalb County Police Department, 404-294-2519; North Precinct, 4453 Ashford-Dunwoody Road, 770-901-6012; www.dekalbpolice.com; DeKalb County Sheriff's Office, 404-298-8145, www.dekalbsheriff.org
Emergency Hospital: Dunwoody Medical Center, 4575 North Shallowford Road, 770-454-2000; www.emorydunwoody.com
Libraries: Chamblee, 4115 Clairmont Road, 770-936-1380; Embry Hills, 3733 Chamblee Tucker Road, Chamblee, 770-270-8230; www. dekalb.public.lib.ga.us
Public School Education: DeKalb County Board of Education, 678-676-1200, www.dekalb.k12.ga.us
Community Publications: *Chamblee-Doraville Neighbor,* 770-454-9388
Community Resources: City of Chamblee, 770-986-5010, www. chambleega.com; Chamblee Antique Row, 770-455-4751, www. antiquerow.com; DeKalb Peachtree Airport, Clairmont Road, Chamblee, 770-936-5440, www.pdkairport.org; DeKalb County Chamber of Commerce, 404-378-8000, www.dekalbchamber.org; DeKalb County Convention & Visitors Bureau, 770-492-5000, www.atlantasdekalb.org; DeKalb History Center, 404-373-8287, www.dekalbhistory.org
Public Transportation: **MARTA**, 404-848-4711, www.itsmarta.com; **Northeast Line stations**: Chamblee and Doraville; **Bus**: 19 Clairmont Road, 25 Peachtree Industrial, 29 Brookhaven/Chamblee, 39 Buford Highway, 65 Chamblee/Chestnut, 70 Chamblee/Doraville, 124 Chamblee Tucker, 129 Chamblee/Dunwoody, 135 North Shallowford

DUNWOODY

The upscale community of **Dunwoody**, north of Chamblee, is a planned suburb originally based around Dunwoody Village, a commercial shopping complex. The neighborhoods surrounding Dunwoody Village are filled with large, traditional-style homes on tree-lined streets with culs-de-sac. And most Dunwoody residents tend to be middle- to upper-middle-class families. But, the recent development of several gated apartment communities has helped make Dunwoody more affordable and, therefore, accessible to the younger crowd, particularly aspiring executives and professionals.

Like neighboring Sandy Springs, which is linked to Dunwoody by Abernathy Road, this area has experienced phenomenal growth in recent years, making it one of the most desired, and most expensive, suburbs in metro Atlanta. In what was once untouched forest, now office parks and strip malls abound. Newly developed upscale restaurants fill the area, as do coffee shops, bookstores, bakeries, and specialty boutiques. Yet, even with all the newly developed retail and office spaces, Dunwoody still has plenty of greenspace and one of the best nature centers in the area. Located on Roberts Drive, the Dunwoody Nature Center offers exhibits, classes, nature trails and a small park. It's open year round, but it's best to call for hours as they vary according to season.

Dunwoody residents enjoy their proximity to Perimeter Mall and the exploding commercial development surrounding it. Perimeter Mall, which rivals Buckhead's Lenox Mall in size and variety of stores, is located about a mile south of the Dunwoody Village neighborhoods. Locals no longer need to travel to the city, since all the amenities they can dream of are now close to home.

Web Site: www.dunwoodynorth.org
Area Codes: 404, 770
Zip Codes: 30038
Post Offices: Dunwoody Post Office, 1551 Dunwoody Village Parkway; Perimeter Station, 4707 Ashford-Dunwoody Road; Dunwoody Carrier Annex, 4444 North Shallowford Road; 800-275-8777, www.usps.com
Police Precincts: DeKalb County Police Department, 404-294-2519; North Precinct, 4453 Ashford-Dunwoody Road, 770-901-6012; www.dekalbpolice.com; DeKalb County Sheriff's Office, 404-298-8145, www.dekalbsheriff.org
Emergency Hospitals: Dunwoody Medical Center, 4575 North Shallowford Road, 770-454-2000, www.emorydunwoody.com; Northside Hospital, 1000 Johnson Ferry Road NE, 404-851-8000, www.northside.com; St. Joseph's Hospital, 5665 Peachtree Dunwoody Road, 404-851-7001, www.stjosephsatlanta.org; Children's Healthcare of Atlanta, 1001 Johnson Ferry Road NE, 404-256-5252, www.choa.org
Library: Dunwoody Branch, 5339 Chamblee-Dunwoody Road, 770-512-4640, www.dekalb.public.lib.ga.us

Public School Education: DeKalb County Board of Education, 678-676-1200, www.dekalb.k12.ga.us

Community Publications: *Dunwoody Crier,* 770-451-4147, www.the crier.net

Community Resources: Dunwoody North Civic Association, www.dunwoodynorth.org; Dunwoody North Home and Garden Club, 770-455-0650; Dunwoody Homeowners Association, 770-817-8100, www.dunwoodyga.org; Dunwoody Nature Center, 770-394-3322, www.dunwoodynature.org; Perimeter Mall, 770-394-4270, www.perimetermall.com; DeKalb County Chamber of Commerce, 404-378-8000, www.dekalbchamber.org; DeKalb County Convention & Visitors Bureau, 770-492-5000, www.atlantas dekalb.org; DeKalb History Center, 404-373-8287, www.dekalb history.org

Public Transportation: **MARTA**, 404-848-4711, www.itsmarta.com; **North Line station**: Dunwoody; **Bus**: 129 Chamblee/Dunwoody, 132 Tilly Mill, 135 North Shallowford, 150 North River

COBB COUNTY

Like much of the area in and around metro Atlanta, Cobb County was once home to the Creek and Cherokee Indian nations. In 1832, after the state parceled out the land by lottery, settlers organized the Cobb County government and named their community after Thomas Willis Cobb, the illustrious politician, who, during the course of his political career, served as a US Representative, a US Senator, and a Supreme Court Judge. Civil War fighting subsequently devastated the Cobb County area. However, by World War I, demand for the region's abundant agricultural products led to an economic growth that continues to this day. During the last three decades, Cobb has increased its population by over 50%. Today there are over 600,000 residents in Cobb County.

Cobb County's booming economy, high standard of living, and safer streets lure many newcomers to the area. Numerous residents from other parts of metro Atlanta have chosen to relocate here as well. Once a bedroom community centered around Marietta and Smyrna, over the last decade Cobb has grown into a suburban megaplex. The area's largest industrial employer, Lockheed Martin, employs over 10,000 workers in its Marietta plant. Fifteen million square feet of office space, located at the intersection of I-75 and I-285 and dubbed the "Platinum Triangle," houses some of the nation's largest companies, including Home Depot, US Sprint, and IBM.

In addition to the Cobb Galleria Centre, with its convention area, convertible arena, and stage seating for athletic events, concerts, and plays,

Cobb is also home to three of the Southeast's largest outdoor theme parks: Six Flags Over Georgia, White Water Park, and American Adventures.

The county has its own public transportation system, Cobb Community Transit, which operates bus service throughout the county and into the Atlanta commercial district. Funded by sales taxes and state money, a massive transportation improvement effort is continuously underway, with almost $900 million being spent on improving Cobb's roadways and bridges.

In addition to the neighborhood profiles below, other Cobb County communities worth investigating include the cities of **Acworth**, www.acworth.org, **Kennesaw**, www.kennesaw.ga.us, and **Powder Springs**, www.cityofpowdersprings.org,

MARIETTA

The Cobb County seat is **Marietta**, with nearly 60,000 residents. Named for Thomas Willis Cobb's wife, this city was settled in 1833 and incorporated in 1852. The town has a rich Civil War history, with many turn-of-the-century private homes still in existence. In fact, Marietta boasts five nationally recognized historical districts, including Cherokee Street and Washington Avenue, where you will find antebellum and High Victorian-style houses, sheltered from the hot Georgia sun by lofty shade trees. The historic town square, in downtown Marietta, is home to Glover Park on the Square, a block of land donated in the mid-1800s by the city's first mayor, John H. Glover, a popular businessman and politician. The square has served generations of Cobb County consumers with its shops and businesses, and it plays host to a variety of free concerts and events throughout the year.

Marietta is also the center of much of Cobb County's cultural life. The Marietta-Cobb Museum of Art, built in the Greek Revival style in the 1930s, features a diverse program of exhibitions throughout the year. Also, the relatively new community theater, Marietta Theatre in the Square, hosts small, local plays as well as upscale, Broadway-type productions such as the "1940s Radio Hour."

The neighborhoods in Marietta and throughout most of East Cobb range from upscale subdivisions of large homes to recently built apartment complexes to blocks of smaller, less expensive houses, perfect for first-time homebuyers. And, unlike many neighborhoods within the Atlanta city limits, where you may pay top dollar for smaller homes with tiny yards, the lots in Cobb tend to be more than generous, with houses to match.

Web Site: www.city.marietta.ga.us
Area Code: 770

Zip Codes: 30008, 30060, 30062, 30064, 30065, 30066, 30067, 30068, 30090

Post Offices: Marietta, Main Post Office, 257 Lawrence Street NE; Gresham Road Station, 1290 Gresham Road; Cumberland Carrier, 1901 Terrell Mill Road; Cumberland Mall, 1101 Cumberland Mall SE; Windy Hill, 3000 Windy Hill Road; Mount Bethel, 4455 Lower Roswell Road; East Cobb, 1395 East Cobb Drive; Sprayberry, 2886 Sandy Plains Road; 800-275-8777, www.usps.com

Police Precincts: City of Marietta Police Department, 770-794-5300, www.city.marietta.ga.us/police; Cobb County Police Department, 140 North Marietta Parkway, 770-499-3900, www.cobbpolice.com

Emergency Hospitals: Wellstar Kennestone Hospital, 677 Church Street, Marietta, 770-793-5000; Wellstar Windy Hill Hospital, 2540 Windy Hill Road, Marietta, 770-644-1000; www.wellstar.org

Libraries: Central Headquarters, 266 Roswell Street, 770-528-2320; East Marietta Branch, 2051 Lower Roswell Road NE, 770-509-2711; Gritters Branch, 880 Shaw Park Road NE, 770-528-2524; Hattie G. Wilson Branch, 350 Lemon Street NE, 770-528-2526; Kemp Memorial Branch, 4029 Due West Road NW, 770-528-2527; Merchant's Walk Branch, 1315 Johnson Ferry Road NE, 770-509-2730; Mountain View Branch, 3320 Sandy Plains Road NE, 770-509-2725; Sibley Branch, 1539 South Cobb Drive SE, 770-528-2520; Stratton Branch, 1100 Powder Springs Road SE, 770-528-2522; www.cobbcat.org

Public School Education: Marietta City Schools, 250 Howard Street, 770-422-3500, www.marietta-city.k12.ga.us; Cobb County School System, 514 Glover Street, 770-426-3300, www.cobb.k12.ga.us

Community Publications: *Marietta Daily Journal/Neighbor Newspapers*, 770-428-9411, www.mdjonline.com

Community Resources: Marietta Welcome Center, Four Depot Street, 770-429-1115; The Marietta Square, www.mariettasquare.com; Marietta-Cobb Museum of Art, 770-528-1444, www.marietta square.com/mcma; Cobb County Chamber of Commerce, 770-980-9510, www.cobbchamber.org; Cobb Galleria Centre, 770-955-8000, www.cobbgalleria.com

Public Transportation: **Cobb Community Transit (CCT)** system, 770-427-4444, www.cobbdot.org/cct.htm; local and express routes throughout Cobb County; **Cobb Rides**, www.cobbrides.com; **Commuter Club**, 770-859-2331, www.commuterclub.com

SMYRNA

The Southeast Cobb County community of **Smyrna**, originally an interdenominational religious camp and frontier village, is today an 11.4-square-mile city dominated by office towers, shopping malls, and vigorous commercial growth, although within this snarl of consumer and business traffic, there are luxury apartment complexes and numerous condominiums.

One of the fastest growing areas in Cobb County, Smyrna is currently home to nearly 41,000 residents, many of them commuting into the City of Atlanta or working at nearby Lockheed Martin or IBM. Yet, despite continuous growth, city planners have been successful at preserving much of this community's charm. Nicknamed "the Jonquil City" for the yellow flowers that bloom here every spring, Smyrna is a pleasant and prosperous place to live. Over the last decade, Smyrna's revitalized downtown area, "the Village Green," has taken on new life, becoming the heart of the city by providing retail development, a community center, and new public library for residents. The library, in fact, is the only independent city library in the state. Originally established in 1936, the new Village Green facility opened in 1991, and offers over 55,000 books and other materials, as well as computers, a conference room, and an art gallery. The Village Green also plays host to many local festivals and family events throughout the year, and is home to Smyrna's city hall, as well as a number of charming homes.

Newer homes in the area range in price from the $300,000's to the low $1 million's and can be found in subdivisions scattered among the office complexes and retail districts. Those looking for more spacious environs, though, should consider the upper northwest corner of the county. This area has been less encroached upon by commercial development, and you can still find farmland and horse ranches.

Web Site: www.ci.smyrna.ga.us
Area Code: 770
Zip Codes: 30080, 30081, 30082, 30339
Post Offices: Smyrna, 850 Windy Hill Road; Concord Square, 3315 South Cobb Drive; 800-275-8777, www.usps.com
Police Precincts: City of Smyrna Police Department, 770-434-9481; Cobb County Police Department, 140 North Marietta Parkway, 770-499-3900, www.cobbpolice.com
Emergency Hospital: Emory-Adventist Hospital, 3949 South Cobb Drive, Smyrna, 770-434-0710, www.adventisthealthsystem.com
Libraries: Lewis A. Ray Branch, 4500 Oakdale Road SE, Smyrna, 770-801-5335, www.cobbcat.org; Smyrna Public Library, 100 Village Green Circle, 770-431-2860, www.smyrna-library.com

Public School Education: Cobb County School System, 514 Glover Street, 770-426-3300, www.cobb.k12.ga.us

Community Publications: *The Bright Side*, 770-423-9555, www.brightsidenews.com

Community Resources: Smyrna Welcome Center, 2861 Atlanta Road, 770-805-4277; Smyrna Museum, 770-431-2858; Smyrna Community Development, 2190 Atlanta Road SE, 770-319-5387; Smyrna Community Center, 200 Village Green Circle, 770-431-2842; Cobb County Chamber of Commerce, 770-980-9510, www.cobbchamber.org

Public Transportation: **Cobb Community Transit** (**CCT**) system, 770-427-4444, www.cobbdot.org/cct.htm; local and express routes throughout Cobb County; **Cobb Rides**, www.cobbrides.com; **Commuter Club**, 770-859-2331, www.commuterclub.com

VININGS

Vinings is a small parcel of land overlapping parts of Smyrna and unincorporated Cobb County. Throughout its history, Vinings has been a strategic gathering place: first for Creek and Cherokee Indians; then for settler Hardy Pace, who launched a prosperous ferry operation here in the 1830s; then for the Western and Atlantic Railroad, which established Vinings as a major crossroads; and finally for Union troops, who descended with General Sherman in 1864 and used Vinings' assets to their advantage when attacking Atlanta.

Today, Vinings' abundant greenspace, high-end shopping options, and elegant charm make it a haven for residents. Nestled within a one-mile radius of just over 5,500 single-family homes, you'll find 10-million square feet of office space and retail shopping establishments. Furthermore, the small bungalows that once housed employees of Lockheed or nearby Dobbins Air Force Base are being torn down to make room for nicely landscaped subdivisions with masonry walls and Bradford pear trees. Many of the new housing developments, like Vinings Estates, offer upscale homes on smaller lots and count their proximity to downtown Atlanta and Buckhead—about 15 to 20 minutes each way—among their strongest selling points.

Web Site: www.viningsga.org
Area Code: 770
Zip Code: 30339
Post Offices: Akers Mill, 2997 Cobb Parkway; Cumberland Mall, 1101 Cumberland Mall SE; 800-275-8777, www.usps.com

Police Precinct: Cobb County Police Department, 140 North Marietta Parkway, 770-499-3900, www.cobbpolice.com

Emergency Hospital: Emory-Adventist Hospital, 3949 South Cobb Drive, Smyrna, 770-434-0710, www.adventisthealthsystem.com

Libraries: Vinings Branch, 4290 Paces Ferry Road, 770-801-5330; Lewis A. Ray Branch, 4500 Oakdale Road SE, Smyrna, 770-801-5335; www.cobbcat.org

Public School Education: Cobb County School System, 514 Glover Street, 770-426-3300, www.cobb.k12.ga.us

Community Publications: *The Bright Side*, 770-423-9555, www.brightsidenews.com

Community Resources: Vinings Estate Community Association, 655 Crescent Ridge Trail SE, 770-745-6615; Vinings Historical Preservation Society, 770-432-3343, www.vinings.org; The Vinings Club, 770-431-9166, www.theviningsclub.com; Cobb County Chamber of Commerce, 770-980-9510, www.cobbchamber.org

Public Transportation: **Cobb Community Transit** (**CCT**) system, 770-427-4444, www.cobbdot.org/cct.htm; local and express routes throughout Cobb County; **Cobb Rides**, www.cobbrides.com; **Commuter Club**, 770-859-2331, www.commuterclub.com

AUSTELL

Beginning as a rail town in 1880, when new rail lines were built from Atlanta to Birmingham, the City of Austell was incorporated in 1885 and named for the late General Alfred Austell, founder of the Atlanta National Bank. Today Austell is home to Six Flags Over Georgia, a popular amusement park and one of Atlanta's major tourist attractions. It's also home to the Lithia Springs Water Company, and Sweetwater Creek State Park, a peaceful tract of wilderness featuring nature trails, fishing lakes, and a visitor's center.

Though long known as a hub of industry, Austell hasn't been so well known for its housing. However, this has begun to change over the last ten years. As more people pour into Cobb County, Austell is becoming a community in demand. In fact, in recent years, Austell has consistently ranked among the top ten in metro Atlanta cities for increases in new and existing home sales. Many residents feel this is due in part to the new, higher-priced homes being developed in beautifully landscaped subdivisions, and to the fact that the community is working to improve the quality of the schools in the area.

Web Site: www.austell.org
Area Code: 770

Zip Codes: 30106, 30168

Post Office: Austell, 2847 Veterans Memorial Highway; 800-275-8777, www.usps.com

Police Precincts: Austell Police Department, 770-944-4318, www.austell.org/police; Cobb County Police Department, 140 North Marietta Parkway, 770-499-3900, www.cobbpolice.com

Emergency Hospital: Wellstar Cobb Hospital, 3950 Austell Road, Austell, 770-732-4000, www.wellstar.org

Library: Sweetwater Valley Branch, 5000 Austell-Powder Springs Road, Austell, 770-819-3290, www.cobbcat.org

Public School Education: Cobb County School System, 514 Glover Street, 770-426-3300, www.cobb.k12.ga.us

Community Publications: *Marietta Daily Journal*, 770-428-9411, www.mdjonline.com

Community Resources: Austell City Hall, 2716 Broad Street SW, 770-944-4300, www.austell.org; Collar Community Center, 2625 Joe Jerkins Boulevard, 770-944-4309, www.austell.org/parks/cc.htm; Six Flags Over Georgia, 770-948-9290, www.sixflags.com/parks/over georgia; Sweetwater Creek State Park, 770-732-5871, www.friendsof sweetwatercreek.org; Lithia Springs Water Company, 770-944-3880, www.lithiaspringswater.com; Cobb County Chamber of Commerce, 770-980-9510, www.cobbchamber.org

Public Transportation: **Cobb Community Transit (CCT)** system, 770-427-4444, www.cobbdot.org/cct.htm; local and express routes throughout Cobb County; **Cobb Rides**, www.cobbrides.com; **Commuter Club**, 770-859-2331, www.commuterclub.com

GWINNETT COUNTY

Driving north, away from Atlanta on I-85, one cannot miss the water tower emblazoned with the pronouncement that "Gwinnett Is Great." Residents must agree, because the Gwinnett County population has more than doubled over the last two decades. In 1984 Gwinnett was named the fastest growing county in the United States, and since then it has consistently held a place in the country's top ten developing counties. From a population of just 72,000 in 1970, Gwinnett now boasts nearly 700,000 residents. It is projected that the county will be home to over 900,000 residents by the year 2010.

Until the early 1990s, Gwinnett was a bedroom community, a 436-square-mile rural outpost 30 miles northeast of Atlanta. Named in 1818 after Button Gwinnett, one of Georgia's signers of the Declaration of Independence, Gwinnett County has always been attractive to those who relish its small towns, farms, and forests.

Gwinnett County residents are more likely to work close to home than in Atlanta, which is good, since the county's population explosion has created severe traffic problems on area highways. Attracted by the area's thriving economy and low taxes, businesses have flocked to Gwinnett. Some 250 international companies, and over 20% of the Fortune 500 companies maintain offices in Gwinnett County, many of them located in Technology Park/Atlanta—a prominent, 600-acre high-tech industrial center. More than 250,000 jobs with major corporations like AT&T, Canon USA, Motorola, General Electric, and Panasonic provide employment for area residents.

The county has grown for more than just economic reasons. Its public school system is one of the finest in Georgia. Gwinnett students consistently excel on standardized tests, and over two thirds continue their studies after graduation. In the last decade, eight of the county's schools earned the distinction of being named National Schools of Excellence. With such a reputation it's no wonder that families relocating to the metro Atlanta area would choose the exceptional educational value that Gwinnett's public school system affords. This influx of families perhaps accounts for Gwinnett's young median age of 30 years.

While the county is known for its commercial development, there are still pockets of greenspace among the gleaming, new office buildings. Travel the old state roads of northeast Gwinnett and you'll find farms and pastures. It's not until you reach the middle of the county, and cities like Norcross and Lawrenceville, that you'll see the office parks, shopping malls, and immaculately landscaped subdivisions.

One advantage to the population explosion occurring outside Atlanta's perimeter is that Gwinnett residents no longer have to travel to Atlanta to get their fill of culture and shopping. Gwinnett Place Mall offers over one million square feet of retail and dining, while the Mall of Georgia offers an amazing 1.7 million square feet of retail space as well as an 80-acre nature park, a 500-seat amphitheater, and a seven-story IMAX theater. In addition to the plethora of shopping opportunities in Gwinnett County, there is also a Fine Arts Center located next to the Gwinnett Civic and Cultural Center. The facility has an exhibition hall, a ballroom, and a 1,200-seat theater, which has been the site of performances by the Gwinnett Ballet Company.

The county's natural recreational sites attract Atlanta nature lovers, who perform a reverse-commute on weekends, exchanging city streets for the incredible beauty of Georgia's forests and rivers. Lake Lanier Island, in Buford, has become the destination of choice for many residents looking for a quick getaway. The island is now home to two large luxury resorts with man-made beaches, golf courses, and a water park. It's one of north Georgia's most popular vacation spots during the warm weather months.

In addition to the two communities profiled below, other Gwinnett County neighborhoods worth looking into include the cities of **Lilburn**,

www.cityoflilburn.com, **Snellville**, www.snellville.org, and **Duluth**,
www.duluth-ga.com.

LAWRENCEVILLE

Homebuyers enjoy a variety of options in Gwinnett's county seat of
Lawrenceville. This busy city was chartered in December 1821, on the third
anniversary of the birth of Gwinnett County, and named for Captain James
Lawrence, a naval hero in the war of 1812. The first courthouse was built in
1824, and the first public school in 1826. Though the community suffered
many human casualties during the Civil War, most of the town was left
standing. In fact, Lawrenceville's historic courthouse was recently restored
and is now listed in the National Register of Historic Places. Today,
Lawrenceville is a large part of the high-tech movement in Gwinnett
County, with new businesses still moving into the area. Of the 23,000 people who make their home here, almost half of them work in the community rather than commute to Atlanta.

Most of the homes here are found in newly developed subdivisions,
though it is possible to find older, brick ranch homes from the 1960s and
1970s, as well as restored turn-of-the-century homes, if that's what you're
looking for. And, as in other metro Atlanta suburbs experiencing phenomenal growth, apartment complexes abound, offering an abundance of rental
opportunities to those who want to live in the area but aren't ready to buy.

Web Site: www.lawrencevillegaweb.org
Area Codes: 770, 678
Zip Codes: 30043, 30044, 30045, 30046, 30049
Post Offices: Main Office, 121 E. Crogan Street; Lawrenceville, 35
   Patterson Road, 800-275-8777
Police Precincts: Lawrenceville Police Department, 770-339-2400,
   www.lawrencevillegaweb.org; Gwinnett County Police Department,
   770-513-5000, www.gwinnettcounty.com; Gwinnett County Sheriff's
   Department, 770-822-3100, www.gwinnettcountysheriff.com
Emergency Hospital: Gwinnett Medical Center, 1000 Medical Center
   Boulevard, Lawrenceville, 678-442-4321, www.gwinnetthealth.org
Libraries: Main Library, 1001 Lawrenceville Highway, 770-822-4522;
   Five Forks Branch, 2780 Five Forks Trickum Road, Lawrenceville, 770-
   978-5600; www.gwinnettpl.org
Public School Education: Gwinnett County School System, 770-963-
   8651, www.gwinnett.k12.ga.us
Community Publications: *Gwinnett Daily Post*, 770-963-9205,
   www.gwinnettdailyonline.com

Community Resources: Lawrenceville Tourism and Trade Association, 678-226-2639, www.visitlawrenceville.com; Historic Downtown Lawrenceville, www.lawrenceville-ga.com; Gwinnett County Chamber of Commerce, 770-232-3000, www.gwinnettchamber.org; Gwinnett Civic and Cultural Center, 6400 Sugarloaf Parkway, 770-813-7501, www.gwinnettcenter.com

Public Transportation: Gwinnett County Transit, 770-822-5010, www.gctransit.com; local bus service throughout Gwinnett County

NORCROSS

Located 20 miles northeast of Atlanta, the City of **Norcross** is another Gwinnett County community benefiting from the area's growing high-tech industry. What started as a small resort town for wealthy Atlantans in 1871 has grown into a highly industrial city of over 8,000 residents. Named for former Atlanta Mayor Jonathan Norcross, this suburb is the second oldest in Gwinnett County, and has managed to retain much of its old, southern charm, despite its growth in recent years. Many early 20th century homes and commercial buildings can still be found here today, most of them lovingly preserved by residents who are proud of their community's history and intent on preserving it. There is even a 112-acre Historic District here, which encompasses a beautifully restored downtown square, fifty private residences, three church buildings, and a library. In fact, Norcross is the only Gwinnett County community to have a district listed in the U.S. Register of Historic Places.

New housing in Norcross is similar to that in Lawrenceville and other Gwinnett County neighborhoods, with apartment complexes and carefully planned subdivisions dominating. In fact, because of the similarity between Gwinnett's communities, many Atlantans have trouble distinguishing where one Gwinnett city ends and another begins.

Nevertheless, Norcross is a popular community for families with young children, who like its comfortable, small-town feel and convenience to local highways. Interstate 85 runs right through Norcross, making it relatively easy to get into Atlanta and to other Gwinnett County communities. The downside is that, as in most north metro suburbs, traffic can be a nightmare during peak commute times, and Gwinnett's public transportation (which has only been operating since 2000) hasn't yet caught on here the way MARTA has in Atlanta's intown communities.

Web Site: www.norcrossga.net
Area Codes: 770, 678
Zip Codes: 30071, 30092, 30093

Post Offices: Gwinnett Place, 3628 Satellite Boulevard; Holcomb Bridge, 8920 Eves Road; Norcross, 265 Mitchell Road; Peachtree Corners, 5600 Spalding Drive; Rockbridge Shopping Center, 4771 Britt Road; 800-275-8777, www.usps.com

Police Precincts: Norcross Police Department, 770-448-2111, www.norcrossga.net; Gwinnett County Police Department, 770-513-5000, www.gwinnettcounty.com; Gwinnett County Sheriff's Department, 770-822-3100, www.gwinnettcountysheriff.com

Emergency Hospitals: Joan Glancy Memorial Hospital, 3215 McClure Bridge Road, Duluth, 678-584-6800, www.gwinnetthealth.org; Gwinnett Medical Center, 1000 Medical Center Boulevard, Lawrenceville, 678-442-4321, www.gwinnetthealth.org

Libraries: Norcross, 6025 Buford Highway, 770-448-4938; Peachtree Corners, 5570 Spalding Drive, 770-729-0931; www.gwinnettpl.org

Public School Education: Gwinnett County School System, 770-963-8651, www.gwinnett.k12.ga.us

Community Publications: *Gwinnett Daily Post*, 770-963-9205, www.gwinnettdailyonline.com

Community Resources: Norcross City Hall, 65 Lawrenceville Street, 770-448-2122; Norcross Community Development, 770-448-4935, www.norcrossga.net; Norcross Youth Soccer, 770-840-7696, www.norcross-soccer.org; Gwinnett County Chamber of Commerce, 770-232-3000, www.gwinnettchamber.org; Gwinnett Civic and Cultural Center, 6400 Sugarloaf Parkway, 770-813-7501, www.gwinnettcenter.com

Public Transportation: **Gwinnett County Transit**, 770-822-5010, www.gctransit.com; local bus service throughout Gwinnett County

CHEROKEE COUNTY

Directly north of Cobb County and bisected by I-575 as it branches away from I-75 to head north into the Blue Ridge Mountains, Cherokee County, once the heart of the Cherokee Nation, is one of the fastest-growing areas in Georgia. The coming of the interstate allowed fast access to Marietta and Atlanta, and since then the population has boomed with shops, businesses, and housing developments springing up in almost alarming numbers off all the exits. Cherokee County, once considered rural and remote, now has a population of nearly 170,000 and is becoming increasingly busy and cosmopolitan.

The original county land covered over 6,900 square miles, over most of North Georgia, and was established by the Georgia Legislature in 1831 while it still belonged to the Cherokee and Creek tribes. These native tribes were unable to keep their land, despite a long struggle to do so, and by

1839, most remaining Indians were rounded up and forced to walk the infamous Trail of Tears to Oklahoma. With the natives gone, white settlers began populating the area. The Industrial Revolution helped provide jobs for them as mills were built to grind corn and process cotton. Discoveries of gold, copper, and marble also attracted many pioneers. During the Civil War, the county's residents united with such a strong, pro-Confederate position that General Sherman ordered much of the area burned in 1864. When the war was over, residents returned to Cherokee to rebuild and recover, and the county soon grew in importance.

During and after World War II, the population swelled, and cotton farming gave way to poultry production. The aerospace company Lockheed, a giant employer located in nearby Marietta, gave people more reason to settle in the area. Today, many commute to Marietta, and even into the heart of Atlanta for work, and traffic jams on I-575 during rush hour are notorious. Although Cherokee, nestled in the foothills of the mountains, offers beautiful scenery and less expensive housing, it is important to consider the increasingly long commute times into the city.

In addition to the two Cherokee County communities profiled here, other area neighborhoods to consider are **Holly Springs**, www.holly springsga.net, **Ball Ground**, 770-735-2123, and **Waleska**, 770-479-2912.

CANTON

From Cherokee County's tumultuous beginnings, five municipalities would emerge as centers of commerce and trade, each with its own identity. As the county seat, **Canton** became the center of government here. Situated on the banks of the Etowah River, from which it took its original name, this frontier settlement changed its name to Canton in 1834 when two town leaders envisioned it becoming the silk center of the West, simulating Canton in China. The Canton Cotton Mill (now completely redeveloped into loft apartments in the center of town) was established in 1899, employed over 1,000 people, and put Canton on the map as word spread of its high-quality denim. Since the closing of the last two mills in 1981, Canton has transitioned nicely from mill town to a prosperous southern city. Now enjoying the greatest economic boom in its history, Canton has invested more than $60 million in residential and commercial development over the last decade. Today, the city is spread out into different sections (Canton is accessible from four exits off I-575), but downtown is the heart of the city, with its government buildings, refurbished theater, restaurants, and shops. As part of the "Streetscapes" program, downtown streets were given a more classic look, with brick pavers added to sidewalks, intersections upgraded, and new lampposts and landscaping added.

Riverstone Parkway, off exit 20 on I-575, has become a focus for residents. Architecturally pleasing shopping centers, stores, restaurants, a movie theater and other businesses line the parkway, and new buildings are being added all the time. Housing, apartment, and hotel developments surround the area.

In 2004, Heritage Park opened. This first phase of the Etowah River Greenway Project offers 30 acres of walking and biking trails as well as a natural amphitheater. In partnership with the Metro Atlanta YMCA, an $8 million community center is being built to include an indoor swimming pool, gymnasium, wellness center, aerobics studio, and more. Phase Two should be completed by 2006, utilizing 60 more acres for recreation. Additionally, the Bluffs at Technology Park, which partially opened in 2004, will be home to 15,000 high-tech jobs when completed, and an ambitious reservoir project, scheduled for completion in 2007, will provide 44 million gallons of water a day, and will be surrounded by 20 acres of public-use parkland.

New apartments, townhomes, and single-family home subdivisions are scattered throughout Canton. According to regional projections, the 14,000 residents today will mushroom to 42,000 by 2025. Bridge Mill on Bells Ferry Road is perhaps the largest development. It offers a variety of dwellings, from condos to estate homes, an 18-hole golf course, a 50-acre athletics club, including tennis courts, aquatic center and recreation clubhouse, jogging paths, playgrounds, and fitness center.

Another burgeoning area is along Highway 20 as it heads into Forsyth County, where well-designed family subdivisions with a rural feel, and the services that support them, are popping up everywhere. Most have swimming pools, walking trails, tennis courts, and homeowner associations. A little to the south of Canton, the area along Sixes Road has also become known for large subdivisions and expensive homes.

Web Site: www.canton-georgia.com
Area Code: 770, 678
Zip Codes: 30114, 30115
Post Offices: Main Street Station, 130 East Main Street, Canton; Canton Branch, 2400 Riverstone Boulevard; 800-275-8777, www.usps.com
Police Precincts: Canton Police Department, 770-720-4883, www.canton-georgia.com; Cherokee County Sheriff's Office, 678-493-4200, www.cherokeega-sheriff.org
Emergency Hospital: Northside Cherokee Hospital, Canton, 770-720-5100, www.northsidecherokee.com
Libraries: R.T. Jones Memorial Library, 116 Brown Industrial Parkway, Canton, 770-479-3090; Hickory Flat Public Library, 2740 East Cherokee Drive, Canton, 770-345-7565; www.sequoyahregionallibrary.org

Public School Education: Cherokee County School System, 770-479-1871, www.cherokee.k12.ga.us

Community Publications: *Cherokee Ledger,* 770-928-0706, www.ledgernews.com

Community Resources: Canton City Information Line, 770-704-1526; City of Canton, Heritage Park, www.canton-georgia.com; Historic Canton Theatre, 770-704-0755, www.cantontheatre.com; Cherokee County Chamber of Commerce, 770-345-0400, www.cherokee-chamber.com; Cherokee County Georgia Online, www.cherokeetrails.org; Cherokee County Arts Center, 770-704-6244, www.cherokeearts.org

Public Transportation: **City of Canton Transit System**, 770-720-7674, www.canton-georgia.com; provides free bus service, Monday-Saturday from 9 a.m. to 4 p.m., throughout the City of Canton

WOODSTOCK

One of the largest communities in Cherokee County, with over 13,000 residents, **Woodstock** was chartered in 1897, and was primarily a farming community, growing cotton and grains for the mills to the north. Some mineral mining also took place here. The Marietta and North Georgia Railroad came to Woodstock in 1879, bringing passengers and freight, but the area remained a sleepy settlement for many years. Not so anymore. Today, the city of Woodstock is growing so fast that the road systems and utility companies can barely keep up. With more and more new businesses and professional services taking advantage of Woodstock's excellent location (where Highway 92 intersects I-575), the area has doubled in size in the last ten years.

The city has two distinct areas: historic Downtown and Towne Lake. The former, with its brick-paved sidewalks and buildings dating back to 1879, has retained its old-South charm. The train depot is the focal point, with an active railway line cutting through the heart of the area. Here, you'll find antique shops, tearooms, hair salons, gift shops, chiropractors, health spas, and more. The Visitors Center at Dean's Store offers information and directions. Woodstock City Park and Dupree Park are both nearby and offer relaxation, recreation, and other activities throughout the year.

Towne Lake, on the east side of Woodstock, is where most people live. This area is characterized by enormous subdivision communities (such as Eagle Watch and The Arbors) of mainly large homes with homeowner associations and recreational facilities that line Towne Lake Parkway on both sides for miles. The area even has its own magazine, *The TowneLaker,* detailing news, people, and events. Two major golf clubs, Towne Lake Hills and Eagle Watch, are professional standard. Servicing the thousands of residents, the district is surrounded by supermarkets, strip malls, specialty shops, restaurants, and businesses. But, as attractive as this area is to families, when commuters leave home on weekday mornings, to make their way to work, they clog up the main arteries to the Interstate and cause huge traffic jams to the south.

Older subdivisions are spread out throughout the city, and tend to contain smaller, less expensive homes on larger lots, and more greenery. Most of these do not have homeowner associations, and houses often need a little upgrading.

Web Site: www.ci.woodstock.ga.us

Area Code: 770, 678

Zip Codes: 30188, 30189

Post Office: Woodstock, 225 Parkway 575, 800-275-8777, www.usps.com

Police Precincts: Woodstock Police Department, 770-592-6030, www.ci.woodstock.ga.us; Cherokee County Sheriff's Office, 678-493-4200, www.cherokeega-sheriff.org

Emergency Hospitals: Northside Cherokee Hospital, Canton, 770-720-5100, www.northsidecherokee.com; Piedmont Mountainside Hospital, Jasper, 706-692-2441, www.piedmontmountainsidehospital.org

Libraries: Woodstock Public Library, 7745 Main Street, 770-926-5859; Rose Creek Public Library, 4476 Towne Lake Parkway, Woodstock, 770-591-1491; www.sequoyahregionallibrary.org

Public School Education: Cherokee County School System, 770-479-1871, www.cherokee.k12.ga.us

Community Publications: *The TowneLaker,* 770-516-7105, www.townelaker.com; *Cherokee Ledger,* 770-928-0706, www.ledger news.com

Community Resources: Dean's Store, 8588 Main Street, Woodstock, 770-924-0406; Woodstock City Park, 678-445-6518, www.ci.woodstock. ga.us; Woodstock Historic Train Depot, 770-592-6001; Cherokee County Chamber of Commerce, 770-345-0400, www.cherokee-chamber.com; Cherokee County Georgia Online, www.cherokeetrails.org; Cherokee County Arts Center, 770-704-6244, www.cherokeearts.org

ADDITIONAL COUNTIES

Of the following metro Atlanta counties, Clayton, Rockdale, and Henry are closest to Atlanta's inner-ring communities, and offer the shortest commute into the city. However, it's important to note that all of these counties are included in the metro area because at least 25% of their residents work in Atlanta. So, while the daily commute may be long and tedious from most of these counties, many people have chosen to do it, despite the fact

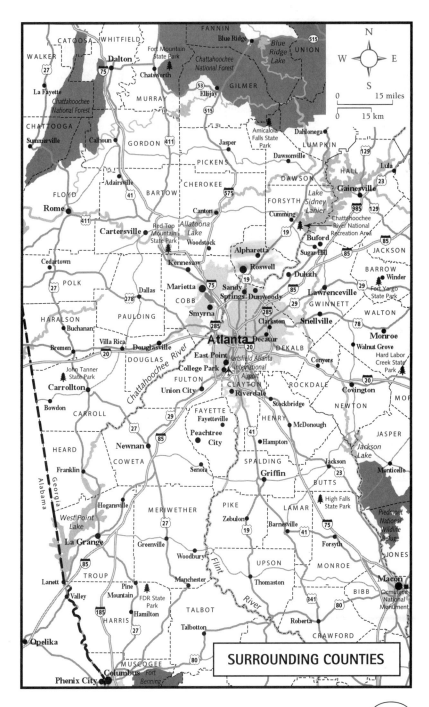

SURROUNDING COUNTIES

that most of them are 40 miles or more, and at least a 90-minute drive, from downtown. Cutting the commute time by one third to one half, however, is the **Xpress** regional bus system, which inaugurated service in 2004 and continues to add express bus routes to downtown Atlanta and outlying MARTA stations (see **Transportation** chapter for more information). It's also important to note that some of these outer-ring counties use the 706 area code, which is long distance from Atlanta.

Regardless of location, each of the counties is home to several communities that may be of interest to newcomers who prefer a small-town lifestyle to the hustle and bustle of the city. For more information, check out the county web sites listed below.

NORTH METRO COUNTIES
Bartow County, www.bartowga.org
Forsyth County, www.forsythcounty.com
Pickens County, www.pickensga-online.com
Dawson County, www.dawsoncounty.org

WEST METRO COUNTIES
Paulding County, www.paulding.gov
Carroll County, www.carroll-ga.org
Douglas County, www.co.douglas.ga.us
Haralson County, www.haralson.org

SOUTH METRO COUNTIES
Clayton County, www.co.clayton.ga.us
Coweta County, www.coweta.ga.us
Fayette County, www.admin.co.fayette.ga.us
Henry County, www.co.henry.ga.us
Heard County, www.heardgeorgia.org
Jasper County, jaspercounty.georgia.gov
Lamar County, lamarcounty.georgia.gov
Meriwether County, www.meriwether.ga.us
Pike County, www.pikecounty.us
Spalding County, www.spaldingcounty.com

EAST METRO COUNTIES
Barrow County, www.barrowchamber.com
Butts County, www.buttscounty.org
Newton County, www.co.newton.ga.us
Rockdale County, www.rockdalecounty.org
Walton County, www.southcomm.com/walton/chamber.htm

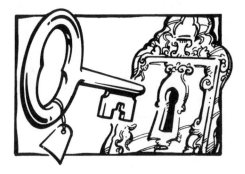

ATLANTA AND ITS SURROUNDING SUBURBS OFFER A WIDE VARIETY of housing options; from old brick apartments and warehouse-style lofts, to sturdy Craftsmans and beautifully restored Victorians, they're all here. The key will be to find your dream home before someone else does! Those interested in a modern apartment complex will find a good selection, but if you're looking to rent or buy a house, you may find the prospects not nearly as ample and the competition heated.

The Atlanta housing market has been in a long-term upswing. The astounding influx of people into metro Atlanta has caused prices to skyrocket in the most popular communities. Generally, the older, more prominent communities, like Buckhead and Virginia Highland, are the most expensive, while the newer subdivisions, particularly those furthest away from Atlanta proper, cost significantly less. For those hailing from a large US metropolitan area, prices here will probably seem comparable or even a bargain, particularly if you're coming from one of the coastal cities of New York, Boston, Los Angeles, or San Francisco.

For newcomers looking for an urban living experience, one of the most popular housing trends is loft living. What started in the old industrial areas of downtown has slowly moved to other intown communities, and it's now possible to find a great loft almost anywhere in the city. Many buildings in Atlanta's downtown and in the Midtown, Virginia Highland, and Buckhead neighborhoods have been converted to lofts that can either be rented or purchased. And many more newly constructed loft condominium buildings are under construction.

Another housing trend is the regentrification of Atlanta's older communities. If you can spot the next up-and-coming neighborhood, buy a home there for a reasonable sum, and then renovate, your investment may appreciate quickly. In recent years, several Atlanta communities, including Kirkwood, East Point, and East Atlanta have all experienced this regentrification trend.

Think carefully about where you want to live in terms of your place of employment. Hours spent each day on the highway will make the perfect four-bedroom, three-bathroom home with a nice yard and two-car garage a lot less appealing.

If all else fails, you can always move into a nice apartment for now, and take your time looking for the right house. Metro Atlanta abounds with large, upscale apartment communities. Many offer such amenities as swimming pools, gyms, and on-site dry cleaning; in fact, some are so nice that residents forego the home-buying quest altogether and opt for long-term apartment living.

APARTMENT HUNTING

Apartment hunting in Atlanta takes time, energy, perseverance, and just a little bit of luck, but if you dedicate yourself to the task, you will find your ideal abode. Because of the suburban nature of the metro area, high-rise apartment buildings are few and far between, except for a smattering in the Buckhead area (and those rents exceed many people's budgets). Instead, metro Atlanta offers rental houses; apartments in houses; duplexes and triplexes; small apartment buildings; and large, low-rise apartment complexes. Generally speaking, the closer in to the city you live, the more likely you will find an apartment in a house or small apartment building. Communities outside the perimeter tend to have larger apartment complexes, often gated communities, with many amenities. And, like the rest of Atlanta, apartments usually offer ample parking.

Apartment prices in Atlanta, by big city standards, used to be anywhere from reasonable to downright cheap. More recently, however, many residents have experienced a bit of sticker shock in regards to apartment rental prices. Over the last five years, rental prices in the metro area have increased by approximately 10% to 15%. Skim the classifieds and you will see that the average price range for a one-bedroom apartment is $700 to $950; and you can expect to pay anywhere from $950 to $1,500 for a two-bedroom; and between $1,500 to $2,500 for a three-bedroom. Of course, rents vary according to location and amenities. If you insist on living in one of the hot intown neighborhoods, or making your home in an upscale apartment complex, you can expect to pay considerably more than you would if you chose a smaller, bare-bones complex or moved into one of the city's outer communities. Remember, good deals do exist in metro Atlanta, but you may need a little patience and persistence to find them.

In the suburbs, space is not generally a problem. Most apartments are roomy, especially compared to more densely populated cities. In parts of the greater metro area, you can rent a two-bedroom duplex with a front porch and spacious backyard for half of what you would pay for a studio in the Big Apple. In fact, porches—especially screened-in porches—are a great selling point in many dwellings. (Because of the intense summer heat, most older houses and apartment buildings were built with at least one screened-in porch.) Other types of apartments that are readily available throughout metro Atlanta are apartment complexes—groupings of identical apartment buildings enclosed by a fence and with a security gate to protect access to the complex. It's sort of like a little city, with a swimming pool, tennis courts, exercise facilities, and other conveniences all at your doorstep. Newcomers, in particular, may benefit from the many social opportunities available at a complex.

One advantage of living in a city composed of suburbs is that many rental houses are available. If you have a roommate, roommates, or a family, this might be your most pleasant and economical option. Many people who buy homes rent out a separate apartment within the house to help pay for their mortgage. Those with large old homes sometimes rent out their accompanying carriage houses to singles or couples.

When searching the classifieds for a place to live, you should learn the lingo and the euphemisms. A "1960s" building probably means that the apartment complex resembles the wing of a chain motel. In certain areas—Buckhead, Midtown, and a stretch on Briarcliff Road, to name a few—1960s apartment buildings are common. "On-street parking" means that the complex does not have its own parking lot. A "terrace apartment" is in the basement. If you see the same ad day after day, this may be an indication that the apartment building in question has a high tenant turnover rate, and that if you live there, you, too, might want to move out soon.

Apartment hunting in metro Atlanta can be competitive year-round, but is especially so in the late summer, when new college students flood the rental market. Get an early start if you are relying on the classifieds—apartments advertised in *Creative Loafing* are often already rented if you wait until afternoon to call. And keep in mind that when you're ready to view a rental property, it is common practice for the management staff to make a copy of your ID for their records before showing you the apartment. Below are some resources to help you find the perfect pad.

NEWSPAPER CLASSIFIEDS

The major sources for classified ads in metro Atlanta are as follows:
- ***The Atlanta Journal-Constitution***, 404-526-5151, www.ajc.com; check the Sunday edition. This paper covers the entire metro Atlanta area, and the online listings are updated daily.
- ***Creative Loafing***, 404-688-5623, www.creativeloafing.com; comes out every Wednesday. This free alternative weekly paper also covers the

entire metro Atlanta area and is a great resource if you're looking for a roommate or a small home or apartment in a funky neighborhood. Many places listed in *CL* may not show up in the *AJC*.

- **Neighbor Newspapers, Inc.**, www.neighbornewspapers.com; includes *The DeKalb Neighbor*; *The Alpharetta Neighbor*; and *The Northside Neighbor*, which come out weekly in many Atlanta communities. If you can't find them at your local bookstore or favorite café, just visit them on the web or call 770-795-3000 to have a copy sent to you.

You can also find a multitude of advertisements for apartment complexes in several free, full-color booklets, all of which can be found near the entrances of local supermarkets, malls, and video rental stores:
- **Apartment Blue Book**, *800-222-3651, www.apartmentbluebook.com*
- **Apartments For Rent**, *866-573-5928, www.forrent.com*
- **Atlanta Apartment Guide**, *770-417-1717, www.apartmentguide.com*

ONLINE RENTAL SERVICES

There are now many online services offering listings of rental properties. Most are affiliated with local newspapers or rental agencies; some charge a nominal fee, some are free. Many sites post apartment listings only; others post home rentals as well, or help to match roommates. A few to consider:
- **Access Atlanta**, www.accessatlanta.com; free online news and classifieds service affiliated with the *Atlanta Journal-Constitution;* offers apartment, home, and roommate listings for the entire metro Atlanta area, including the outermost counties.
- **Apartment Ratings**, www.apartmentratings.com; not an apartment listing service, but rather a no-charge, nationwide rating service with residents posting assessments and reviews of the metro Atlanta apartments they've lived in (good or bad), for the benefit of others.
- **Apartment Selector**, www.aptselector.com; free online service offering detailed nationwide apartment listings, including listings from all areas of metro Atlanta.
- **Atlanta Rental Homes**, www.atlantarentalhomes.com; free online service offering home, townhome, and condo listings from around the metro Atlanta area.
- **Craig's List**, http://atlanta.craigslist.org; the Atlanta component of this popular web site posts listings for fee and no-fee apartment rentals, roommates, and sublets.
- **Creative Loafing Online**, www.creativeloafing.com; free online version of Atlanta's local, alternative newspaper; offers updated apartment, home, and roommate listings for the entire metro Atlanta area.

- **Lofts Atlanta**, www.lofts-atlanta.com; listings of Atlanta-area loft properties owned and managed by Aderhold Properties, Inc., available for no fee.
- **Rent.com**, www.rent.com; a free online rental service with nation-wide listings for apartments, homes, and roommates. Covers the metro Atlanta area.
- **RentNet**, www.rentnet.com; free nationwide apartment guide, includes listings of available metro Atlanta units.
- **Roommates.com**, www.roommates.com; online roommate match-ing service. Basic membership is free and includes general listings and searches. "Choice membership" offers advanced search and posting options, as well as the ability to receive messages from other members. A three-day trial costs $5.99.

DIRECT ACTION

If you're tired of apartment shopping from the smudgy pages of the news-paper or the flickering screen of a computer monitor, get in your car and cruise around the neighborhood you want to live in. Often the best apart-ments are not advertised. Instead, landlords place "for rent" signs in their front yards with their phone numbers printed on them. Be sure to bring pencil, paper, and cell phone.

While you're in the neighborhood, stop by the local café or bookstore, where you might find a community bulletin board with "apartment for rent" or "roommate wanted" notices. Ask the friendly people preparing your latte if they know of any apartments for rent in the area. A person's friend's cousin may have just vacated the perfect place . . . you never know.

Finally, even if a building you are particularly fond of does not have a rental sign posted out front, call the manager anyway. Someone might be moving out, and you may just get yourself a great new place.

APARTMENT SEARCH FIRMS

If you lack the time and energy to look for an apartment yourself, you can always try an apartment locator service. When you contact the apartment locator, you should first ask if there is a charge for the service. Fees vary, depending on the company. In some locations, the apartment owners pay the locator and in others the renters pay.

To find a successful match, your agent will ask you a series of detailed questions about apartment options, and you should consider your prefer-ences beforehand so that you will be ready to answer. You should have an idea about which area of town you want to live in and how much rent you can afford to pay. Also, you should decide whether you want to live in an apartment complex managed by an on-site staff or whether you would prefer to deal with a landlord. Another question to consider is how much space and storage you will need in your new place, and let the agency know if you have pets, particularly a dog. Most of the apartment complexes in metro Atlanta accept pets, though some may have size limitations. So be sure you research this, or have the search firm check on this upfront.

In addition, you will probably want to make a list of the amenities that are necessary for your happiness and well-being. Some hearty individuals can live here without air-conditioning, but for most people in Atlanta it's a must. Do you want washer/dryer facilities in your apartment or on the premises, or do you mind paying less and lugging your washables to the Laundromat? Is it difficult to imagine living without a dishwasher or do you eschew modern conveniences? If you're moving to metro Atlanta from a colder climate, you might want to spend your summer weekends in the sun and treat yourself to a place with a pool.

Most apartment search firms serve the entire Atlanta area, and some have several offices. The following listed firms will help you find a unit that meets your needs, answer questions about the neighborhoods you're considering, and tour potential apartments with you. Check "Apartment Finding and Rental Services" in the Atlanta Yellow Pages for more options:

- **A&A Apartment Locators**, 770-594-1110, 866-237-1401, www.free apartmentlocators.com
- **Apartment Selector**, 770-643-5313, www.aptselector.com
- **Promove**, 404-848-0074, 800-742-1883, www.promove.com

REAL ESTATE FIRMS

Many local real estate brokers handle rental properties and are very knowledgeable about the neighborhoods or communities they represent. Additionally, they often have access to properties that aren't yet listed in the *AJC* or *Creative Loafing*. Some firms may charge the apartment hunter a nominal fee for using their leasing services, though most often the landlord pays this fee. Be sure to ask. A few local real estate firms to consider when looking for an apartment include (check the Atlanta Yellow Pages under "Real Estate" for a complete listing):

- **Coldwell Banker**, 404-705-1798, www.coldwellbankeratlanta.com; covers the greater metro Atlanta area. Offers a large selection of rental properties, as well as a professional leasing staff. Property details and agent contact information is available online. Service fees are paid by the property owner.
- **Excalibur Group**, 678-825-1400, 877-381-3800, www.excal homes.com; offers a large selection of rental properties throughout

metro Atlanta, including houses, townhomes, and condos. Online listings include property details, photos, and agent contact information.
- **Harry Norman Realtors**, 404-256-0033, 800-774-1033, www.harry norman.com; covers the greater metro Atlanta area. Rental properties are available for viewing online. Service fees are paid by the property owner.
- **Prudential Atlanta Realty**, 678-352-3310, www.prudentialgeorgia. com; offers a large selection of rental properties throughout metro Atlanta. Online listings include photos, property details, neighborhood information, and agent contact information.

CHECKING IT OUT

So, you've just moved to the city and you're desperate to find a place to call your own. You see an ad in the paper that sounds perfect, so you call to make an appointment and to meet the landlord and tour the place, only to have him tell you that there are ten other people who have already been by and are ready to sign the lease. What do you do? First, don't panic. Landlords have been known to use this tactic to pressure prospective tenants into taking a place that has been difficult to let. When viewing units, take your time and examine the space to make sure it is exactly or close to exactly what you want. Even if the market is tight, don't commit to an apartment with which you are not comfortable. When checking out prospective apartments, here are a few things keep in mind:
- Are the kitchen appliances clean and in working order? Do the stove's burners work? How about the oven? Is there enough counter and shelf space? Does it smell funny in the kitchen space—or anywhere else for that matter? Most Atlanta apartments and rental homes come furnished with refrigerator and stove, though the landlord is not required to provide them. Be sure to ask about this ahead of time, so you'll know exactly what you're getting.
- What is included in the rental price? Are you responsible for the monthly utilities or are they paid by the landlord? Again, find out so that you can budget accordingly. Generally, water and trash pickup are paid for by the landlord, though this may not always be the case.
- Does the apartment come with central air? If not, will you have a window unit for the hotter months? Summers in Atlanta can be nearly unbearable, with high temperatures and even higher humidity. All of the newer apartment complexes offer central air.
- Does the building allow pets? If so, what is the maximum size and weight? Are additional pet fees or deposits required? Are there places set aside outside for pets to walk or go off-leash?

- Are there any signs of pests or vermin? Even the nicest apartments can have bug problems, so be sure to ask, and find out what the landlord does in terms of pest control. Most of the newer apartment complexes provide monthly pest control for their tenants, at no additional cost.
- Make sure you check all of the windows in the apartment. Do they open, close, and lock easily? Do they seem secure? Do the windows open onto a noisy or potentially dangerous area?
- Is there enough closet and storage space? Many intown apartments, especially the older ones, lack the closet space that the new complexes offer; though some may make up for that by offering additional storage space elsewhere in the building, like a basement or attic. Be sure to ask; you'll want to know that you'll have the space you need before signing the lease.
- If you're living with roommates, are there enough provisions, particularly bathrooms and closets, for everyone? Older Atlanta apartments typically offer only one bathroom; newer complexes and rental homes can have two or more, even in a two-bedroom unit.
- Are there enough electrical outlets for all your needs? Do the outlets work? Is it wired for cable or DSL?
- How's the water pressure? You may want to run the faucets and shower, and flush the toilet to check. You can also ask how big the water tank is and whether or not it serves more than one unit.
- For safety reasons, make sure any home or apartment you're considering has a second exit and comes with working smoke or heat detectors. You may also want to ask whether fire extinguishers, carbon monoxide detectors, and/or fire alarms are included.
- Does the apartment come with a washer and dryer, or at least a washer/dryer hookup? If not, check if there are laundry facilities in the building or nearby.
- Do you feel comfortable in the neighborhood? Will you feel safe here at night? Is it too loud, particularly on weekend nights? Or does it feel too isolated? Is the street well lit?
- Is the building or apartment community convenient to public transportation and shopping? Have you considered your possible routes to work? How is traffic during rush hour along the routes you would take? In metro Atlanta, traffic is a big problem, so this is something to seriously consider before signing a lease.
- Whom do you contact in case of emergency?

Ed Sacks' *Savvy Renter's Kit* contains a more thorough renter's checklist for those interested in augmenting their own.

If it all passes muster, be prepared to stake your claim without delay!

STAKING A CLAIM

When touring apartments, make sure you come prepared for the business of renting, so that when you find the place you want you can act on it. Most likely you will need to fill out an application, which will require your bank account information, other credit information, and past rental references. A picture ID is usually required; the landlord will make a copy of it to keep with your application.

Credit checks are the norm when renting or buying and the fee is generally around $50. A check for that amount plus a security deposit will usually suffice in holding an apartment for you while you're awaiting approval. Keep in mind, though, that when applying for an apartment, you may also be asked to pay first and last month's rent up front, so be prepared. Ask ahead of time so that you know the total cost before you get too far into the paperwork. If it turns out your application is not approved, the deposit check will be returned to you minus the fee for the credit check.

LEASES AND SECURITY DEPOSITS

Georgia law is not particularly tenant-friendly. When looking at leases and security deposits, the best advice is "buyer beware." Know what you're signing/understand the terms of the lease. And, unless you're desperate, if a rental situation seems difficult from the start, you should probably walk away and find something else.

LEASES

In Georgia, a lease is a negotiable contract between the landlord and tenant. Leases run the gamut—from the standard residential forms used by most apartment complexes to documents drawn up by individual landlords. They are serious business and can vary greatly depending on the landlord. And there is no particular practice or condition that is considered illegal, except for "self help eviction," meaning that a landlord must execute proper eviction procedures through the courts if he/she wants to evict a tenant.

Rental leases in Georgia are legal contracts and thus difficult to alter once both parties sign on the dotted line. With this in mind, before signing be sure to find out as much as possible about the landlord and the apartment you are renting, and to clarify any cloudy issues included in the lease. Three items of common concern include apartment shares, pets, and sublets: If you plan to share your apartment with someone else, you'll both have to be on the lease; a "no pets" clause on the lease means no pets; and subletting is generally not allowed in metro Atlanta, so check with the landlord if this may be something you are interested in doing at a later date—or if you are investigating a sublet housing situation for yourself. It's better to be upfront about your requirements and the landlord's expectations in the beginning. If there are items in the lease that are not to your liking, negotiate changes before signing. For example, if you think your job might relocate you before your lease is up, you may want to ask your landlord to insert an early transfer clause in the lease. If an early transfer clause is not an option, you may be able to get a short-term or month-to-month lease for a slightly higher rental rate.

SECURITY DEPOSITS

In Georgia, a landlord can charge whatever the market will bear for a security deposit; generally speaking, however, you can expect to be charged one month's rent or less. If you think an apartment's security deposit is too high, look elsewhere.

According to Georgia law, landlords must put your security deposit in an escrow account. They are not, however, required to place security deposits in an interest-bearing account, nor are they legally obligated to pay the tenant any interest earned. If you decide to move out once your lease is up, your landlord is required to return your deposit to you within thirty days of vacating the apartment—minus the cost of repairs for any damages beyond the usual wear and tear. However, he/she must inform you in writing within ten working days to explain the reasons for the deductions. If you do not receive a written explanation, or if your security deposit does not arrive within 30 days, you can file for its return in the your city's magistrate court.

For more information regarding security deposits, you can contact **Georgia Legal Services**, 404-206-5175, www.glsp.org, and ask for "Residential Security Deposits," a free booklet that outlines your rights and responsibilities as a tenant under Georgia Law.

TENANT RESOURCES

If you have questions about tenants' rights in Georgia, if you want to lodge a complaint against a landlord, or if you have issue with your lease or your security deposit, try the following agencies:
- **Atlanta Legal Aid Society, Inc.**, 404-524-5811 (Atlanta); 404-377-0701 (DeKalb); 404-669-0233 (South Fulton/Clayton); 770-528-2565 (Cobb); 678-376-4545 (Gwinnett); www.atlantalegalaid.org
- **Georgia Department of Community Affairs, Affordable Housing Division,** www.dca.state.ga.us/housing/index.html

- **Georgia Governor's Office of Consumer Affairs**, 404-651-8600 or 800-869-1123; www2.state.ga.us/gaoca
- **Georgia Commission on Equal Opportunity, Fair Housing Division**, 404-656-7708, 800-473-OPEN, www.gceo.state.ga.us/housing.htm
- **Georgia Landlord/Tenant Hotline**, 404-463-1596, 800-369-4706, www.glsp.org
- **Metro Atlanta Fair Housing Services**, 404-221-0147, 800-441-8393

RENTER'S/HOMEOWNER'S INSURANCE

Once you've settled on a place to live, you will want to consider purchasing property insurance. Regardless of whether you're renting or buying your home, a good insurance policy should be a priority. It's especially important here in the South where damaging tornadoes and thunderstorms are common summertime occurrences.

A typical renter's insurance policy will cover damages to your belongings in cases of fire, theft, or water damage, though you may also have the option of additional coverage, including personal liability. The good news is that rental policies are fairly inexpensive. Depending on your possessions, you can expect to pay somewhere between $150 and $300 a year for coverage. That's a small price to pay for peace of mind, especially when you consider what it would cost to replace your possessions.

While renters in metro Atlanta have a choice in whether to purchase property insurance, buyers here typically do not. For most everyone dealing with a bank when buying a home, purchasing a homeowner's policy will undoubtedly be a necessary part of the process. Rates for homeowner's insurance vary depending on the value of your property and the estimated worth of your possessions. Most policies include coverage for personal liability, fire, water damage, theft, electrical problems, and more. Be sure to ask questions and go over the details of the policy with your insurance agent to make sure you have the coverage you'll need.

The ideal renter's or homeowner's policy will provide "replacement value" coverage. Unfortunately, most insurance companies no longer offer replacement value policies; instead maximum coverage is 120% to 125% of the face value of your house and belongings.

For more information on renter's or homeowner's insurance in metro Atlanta, contact the **Georgia Insurance Commissioner's Office of Consumer Services**, 404-656-2070, 800-656-2298, www.gainsurance.org. You can also research insurance policies and compare quotes online at **Insure.com**, www.insure.com; and **Quicken Insurance**, www.quickeninsurance.com.

To find an insurance agent in your neighborhood, check the local Yellow Pages, where offices are listed by county or community, or contact the following:

- **AllState Insurance**, 847-402-5000, www.allstate.com; several offices throughout metro Atlanta
- **Cotton States Insurance**, 800-282-6536, www.cottonstatesinsurance.com; several offices throughout metro Atlanta
- **State Farm Insurance**, www.statefarm.com; several offices throughout metro Atlanta; local agent information (including toll-free numbers and 24-hour service) can be located online by entering your zip code
- **Travelers**, 800-252-4633, www.travelers.com; several offices throughout metro Atlanta

BUYING A HOME

Buying a home can be a complex, time-consuming, and even stressful process. The resources and suggestions that follow can assist with the home-buying process.

The first thing you need to consider when buying a house is how much you can spend. Start with your gross monthly income, then tally up your monthly debt load: credit cards, car loans, personal debt, child support, alimony, etc. For revolving debt (like credit card debt), use your minimum monthly payment for the calculation. For the purposes of this calculation, ignore any debts you expect to have paid off entirely within six months' time. As a rule, your monthly housing costs shouldn't exceed 28% of your total monthly income, and your debt load shouldn't exceed 36% of it. That said, these days lenders might tailor the 28/36 ratio depending on your situation (assets, liability, job, credit history). When calculating your budget, don't forget to factor in closing costs, which may include insurance, appraisals, attorney's fees, loan fees, and transfer taxes. Fees normally range from 3% to 7% of the purchase price. Likewise, when figuring out your budget, be sure to factor in the additional monthly outgoes of homeowner's insurance, property taxes (tax deductible), utilities, condo fees, improvements, and maintenance.

Once you've figured out what you can afford to spend on a house, there will be other things to consider:

- How much space will you need? Are you single or married? Do you have children now or are you planning to have children in the future? What about pets? And will you need space for a home office?
- What kind of house do you want? While single-family homes are the most abundant option in metro Atlanta, condos and townhomes are popular as well. Are you looking for old or new? A vintage home can be

an absolute gem once renovations have been made, but this is not always an easy or inexpensive task.

- What type of neighborhood will make you happy? Metro Atlanta offers great, intown neighborhoods as well as numerous suburbs. Consider your proximity to work, shopping, and nightlife when determining where you'll buy. If you have children, you'll also want to check out the local school systems, nearby parks, crime rates, and traffic. And finally, take a look at property values throughout the city. Even if these factors aren't crucial to you personally, they are important, as they can affect the appreciation of your home and therefore the value of your investment.
- When looking at particular neighborhoods, pay attention to how quickly homes sell and whether or not there are significant gaps between asking price and sale price. Buying a home in an up-and-coming community can be a great investment, but keep in mind that not all up-and-coming areas come up.

REAL ESTATE AGENTS

The Atlanta area has no shortage of agents and brokers. Because the city and surrounding suburbs cover such a large geographic area, many companies specialize in specific communities. To get a feel for metro Atlanta's neighborhoods and begin your home search, start with the **Neighborhoods** chapter of this book. Cruise the areas that you like and make a list of brokers working in that area for clues on who knows the local properties; almost all listed single-family homes and condos will have a sign in the yard. Also, be sure to ask around. Chances are someone you know or meet in Atlanta will have an opinion on a broker. Investigate the *Atlanta Journal-Constitution's* Sunday classifieds, which contain a market area map, as well as other community newspapers (listed in the rental section of this chapter). The Atlanta Yellow Pages lists hundreds of real estate agents and brokers with an indication of the areas that they serve. A few of the larger companies, all of which cover metro Atlanta, include:

- **Buy Owner**, 800-771-7777, www.buyowner.com
- **Century 21**, 800-4-HOUSES, www.century21.com
- **Coldwell Banker**, 404-705-1798, www.coldwellbankeratlanta.com
- **Harry Norman Realtors**, 404-256-0033, 800-774-1033, www.harrynorman.com
- **Metro Brokers**, 404-843-2500, www.metrobrokers.com
- **Prudential Atlanta Realty**, 678-352-3310, www.prudentialgeorgia.com
- **Re/Max Atlanta**, www.remax.com/residential; go online for contact information for various Atlanta offices

FINANCING

Most buyers need a **mortgage** to pay for a house. A typical house mortgage is for either 15 or 30 years and consists of four parts, commonly referred to as "PITI" (principal, interest, taxes, and insurance). The **principal** is the flat sum of money that you borrowed from the lender to pay for the property. The larger the down payment, the less you will need to borrow to meet the total purchase price of your home. The lender charges **interest**, a percentage of the principal, as repayment for the use of the money that you've borrowed. (Points, each one equal to 1% of the amount you borrow for your mortgage, might also contribute to the interest.) Your community charges you **taxes** based on a percentage of your property value, which you'll continue paying even after your mortgage is paid off. The final component of PITI is house **insurance** against calamities such as fire, theft, and natural disasters. In many cases, people deposit funds into an escrow or trust account to cover insurance and taxes. Within three business days of applying for your loan, your lender must give you a "good faith estimate" of how much your closing costs will be.

There are many loan programs around. Search the internet, newspapers, and books, and speak with financial planners, real estate agents, and mortgage brokers to find out what's available. Direct lenders (banks) and mortgage brokers are the most common places to go for a loan. A **direct lender** is an institution with a finite number of in-house loans, whose terms and conditions are controlled by the lender. A **mortgage broker**, on the other hand, is a middleman who shops around to various lenders and loan programs to find what's best for your needs. Because brokers shop around for the best interest rates, it's often worth paying their fee. To find a good local lender or mortgage broker you can call any of the real estate brokers listed below and ask for recommendations. They are usually more than happy to put you in touch with area lending institutions or mortgage brokers they've worked with in the past. Or contact the **Georgia Association of Mortgage Brokers**, 770-993-5507, www.gamb.org. (See the **Money Matters** chapter for a list of local and national banks.)

When educating yourself about mortgages, be sure to take the time to research institutions' loan costs and restrictions: interest rates, broker fees, points, prepayment penalties, loan term, application fees, credit report fees, and cost of appraisals.

PRE-QUALIFICATION/PRE-APPROVAL/CREDIT BUREAUS

Lenders suggest that you "pre-qualify" or, better still, get "pre-approved" for a loan. **Pre-qualification** is, in essence, an educated guess as to what you'll be able to afford for a loan. To be **pre-approved**, your loan officer will review your financial situation (by running a credit check, going over your proof of employment, savings, etc.) and then you will be given a letter documenting that the bank is willing to lend you a particular amount based on your proven financial situation. Pre-approval is a bit more labor-intensive for you and the lender, but sellers and real estate agents will take you more seriously if you show up with a pre-approval letter in hand.

For either pre-qualification or pre-approval of a loan, go to your lender with documentation of your financial history and a list of your debt load, and contact the three major credit bureaus (listed below) beforehand to make sure your credit history is accurate (visit www.annualcredit report.com for online access to all three). It's best to get a copy of your credit report from each bureau, as each report may be different. You will need to provide your name, address, previous address, and social security number with your request. A credit report will list your credit activity for the past seven years, including your highest balance, current balance, and promptness or tardiness of payments. After seven years, the slate is wiped clean for any credit transgressions, except in the case of bankruptcy and foreclosure, which will appear on your record for 10 years. Your credit report will have a FICO (Fair Isaac and Company) score. Typically, lenders will give a standard loan for scores of 650+; if your score is lower, you'll probably get a sub-prime loan (from a non-major lender and with a higher interest rate). If you find your credit score is not as good as it could be, keep in mind that lenders are more concerned with your most recent track record than how you behaved seven years ago. It's best to try to pay all your bills in full and on time for at least a year before you apply for a loan, and be aware that even if you pay your bills on time, having too much credit can be a problem. Even if your credit report isn't stellar, you most likely can still get a loan, though your rates (interest and fees) may be higher. A substantial down payment can counteract credit flaws as well.

If you discover any inaccuracies on your credit report, you should contact the service immediately and request that it be corrected. By law, credit bureaus must respond to your request within 30 days. If you have questions about your credit record, call Fannie Mae's nonprofit credit counseling service at 800-732-6643 before you apply for a mortgage. Be aware that too many credit record inquiries can lower your credit status.

The major **credit bureaus** are:
* **Experian**, P.O. Box 2104, Allen, TX 75002-2104, 888-397-3742
* **TransUnion**, P.O. Box 390, Springfield, PA 19064-0390, 800-916-8800
* **Equifax**, P.O. Box 105873, Atlanta, GA 30348, 800-685-1111

DOWN PAYMENT

Down payments vary. Some lenders offer programs that require as little as 5% down or even zero down. An example of these programs is Fannie Mae's three/two loan program, which gives a first-time buyer 95% of the price of a home. The buyer is required to supply 3% of the down payment; the other 2% can be a gift from family, a government program, or a non-profit agency. Programs requiring no down payment may sound like a dream come true, but the interest will be about 2% higher than what you'd pay at 20% down. The best interest rate can be obtained with at least 20% down. (A down payment of less than 20% will require private mortgage insurance.) If you are a first-time buyer, which is defined as someone who hasn't owned property within the past three years, you may qualify for state-backed programs that feature lower down payment requirements and below-market interest rates.

MAKING AN OFFER, CONTINGENCIES, PURCHASE AND SALE (P&S) AGREEMENT

If you want your offer to be seriously considered, particularly in a tight market, be sure to offer a fair market price, include a statement of the source of your down payment, your pre-approval letter, and even a note to the seller about why/how much you want the house. Buyers offering cash, or with a pre-approval in hand, will be more attractive to the seller.

Common **contingencies** include an appraisal of the house that is satisfactory to the bank, financing (in cases where the buyer has not been pre-approved), a free and clear title, selling a current residence, and receiving a satisfactory inspection report of the property from a licensed inspector (see below). Some buyers put into their offer "on terms to be approved by the buyer's attorney."

The closing is just signing the paperwork that finalizes what you agreed to in your offer. If the seller agrees to your written offer, it becomes a binding sales contract, called a **purchase and sale (P&S) agreement**. If you default on this contract, you can lose your deposit money. If the seller defaults, you can sue him to force the sale to which he agreed in writing.

That said, after you make an offer, the buyer will accept it, reject it, or make a counter-offer; at which point you may accept, reject, or change the counter-offer, and so on. When both parties agree, it becomes a binding purchase agreement.

INSPECTION

Choosing an inspector who is a member of the **American Society of Home Inspectors** (**ASHI**) will narrow the field of the many companies who offer inspection services; contact ASHI for recommendations or check with your real estate agent or broker, who will probably have several leads. The following organizations should be able to make referrals for more specialized testing of home environmental toxins such as mold, lead, asbestos, and radon, which are *not* covered in a standard home inspection:

- **American Society of Home Inspectors**, 800-743-2744, www. ashi.org
- **Georgia Association of Home Inspectors**, 770-952-7811, 800-521-5193, www.gahi.com
- **National Association of Certified Home Inspectors**, www. nachi.org

Should your inspector's report find that major repairs will be likely, you may be able to negotiate thousands of dollars off the purchase price. Or you might just decide to keep looking.

CLOSING

Assuming the inspection goes well and/or all issues are resolved to your satisfaction, it is time for closing. At the closing, also known as "settlement" or "escrow," costs, such as transfer taxes, closing costs, legal fees, and adjustments are paid. This is a brief process in which the title to the property is transferred from seller to buyer; the seller gets his payment and you get the keys, and the closing agent officially records your loan.

HOUSES AND CONDOS

Newcomers looking to buy a house, build a house, or invest in a condo should have no problems finding the right community. Like rental properties, home prices will vary depending on location. Generally, homes inside the perimeter, and particularly in Buckhead and Virginia Highland, will be most expensive, and homes furthest away from the perimeter, in surrounding suburbs will be the least expensive. Metro Atlanta home prices can range from the mid $100,000s to well over $1 million. If you'd like to research average home prices based on neighborhood, check out the online version of the *AJC Homefinder*, www.ajchomefinder.com.

Single-family homes are, by far, the most common properties available. Your best bet is to drive through the neighborhoods you are interested in and see what's available. It's also a good idea to check out the real estate section of the *Atlanta Journal-Constitution's* Sunday edition, either online or in print. If possible, study it over the course of a few weeks to see which properties go the fastest and which are harder to sell. This may help in your negotiations when you are ready to make an offer on something.

Though not as prevalent as single-family homes, condos are another option in metro Atlanta. Most of the older, intown neighborhoods offer condos for sale, usually in large renovated buildings, though new condo construction is also on the rise throughout the metro area.

In Atlanta, a condo may be a single unit located in a building of many units, or a townhouse with a small deck or yard. In either case, the home will be yours, but the land and common areas will be community property, jointly owned by the condo association, of which you will be a member. As a member, you'll be required to pay monthly or quarterly dues to help cover basic community expenses like property maintenance and repairs, landscaping, and trash pickup. Membership fees may also be used to pay for maintenance and upkeep on any amenities your building offers, such as a hot tub, pool, or fitness center. It's a good idea to check out an association's financial reports upfront to get an idea of how often their fees have gone up, how much they typically increase, and what the funds are used for. At the same time, you will also want to get a list of the association's rules and regulations.

As owner of your individual unit, you will generally be allowed to make improvements to the space, rent it out, or resell it as you see fit, though this may not always be the case. Some associations are very strict about what is allowed on the premises. To avoid any surprises down the road, make sure you understand the rules before you buy.

ONLINE RESOURCES—HOME LISTINGS

Most real estate agents offer home listings on their web sites. Be sure to check the ones listed above. For additional listings as well as real estate links, tips, and demographic information for metro Atlanta you may also want to consider:

- **Atlanta Board of Realtors**, 404-250-0051, www.abr.org
- **AJC Homefinder**, www.ajchomefinder.com
- **Cyberhomes**, www.cyberhomes.com
- **HomeSeekers**, www.homeseekers.com
- **HomeStore**, www.homestore.com
- **MSN House & Home**, www.houseandhome.msn.com
- **National Association of Realtors**, www.realtor.com
- **New Homes Atlanta**, www.newhomesatlanta.com
- **Owners.com**, www.owners.com

- **Realtor.com**, www.realtor.com
- **Realty Locator**, www.realtylocator.com
- **Yahoo! Real Estate**, http://realestate.yahoo.com
- **ZipRealty**, www.ziprealty.com

ONLINE RESOURCES—MORTGAGES

If basic information and current mortgage rates are what you're looking for, you may want to check out the following web sites. These online mortgage service companies can explain the loan process to you, and provide updated rates and other useful information:

- **Bankrate.com**, www.bankrate.com; everything about mortgages and lending
- **Countrywide Financial**, www.countrywide.com; nationwide mortgage rates, credit evaluations, etc.
- **Dirs.com**, www.dirs.com; links and information on mortgages and home equity loans
- **Fannie Mae**, www.fanniemae.com; loans for real estate purchases; dedicated to helping Americans achieve the dream of homeownership
- **Freddie Mac**, www.freddiemac.com; provides information on low-cost loans, a home inspection kit, and tips to help avoid unfair lending practices.
- **Georgia Association of Mortgage Brokers**, www.gamb.org
- **Interest.com**, www.interest.com; shop for mortgages and rates
- **The Mortgage Professor**, www.mtgprofessor.com; demystifies and clarifies the confusing and often expensive world of mortgage brokers, helpfully written by an emeritus Wharton professor who answers questions (!), useful calculators.
- **Owners.com**, www.owners.com; all things mortgage and home sale related
- **Quicken Home**, www.quickenloans.com

ADDITIONAL RESOURCES—BUYING A HOME

Finally, aside from the selection of books you can pick up at your local bookstore or at an online bookseller, consider the following resources and publications:

- *100 Questions Every First Time Homebuyer Should Ask: With Answers from Top Brokers from Around the Country*, 2nd edition (Three Rivers Press), by Ilyce R. Glink
- *The 106 Common Mistakes Homebuyers Make (and How to Avoid Them)*, 3rd edition (Wiley) by Gary W. Eldred

- *The Co-Op Bible: Everything You Need to Know About Co-Ops and Condos: Getting In, Staying In, Surviving, Thriving* (Griffin Trade Paperback) by Sylvia Shapiro
- **Opening the Door to a Home of Your Own**: a pamphlet by Fannie Mae for first-time homebuyers. Call 800-834-3377 for a copy.
- **Score Card**; if you're particularly concerned about environmental toxins at your new property, check out www.scorecard.org, a site sponsored by the Environmental Defense Fund.

BEFORE STARTING YOUR NEW LIFE IN METRO ATLANTA, YOU AND your worldly possessions will have to get here. How difficult and expensive that will be depends on how much stuff you've accumulated, what your budget is, and where you're coming from.

TRUCK RENTALS

The first question you need to answer is: Should I move myself, or have someone else do it for me? If you'd rather do it yourself, you can just rent a vehicle and head for the open road. Look in the Yellow Pages under "Truck Rental" or "Moving," and then call around to compare prices. Below we list four national truck rental firms, their toll-free numbers, and their web addresses, but for the best information you should call a local office. Note that most truck rental companies now offer "one-way" rentals (don't forget to ask whether they have a drop-off/return location in or near your destination), as well as packing accessories and storage facilities. Of course, these extras are not free, and if you're cost conscious you may want to scavenge boxes in advance of your move or buy some directly from a box company. Those moving locally should check neighborhood **FedEx Kinko's** locations, www.fedexkinkos.com, which frequently offer empty boxes in their self-serve area.

If you're planning on moving during the peak moving months (May through September), be sure to reserve your truck well in advance, at least a month ahead of when you think you'll need the vehicle. Remember, too, that the beginning of the month and Saturdays are extremely popular times to move. You may be able to get cheaper rates if you book a different day.

Once you're on the road, keep in mind that your rental truck may be a tempting target for thieves. If you must park it overnight or for an extended period (more than a couple of hours), try to find a safe place, preferably somewhere well-lit and easily observable by you, and do your best not to leave anything of particular value in the cab. Make sure the back door is locked and, if possible, use a steering wheel lock or other easy-to-purchase safety device.

- **Budget**, 800-428-7825, www.budget.com
- **Penske**, 800-222-0277, www.penske.com
- **Ryder**, 800-297-9337, www.ryder.com (now a Budget company, though still operating under the Ryder name)
- **U-haul**, 800-468-4285, www.uhaul.com

Not sure if you want to drive the truck yourself? Commercial freight carriers, such as **ABF U-PACK**, 800-355-1696, www.upack.com, offer an in-between service; they'll deliver a 28-foot trailer to your home, you pack and load as much of it as you need, and then they'll drive the vehicle to your destination (often with some other freight filling up the empty space). However, if you have to share truck space with another customer, you may arrive far ahead of your boxes and furniture. Try to estimate your needs beforehand and ask for your load's expected arrival date. You can get an online estimate from some shippers, so you can compare notes.

If you aren't moving an entire house and can't estimate how much truck space you'll need, keep in mind this general guideline: Two to three furnished rooms equal a 15-foot truck; four to five rooms, a 20-foot truck.

MOVERS

INTERSTATE

First, the good news: Moving can be affordable and problem-free. The bad news: If you're hiring a mover, the chances of it being so are dramatically reduced.

Probably the best way to find a mover is by **personal recommendation**. Absent a friend or relative who can recommend a trusted moving company, you can turn to what surveys show is the most popular method of finding a mover: the **Yellow Pages**. Then there's the **internet**; just type in "movers" on any of the major search engines and you'll be directed to dozens of more or less helpful moving-related sites.

In the past, **Consumer Reports**, www.consumerreports.org, has published useful information on moving. You might also ask a local realtor, who may be able to steer you towards a good mover, or at least tell you which ones to avoid. Members of the American Automobile Association have a valuable resource at hand in **AAA's Consumer Relocation Services**, which will assign the member a personal consultant to handle every detail of the move free of charge and which offers savings from discounts arranged with premier moving companies. For more information, call 800-839-MOVE, www.aaa.com.

But beware! Since 1995, when the federal government eliminated the Interstate Commerce Commission, the interstate moving business has degenerated into a wild and mostly unregulated industry with thousands of unhappy, ripped-off customers annually. In fact, there are so many reports of unscrupulous carriers that we no longer list movers in this book. Since states don't have the authority to regulate interstate movers and the federal government has been slow to respond, you are pretty much on your own when it comes to finding an honest, hassle-free mover. That's why we can't emphasize enough the importance of carefully researching and choosing who will move you.

To aid in your search for an **interstate mover**, we offer a few general recommendations: First, get the names of at least a half-dozen movers and check to make sure they are licensed by the **US Department of Transportation's Federal Motor Carrier Safety Administration** (**FMCSA**). With the movers' Motor Carrier (MC) numbers in hand, call 888-368-7238 or 202-358-7000 (offers the option of speaking to an agent) or go online to www.fmcsa.dot.gov to see if the carriers are licensed and insured. If the companies you are considering are federally licensed, your next step should be to check with the **Better Business Bureau**, www.bbb.org, in the state where the moving companies are licensed, to find out if there are any complaints against them. You can also check with the states' consumer protection boards or attorney generals (in metro Atlanta, contact the **Governor's Office of Consumer Affairs**, 404-651-8600, 800-869-1123, www2.state.ga.us/gaoca). You may also want to check out **FMCSA's Household Goods Consumer Complaints** site, www.1-888-dot-saft.com, where they maintain complaints that have been filed on interstate movers. Assuming there is no negative information, you can move on to the next step: asking for references. Particularly important are references from customers who did moves similar to yours. If a moving company is unable or unwilling to provide references, eliminate it from your list. Unscrupulous movers have been known to give phony references who will sing the mover's praises, so make sure you talk to more than one reference and ask questions. If something feels fishy, it probably is. Another way to learn more about a prospective mover: Ask them if they have a local office (they should) and then walk in and check it out in person.

Once you have at least three movers you feel reasonably comfortable with, it's time to ask for price quotes. These should always be free. Best is a binding "not-to-exceed" quote, in writing of course. This will require an on-site visual inspection of what you are shipping. If you have any doubts about a prospective mover, drop it from your list before inviting a stranger into your home to catalog your belongings.

Recent regulations by FMCSA require movers to supply several documents to consumers before executing a contract. These include a booklet titled, *Your Rights and Responsibilities When You Move;* a concise and accurate written estimate of charges; a summary of the mover's arbitration program; the mover's customer complaint and inquiry handling procedure; and the mover's tariff, containing rates, rules, regulations, classifications, etc. For more information about FMCSA's role in handling household goods, visit its consumer page at www.fmcsa.dot.gov/factsfigs/moving.htm.

Additional moving recommendations:

- If someone recommends a mover to you, be sure to get names (the salesperson or estimator, the drivers, the loaders). To paraphrase the NRA, moving companies don't move people, people do. Likewise, if someone tells you he had a bad moving experience, note the name of the company and try to avoid it.

- Remember that price, while important, isn't everything, especially when you're entrusting all of your worldly possessions to strangers. Be sure to choose a mover you feel comfortable with.

- Legitimate movers generally charge by the hour (for local moves, under 100 miles), and by weight/mileage (for long-distance moves). Be wary if the mover wants to charge by cubic foot.

- In general, ask questions and if you're concerned about something, ask for an explanation in writing. If you change your mind about a mover once you've signed on the dotted line, write the company a letter explaining that you've changed your mind and that you won't be using its services. Better safe than sorry.

- Ask about insurance; the "basic" 60 cents per-pound, industry-standard coverage is not enough. If you have homeowner's or renter's insurance, check to see if it will cover your belongings during transit. If not, ask your insurer if you can add that coverage for your move. Otherwise, consider purchasing "full replacement" or "full value" coverage from the carrier for the estimated value of your shipment. Though it's the most expensive type of coverage offered, it's probably worth it. Trucks get into accidents, they catch fire, they get stolen—if such insurance seems pricey to you, ask about a $250 or $500 deductible. This can reduce your cost substantially while still giving you more comprehensive protection in the event of a catastrophic loss.

- Whatever you do, do not mislead a salesperson about how much and what you are moving. And make sure you tell a prospective mover about how far they'll have to transport your stuff to and from the truck, as well as any stairs, driveways, obstacles or difficult vegetation, long paths or sidewalks, etc. The clearer you are with your movers, the better they will be able to serve you.

- Think about packing. If you plan to pack yourself, you can save a lot of money, but if something is damaged because of your packing, you may not be able to file a claim for it. On the other hand, if you hire a mover to do the packing, they may not treat your belongings as well as you will. They will certainly do it faster, that's for sure. Depending on the size of your move and whether or not you are packing yourself, you may need a lot of boxes, tape, and other packing materials. Mover boxes, while not cheap, are usually sturdy and the right size. Sometimes a mover will give a customer free used boxes. It doesn't hurt to ask. Also, don't wait to pack until the last minute. If you're doing the packing, give yourself at least a week to do the job; two or more is better. Be sure to ask the mover about any weight or size restrictions on boxes.

- You should transport any irreplaceable items such as jewelry, photographs, or key work documents personally. Do not put them in the moving van! For less precious items that you don't want to put in the moving truck, consider sending them via the US Postal Service or by UPS.

- Ask your mover what is not permitted in the truck: usually anything flammable or combustible, as well as certain types of valuables.

- Although movers will put numbered labels on your possessions, you should make a numbered list of every box and item that is going in the truck. Detail box contents and photograph anything of particular value. Once the truck arrives on the other end, you can check off every piece and know for sure what did (or did not) make it. In case of claims, this list can be invaluable. Even after the move, keep the list; it can be surprisingly useful.

- Movers are required to issue you a "bill of lading." Do not hire a mover who does not use them.

- Consider keeping a log of every expense you incur for your move, e.g., phone calls, trips to Atlanta, etc. In many instances, the IRS allows you to claim these types of expenses on your income tax. (See Taxes, below.)

- Be aware that during the busy season (May through September), demand can exceed supply, and moving may be more difficult and more expensive than during the rest of the year. If you must relocate during the peak moving months, call and book service well in advance of when you plan on moving—a month at least. If you can book service well in advance, say four to six months early, you may be able to lock in a lower winter rate for your summer move.

- Listen to what the movers say; they are professionals and can give you expert advice about packing and preparing. Also, be ready for the truck on both ends—don't make them wait. Not only will it irritate your movers, but it may also cost you. Understand, too, that things can happen on the road that are beyond a carrier's control (weather, accidents, etc.), and your belongings may not get to you at the time or on the day promised.

- Treat your movers well, especially the ones loading your stuff on and off the truck. Offer to buy them lunch, and tip them if they do a good job.
- Before moving pets, attach a tag to your pet's collar with your new address and phone number in case your furry friend accidentally wanders off in the confusion of moving. Your pet should travel with you, and you should never plan on moving a pet inside a moving van.
- Be prepared to pay the full moving bill upon delivery. Cash or bank/cashier's check may be required. Some carriers will take VISA and MasterCard, but it is a good idea to get it in writing that you will be permitted to pay with a credit card since the delivering driver may not be aware of this and may demand cash. Unless you routinely keep thousands in greenbacks on you, you could have a problem getting your stuff off the truck.

INTRASTATE AND LOCAL MOVERS

The Georgia **Department of Motor Vehicle Safety** (**DMVS**), 678-413-8732, www.dmvs.ga.gov/cvc, regulates the licensing, rates, and rules of the Household Goods Moving Industry within Georgia. All companies involved in the moving business must be insured and hold a license that permits them to provide moving services within or from/to Georgia. Most movers list their state license number in their advertisements. If the number is not listed, or if you use a mover recommended by a friend or family member, be sure to ask for their license number up front. You can also verify certification of your chosen mover and see whether any complaints have been filed against them within the last three years, by going online to www.dmvs.ga.gov/cvc/carriersdata.asp. The DMVS site also offers important information on moving within Georgia: www.dmvs.ga.gov/cvc/movingguide.asp.

For moves within Georgia, DMVS regulations require all movers to provide each client with a written estimate before the move commences. The estimate should clearly state all decisions about what you want moved, what services will be included, the mover's liability for loss or damage, and an estimated price. In Georgia, three possible estimates are allowed: a "non-binding estimate," a "binding estimate," or, ideally, a "not-to-exceed price" estimate. Research these options ahead of time, to ensure you're getting the estimate that works best for you. Once all of this is worked out, you'll be presented with an Agreement for Service form. The mover will have you sign this form before the move begins. And you'll want to be sure that the mover signs it as well.

CONSUMER COMPLAINTS—MOVERS

If a **move goes badly,** and you blame the moving company, you should first file a written claim with the mover for loss or damage. If this gets you nowhere and it's an **intrastate** move, contact the **DMVS**, 404-413-8732. They will typically suggest that you send them a letter of complaint, stating the following: the address of the point of origin and final destination; the nature of the complaint; all verbal and written correspondence with the carrier; and the course of action needed to resolve the issue. You will also be asked to enclose a copy of the estimate, the Bill of Lading, and any written correspondence between the carrier and yourself.

If your grievance is with an **interstate carrier**, your choices are unfortunately limited. Interstate moves are regulated by the **Federal Motor Carrier Safety Administration (FMCSA)**, 888-368-7238, www.fmcsa.dot.gov, an agency under the Department of Transportation, with whom you can file a complaint against a carrier. While its role in the regulation of interstate carriers has historically been concerned with safety issues rather than consumer issues, the recent upsurge in unscrupulous movers and unhappy consumers has led the FMCSA to respond by issuing a set of rules "specifying how interstate household goods (HHG) carriers (movers) and brokers must assist their individual customers shipping household goods." According to its consumer page, carriers in violation of said rules can be fined, and repeat offenders may be barred from doing business. In terms of loss, however, "FMCSA does not have statutory authority to resolve loss and damage of consumer complaints, settle disputes against a mover, or obtain reimbursement for consumers seeking payment for specific charges. Consumers are responsible for resolving disputes involving these household goods matters." It is not able to represent you in an arbitration dispute to recover damages for lost or destroyed property, nor can it enforce a court judgment. If you have a grievance, your best bet is to file a complaint against the mover with the FMCSA and with the **Better Business Bureau,** www.bbb.org, in the state where the moving company is licensed, as well as with that state's attorney general or consumer protection office. To seek redress, hire an attorney.

STORAGE WAREHOUSES

Storage facilities may be required when you have to ship your belongings before you've found an apartment, or if your new home is too small. If your mover maintains storage facilities in the metro area, as many do, you may opt to store with them. Some even offer one month's free storage. Otherwise, look in the Yellow Pages under "Storage," and then shop around for the best and most convenient deal. Below are a couple of major moving/storage companies. Listing here does *not* imply endorsement by First Books.

- **Door to Door Storage**, 888-366-7222, www.doortodoor.com, several locations throughout metro Atlanta, offering warehousing for cargo containers, which are delivered to you for packing, and are then picked up and transported back to the storage facilities.
- **Public Storage**, 800-447-8673, www.publicstorage.com, offers locations throughout metro Atlanta and the rest of the country for self-service storage, pickup service and storage, full-service moving, and/or local and long-distance truck rentals.

SELF-STORAGE

The ability to rent anything from 5' x 5' rooms to storage rooms large enough to accommodate a car is a great boon to urban dwellers. Collectors, people with old clothes they can't bear to give away, and those with possessions that won't fit in their home or apartment all find mini-warehouses a solution to too-small living spaces.

Rates for space in metro Atlanta self-storage facilities are competitive. Expect to pay at least $65 per month for a basic 5' x 5' (25 square foot) climate-controlled unit, $95 per month for a 5' x 10' (50 square foot) space, and so on. Some offer free pickup; otherwise you or your mover delivers the goods. If you're looking for lower rates, inquire with the storage facility about move-in specials or other locations.

As you shop around, you'll probably want to check the facility for cleanliness and security. Does the building have sprinklers in case of fire? Does it have carts and hand trucks for moving in and out? Will you be billed monthly, or will the storage company automatically charge the bill to your credit card? Is the rental month to month or is there a minimum lease? Access should be 24-hour or nearly so. And, remember, some units are air-conditioned, an asset if you plan to visit your locker in the summer, or if you are storing items that can be damaged by excessive heat or humidity.

Finally, a word of warning: Unless you no longer want your stored belongings, pay your storage bill and pay it on time. Storage companies may auction off the contents of delinquent customers' lockers.

Here are a few local self-storage companies. For additional options, check the Yellow Pages under "Storage."

- **A Action Self-Storage**, www.atlantaactionstorage.com; several locations in metro Atlanta, including 1170 Howell Mill Road, 404-881-0100, and 4695 Hammermill Road, Tucker, 770-934-5310.

- **Buford Highway Mini-Storage**, 4206 Buford Highway NE, 404-636-6244; locally owned storage facility located east of Downtown Atlanta, in Chamblee.
- **Midtown Storage at Monroe**, 2115 Monroe Drive, 404-888-9388, www.midtownstorage.com; locally owned storage facility housed in a two-story, climate-controlled building in Midtown Atlanta.
- **Public Storage**, 800-447-8673, www.publicstorage.com; multiple locations throughout metro Atlanta, including Downtown, Alpharetta, Decatur, Lawrenceville, Marietta, Norcross, Roswell, Sandy Springs, Smyrna, and Stone Mountain.
- **Shurgard Storage Center**, 866-866-6199, www.shurgard.com; several locations throughout metro Atlanta, including Brookhaven, Decatur, Gwinnett Place, Lawrenceville, Norcross, Roswell, and Stone Mountain.
- **U-Haul Self-Storage**, 800-GO-UHAUL, www.uhaul.com; has 16 locations throughout metro Atlanta, including College Park, Decatur, Doraville, Midtown, and Smyrna.

CHILDREN AND MOVING

Studies show that moving, especially frequent moving, can be hard on children. According to an American Medical Association study, children who move often are more likely to suffer from such problems as depression, low self-esteem, and aggression. Often their academic performance suffers as well. Aside from not moving more than is necessary, there are a few things you can do to help your children through this stressful time:

- Talk about the move with your kids. Be honest but positive. Listen to their concerns and involve them in the moving process as much as you can.
- Make sure your children have their favorite possessions on the trip; don't pack "blankey" in the moving van.
- Make sure you have some social activities planned on the other end. Your children may feel lonely in your new home and such activities can ease the transition. If you move during the summer you might consider finding a local day camp they can sign up for, as a way to make new friends. Check with the YWCA or YMCA, as well as places like Zoo Atlanta, Fernbank, and The Atlanta Botanical Gardens.
- Keep in touch with family and loved ones as much as possible. Photos and phone calls are important ways of maintaining links to the important people you have left behind.
- If your children are of school age, take the time to involve yourself in their new school and in their academic life. Don't let them fall through the cracks. Additionally, try to schedule your move during the summer, so that they can start their new school at the beginning of the term.

- If possible, spend some time in the area you're moving to prior to the move, doing fun things like exploring the neighborhoods, visiting local playgrounds and parks, or checking out the malls with your teenagers. With any luck, they'll meet some other kids their own age.

For children ages 6-11, *The Moving Book: A Kids' Survival Guide* by Gabriel Davis is a wonderful gift. For general guidance, read *Smart Moves: Your Guide Through the Emotional Maze of Relocation* by Nadia Jensen, Audrey McCollum, and Stuart Copans.

TAXES

If your move is work-related, some or all of your moving expenses may be tax-deductible—so you may want to keep those receipts. Though eligibility varies, depending for example, on whether you have a job or are self-employed, generally, the cost of moving yourself, your family, and your belongings is tax deductible, even if you don't itemize. The criteria: In order to take the deduction, your move must be employment-related, your new job must be more than 50 miles away from your current residence, and you must be there for at least 39 weeks during the first 12 months after your arrival. If you take the deduction and then fail to meet the requirements, you will have to pay the IRS back, unless you were laid off through no fault of your own or transferred again by your employer. It's probably a good idea to consult a tax expert regarding IRS rules related to moving. However, if you're a confident soul, you can get a copy of IRS Form 3903 at www.irs.gov, and try figuring it out yourself!

ADDITIONAL RELOCATION AND MOVING INFORMATION

- **American Car Transport**, www.american-car-transport.com, can assist you if you need help moving your car.
- **Best Places**, www.bestplaces.net, compares quality of life and cost-of-living data of US cities.
- **Data Masters**, www.datamasters.com, provides basic community statistics by zip code.
- **The Employee Relocation Council**, www.erc.org, is a professional organization offering members specialized reports on the relocation and moving industries.

- **First Books**, www.firstbooks.com, relocation resources and information on moving to Atlanta, Boston, Chicago, Los Angeles, Minneapolis-St. Paul, New York, San Francisco, Seattle, and Washington, DC, as well as London, England. Also publisher of the *Newcomer's Handbook®* for *Moving to and Living in the USA, The Moving Book: A Kids' Survival Guide,* as well as *The Pet-Moving Handbook.*
- *How to Survive A Move,* edited by Jamie Allen and Kazz Regelman, is a **Hundreds of Heads** guide (www.hundredsofheads.com). Divided into sections ranging from planning a move to packing tips, moving with kids, and worst moves ever, this easy-to-digest book provides the wisdom, dispensed mostly in single-paragraph bites, of hundreds of people who've lived through the experience.
- **HomeStore**, www.homestore.com, provides numerous relocation resources, including a handy salary calculator that will compare the cost of living in US cities.
- **The Riley Guide**, www.rileyguide.com/relocate.html, is an online moving and relocation clearinghouse. It offers lists of moving and relocation guides and web sites, as well as links to sites that cover cost-of-living demographics, real estate, school, and healthcare directories.
- **The United States Postal Service**, www.usps.com, offers helpful relocation information.

A S SOON AS YOU HAVE YOUR NEW ADDRESS, YOU WILL PROBABLY want to open a bank account. Read on for information about Atlanta banks and credit unions; credit cards; credit reports; city, state, and federal income taxes; and moving or starting a business.

FINANCIAL INSTITUTIONS

Many banks in Atlanta maintain branch offices in numerous locations around the metropolitan area. In addition, these banks operate a multitude of ATMs for 24-hour banking convenience.

When shopping around for a bank, you can choose a giant conglomerate that operates in several states, or you can choose a locally run bank. Either way, you should compare bank services and fees to find the best deal for your financial needs. Some banks offer free checking under certain conditions, such as maintaining a minimum balance in your account. Some offer reduced monthly fees for people who bank mostly by ATM. And, many banks offer special deals to new customers, such as a waiver of check fees or safe deposit rent. Though most people withdraw money from ATMs, many choose to execute other transactions, such as deposits, at the bank itself. Choosing a bank that has a branch in your neighborhood as well as one near your place of employment guarantees access to your bank during business hours. However, if you don't need a branch on every corner, you should look into a smaller bank that may be in your neighborhood. Local institutions may offer lower fees and friendlier service than their mega-bank competitors.

Due to recent changes in banking regulations, some of the old familiar names have merged with larger banks, and some who merged just a year or two ago are now in the second generation of name changes. Some of Atlanta's largest banks are listed below. These banks will not only administer your checking and savings accounts, but they can also help you with CDs, money market accounts, and other investment products such as mutual funds.

- **BB&T**, www.bbandt.com, 800-226-5228, 25 metro Atlanta locations
- **Bank of America**, www.bankofamerica.com, 800-299-2265; over 75 locations in metro Atlanta
- **Colonial Bank**, www.colonialbank.com, 877-502-2265; 12 Atlanta locations
- **Main Street Bank**, www.mainstreetbank.com, 770-786-3441; Atlanta-based bank with 20 locations
- **SouthTrust Bank**, www.southtrust.com, 800-225-5782 or 770-612-6500; over 50 locations in the metro Atlanta area
- **SunTrust Bank**, www.suntrust.com, 800-SUNTRUST or 404-230-5555; over 75 locations in the metro Atlanta area
- **Wachovia**, www.wachovia.com, 800-788-7000; over 50 locations in the metro Atlanta area
- **Washington Mutual**, www.wamu.com, 800-788-7000; over 20 locations in the metro Atlanta area

CREDIT UNIONS

If membership in a credit union is an option, this may be the best place to go for your banking needs. Credit unions are typically run by a volunteer board and offer significantly lower fees on savings and checking accounts, short-term loans, and credit cards. According to *American Banker's* annual survey, credit unions rank high in customer satisfaction. Because credit unions limit membership based on set criteria, you'll need to investigate a few for a match. Organizations such as employers, unions, professional associations, churches, and schools (alumni associations) typically provide membership. The down side is that credit unions are usually unable to provide the wider variety of financial products and services, such as mutual funds, CDs, and other investment vehicles. Additionally, credit union members may find it difficult to get to their union's offices. Unlike large banks, credit unions may have one or two locations, rather than branch offices throughout the city.

For a complete list of local credit unions or information about them, you can visit the **National Association of Credit Union Service Organizations**, www.nacuso.org, or the **National Credit Union Administration** (**NCUA**), http://ncua.gov. Some of the larger credit unions in metro Atlanta are:

- **Atlanta Postal Credit Union**, 800-849-8431, www.apcu.com; for Atlanta area postal workers
- **CDC Federal Credit Union**, 404-325-3270, www.cdcfcu.com; for Centers for Disease Control employees
- **Delta Employees Credit Union**, 404-715-4725, www.decu.org; for Delta Airline employees
- **Emory Federal Credit Union**, 404-329-6415, http://portal.fxfn.com/zefcudg; for employees of both Emory Hospital and Emory University
- **Georgia Federal Credit Union**, 770-621-5410, www.gfcu4u.org; for local school system employees and county employees

CHECKING ACCOUNTS

Most banks offer checking accounts in a variety of shapes and sizes. You may choose from a no-frills economy account with a low maintenance fee and limited withdrawals or a flat fee account with unlimited transactions. Generally, though, if you maintain a certain minimum balance in your account, the bank will waive any service charges.

To set up a checking account, most banks require the address and phone number of your current employer; two signed pieces of identification; such as a driver's license, credit card, or student ID; and a minimum start-up deposit. Some banks now also run a credit check on your social security number while you wait. If you have a bad credit record or a history of bouncing checks, you may not be allowed to open an account. Also, be aware that if you do open an account, there is usually a waiting period, from five to seven days, before you can access funds in that account.

SAVINGS ACCOUNTS

Many people choose to open a savings account along with their checking account. And just as your bank offers you several checking options, it will probably offer you more than one savings plan from which to choose. If you have only short-term savings needs, you might choose an account that sets aside a small amount from your checking account each month and credits your savings. On the other hand, if you have a large sum of cash, you may want to open a savings account that gives you a higher interest rate in exchange for maintaining a minimum balance in your account. As with a checking account, employment information, identification, and a minimum start-up deposit will most likely be required.

CONSUMER COMPLAINTS—BANKING

Federal and state government regulate bank policies on discrimination, credit, anti-redlining, truth-in-lending, etc. If you have a problem with your bank, you should first attempt to resolve the issue directly with the bank. Should you need to file a formal complaint against your financial institution, you can do so through the Board of Governors of the Federal Reserve System, Division of Consumer and Community Affairs. For specific information, call 202-452-3693 or go online to www.federal reserve.gov/pubs/complaints. You can also pursue the issue with the following agencies:

- Nationally chartered commercial banks go through the **US Comptroller of the Currency, Customer Assistance Group**, 1301 McKinney Street, Suite 3710, Houston, TX 77010; 800-613-6743; www.occ.treas.gov.
- **US Office of Thrift Supervision**, 1700 G Street NW, Washington, D.C. 20552, 202-906-6000, www.ots.treas.gov; for thrift institutions insured by the Savings Association Insurance Fund and/or federally chartered (i.e., members of the Federal Home Loan Bank System).
- For **state-chartered banks**, contact the **Georgia Department of Banking and Finance**, 2990 Brandywine Road, Atlanta, 770-986-1633, 888-986-1633, www.ganet.org/dbf. State-chartered banks that are members of the Federal Reserve System should contact the **Federal Reserve Bank of Atlanta**, 1000 Peachtree Street NE, Atlanta, 404-498-8500, www.frbatlanta.org; or the **Federal Deposit Insurance Corporation** (**FDIC**), 10 Tenth Street NE, Atlanta, 800-765-3342, www.fdic.gov.
- Federally chartered credit unions or state-chartered credit unions with federal insurance: **National Credit Union Administration**, 9 Washington Square, Washington Avenue Extension, Albany, NY 12205, 518-862-7400, www.ncua.gov

CREDIT CARDS

The internet is a valuable resource when it comes to getting information about credit cards. A list of low-rate card issuers can be found online at **CardWeb**, www.cardweb.com, or by calling 800-344-7714; **Consumer Action**, www.consumer-action.org; and **Credit Cards Comparison**, www.credit-cards-comparison-charts.com.

For more information about a specific card, to request an application or to apply online, you can contact the following:

- **American Express**, 800-THE-CARD, www.americanexpress.com
- **Diner's Club**, 800-2-DINERS, www.dinersclubnorthamerica.com
- **Discover Card**, 800-347-2683 (or apply at any Sears location), www. discovercard.com
- **VISA** and **MasterCard** are available from banks and other financial service associations. Terms may very widely, so shop around for the lowest interest rate and annual fees. And be sure to read the fine print. A card may offer a fabulous deal for six months and then charge an exorbitant rate after that—just when you've made all your Christmas purchases.
- **Department store credit cards** can be acquired at checkout counters and customer service desks. Most stores offer instant credit for those who qualify. Usually, you can get a discount on one day's purchase when you sign up for a department store credit card. Store charge accounts also offer advantages beyond credit, such as advance notice of sales, mail or phone orders, and free shipping.

BANKING & CREDIT RESOURCES

For a list of articles about trends in banking, and links to the Federal Trade Commission and other consumer protection agencies, visit the **National Institute for Consumer Education** web site at www.nice.emich.edu. To look up current interest rates on deposits, go to www.rate.net or www.bankrate.com.

If you're buying a car or boat, renovating your new fixer-upper, or sending the kids to college, you can still shop for loans the old-fashioned way, using the Yellow Pages and the financial section of the newspaper, but the internet can make the job a lot easier. Online loan calculators let you experiment with different payment plans. There are several loan calculators on bankrate.com but you can look at other sites as well:

- **www.myfico.com**
- **www.411-loans.com**
- **Eloan**, www.eloan.com,
- **Financial Power Tools**, http://financialpowertools.com
- **Women's Financial Network**, www.wfn.com
- **The Motley Fool**, www.fool.com (an excellent place to learn about money, investing and banking. They offer online seminars, well-written articles, and an active discussion board.)

Obtain copies of your **credit report** from the three major credit bureaus at **www.annualcreditreport.com**. Avoid ordering your credit report more than once a year, though—frequent requests could adversely affect your credit rating.

TAXES

,partment of Revenue, 404-417-4477, www.gatax.org, ..pal tax collecting agency for the state. The Department, led by ..evenue Commissioner, is charged with the administration and enforcement of nearly all of the Georgia's tax laws, pertaining to everything from state income tax and sales tax, to ad valorem and property tax. The Department of Revenue is headquartered at 1800 Century Center Boulevard, NE, Atlanta, though several of their departments are located in other locations around town.

SALES TAX

Georgia State Sales Tax is currently 4%, with each county or municipality having the power to levy additional sales taxes by popular vote. Added taxes are used for such local needs as building schools, improving local roads, and other special uses the county or city deems necessary. What follows is a sampling of metro area sales taxes, and how the tax funds are allocated:

- **City of Atlanta**: 7% sales tax (4% Georgia, 1% for MARTA, and 2% for local special needs)
- **Fulton County**: 7% sales tax (4% Georgia, 1% for MARTA, and 2% for local needs and education)
- **DeKalb County**: 7% sales tax (4% Georgia, 1% for MARTA, 1% homestead, and 1% education)
- **Cobb County**: 5% sales tax (4% Georgia, and 1% for education)
- **Gwinnett County**: 6% sales tax (4% Georgia, and 2% for special purpose education)

It's important to note that Georgia holds two tax-free days each year; generally in late winter/early spring, and again in the late summer, just in time for back-to-school shopping. Many items are sold minus sales tax during tax-free days, including clothing, shoes, computers, and school supplies. For more information about Georgia's tax-free days, including a complete list of goods that qualify for tax-free status and the upcoming tax-free day schedule, visit the **Georgia Department of Revenue Tax-Free Page**, www2.state.ga.us/departments/dor/QA.shtml.

PROPERTY TAX

Georgia residents are required to pay property tax on any personal real estate (including their primary residence) or commercial property that they own in the state. This property tax is the primary source of revenue for local counties, cities, and public schools in Georgia. Each of the state's 159 counties, including the 28 counties that make up metro Atlanta, operates tax offices that assess and collect the tax. For more information on property tax collection in Georgia, contact the **Georgia Department of Revenue, Property Tax Division**, 404-968-0707, www2.state.ga.us. You can also find county-by-county tax information, including contact information for your local tax commissioner, at the **Georgia Department of Revenue County Contact Page**, www2.state.ga.us.

MOTOR VEHICLE TAX

In addition to collecting property tax, it's also the responsibility of **Georgia's Department of Revenue, Property Tax Division,** to value motor vehicles for taxation. All Georgia residents who own a car must register it with their county tax commissioner and pay an annual motor vehicle ad valorem tax. For more information about motor vehicle registration, tags, titles, and taxes, contact the state **Department of Motor Vehicles**, 404-362-6500, www.dmvs.ga.gov, or the tax commissioner's office in your county.

STATE INCOME TAX

The State of Georgia requires that income tax be withheld from wages paid to all resident and nonresident employees who work within the state. Residents are also required to pay state income tax on wages earned outside of Georgia (unless a state tax has already been withheld in another state). The deadline for filing a Georgia income tax return is April 15th. For more information on Georgia's state income tax, or to request a copy of Georgia's tax forms, contact the **Georgia Department of Revenue, Income Tax Division**, 404-417-3210, www2.state.ga.us. Georgia tax forms are available at most metro Atlanta post offices and public libraries.

FEDERAL INCOME TAX

Federal Income Tax forms can be obtained by calling 800-829-3676 or by picking them up during tax season at any local post office or public library. If you need additional federal income tax information, the resources here can help:
- **IRS Tax Help Line**, 800-829-1040, 800-829-4059 (TDD), www.irs.gov; for consumers with questions and/or in need of forms
- **Federal Teletax Information Line**, 800-829-4477
- **IRS Atlanta Office**, 401 West Peachtree Street, NW, Atlanta, 404-338-7962, www.irs.gov

If you'd like someone else to prepare your tax return, professional tax services are listed in the Yellow Pages or you can search the internet Yellow Pages at: www.yp.bellsouth.com. Of the many firms listed, here are a few for consideration:

- **H & R Block**, 800-472-5625, www.hrblock.com; over 100 locations throughout metro Atlanta
- **Jackson Hewitt**, 800-234-1040, www.jacksonhewitt.com; over 100 locations in metro Atlanta
- **Townsend Income Tax & Accounting**, 770-433-0606, www.1040. com/townsend; locally owned, with five offices throughout metro Atlanta

ELECTRONIC INCOME TAX FILING

These days, many people are choosing to file their taxes electronically, by purchasing or downloading tax software, using an online tax service, or going through an accredited agency. According to the IRS, electronic filers receive their refunds in about half the time of people who file through the mail, and e-filing, as it's called, costs less and is more accurate than doing it the old fashioned way.

To research the many tax filing software options, go to your search engine and type in "tax software." **Quicken Turbo Tax**, www.turbo tax.com, is just one of many that are available.

For more information on electronic filing, check out **IRS E-file**, www.irs.gov/efile. This site includes features such as convenient payment options or direct deposit for those expecting a return, and offers a list of software brands and internet sites that are capable of handling both federal and state returns.

If you'd like to file your Georgia State Income Tax online, visit the **Georgia Department of Revenue, Taxpayer Services Division** web site, www2.state.ga.us.

STARTING OR MOVING A BUSINESS

If you are interested in starting a new business, or relocating your existing business to metro Atlanta, you may want to consider consulting an attorney who is familiar with the process and with the city itself. The following resources will give you an idea of how to get started, what to expect, and where to turn for information:

- **Metro Atlanta Chamber of Commerce**, **Business Recruitment Department**, 404-586-8446, www.metroatlantachamber.com; specializes in assisting companies who are planning a move into metro Atlanta, offering information on everything from commercial and residential real estate and employee training, to local business taxes and incentives.

- **First Stop Business Information Center**, 404-656-7061, 800-656-4558, www.sos.state.ga.us/firststop/default.htm; a great source for the information and contacts necessary for doing business in Georgia. Here you'll find county contacts (where you will be required to go for your business license), state regulatory reqirements, and informative articles on running a business.
- **Internal Revenue Service**, 800-829-1040, www.irs.gov; offers information on applying for an employer tax ID number.
- **US Small Business Administration**, 800-827-5722, www.sba.gov; provides information, aid, counseling, and assistance for those interested in starting and running a small business.

ONGRATULATIONS! YOU'VE FOUND A PLACE TO LIVE AND NOW IT'S just a matter of settling in before you'll start to feel like a true Atlantan. The crucial tasks of setting up your utilities, hooking up cable TV, getting online, registering your car, and signing up to vote are now at hand. Perhaps you'd also like to subscribe to the local paper, find a family doctor, and get a library card. Details follow.

UTILITIES

Houses and apartments in metro Atlanta are equipped either solely with electricity or with a combination of electricity and gas. Even if you have an electric stove, you may still have a gas-powered water heater, so check the basement appliances or ask your landlord about your apartment's utilities.

ELECTRICITY

If you are renting a house or apartment, your leasing agent or landlord will tell you which power company serves your new home. Some rentals include electric power with the monthly rent, though most do not, so it will be up to you to make arrangements with the power company to have the electricity turned on in your name.

For electric service in the City of Atlanta and much of Fulton, DeKalb, Cobb, and Gwinnett counties (especially the portions closer in to the city), contact **Georgia Power**, 404-325-4001, www.georgiapower.com. A $22 establishment fee will appear on your first bill, and an additional deposit (not exceeding $150) may be required if you are a new Georgia Power customer. Power will be turned on within 24 hours. If the power is already on when you move in, they will begin billing you after you put the account in your name. You may want to consider Georgia Power's Budget Billing Plan to soften the periodic shocks of peak electric bills throughout the year. The plan averages the power bills over a year into 12 equal payments. The good news is that if your service totals less than the estimated average at the end of the year you'll receive a refund. But, if it is more, the difference will be added to the monthly bills for the next year. Either way, Budget Billing helps you avoid $200 electric bills during the summer when temperatures soar and the air conditioner will be in high use.

Depending on your address, you may be serviced by a different power company. If in doubt, call Georgia Power, and they will be able to tell you which company to call.

Parts of DeKalb County are served by **Snapping Shoals EMC**, 770-786-3484, www.ssemc.com. This company is one of the Electric Membership Corporations originally established to offer power to rural areas of the state. Today they serve 74,000 residential and commercial customers in metro Atlanta and seven other counties southeast of the city. Membership is $10, and a $40 connection fee is required.

Walton EMC, 770-972-2917, 800-342-6582, www.waltonemc.com, and **Jackson EMC**, 770-963-6166, www.jacksonemc.com; both cover some parts of Gwinnett County as well other northeast Georgia counties. Each requires a $5 membership fee and $20 connection fee to establish service. Additional deposits may also be required, though the EMCs will sometimes accept a letter of credit from your previous electric company in lieu of this.

In addition to Georgia Power and the EMCs, Gwinnett County also receives power from several other sources, including the following municipalities: **City of Norcross**, 770-448-2122, www.norcrossga.net; **City of Buford**, 770-945-6761; **City of Lawrenceville**, 770-963-2414, www.lawrencevillegaweb.org. Minimal connection fees and deposits may be required by each.

Georgia Power (see above for phone number) serves most of Cobb County, including the cities of Austell, Marietta, and Smyrna. In some northeast and western portions of Cobb County, though, service is provided by **Cobb EMC**, 770-429-2100, www.cobbemc.com. Cobb EMC requires an establishment fee and credit check before establishing service. For electric service in the **City of Acworth** call 770-974-5233, www.acworth.org; service requires a deposit as well as a non-refundable application fee.

Sawnee EMC, 770-887-2363, www.sawnee.com, provides power to a limited number of Fulton County residents in the Alpharetta and Roswell areas, though most homes in these suburbs are served by Georgia Power. Sawnee EMC also covers additional north Georgia counties, including Forsyth, Dawson, and most of Cherokee. A $5 membership fee and $25 connection fee is required to establish service. Additional deposits (not to exceed $200) may also be required.

NATURAL GAS

The state's natural gas deregulation in the late 1990s may have given Atlanta residents increased options in gas providers, but it also led to some confusion. Which company should you use? What are the differences between the providers? Are the rates basically the same or are some of the providers significantly less expensive than the others? Because of increased competition, many of the state's gas providers offer incentives to new customers, so be sure to ask when calling around. You will also want to inquire about the rate "per therm" and any additional charges that may appear on your bill. Some gas companies require an initial deposit as well as a contract and connection fee, others don't. Do your research ahead of time to make sure you're choosing the company that will best meet your needs. A few of the largest gas companies serving metro Atlanta are:

- **Atlanta Gas Light**, 770-994-1946, www.atlantagaslight.com
- **Georgia Natural Gas**, 770-850-6200, www.georgianaturalgas.com
- **Scana**, 877-467-2262, www.scana.com
- **Southern Company Gas**, 866-762-6427, www.southerncompany gas.com

Keep in mind that if you are renting an apartment in a large complex, the owner may have contracted with one of the gas companies to serve all of the apartments in that community, so your choice will be made for you. Remember to bring this up with the leasing agent before you move in.

For additional information about gas deregulation and providers in the State of Georgia, contact the **Georgia Public Service Commission**, 404-656-4501, www.psc.state.ga.us. They can explain deregulation, offer you a checklist of what to look for in a natural gas provider, and assist you if you have complaints.

TELEPHONE

BellSouth, 404-780-2355, 800-356-3094, www.bellsouth.com, is the primary provider of local, landline telephone service in metro Atlanta, although a handful of other companies have recently entered the competition. Besides basic, residential service, BellSouth also offers optional services, for a fee, including call waiting, caller ID, voice mail, and call forwarding. A $50 connection fee is required for new service, and will be included on your first month's bill. A credit check determines whether or not you'll be charged an additional deposit.

Establishing your local service is also your opportunity to choose a long distance carrier (see below). Many of metro Atlanta's local phone service companies, including BellSouth and AT&T, also provide long distance service. The benefit of using one company for both local and long distance calls is that you only receive one phone bill each month. You may also receive discounted rates by combining service into one plan. This option may not be offered in all parts of the metro area though, so be sure to ask up front if this is something you're interested in.

• **Alltel**, 800-501-1754, www.alltel.net
• **AT&T**, 800-222-0300, www.att.com
• **MCI**, 800-444-3333, www.mci.com

LONG DISTANCE SERVICE PROVIDERS

When researching a long distance company be sure to call around and ask for their best deals until you find the plan that best meets your needs. Carriers frequently advertise low per-minute rates, but make sure you read the fine print. If you have to pay a higher monthly fee to get the lower per-minute rate, and you don't make many long distance calls, it may make more sense for you to use a pre-paid calling card, or your cell phone for long distance, omitting the need for a long distance provider entirely. The major long distance carriers in metro Atlanta are:

• **AT&T**, 800-222-0300, www.att.com
• **BellSouth**, 404-780-2355, 800-356-3094, www.bellsouth.com
• **MCI**, 800-444-3333, www.mci.com
• **Sprint**, 800-877-4646, www.sprint.com
• **Verizon**, 800-343-2092, www22.verizon.com

For help comparing long distance and wireless calling plans, you may want to visit the **Telecommunications and Research Action Center (TRAC)**, www.trac.org, or call them at 202-263-2950. TRAC, which is not affiliated with the communications industry, publishes TeleTips, which are residential and small business long distance charts to assist consumers with their long distance options. The TRAC site also provides directory assistance via the Internet.

If you are ever the victim of an unfair business practice, such as "slamming" (switching your long distance service without your consent), contact the **Department of Consumer Affairs** through the governor's office, 404-651-8600, 800-869-1123, www2.state.ga.us/gaoca. For more information on how to protect yourself from consumer fraud, see the **Consumer Protection** section below.

CELL PHONES

The Atlanta Yellow Pages devotes several pages to cell phone providers in the metro area. Because of competition, it's now possible to find a great service plan, with extra features, for relatively small fees. Be sure to ask what services are available when calling to establish your cell phone service A few to consider are:

- **Cingular**, 800-331-0500, www.cingular.com
- **Metro PCS**, 888-863-8768, www.metropcs.com
- **Nextel**, 800-639-6111, www.nextel.com
- **Sprint PCS**, 888-211-4727, www.sprintpcs.com
- **T-Mobile**, 800-T-Mobile, www.t-mobile.com
- **Verizon Wireless**, 800-922-0204, www.verizonwireless.com

AREA CODES

Area code 404 covers Atlanta city limits, as well as most of Fulton County, most of DeKalb County, and a portion in the north of Clayton County. Area code 770 covers the surrounding suburbs, such as those in Gwinnett County, Cobb County and most communities outside the I-285 perimeter; further out is area code 706. Area codes 678 and 470 cover Alpharetta as well as other suburbs north of the perimeter, and are also the area codes assigned to most new cell phone numbers established in metro Atlanta.

When dialing from the 404 area to the 770 or 678 area—or vice versa—dial only 10 digits: the area code plus the number. Do not dial a one or a zero before the number or you will reach a recorded message. Some programmable dialing systems automatically insert a "1" before dialing 10-digit numbers, so you should make sure your equipment will dial correctly.

INTERNET SERVICE PROVIDERS (ISPs)

Internet service in metro Atlanta varies from traditional modem dial-up over your home phone line to cable modems and DSLs. Dial-up provides you the most basic of online services, typically just standard internet access and email, and is slow (the trade-off, of course, is that it is generally much less expensive than cable and DSL).

For high-speed internet access, a digital subscriber line (DSL) or cable modem access cannot be beat. DSL runs on copper wires like those used for telephone service, but on a separate line. Unlike dial-up, a DSL connection is always on, so logging onto the internet is nearly instantaneous. Cable internet access is available from your local cable television provider. And, like DSL, the cable modem is "always on." However, there is a possibility that your access speed could be decreased if your neighbors also have cable access. Before you sign up for a cable modem, make sure you determine what speed is guaranteed. Cable modem and DSL availability vary according to the building or area you in which you reside.

When establishing your ISP consider "bundling." This is where your digital cable, telephone, and/or internet service are all grouped together on one plan. The main benefit of bundling is that you receive one bill from one provider for the entire amount each month, typically at a discount. Currently, Comcast, BellSouth, and AT&T (Cingular) offer bundling packages in Atlanta area. To find out whether or not your neighborhood is included, contact the providers directly.

For a complete listing of internet service providers in your area, check the Yellow Pages under "Internet Access Providers." In the meantime, here are a few metro Atlanta providers who offer dial-up access, cable modem, and/or DSL:

- **Alltel**, 800-501-1754, www.alltel.com
- **America Online**, 888-265-8003, www.aol.com
- **AT&T Worldnet**, 800-967-5363, www.att.com
- **Bellsouth Internet Services**, 888-321-2375, www.bellsouth.com
- **Comcast**, 800-COMCAST, www.comcast.com
- **Earthlink**, 800-511-2041, www.earthlink.com
- **Microsoft**, 800-426-9400, www.msn.com
- **Net Zero**, 877-665-9995, www.netzero.net

WATER

Drinking water for the metro Atlanta area comes from the north, in the Georgia Mountains, travels south via the Chattahoochee River to Lake Lanier and then further south to collecting and processing plants closer to the city. The city's water department is Georgia's fourth largest utility and the third largest water system in the southeast. It serves nearly two million customers in the metro areas of Fulton and DeKalb counties, and sells water to many of the nearby municipalities who, in turn, bill their residents through their own local water departments.

City officials tout the fact that Atlanta's water continues to meet or exceed national water standards established by the US Environmental Protection Agency (EPA). Recent water quality reports for metro Atlanta can be accessed online through the **City of Atlanta Bureau of Water**, http://apps.atlantaga.gov/citydir/water/waterquality.htm. For additional information about Georgia's water standards, or about metro Atlanta's water supply, contact **Clean Water Atlanta**, 404-529-9211, www.clean wateratlanta.org, or the **City of Atlanta Department of Watershed Management**, 404-330-6081, www.atlantaga.gov/government/water shed.aspx.

In most rental situations, the landlord will include water in the monthly rent, but remember to ask about this up front. If you are responsible for your own water, a deposit as well as a copy of your lease and a picture ID will most likely be required to initiate service. When the bill arrives, expect to be charged for water consumption, as well as a sewer fee, which is based on a portion of the water consumption. Though local water services are a value by national standards, it is a good idea to ask about the consumption history of the home or apartment you are considering. And, once you move in, be sure to check periodically for toilets that run excessively, faucets with pesky drips, and outside hose bibs that leak. A toilet with an unchecked faulty valve can send your water bill up to the level of your monthly car payment.

To establish service or to get more information about water service within the city limits, contact the **City of Atlanta Bureau of Water**, 404-658-6500, http://apps.atlantaga.gov/citydir/water/index.htm. For water service outside the city, in DeKalb County, contact the **DeKalb County Water and Sewer Division**, 770-621-7200, http://dekalbwater sewer.com; in North Fulton County, contact the **Fulton County Water & Sewer Billing Division**, 404-730-6830, www.co.fulton.ga.us; in Cobb County contact the **Cobb County Water System**, 770-423-1000, www.cobbwater.org/home/index.asp; Gwinnett County residents should contact the **Gwinnett County Department of Public Utilities**, 678-376-6800, www.co.gwinnett.ga.us.

GARBAGE AND RECYCLING

Trash collection and recycling differ from neighborhood to neighborhood in the metro Atlanta area. The following section should provide you with enough information to help you figure out what works in your community. And remember, when in doubt, ask your leasing agent, landlord, or real estate broker to answer any questions you have concerning your new home, including trash collection and recycling procedures.

TRASH REMOVAL

Apartment dwellers usually deposit household trash in a designated common container, a dumpster, within the apartment complex. It is then management's responsibility to have the container emptied on a regular basis, usually once or twice a week. Garbage fees are generally included in your monthly rent. However, if you are renting a house or duplex or purchasing a home or condominium, you will need to know who to call to begin trash pickup.

In the **City of Atlanta**, wheeled "Herby Curby" trash receptacles made of heavy-duty plastic are available to residents, and curbside trash pickup is provided once a week. Ask your neighbor or call 404-659-6757 to find out what day trash is collected in your neighborhood. The charge for sanitation service within the city limits is about $275 per year, and is billed to the property owner every July. If you are renting, you should not receive the bill. However, if the bill is sent to you by mistake, notify your landlord immediately so that he can pay it before the August 15th deadline. Otherwise, you may find yourself without trash pickup. If you'd like more information, contact the **City of Atlanta Bureau of Solid Waste, Sanitation Department**, www.atlantaga.gov, 404-330-3333.

- Unincorporated **Fulton County**, 404-730-4000, www.co.fulton. ga.us, uses private garbage haulers for residential service. Haulers must be registered with the county and satisfy various insurance and Environmental Protection Division (EPD) requirements. A list of approved private companies, along with their designated areas of service, can be obtained by contacting the county directly.

- **DeKalb County**, 404-294-2900, www.co.dekalb.ga.us, provides curbside pickup twice a week for household garbage, and once a week pickup for yard debris. Homeowners provide 20- to 30-gallon cans, and no special bags are required for household trash. Yard debris should be in paper bags and not mixed in with anything else. The charge for sanitation service in DeKalb County is generally about $200 per year, billed quarterly to the homeowner.

- The **City of Decatur**, which is in DeKalb County, has a unique plan, which is now being used by several other metro Atlanta cities. Called the "Pay As You Throw" program, this plan offers residents an incentive to recycle. The program requires an annual fee of $150, billed in the spring, for collection of household garbage and yard trimmings. Residents must then purchase special garbage bags from local supermarkets and hardware stores. Trash will only be collected if it is contained in these bags, which range in price from 15 cents to $1, depending on size. Under this system, residents who recycle more or have less trash to dispose of will pay less than households with larger garbage amounts simply because they use fewer bags. Contact the **City of Decatur Sanitation Department**, 404-377-5571, www. decatur-ga.com, for more information.

- The **City of Austell**, part of Cobb County, uses the same plan as Decatur, with bags costing $1.50 and $2.75, depending on size. No additional charge is levied on residents. Residential trash pickup is Monday. For more information, contact the **Austell Solid Waste Division**, 770-944-4300, www.austell.org.

- The **City of Marietta** requires that all residential trashcans display an official city decal in order to be emptied. Decals can be obtained through **Marietta Powers Customer Service Department**, 675 North Marietta Parkway, 770-794-5150. The city also requires that trash cans not exceed 32 gallons in size. If curbside cans gallons, the homeowner will be charged an additional $10 per c empty them. For more information, including trash collection dates, contact the **Marietta Sanitation Department**, 770-794-5581, www.city.marietta.ga.us.

- In **Smyrna**, residential trash is collected, curbside, twice a week. Days vary depending on your address. The charge for sanitation service in Smyrna is about $17 per month is billed monthly to the homeowner. For additional information, contact the **Smyrna Sanitation Department**, 770-319-5338, www.smyrnacity.com.
- Unincorporated **Cobb County** uses private haulers with the same insurance and registration requirements as Fulton County. For a complete list call 770-528-2500, or go online to www.cobbcounty.org.
- **Gwinnett County** also employs private companies for residential trash pickup. For a current list of haulers and their requirements, contact **Gwinnett Clean and Beautiful**, 770-822-5187, www. gwinnettcb.org.

RECYCLING

Most cities and communities in metro Atlanta have established recycling programs, either in the form of curbside pickup or drop-off sites. The **City of Atlanta**, for instance, offers curbside pickup to over 87,000 single-family residences. For more information, contact the **Atlanta Recycling Hotline** at 404-792-1212 or visit www.dreamsan.com/atlantarecycling.htm.

If you live outside the city limits and would like to know more about recycling in your neighborhood, contact the appropriate county office:
- **Fulton County**, 404-730-8097, www.co.fulton.ga.us
- **DeKalb County**, 404-294-2900, www.co.dekalb.ga.us
- **Cobb County**, 770-528-1135, www.cobbcounty.org
- **Gwinnett County**, 770-822-5187, www.gwinnettcb.org

Additionally, several volunteer organizations in Atlanta and the surrounding communities also provide useful information about recycling efforts as well as the location of recycling centers. For details, contact the agency nearest you:
- **Gwinnett Clean and Beautiful**, 770-822-5187, www.gwinnett cb.org
- **Keep Atlanta Beautiful**, 404-330-6972
- **Keep Cobb Beautiful**, 770-528-1135, www.cobbcounty.org
- **Keep DeKalb Beautiful**, 404-371-2654, www.co.dekalb.ga.us/ beautiful

- **Keep Georgia Beautiful**, www.keepgeorgiabeautiful.com, provides a list of local offices, by county, throughout the metro Atlanta area
- **Keep Marietta Beautiful**, 770-794-5606, www.city.marietta.ga.us
- **Keep Roswell Beautiful**, 770-594-6451, www.ci.roswell.ga.us
- **Keep Sandy Springs/North Fulton Beautiful**, 770-551-7766, www.kssnfb.org
- **Keep Smyrna Beautiful**, 770-431-2863, www.ci.smyrna.ga.us
- **Keep South Fulton Beautiful**, 770-969-9324, www.ksfb.info

If you wish to dispose of household recyclables on your own, you can find a comprehensive listing of local recycling centers online at **Earth 911**, www.earth911.org. Just enter your zip code and you'll be directed to a page that lists centers for recycling paper, plastic, scrap metal, and more in your neighborhood. You can also find listings in the **Atlanta Yellow Pages**, under **Recycling Centers**.

CONSUMER PROTECTION—UTILITIES COMPLAINTS

With the recent deregulation of local gas companies, various long distance providers vying for your business, and issues over what fees are possible for electric companies to charge when computing monthly billing, it is little wonder consumers are confused about their rights. If you have any questions or feel your rights as a consumer have been violated, the following consumer protection organizations should be able to help:
- If you have questions or complaints about your utility services and feel that your problems have gone unanswered by the individual company providers, contact the **Georgia Governor's Office of Consumer Affairs**, 404-651-8600, 800-869-1123, www2.state.ga.us/gaoca, or the **Office of the Attorney General of Georgia**, 404-656-3300, http://ganet.org/ago. Both offices are responsible for protecting the rights of Georgia consumers, and enforcing the state's consumer protection laws, including Georgia's Fair Business Practices Act.
- The **Georgia Public Service Commission** (**GPSC**), 404-656-4501, 800-282-5813, www.psc.state.ga.us, is another excellent source of information and assistance. As the official regulatory agency for utilities operating in Georgia, their job is to ensure that consumers receive safe, reliable and reasonably priced utility services from "financially viable and technically competent companies." The GPSC provides helpful tips for utilities customers, answers to frequently asked questions, and even an online link through which consumers can file their complaints.
- For those seeking a more public forum for consumer complaints, WSB-TV and radio offers Georgia's best known and respected consumer rights guru, **Clark Howard**. His regular show airs complaints by con-

sumers and offers connections between those with problems and those with the answers. Howard also writes a weekly column for the *Atlanta Journal-Constitution* newspaper and maintains a **Consumer Action Line** at 404-892-8227. Howard's persistence on behalf of consumers has prompted many to say, "If Clark can't help you, nobody can!"

DRIVING IN GEORGIA

DRIVER'S LICENSES, AUTOMOBILE REGISTRATION AND STATE IDS

If you have an out-of-state driver's license, Georgia law requires that you obtain a Georgia driver's license within 30 days. To purchase your license, bring your previous driver's license or two other pieces of identification, proof of Georgia residency (such as a utility bill or copy of your lease), and $15 cash. If your name is different than the one on your previous driver's license or ID, you will also be required to show official documentation of the name change (e.g., your marriage license or divorce papers). New residents over 18, with a valid out-of-state license, need only pass an eye exam to exchange the out-of-state license for a Georgia license. New residents under 18, or those whose out-of-state license has expired, must also pass the written road rules and sign tests as well as the driving test.

For additional information regarding requirements and exam times, as well as a full listing of local exam offices, contact the **Department of Motor Vehicle Safety**, 678-413-8400, www.dmvs.ga.gov. Following is a short list of examination stations to get you started:

- **Atlanta**, 1296 Moreland Avenue; open Tuesday-Saturday, 9 a.m. to 5 p.m.
- **Downtown Atlanta**, 146 Memorial Drive; open Monday-Friday, 9 a.m. to 5 p.m.
- **Sandy Springs**, 8610 Roswell Road; open Tuesday-Saturday, 9 a.m. to 5 p.m.
- **Marietta**, 1605 County Services Parkway; open Tuesday-Saturday, 9 a.m. to 5 p.m.
- **Lawrenceville**, 310 Hurricane Shoals Road; open Tuesday-Saturday, 9 a.m. to 5 p.m.

STATE IDS

State IDs can be obtained at any state driver's license exam office, with proof of residency. The cost is $10. For more information visit any of the office locations listed above, go online to www.dmvs.ga.gov, or call 404-657-9300.

AUTOMOBILE REGISTRATION

If you own a car, you must purchase Georgia tags within thirty days of establishing residency. You will need to bring your valid insurance card to register your car in Georgia. You are required by law to possess liability coverage, and you must have an insurance identification card with you when you drive.

In addition, you will also need your car's title, the name and address of lienholder or copy of lease agreement, current tag registration, vehicle mileage reading, and a valid, original certificate of emission (Fulton, DeKalb, Cobb, and Gwinnett counties require all gas-burning vehicles be checked for emission standards once every other year). Have your car inspected at a state-designated inspection site (many gas stations provide this service); the cost is generally around $25.

Tag registration costs $20, and, in addition, you will also have to pay an *ad valorem* tax (property tax). Your county's Motor Vehicle Division will assess this tax according to information you provide on your application for registration. Also, if your car is new to the State of Georgia, you will have to pay an "impact" fee of anywhere from $40 to $200, based on its value. The following County Tax Commissioner Tag Offices handle license tags and car registration:

- **Fulton County**, 404-730-6100, www.fultoncountytaxes.org; tag offices are open Monday-Friday. Office hours vary by location:
- 3000 Old Alabama Road, Alpharetta
- 289 South Main Street, Alpharetta
- 677 Fairburn Road, Atlanta
- 2636 Martin Luther King Jr., Atlanta
- 3425 Cascade Road, Atlanta
- 141 Pryor Street, Atlanta
- 7741 Roswell Road, NE, Atlanta
- 5600 Stonewall Tell Road, College Park
- 6500 Vernon Woods Drive, Sandy Springs
- **DeKalb County**, 404-298-4000, www.co.dekalb.ga.us/taxcommissioner; tag offices are open 8 a.m. to 4:30 p.m., Monday-Friday:
- 1358 Dresden Drive, Atlanta
- 4380 Memorial Drive, Decatur
- 2389 Wesley Chapel Road, Decatur
- **Cobb County**, 770-528-TAGS, www.cobbtax.org; tag offices are open 8:30 a.m. to 4:45 p.m., Monday-Friday:
- 700 South Cobb Drive, Marietta
- 4400 Lower Roswell Road, Marietta
- 2950 Canton Highway, Marietta
- 4700 Austell Road, Austell

- **Gwinnett County**, 770-822-8818, www.co.gwinnett.ga.us; tag offices are open 8:30 a.m. to 5 p.m., Monday-Friday:
- 750 South Perry, Lawrenceville
- 5030 Georgia Belle Court, Norcross
- 5270 Peachtree Parkway, Norcross
- 2280 Oak Road, Snellville

For additional information about tag registration in metro Atlanta, or to find tag offices in counties other than the ones listed here, visit the **Department of Motor Vehicle Safety** web site at www.dmvs.ga.gov.

AUTOMOBILE SAFETY

Words to the wise on Georgia's drunk driving laws: the attitude here is "zero tolerance" for drunk driving. Local intoxication limits are .04 for impairment and .10 for legally drunk. If you are under the age of 21, .02 will get you arrested. Those limits translate to roughly two and a half 12-ounce beers in one hour for the average 160-pound person to reach the impairment stage.

Georgia also enforces state seatbelt laws: It is permissible for an officer to stop a vehicle and cite the driver for a seatbelt violation only. Anyone in the front seat of a car must wear a seatbelt. Anyone 18 or younger in the front or back seat must wear a seatbelt. By definition, Georgia law means a shoulder strap and lap belt when the word seatbelt is used. Children age four and under must ride in a child safety-restraining seat, which must be installed according to manufacturer's recommendations. It is not permitted for an adult to hold a child or restrain both with one belt. For tips on properly installing car seats, or to stay up-to-date on child safety laws in Georgia, check www.safekids.org.

AUTOMOBILE INSURANCE

Georgia is a tort state, which means that drivers here are financially responsible for any property damage and personal injury they cause during an auto accident. Therefore, Georgia drivers are legally required to carry automobile insurance—the minimum being liability coverage of 25/50/25. This means that, in the event of an accident, you're covered for $25,000 per person for injuries to the other party, up to $50,000 for all, and $25,000 for damage caused to the other party's property. However, keep in mind that these are only minimums, and most insurance agents will recommend higher levels of protection. Additionally, if your car is financed, your lien holder will most likely require that you carry comprehensive insurance coverage.

In addition to liability and comprehensive policies, most Georgia insurance companies also offer additional coverages, such as collision, medical, and uninsured motorist coverage. The uninsured motorist coverage, in particular, is worth considering, as it is designed to help cover the cost of your injuries and property damage should you be involved in an accident with a uninsured, or underinsured driver.

For additional information on auto insurance within Georgia, contact the **Georgia Insurance Commission**, 404-656-2070, www.inscomm. state.ga.us.

The **Atlanta Yellow Pages** lists about thirty pages of insurance brokers and companies operating throughout the metro Atlanta area. All major national companies are represented, so chances are, if you already have auto insurance with a major provider, your transition to Atlanta will only require a phone call to your present company.

If you prefer to look up insurance companies and information online, the key words "Georgia Auto Insurance" bring up hundreds of web sites, many offering free quotes, policy comparison, and state insurance information. You can also check **Insure.com**, www.insure.com, or **InsWeb**, www.insweb.com, for similar details. Direct site addresses for a few auto insurance companies are:

- **Allstate**, www.allstate.com
- **Geico**, www.geico.com
- **Liberty Mutual**, www.libertymutual.com
- **Progressive**, www.progressive.com
- **State Farm**, www.statefarm.com

PURCHASING AN AUTOMOBILE

Metro Atlanta has a car dealer for almost any type of new or used vehicle you can imagine. The Atlanta Yellow Pages, in fact, offers 13 pages of dealership listings. The major dealerships run spots on local TV stations and advertise in all the Atlanta newspapers. Used cars are generally advertised in classified sections, and there are also several local magazines devoted to cars for sale by owners and dealers. You can find these in most bookstores, grocery stores, and convenience stores.

Purchasing a car can be both exciting and a hassle, and always a big expense. It pays to conduct research beforehand to determine the worth of the car you're thinking of purchasing. For used cars, check out the Kelley Blue Book site at www.kbb.com. To research dealer invoice prices for new cars, check www.autovantage.com. AAA offers a walk-in vehicle pricing report service to members and non-members for a nominal fee. Also *Consumer Reports* offers a low-cost auto pricing information service, available via their web site: www.consumerreports.org.

If you are looking at used cars, the **US Department of Transportation's Auto Safety Hotline**, 888-327-4236, www-odi.nhtsa.dot.gov/ivoq, is a good place to get information about vehicle recalls. Locally, you can call 404-327-8200 for free information on new or used vehicles.

CONSUMER PROTECTION—LEMON LAW

In 1990, Georgia state legislators passed the **Motor Vehicle Warranty Rights Act**, thereby establishing one of the country's most comprehensive "lemon laws." Georgia's law recognizes and states that the purchase of a new vehicle is a major one for consumers, and that buying a defective vehicle creates undue hardship on the consumer and could even be the cause of injury or death. As a result, automobile manufacturers are now legally required to repair any and all defects that affect the use, value, or safety of the vehicles they sell within the first 12 months or 12,000 miles (whichever comes first).

Georgia's lemon law also provides an accessible, self-help complaint process for consumers who experience problems with newly purchased or leased vehicles that are registered in the state. If you're having continuous, recurring problems with your new car, and the automobile manufacturer fails to fix it after a "reasonable" number of repair attempts, you may request a state arbitration hearing. There, a panel of arbitrators will hear your complaint and decide whether or not you are eligible for a replacement vehicle or a full refund of the purchase price.

To find out more about the lemon law, or to file a complaint, contact the **Georgia Governor's Office of Consumer Affairs**, 404-651-8600, 800-869-1123, www2.state.ga.us/gaoca.

PARKING

Because suburbs comprise most of the Atlanta metropolitan area, parking is generally not much of a problem when compared to many major cities. Almost anywhere you drive your car you will have little trouble finding a place to park, with "difficult parking" defined as a one- or two-block walk to a restaurant, the true exceptions being major malls on weekends, the airport, and downtown sporting events. (The ever-popular alternative to driving is taking MARTA (see **Transportation** chapter). A MARTA train will take you to all the downtown sports venues, and will whisk you straight to the airport. MARTA even has a stop at Lenox Square mall, if you want to go shopping without your car.) To avoid driving endlessly around an enormous mall parking lot, make your mall visits on weekday evenings when crowds are smaller.

PARKING GARAGES AND LOTS

Suburban office complexes always have on-site parking for employees, most at no charge. If you work downtown, however, you will most likely be responsible for finding a space on your own. Many businesses have arrangements with parking garages close to the office. This is usually something discussed during the interview phase of a job search, since you may have to pay for your own parking. If you do have to pay, remember that you do have a few options. You can pay by the day and try to park in the least expensive lots whenever possible, or you can stick with the lot with which you feel most comfortable, and buy a monthly parking pass. Most lots charge anywhere from $5 to $10 per day, but if a convention is in town and lots are filling up, the rates can go as high as $20 per day. With a monthly parking pass, your rate is secured regardless of what event may be taking place. For monthly parking passes, the best lots charge anywhere from $75 to $150. Parking on the periphery and walking a few blocks may get you the best deal—both financially and health wise.

For downtown parking locations call a couple of the larger lot management companies. **AAA Parking**, 404-525-5959, www.aaaparking online.com; and **Parking Management, Inc.**, 404-755-0303 are two of the bigger ones. Additional listings can be found in the Atlanta Yellow Pages under "Parking Facilities."

To avoid the hassle of finding parking downtown, remember that riding MARTA alleviates any need for parking worries. It's also much less expensive than paying for downtown parking. You can ride the rails (or the buses) one-way for a mere $1.75. MARTA also offers a monthly pass for $52.50, which offers unlimited access to the trains and buses for one low price. Schedules and routes for MARTA are available by calling 404-848-4711 or online at www.itsmarta.com. Park & Ride lots are strategically located all along the MARTA routes, and some lots even offer overnight parking for those headed to the airport. The transit system moves over 300,000 passengers daily and provides rail and interconnecting bus service throughout the city. If you are going to a sporting event, any downtown festival or concert, or to the airport, MARTA is the best choice. See the **Transportation** chapter for more information on MARTA.

TOWED OR STOLEN AUTOMOBILES

Regardless of where you park in metro Atlanta, it pays to be aware of "No Parking" zones—even in parking lots. If you do park illegally and end up with a parking ticket, you can expect to pay $25 to $50 for parking in a restricted area, at least $10 for overtime parking, and $60 to $100 for parking in a handicapped area. Your ticket will detail the citation and direct you on how to pay. Most fines are paid at 104 Trinity Street, Atlanta; call 404-658-6935 for more information.

Impound areas are clearly posted, so pay attention to the signs. If you are unlucky enough to have your car towed in the city due to a parking violation, call the **Atlanta Police Department, Impounded Vehicle Division**, 404-853-4330, for the location of the lot holding your vehicle. In areas outside the city limits, a sign will be posted on site identifying the towing company and a phone number to call. An impounded vehicle can cost as much as $200, and impound lots do not take checks. When you go to retrieve your car, make sure you have cash or credit card for the entire amount due, a photo ID, and proof that the vehicle is yours. A title, insurance policy, or registration receipt will suffice.

If it turns out your car has been **stolen**, rather than towed, you should call the police immediately. They will need your license and tag numbers, the car's year, make, model and color, and the vehicle's identification number. Most of this information can be found on your car title or insurance policy.

Unfortunately, many stolen cars end up stripped and sold for parts, so to have any hope of getting any of your "parts" back, you should mark your car's accessories in some way. For instance, if your car has a stereo, radar detector, or car phone, it's a good idea to write your driver's license number on them.

BROADCAST AND PRINT MEDIA

TELEVISION

Atlanta is the home of TBS Superstation, as well as cable stations CNN, Turner Classic Movies, TNT, and the Cartoon Network. Reception here without cable or satellite is pretty good for most of the major networks and the public broadcasting channels, though you may still want to invest in a good antenna or "rabbit ears" to get your best non-cable signal. If you do not opt for cable or satellite service, your television menu will look like this:

NATIONAL AFFILIATES

Channel 2 . . . . . . WSB-TV . . . . **ABC**; www.wsbtv.com
Channel 5 . . . . . . WAGA . . . . . . **Fox**; www.fox5atlanta.com
Channel 8 . . . . . . WGTV . . . . . . **PBS (Georgia Public Television)**;
www.gpb.org/gptv
Channel 11 . . . . . WXIA . . . . . . **NBC**; www.11alive.com

Channel 30 . . . . . WPBA . . . . . . **PBS (Atlanta Public Television)**;
www.wpba.org
Channel 36 . . . . . WATL . . . . . . **Warner Bros.**; www.wb36.com
Channel 46 . . . . . WGCL . . . . . . **CBS**; www.cbs46.com
Channel 69 . . . . . WUPA . . . . . . **United Paramount**; www.upn69.com

LOCAL INDEPENDENT BROADCAST CHANNELS

Channel 14 . . . . . WPXA . . . . . . **Pax**; www.pax.tv
Channel 17 . . . . . WTBS . . . . . . **TBS Superstation**; www.tbs17.com
Channel 63 . . . . . WHSG . . . . . . **Trinity Broadcasting Network**;
www.tbn.com

INTERNATIONAL TELEVISION

Channel 34 . . . . . WUVG . . . . . **Univision**; www.univision.com

CABLE TELEVISION

Cable TV service throughout all metro Atlanta counties is primarily offered by four cable service providers. The cable company that serves you will depend on your address. For more information, or to find out which companies offer service in your neighborhood, contact the following:
• **Adelphia**, 888-683-1000, www.adelphia.com
• **Americast (from BellSouth)**, 770-360-4990, http://bims.bell south.com; also offers internet service/bundling in some areas
• **Charter Communications**, 770-333-6400, www.charter.com
• **Comcast Cable**, 404-266-2278, www.comcast.com; also offers internet service/bundling

RADIO

Metro Atlanta offers diverse, high-quality radio programming. Here, you'll find everything from jazz to top 40, hard rock to gospel. In addition, the college stations in the area provide an eclectic mix of rap, alternative, ethnic, and spoken shows.

FM DIAL
88.5 . . . . WRAS . . . . . . Georgia State University radio; diverse
format, www2.gsu.edu
89.3 . . . . WRFG . . . . . . blues, jazz, www.wrfg.org
90.1 . . . . WABE . . . . . . Public Broadcasting Atlanta and NPR,
www.wabe.org

90.5 . . . . WUOG . . . . . University of Georgia student radio; diverse format, www.uga.edu/~wuog
91.1 . . . . WREK . . . . . . Georgia Tech University radio; eclectic, www.wrek.org
91.9 . . . . WCLK . . . . . . Clark Atlanta college radio; jazz, soul, www.wclk.com
92.9 . . . . WZGC . . . . . Dave FM; classic and current rock hits, www.929dave.fm
94.1 . . . . WSTR . . . . . . top 40, www.star94.com
94.9 . . . . WPCH . . . . . . light rock/easy listening, www.peach949.com
95.5 . . . . WBTS . . . . . . rock, pop, hip hop, http://955thebeat.com
96.1 . . . . WKLS . . . . . . album rock, www.96rock.com
97.1 . . . . WFOX . . . . . . hits from the 1980s, 90s and now, http://971jamz.com
98.5 . . . . WSB-FM . . . . soft rock/adult contemporary, http://b985.com
99.7 . . . . WNNX . . . . . new rock and alternative rock, www.99x.com
100.5 . . . . WWWQ . . . . top 40, www.q100atlanta.com
101.5 . . . . WKHX . . . . . . country, www.wkhx.com
102.3 . . . . WLKQ . . . . . . oldies; www.lake102fm.com
103.3 . . . . WVEE . . . . . . urban/R&B, www.v-103.com
104.1 . . . . WALR . . . . . . R&B, http://kiss1041fm.com
104.7 . . . . WFSH . . . . . . contemporary Christian, www.thefish atlanta.com
105.7 . . . . WGST . . . . . . news and talk, www.wgst.com
106.7 . . . . WYAY . . . . . . country classics, www.eagle1067fm.com

AM DIAL
550 . . . . WDUN . . . . . news, talk and sports, www.accessnorth ga.com/wdun
590 . . . . WDWD . . . . . Radio Disney, http://radio.disney.go.com
610. . . . . WPLO . . . . . . Hispanic, www.radiomex610atlanta.com
640 . . . . WGST . . . . . . news and talk, www.wgst.com
680 . . . . WCNN . . . . . news, www.680thefan.com
750. . . . . WSB . . . . talk radio, sports, Braves games, www.wsbradio.com
790 . . . . WQXI . . . . . . sports talk, www790thezone.com
860 . . . . WAEC . . . . . . Christian, www.streamingfaith.com
920 . . . . WAFS . . . . . . Christian, www.920wafs.org
970 . . . . WNIV . . . . . . Christian talk, www.wniv.com

1010	WGUN	Christian, http://66.70.166.88/wgun2.htm
1050	WPBS	gospel, www.wpbsradio.com
1080	WFTD	traditional Mexican and Latin pop, www.radiolaley.com
1190	WGKA	news and talk, www.themighty1190.com
1340	WIGO	sports, news, www.talkradio1340.com
1380	WAOK	Black news and talk, www.waok.com
1400	WNIV	Christian talk, www.wniv.com
1460	WXEM	regional Mexican, www.radiolafavorita.com
1470	WRGA	news and talk, www.wrgarome.com
1550	WAZX	regional Mexican "Radio Exitos," www.enespanol.com/radio.exitos
1600	WAOS	regional Mexican "La Favorita," www.radiolafavorita.com
1690	WWAA	Air America Talk, www.airamericaradio.com

NEWSPAPERS & MAGAZINES

Metro Atlanta is home to a wide variety of newspapers and periodicals. From Atlanta business to Atlanta fashion to neighborhood news and information, if you have a specific interest, there's sure to be a paper or magazine that covers it. Most of the magazines can be found at newsstands and bookstores throughout the city, and many of the papers can be picked up for free at area restaurants or you can have them delivered straight to your door. For more information, call the numbers, or visit the web sites listed below:

NEWSPAPERS

- *Alpharetta-Roswell Revue and News*, 319 North Main Street, Alpharetta, 770-442-3278, www.northfulton.com; covers news and local interest for these two communities.
- *Atlanta Buckhead; Atlanta Intown*, 1280 West Peachtree Street, Suite 220, Atlanta, 404-586-0002, www.atlantanewsgroup; two monthly newspapers offering community-focused news and real estate information to Atlanta's intown neighborhoods
- *Atlanta Daily World*, 145 Auburn Avenue, Atlanta, 404-659-1110, www.atlantadailyworld.com; covers African-American news and entertainment

- *Atlanta Jewish Times*, 6065 Roswell Road NE, Atlanta, 404-252-1600, www.atljewishtimes.com; covers news of interest to Atlanta's Jewish community
- *The Atlanta Journal-Constitution*, 72 Marietta Street NW, Atlanta, 404-526-5151, www.ajc.com; metro Atlanta's main daily newspaper.
- *Creative Loafing*, 750 Willoughby Way, Atlanta, 404-688-5623, www.creativeloafing.com; Atlanta's free weekly paper, highlighting news, events and entertainment throughout the city.
- *Decatur DeKalb News Era*, 739 DeKalb Industrial Way, Decatur, 404-292-3536; weekly paper providing news and information for the Decatur area.
- *Gwinnett Daily Post*, 166 Highway 20 NE, Lawrenceville, 770-963-9205, www.gwinnettdailyonline.com; provides news and local interest stories for and about Gwinnett County.
- *Marietta Daily Journal/Neighbor Newspapers*, 580 Fairground Street SE, Marietta, 770-428-9411, www.mdjonline.com; a main newspaper serving Marietta and Cobb County. Also offers several smaller, neighborhood editions specializing in local interest news and events.
- *Southern Voice*—1095 Zonolite Road NE, Atlanta, 404-876-1819, www.sovo.com; metro Atlanta's premier gay and lesbian newspaper
- *Thrifty Nickel*—1468 Roswell Road NE, Marietta, 770-971-8333, www.americanclassifieds.com; free from boxes usually located in shopping areas. Offers classified ads for just about anything for sale around town.

For a more complete listing of newspapers throughout the state of Georgia, check out the **Georgia Department of Defense UPAR Center**, **Georgia Newspaper List**, www.dod.state.ga.us/upar/newspaper addresses.html.

MAGAZINES

- *Atlanta Magazine*, 1330 West Peachtree Street NW, Atlanta, 404-872-3100, www.atlantamagazine.com; monthly publication with features on food, entertainment, arts, and travel
- *Atlanta Parent Magazine*, 2346 Perimeter Park Drive, Chamblee, 770-454-7599, www.atlantaparent.com; family publications featuring resources and information for parents
- *Atlanta Sports and Fitness*, 3535 Piedmont Road, Building 14, Suite 1200, Atlanta, 404-870-0123, www.atlantasportsmag.com; features news and information on what's hot in Atlanta sports and fitness
- *Atlanta Tribune*, 875 Old Roswell Road, Roswell, 770-587-0501, www.atlantatribune.com; monthly newsmagazine for metro Atlanta's African-American community

- **Atlanta Wine Report**, 2200 Parklake Drive, Atlanta, 678-985-9494, www.atlwine.com; bi-monthly magazine for metro Atlanta wine enthusiasts
- **Business To Business/Catalyst Magazine**, 3379 Peachtree Road NE, Atlanta, 404-888-0555, www.btobmagazine.com and www.catalyst magazine.com; two monthly business magazines rolled into one, bound together with a unique cover for each and a format that meets in the middle. This publication features business news, and profiles of Atlanta companies and top executives.
- **Competitive Edge Magazine**, 6075 Atlantic Boulevard NW, Norcross, 770-242-2626, www.compedgemag.com; features practical business information and ideas and profiles of Atlanta area businesses and executives
- **Georgia Trend**, 5880 Live Oak Parkway, Norcross, 770-931-9410, www.georgiatrend.com; monthly publication covering Georgia news, business, and politics
- **Georgia Voyager Magazine**, 6063 Peachtree Parkway, Norcross, 800-243-6991, www.gavoyager.com; quarterly educational and historical publication for adults and kids
- **Know Atlanta Newcomer Guide**, 7840 Roswell Road, Dunwoody, 770-512-0016, www.knowatlanta.com; provides information on places, people and things to see in metro Atlanta
- **Southern Flair Magazine**, 403 West Ponce de Leon Avenue, Decatur, 404-377-9998, www.southernflair.com; features the latest in who's who and what's what with Atlanta's elite

OFFICIAL DOCUMENTS

VOTER REGISTRATION

You must register to vote in the county of your residence at least 30 days prior to an election. You can register either by mail or in person. You can register to vote at most local banks, colleges, city halls, and county offices. Also, in accordance with the motor voter law, you can register to vote when you obtain or renew your driver's license (see above section for locations). County voter registration offices can be accessed at the following locations:

- **Fulton County**: Control Office, 141 Pryor Street, Suite 4085, Atlanta, 404-730-7072; South Annex, 5600 Stonewall Tell Road, Room 218, College Park, 770-306-3050; North Annex, 7741 Roswell Road NE, Room 222, Atlanta, 770-551-7675

- **DeKalb County**: 4380 Memorial Drive, Suite 300, Decatur, 404-298-4020
- **Cobb County**: 47 Waddell Street, Building F, Marietta, 770-528-2581
- **Gwinnett County**: 75 Langley Drive, Lawrenceville, 770-822-8787

For additional information about voter registration in Georgia or to find registrar offices in counties other than the ones listed above, contact the **Georgia Secretary of State, Elections Division**, 404-656-2871, 888-265-1115, www.sos.state.ga.us/elections.

If you'd like more information about local and national party affiliations, contact:

- **The Democratic Party of Georgia**, 404-870-8201, www.georgia party.com
- **The Georgia Green Party**, 404-806-0480, www.greens.org/georgia
- **The League of Women Voters (Georgia)**, State Office, 678-547-0755, www.lwvga.org; Fulton County/Atlanta, 404-577-8683; DeKalb County, 404-321-0913; Cobb County/Marietta, 770-592-0625
- **The Libertarian Party of Georgia**, 404-888-9468, www.lpgeorgia. com
- **The Republican Party of Georgia**, 404-257-5559, www.gagop.org

LIBRARY CARDS

Atlanta's central library is located downtown at One Margaret Mitchell Square. Other library branch addresses are listed in the **Neighborhoods** chapter of this book. All libraries within each county are interconnected, so if you check out a book at one location, you can return it to another branch in the same county. If you are looking for more obscure materials that public libraries may not have, check the area's university libraries. While you may not be able to obtain check-out privileges, you can still peruse materials on site.

To obtain a library card in **Fulton County**, you'll need to bring one piece of identification such as a driver's license, and a recent piece of mail or a bill showing your address in Fulton County. For a library card in **DeKalb**, **Cobb**, and **Gwinnett** counties, you need only bring one recent proof of residence in your particular county. A driver's license, rent receipt, utility bill, check, or postmarked piece of mail with your name and current address will do.

For more information on area libraries, see the **Literary Life** section in the **Cultural Life** chapter.

PASSPORTS

If you're interested in getting a passport or renewing an old one, you have several options in metro Atlanta. Passport applications can be found online, as well as in most local post offices, libraries, courts, and county offices.

Depending on your needs, you may apply for a passport either in person or through the mail. However, you must apply for your passport in person if you are applying for the first time; your previous passport was lost or damaged; your previous passport was issued over 15 years ago and has expired; your name is different than it was on your last passport and you don't have legal proof of the change; or you are between the ages of 14 and 17 years old. Otherwise, you may apply through the mail. Either way, you should allow at least six weeks for processing.

Passport application forms are available through the **US Department of State, National Passport Information Center**, http://travel.state.gov/get_forms.html, or call them at 877-487-2778, TDD 888-874-7793, Monday-Friday 8 a.m. to 8 p.m. EST. (General travel information and advisories are available at the Bureau of Consular Affairs' home page, www.travel.state.gov.) This government site provides answers to many questions regarding the passport application process, as well as pages of additional, helpful information—including a detailed listing of passport acceptance facilities throughout metro Atlanta.

When you apply for your passport, keep in mind you'll need not only to fill out the application form but also to provide the following: your social security number, proof of US citizenship and identity, and two passport photos. Acceptable documents proving your citizenship include a previous passport, certified birth certificate, consular report of birth abroad, naturalization certificate, or certificate of citizenship. Acceptable documents proving your identity include a previous passport, naturalization certificate, certificate of citizenship, or a current and valid ID (driver's license, state ID, military ID). Passport photos, two identical 2" x 2" photos, either black and white or color, are easily obtained at many local photo shops, AAA offices, or FedEx Kinko's locations.

A new passport costs $97 for those 16 years old and older and $82 for those under 16; renewals are $67. Allow six weeks for your completed passport to be processed. For expedited service, add $60; you can expect to receive your passport in two weeks. New applications for passports use form DS-11, and for minors under age 14 an additional consent form, DS-3053 is required. You will find the necessary forms at many post offices and libraries, at county court offices, or online at the State Bureau of Consular Affairs. You must appear in person to get your first passport; this includes minors. Most passport acceptance facilities accept payment for passport fees in the forms of check, money order, or bank draft made payable to the Department of State. (The facility's processing fees may be payable by debit or credit card.)

If you are in a hurry, consider **Instant Passport**, 800-284-2564, www.instantpassport.com, which can get you a passport in about one week. There is a $100 charge on top of the regular passport fees for the service. If even that's not fast enough, Instant Passport also offers a 24-hour emergency passport service, which can cost anywhere from $300 to $500.

FINDING A HEALTH CARE PROVIDER

If you have health insurance through one of the many HMO companies operating in Georgia, then choosing a physician is easily accomplished by checking the approved list that will accompany your health care plan booklet. If you do not use an HMO provider, it is often a good idea to get a recommendation from a friend or co-worker. You can also check out the nearly one hundred pages of physician listings in the Atlanta Yellow Pages.

If you prefer to use a referral service, rather than spend hours researching and calling various doctors' offices, there are several in metro Atlanta to consider:

- **Atlanta Medical Center Physician Referral**, 404-265-3627, www.atlantamedcenter.com
- **Children's Healthcare of Atlanta**, 404-250-KIDS, www.choa.org
- **DeKalb Medical Center Physician Referral**, 404-501-9355, www.drhs.org
- **Emory Health Connection**, 404-778-7777, www.emoryhealthcare.org
- **Georgia Academy of Family Physicians**, 800-392-3841, www.gafp.org
- **Millennium Alternative Healthcare**, 770-390-0012, www.millennium-healthcare.com
- **Promina Health System Physician Referral**, 404-541-1111, www.promina.org

Once you've narrowed your list of prospective physicians, you may want to research them further by utilizing the following online resources:

- **American Board of Medical Specialties Certification Verification**, 866-ASK-ABMS, www.abms.org; contact to see if your specialist is certified by the national board
- **Healthgrades**, 303-716-0041, www.healthgrades.com; purchase a complete report on your physician or health care facility for $10
- Georgia's **Composite State Board of Medical Examiners**, 404-656-3913, http://medicalboard.georgia.gov; verify that your physician is licensed to practice medicine and check for recent disciplinary actions. The CSBME is also the office to contact if you encounter problems with your health care provider or want to file a complaint.

PETS

It is easy to be a dog or cat owner in metro Atlanta. Most apartment complexes and landlords allow for pets, though they may have size or weight limitations, and they will most definitely charge an additional pet deposit. Landlords that do not allow pets will usually state that restriction in their classified ads and on the "for rent" signs in front of the rental property. One of the great things about owning pets in metro Atlanta is that many of the homes here (both intown and in the suburbs) are set on nice-sized lots, offering plenty of outdoor space for pets.

There are few restrictions for pet owners in Atlanta, and the laws that are on the books aren't always enforced. The main laws regarding pet ownership are highlighted below, though, of course, they may not be relevant to all counties in the metro area.

Also, it's important to keep in mind that this section deals primarily with laws and information pertaining to dogs and cats. If the pet you own, or are considering owning, is of the more exotic variety, you will definitely want to check in with the animal services department of the county in which you reside, as they will most likely have specific ordinances pertaining to the types of pets that are allowed, and how they must be kept. You may also find *The Pet Moving Handbook: Maximize Your Pet's Well-Being and Maintain Your Sanity* (FirstBooks) a helpful resource.

LICENSING

The City of Atlanta and many of its surrounding counties require dogs and cats to be licensed. A rabies vaccination certificate from a vet or shelter must be presented, along with the appropriate license fee, upon application. In most cases, pet owners can apply by mail—ask the vet or shelter for an application, or download the application online from your local licensing agency's web site. For more information on obtaining a pet license tag, contact the pet licensing office in your county:

- **Cherokee County Marshal's Office, Animal Control**, 678-493-6200, www.cherokeega.com
- **Cobb County Animal Control**, 770-499-4136, www.cobbanimal control.org
- **DeKalb County Animal Control**, 404-294-2996, http://dekalb police.com/ac
- **Fulton County Animal Services**, 404-794-0358, www.fulton animalservices.com
- **Gwinnett Animal Welfare and Enforcement**, 770-339-3200, www.co.gwinnett.ga.us

LEASH LAWS

All metro Atlanta counties have "running at large" ordinances in place, prohibiting pet owners from letting their dogs run loose. It is strongly recommended that dogs remain on-leash anytime they are out of their yards, particularly if you have them out in the traffic-heavy, retail areas around town. However, there is some leniency with this law, as well-behaved dogs that respond to voice commands are generally allowed to be off-leash, with their owners, in their neighborhoods without legal repercussions. Well-behaved dogs can often be found off-leash at most of the area's city and county parks, though it's important to reiterate that the City of Atlanta, and most of the surrounding counties, *does* have leash laws in place, restricting dogs from being off-leash on public property.

A handful of communities throughout metro Atlanta have developed neighborhood dog parks and dog runs—safe places for pets and their owners to spend time outdoors, running and playing without the leash:

- **DeKalb County's Mason Mill Park**, 404-371-2631, www.co. dekalb.ga.us/parks; a half-acre dog park with high and low water fountains, a new fence, wood chips, benches, and pooper scoopers.
- **Piedmont Park Off Leash Dog Park**, 404-875-7275, www.pied montpark.org; 1.5 acres of leash-free greenspace, located at Monroe Drive and Park Drive. Open to the public.
- **Royal Paws Dog Park of Alpharetta**, 770-619-3235, http://royal paws.com; access to this dog park can be gained through Paws membership, or as a valued day pass visitor. For more information, including rates, contact the park at the number or web address above.

In addition to area leash laws, all metro Atlanta counties have scoop-the-poop laws in place.

VETERINARIANS

As a pet owner, you will want to have a vet lined up before you actually need one. Start by contacting the **Georgia Veterinary Medical Association**, 678-309-9800, www.gvma.net, for a list of accredited vets in your neighborhood. You may also want to check with pet-owning friends and neighbors, or visit local parks frequented by dog owners, to glean information on local vets. Choosing a vet, like choosing a physician, is a largely subjective thing. Beyond the cleanliness and friendliness of the establishment, both you and your pet will want to be comfortable with the vet you choose. You may also want to inquire to be sure your vet is available or covered after hours by an answering service.

In case of serious pet emergencies after-hours and on weekends, contact one of the following:
• **Animal Emergency Center of Sandy Springs**, 404-252-7881.
• **Cobb Emergency Veterinary Clinic**, 770-424-9157, www.cobb evc.com
• **DeKalb-Gwinnett Animal Emergency Clinic**, 770-491-0661
• **Georgia Veterinary Specialists**, 404-459-0903, www.gvsvets.com

PET SERVICES

Dogs typically need to be walked at least three times a day, not a problem if you work from home or live with someone who is home during the day. Being social animals, they suffer more than cats from being left alone for long periods. You may want to consider the proposition that two dogs are not much more bother than one, and both are happier together than one alone. In any case, if you are away for more than eight hours a day, you will probably need a **dog walker**, a person who has your keys and who will come in and take your dog out for at least 15 minutes. While this can be expensive, you may find the happiness and well-being of your dog is more than worth the cost. To find a reliable dog walker, check with other dog owners and your vet for recommendations. Some of the better pet-care establishments keep a list of walkers whose credentials they can vouch for. Some dog walkers will also pet-sit when you are away, either staying in your home to care for your pets and plants or visiting three times a day to feed, water, play with, and walk your pet. The going rate for pet sitting in metro Atlanta is currently about $16 a day for cats, and $20 a day for dogs, though prices can be higher in some neighborhoods.

In addition to dog walkers, metro Atlanta is now home to more than a few "**doggy daycares.**" These facilities are designed to offer pet care and socialization opportunities for dogs that would otherwise be home alone all day. Most offer indoor and outdoor play areas, doggy lunch and/or snack, nap breaks, and more. Dogs are typically grouped according to size and temperament, and are generally required to have been spayed or neutered, and up to date on vaccinations. A few area daycares to consider are:

• **Barking Hound Village**, www.barkinghoundvillage.com/daycare; has five locations throughout metro Atlanta. Also offers boarding and dog grooming services.

• **Camp Woof**, 404-499-9008, www.campwoof.com; this Decatur area doggy daycare also provides pet boarding and dog training services.

• **Piedmont Bark Doggy Daycare**, 404-873-5400, www.piedmont bark.com; this daycare, located in Midtown, near Piedmont Park, also offers pet boarding and dog washing services.

ACQUIRING A PET

If you are interested in acquiring a pet once you've settled into your new home, you may want to consider checking the *Atlanta Journal-Constitution*'s Sunday classifieds. There you'll find listings for a variety of pets—some of them free to a good home, and many of them purebreds that will cost you anywhere from $300 to $1,000.

You may also want to consider pet adoption. Adoption fees are generally $60 for cats, $85 for dogs, and $15 or less for smaller pets such as rabbits and hamsters. Those fees typically include the cost of vaccinating, and spaying or neutering the pet. Most shelters require that you be at least 18 years old to adopt, and you must be able to show proof of age and current residence. If you rent, rather than own your home, you must also bring in a copy of your lease indicating your landlord's pet policy.

All of the metro Atlanta counties run animal shelters and/or humane societies, and it's nearly impossible *not* to find a pet to fall in love with at one of them. You don't have to live in the county you adopt from, so it's a good idea to check out all of the local shelters to find the pet that will be just right for you. Adopting a pet is a big responsibility, so be sure you consider your lifestyle and your potential pet's temperament and needs before making a final decision.

To begin your search, check out the following shelters and humane societies; most of them offer photos, pet descriptions, and adoption information online for your convenience:

- **Atlanta Humane Society**, 404-875-5331, www.atlantahumane.org
- **Cherokee County Humane Society**, 770-928-5115, www.cchumanesociety.org
- **Cobb County Humane Society**, 770-428-5678, www.humanecobb.org
- **PAWS Atlanta** (the DeKalb County Humane Society), 5287 Covington Highway, Decatur, 770-593-1155, www.pawsatlanta.org
- **Fulton County Animal Shelter**, 404-794-0358, www.fultonanimalservices.com
- **Gwinnett County Humane Society**, 770-798-7711, www.gwinnethumane.com

CRIME AND SAFETY

As in any major urban area, crime occurs regularly in metro Atlanta. However, unlike many other cities, street muggings are not particularly common. Rather, Atlanta's suburban sprawl has encouraged crimes in mall parking lots, wooded parks, and out-of-the-way, dimly lit automated teller machines. Over the last ten years, there have been numerous reports of carjackings, robberies, and even abductions at these more remote locations. A good rule of thumb is to never walk alone at night, especially downtown. Remember to jog after dark only with a group of people, even in your own neighborhood. Avoid ATMs late at night unless they are well lit and situated in a highly traveled area, such as a busy shopping center. And, at the mall, park in well-lit areas, pay close attention to your surroundings when you return to your car laden with packages, and if you feel uncomfortable walking out alone, request that someone from mall security escort you to your vehicle. Be aware that crimes frequently occur in covered mall parking lots, even in broad daylight.

In addition to parking lot crimes, Atlanta has been experiencing a rise in stolen cars, and car and home break-ins. Do your best to prevent these types of crimes by installing alarms on both your home and vehicle; keeping doors and windows locked at all times; and never leaving valuables in plain view in your car. It's also important, when you move into your new community, to check and see if there is a Neighborhood Watch program. It's a great way to meet your neighbors and a wonderful way to help protect your community. Being part of the Neighborhood Watch will also help keep you informed of any criminal activity that has occurred recently in the neighborhood. Neighborhood Watch programs can be official (with city-provided signs) or unofficial (with signs and organization provided by your block). To find out if there is a program in your neighborhood, or to set one up if there isn't, you can contact the **Atlanta Police Department Safe Neighborhood Task Force**, 404-853-7240, www.atlantapd.org. Or check out the police precincts in your area by calling the numbers listed after each neighborhood profile in the **Neighborhoods** chapter of this book.

POLICE COMPLAINTS

If you have a complaint about a specific officer, or the police force in your area, you will want to contact the city or county police departments directly at the main numbers below:

- **Atlanta Police Department**, 404-853-3434, www.atlantapd.org
- **Cherokee County Sheriff's Office**, 678-493-4200, www.cherokeega-sheriff.org
- **Cobb County Police Department**, 770-499-3900, www.cobbcounty police.com
- **DeKalb County Police Department**, 404-294-2519, www.dekalbpolice.com;
- **Fulton County Police Department**, 770-495-8738, www.fulton police.org

- **Gwinnett County Police Department**, 770-513-5000, www.gwinnettcounty.com
- **State Patrol Office**, 404-624-7000, http://dps.georgia.gov

If you feel you're not getting anywhere with your complaints against the local police department, you may also want to contact the national **Police Complaint Center**, http://policeabuse.org, an organization dedicated to investigating accusations of police misconduct, and assisting citizens in filing police complaints throughout the country.

N OW THAT YOU'VE FOUND A NEW HOME, AND HAVE TAKEN CARE of the basics like getting electricity and water, you may want to take advantage of some of metro Atlanta's helpful services. Some of these services, including mail receiving/shipping and house cleaning, can make your life far simpler. Also here, you'll find services for people with disabilities, a section for immigrant newcomers, and a section on gay and lesbian life. Read on.

DOMESTIC SERVICES

If you're interested in finding someone to help keep your house clean, you may want to check the bulletin board postings at your neighborhood grocery stores, or contact local college placement services for a list of students looking for work. Another option is to hire a professional cleaning service. Most house cleaning agencies are bonded and will give you a free estimate. A few to consider are:

- **A-1 Cleaning Services**, 404-230-9344, http://yp.bellsouth.com/ sites/a1cleaningservices
- **Brittany Maids**, 404-633-5152, www.realpagessites.com/brittany maids
- **Happy Home House Cleaning**, 770-879-5922, www.happyhome housecleaning.com
- **Mopping Moms Organic Cleaning Service**, 678-296-9199, www.moppingmoms.com
- **Touch of Class Maid Service**, 770-262-9778, www.touchofclass maids.com

PEST CONTROL

Most apartment complexes handle periodic pest control for residents, so check your lease or ask your landlord about pest abatement in your building. Though metro Atlanta is not a tropical locale where you would expect major problems with pest control, the relatively warm winters and extended fall temperatures mean that bugs survive better here than in more northern climes. The most common pests are termites, ants, and small brown roaches that like to congregate around the kitchen. If you have pets, be diligent about flea control. A regular flea prevention and treatment from your local vet will not only keep your pet comfortable but also save you money on exterminating fees.

The Atlanta Yellow Pages lists over ten pages of pest control companies who will rid your house of everything from ants to squirrels. Several of these companies will also trap larger animals and humanely relocate them outside the city. A few of the larger pest control companies include:

- **Chemical Technologies of Georgia**, metro Atlanta, 770-237-3244, www.chemical-tech.com
- **Do-It-Yourself Pest Control**, metro Atlanta, 770-458-5090, www.doityourselfpestcontrol.com
- **North Fulton Exterminating**, North Fulton, 770-475-7419, www.northfultonexterminating.com
- **Orkin Pest Control**, metro Atlanta, www.orkin.com
- **Pest USA Exterminating Company**, Lawrenceville, 770-985-4444, www.pestusainc.com
- **Terminix Pest Control**, metro Atlanta, 800-TERMINIX, www.terminix.com

A word on termite protection: If you are a homeowner or are house hunting, Georgia law requires termite inspection prior to selling, and treatment if termites are found. For this reason, you may want to ask the pest control companies about a yearly contract, where you will receive annual inspections and minor treatments if needed.

MAIL AND SHIPPING SERVICES

MAIL DELIVERY

Atlanta is the hub for much of the mail delivery in the Southeast, so fast delivery is the norm. However, if you do have a problem with your postal delivery, you can contact the **Governor's Office of Consumer Affairs**, 404-651-8600, www2.state.ga.us/gaoca. For zip code information, contact the **United States Postal Service**, 800-275-8777, http://zip4.usps.com/zip4/welcome.jsp. For general information, call 800-275-8777, or visit www.usps.com.

Atlanta's **Main Post Office**, 3900 Crown Road SW, Atlanta, 404-684-2308, is open 24 hours and handles the bulk of the mail processing in the city. Because of the large geographic area served, however, the postal system here is well covered by branches located throughout the entire metro area. The USPS 800 number and web address (listed above) or the Blue Pages of the phone book, "US Government, Postal Service," will guide you to the post office nearest you. You can also use the listings at the end of each neighborhood profile in the **Neighborhoods** section of this book.

JUNK MAIL

Junk mail will surely follow you to your new home. In order to curtail this kind of unwanted mail, we suggest you send a written letter, including name and address, asking to be purged from the **Direct Marketing Association's** list (Direct Mail Association's Mail Preference Service, Box 643, Carmel, NY 10512). Some catalogue companies will need to be contacted directly with a purge request. Another option is to call the "opt-out" line at 888-567-8688, and request that the main credit bureaus not release your name and address to interested marketing companies. For **junk e-mail**, you may also go to Direct Marketing Association's web site, www.dmaconsumers.org/optoutform, and request an opt-out service for your e-mail address. The service will accept three non-business e-mail addresses at a time. This should reduce the amount of spam you receive from national lists. The Georgia **Governor's Office of Consumer Affairs** web site, www2.state.ga.us/gaoca, also offers information on decreasing your flow of junk mail, or you can check out the *JunkBusters Guide to Reducing Junk Mail* at www.junkbusters.com. (To **curb phone solicitations**, contact the government's "do not call" registry at 888-382-1222, TTY 866-290-4236; online at www.donotcall.gov.)

MAIL RECEIVING SERVICES

If you haven't yet settled at a permanent address, a number of companies will receive your mail for a fee. Renting a box at your neighborhood post office is a convenient option, and many metro Atlanta area post offices are being remodeled to provide after-hours access for mail retrieval. For full mail services, including mail forwarding and UPS delivery, try the following companies:

- **AAA Mail Center**, 3530 Ashford-Dunwoody Road NE, Atlanta, 770-457-8535
- **Mail Bag**, 2655 North Decatur Road, Decatur, 404-373-2547
- **Mail It Here**, 3100 Briarcliff Road NE, Atlanta, 404-321-3937
- **Mail Safe**, 3277 Roswell Road NE, Buckhead, 404-231-0649; 6065 Roswell Road, Sandy Springs, 404-256-3113

- **UPS Store**, several locations throughout metro Atlanta, 888-346-3623, www.theupsstore.com

SHIPPING SERVICES

Most mail receiving service centers will also ship your packages for you via one of the large national carriers. **Pak Mail Centers of America**, with five metro locations, will also custom pack and ship for you. Call 770-623-3744 for the location nearest you. Other major shipping companies to consider are:

- **DHL**, 800-225-5345, www.dhl.com
- **Delta Dash**, 800-352-2746, www.delta.com/prog_serv/cargo/dash/index.jsp
- **FedEx**, 800-463-3339, www.fedex.com
- **Roadway Express**, 888-550-9800, www.roadway.com
- **UPS**, 800-742-5877, www.ups.com
- **US Postal Service Express Mail**, 800-222-1811, www.usps.com

CONSUMER PROTECTION

"Buyer beware" may be a cliché, but it is the best line of defense against fraud and consumer victimization. If you feel you've been had, here are some agencies that, depending on your concern, may be able to help you on your quest for justice:

- **Atlanta Bar Association**, metro Atlanta, 404-521-0781, www.atlantabar.org; can assist the public with locating attorneys who are qualified to handle all areas of law
- **Atlanta Legal Aid Society**, Atlanta, 404-524-5811; Cobb, 770-528-2565; DeKalb, 404-377-0701; Gwinnett, 678-376-4545; South Fulton/Clayton, 404-669-0233, www.atlantalegalaid.org; represents metro Atlanta's low-income residents in civil legal cases, including those concerned with safe homes, education, protection against fraud, and personal safety
- **Better Business Bureau of Metropolitan Atlanta**, 404-766-0875, www.atlanta.bbb.org; handles complaints about local businesses, and will work as an intermediary to help resolve disputes. They can also provide helpful information on ethical business practices.
- **US Public Interest Research Group** (**USPIRG**), metro Atlanta, 404-575-4060, www.uspirg.org/south; the Southern Field Office of the USPIRG is currently working on federal energy legislation and the implementation of an environmental health tracking system. They can also assist you with questions or complaints about predatory lenders.

- **WSB Consumer Action Center**, 404-892-8227, www.wsbtv.com/ money/index.html; answers consumer questions and complaints in association with the Clark Howard TV and radio show. You can also reach **Clark Howard** with consumer questions by calling 404-872-0750 (Monday-Friday, 1 p.m. to 4 p.m.), or by visiting his web site, www.clark howard.com. It's been said that if Howard, who also has a regular column in the *Atlanta Journal-Constitution*, can't help you, no one can.

The following are state and federal agencies worth considering:
- **Consumer Product Safety Commission**, 800-638-2772, www.cpsc.gov; this office works to inform and protect consumers from unreasonable risks of injury or death that could be caused by the more than 15,000 types of products currently under the agency's jurisdiction—including toys, cribs, power tools, cigarette lighters, household chemicals, and more.
- **Federal Trade Commission**, 877-382-4357, www.ftc.gov/ftc/ consumer.htm; offers valuable information on consumers' rights, enforces a variety of consumer protection laws enacted by Congress, and works to protect consumers against unfair, deceptive, or fraudulent business practices
- **Governor's Office of Consumer Affairs**, 404-651-8600, www2.state.ga.us/gaoca; enforces Georgia's Fair Business Practices Act, as well as other consumer protection laws—both civil and criminal.
- **Office of the Georgia Attorney General, Consumer Protection**, 404-656-3300, http://ganet.org/ago/consumer_info.html; advises and represents all state agencies that protect the rights of Georgia consumers. This office has the authority to shut down loan sharks, fraudulent telemarketing schemes, sweepstakes scams, merchants that engage in price gouging during times of emergency, and other illegal practices aimed at Georgia citizens.
- **State Insurance Commissioner, Consumer Services**, 404-656-2070, www.inscomm.state.ga.us/consumers/home.asp; this division of the Department of Insurance assists Georgia citizens who have questions or complaints about any phase of the insurance process, whether the insurance is for home, auto, health, or business. Consumer Services can also investigate and help mediate or resolve any disputes that Georgia consumers may have with their insurance company.

SERVICES FOR PEOPLE WITH DISABILITIES

A number of organizations in metro Atlanta cater specifically to the needs of the disabled. For information about local resources, contact **disAbility Link**, 404-687-8890, www.disabilitylink.org, or visit their offices at 755

Commerce Drive in Decatur. You can also contact **Friends of Disabled Adults and Children**, 770-491-9014, www.fodac.org, a local volunteer organization, offering important information and medical equipment to low-income, disabled residents throughout metro Atlanta. **The Shepherd Center**, 404-352-2020, www.shepherd.org, a medical, resource, therapy, and informational facility located at 2020 Peachtree Road NW, also offers a large outreach and assistance program for disabled citizens.

For those with hearing impairments, the **Georgia Council for the Hearing Impaired**, 404-292-5312, www.gachi.org, is a Decatur-based, community service organization that offers individual and family counseling as well as advocacy for the hearing-impaired throughout the metro area. The **Center for the Visually Impaired**, 404-875-9011, www.cviatlanta.org, located at 763 Peachtree Street NE, offers support and services for local blind and visually impaired individuals of all ages.

If you have a child with a disability, the **Georgia Learning Resources System (GLRS)**, www.glrs.org, can help you find a program suited to his or her needs; it also provides referral information about services for disabled students, as well as workshops and specialized materials for parents, teachers, and others who work with children with disabilities. Georgia Learning Resources System (GLRS) is available in the **East Metro** area (including DeKalb, Fulton and Gwinnett counties; as well as the cities of Buford and Decatur) at 678-676-2400, and in **West Metro** (including Clayton, Cobb and Douglas counties; and the cities of Atlanta and Marietta) at 770-432-2404.

The **Atlanta Alliance on Developmental Disabilities**, 404-881-9777, www.aadd.org, is a primary service provider and support network for metro Atlanta children, adults, and families living with developmental disabilities. The AADD offers valuable information on public policy and legislation, recreational opportunities, health and wellness, and more.

GETTING AROUND

Applications for handicapped parking permits are available through the **Georgia Department of Motor Vehicle Safety**, 678-413-8400, www.dmvs.ga.gov. Look online under "forms and manuals" for downloadable form DS-29. As of August 2004, completed applications can be submitted in person at any local DMVS exam station, or mailed to: Georgia DMVS, Attention Special Issuance, P.O. Box 80447, Conyers, GA 30013. Along with the application, you must supply a notarized letter from your doctor, explaining why and for how long you will need the permit. If mailing in the application, you should expect to receive the permit within seven to ten days. For more information about parking permits, or to locate an exam office in your neighborhood, contact the DMVS at the phone number or web address above.

On **MARTA**, 404-848-4711, www.itsmarta.com, elderly and handicapped customers can ride trains and buses for half price with a half-fare card. These cards can be obtained free of charge from the Five Points station or from the MARTA headquarters office, located at 2424 Piedmont Road across from Lindbergh Station. One hundred of MARTA's 150 bus routes and all of the rail stations now offer wheelchair accessibility. To find out if your neighborhood bus route has this convenience, contact MARTA at the number or web address above. If you'd like to request that your particular route become wheelchair accessible, call 404-848-5618. In addition to half-fare prices and wheelchair accessibility, MARTA also provides an **ADA Complementary Paratransit Service**, offering special lift-equipped vans on a curb-to-curb, shared ride basis, to eligible residents with disabilities who are unable to board, ride, or disembark from MARTA's regular buses or trains. Individuals who already have a MARTA ADA photo ID card may contact **MARTA's Paratransit Reservation Office**, 404-848-5826, www.itsmarta.com/howto/special/para.htm, to schedule a ride. The cost is $3.50 per one-way trip. For more information about MARTA's Paratransit Services, or to receive an application, call MARTA's Eligibility and Certification staff at 404-848-5389.

For private transportation within the metro area and to the airport, there are a number of special needs transportation companies operating much like a taxi service. A few to consider are **Ace Medical Transport**, 678-969-0007, www.acemedicaltrans.com, offering on-call service for transportation to doctor's or physical therapy appointments throughout metro Atlanta; **Eagle Wings Transportation**, 770-993-7193, offering dispatched vans equipped for the disabled; and **Walker & Walker Transportation**, 770-739-8525, offering non-emergency transportation services in south metro Atlanta.

COMMUNICATION

Free library services are available for the visually impaired and the physically disabled from the **Georgia Library for Accessible Services**, 1150 Murphy Avenue SW, Atlanta, 404-756-4619, www.georgialibraries.org. Patrons can get books in Braille and on cassette at the library or through the mail. To apply for service, contact the library and leave your name and address. They will mail you an application, which must be certified by your doctor. Upon approval of your application, the library will mail you a cassette recorder and a few titles. You can then select your own titles; the entire service, including the cassette recorder, is free of charge. For more information about this library's services, contact them at the number or web address above.

A few **important TTY phone numbers** to keep on hand are:
- **Emergency Mental Health**, 800-255-0056, throughout metro Atlanta
- **Fire, Police, and Ambulance Services**, 404-525-1122 in Atlanta; 911, Cobb County; 404-294-2677, DeKalb County; 404-730-7109, Fulton County; 770-962-7938, Gwinnett County
- **Georgia Poison Center**, 404-616-9287

The **Georgia Relay Center**, 800-225-0135, TTY 800-255-0056, www.georgiarelay.org, operates 24 hours a day, seven days a week. The center provides relay services for telephone calls to or from speech- or hearing-impaired telephone customers anywhere in the United States and internationally to English-speaking countries. A communication assistant will answer, and local calls are free. For information on telecommunications equipment, contact the **Georgia Council for the Hearing Impaired**, 800-541-0710, www.gachi.org.

For sign language interpreting services, you may want to consider the **Georgia Interpreting Services Network**, 404-521-9100, 800-228-4992, www.gisn.org; or **Sign Language Interpreting Specialists**, 770-531-0700, TTY 770-287-9479, www.slisinc.com. You can also find additional sign language information and listings at the **Georgia Registry of Interpreters for the Deaf** web site, www.garid.org.

HOUSING

Most new apartment complexes have units dedicated to residents who require wheelchair access and other handicapped services. Any of the locator services listed in **Finding a Place to Live** chapter should be able to assist you with an apartment search. For other housing choices, contact the **Disability Action Center of Georgia, disAbility Link**, 404-687-8890, www.disabilitylink.org.

ADDITIONAL RESOURCES

Following is a list of resources, both governmental and nonprofit, that may be of use to those with special needs.
- **Southeastern Guide Dogs, Inc.**, www.guidedogs.org; offers information on guide dogs for the visually impaired, and lists a number of resources by region and state
- **Epilepsy Foundation of America (Georgia Chapter)**, Atlanta, 800-527-7105, www.epilepsyfoundation.org/local/georgia
- **Down Syndrome Association of Atlanta**, 404-320-3233, www.down-syndrome-atlanta.org

- **Atlanta Area School for the Deaf**, 890 North Indian Creek Drive, Clarkston, 404-296-7101, www.aasdweb.com
- **The ALS Association of Georgia**, 1955 Cliff Valley Way, Atlanta, 404-636-9909, www.alsaga.org; provides information and support for individuals living with ALS (also known as Lou Gehrig's Disease)
- **Americans With Disabilities Act, State of Georgia ADA Coordinator**, 404-657-9993 (TTY), 404-657-7313 (voice), www.state. ga.us/gsfic/ada; can answer questions about the Americans with Disabilities Act
- **Shepherd Center Wheelchair Sports Teams**, 404-367-1287, www.shepherd.org; provides information on joining local wheelchair sports teams
- **National Center on Physical Activity and Disability**, 800-900-8086, www.ncpad.org, offers free information for Americans with disabilities looking for an appropriate exercise plan

One last tip: **On A Roll**, a syndicated talk radio program hosted by "The Strength Coach," Greg Smith, airs Sundays from 9:00 a.m. to 11:00 a.m. with information, resources and topics for discussion applicable to the lives of people with disabilities. Though the nearest station to Atlanta currently carrying the show is in Knoxville, Tennessee, you can still find out about recent shows, order tapes, and subscribe to the show's newsletter via their web site at www.thestrengthcoach.com.

IMMIGRANT NEWCOMERS

Atlanta has long considered itself the International City of the South; with nearly 500,000 foreign-born residents from dozens of countries settled into the area, it is a valid claim. Those new to metro Atlanta, and to the USA, may find the following listings helpful:

- **Atlanta Celtic Festival, Inc.**, 404-572-8045, www.atlantaceltic festival.org; a local, cross-Celtic organization dedicated to celebrating and broadening awareness of Celtic heritage and cultures through public education and entertainment. In addition to the annual Celtic Festival, the ACF also publishes a quarterly newsletter for members.
- **Center for Pan Asian Community Services, Inc.**, Doraville, 770-936-0969, www.cpacs.org; a private, nonprofit organization dedicated to providing comprehensive social and health services to metro Atlanta's pan-Asian community.
- **The International Community School**, 404-499-8969, www.int comschool.org; a private, multi-cultural and multi-lingual elementary school for refugee and immigrant school children in Atlanta.

- **The International Rescue Committee of Atlanta**, 404-292-7731, www.theirc.org/atlanta; a nonprofit, non-sectarian refugee resettlement agency dedicated to assisting refugees and their families from around the world as they resettle in the metro Atlanta area.
- **Latin American Association**, 404-638-1800, www.latinamerican assoc.org; a nonprofit organization providing comprehensive transitional services and programs for Latino families in the metro Atlanta area.
- **Metro Atlanta Indian American Community**, 678-405-4440, www.ipnatlanta.net; local organization providing information, events calendar, and links to various Indian and South Asian groups and associations throughout metro Atlanta.
- **The National Association of Chinese-Americans**, Atlanta, 770-394-6542, www.naca-atlanta.org; a nonprofit organization dedicated to promoting cultural, educational, scientific and business relationships between the Chinese community and local government, community, and business leaders.
- **Polish American Chamber of Commerce of the Southeast United States**, Atlanta, 404-724-4500, www.pacc-south.com; promotes business and cultural ties between the USA, Poland, and other Central and Eastern European nations, through business programs and social forums.
- **Refugee Women's Network, Inc.**, 404-299-0180, www.riwn.org; a nonprofit organization serving refugee and immigrant women through leadership training, education, and advocacy.
- **Russian Atlanta.Net**, www.russianatlanta.net; an online resource providing the latest news on Russian culture, business, and events in metro Atlanta.

CONSULATES

There are over 20 consulates and honorary consulates in metro Atlanta. Here are a few:
- **Consulate General of Argentina**, 245 Peachtree Center Avenue, Atlanta, 404-880-0805, www.consuladoargentinoatlanta.org
- **Consulate General of Australia**, 3353 Peachtree Road, Atlanta, 404-760-3400, www.austemb.org/govaddr.htm
- **Consulate General of Belgium**, 230 Peachtree Street, Atlanta, 404-659-2150, www.diplobel.org/usa
- **Consulate General of Canada**, 1175 Peachtree Street NE, Atlanta, 404-532-2000, www.dfait-maeci.gc.ca/can-am/atlanta
- **Consulate General of the Democratic Republic of Sao Tome & Principe**, Atlanta, 404-221-0203, www.saotome.org

- **Consulate General of France**, 3475 Piedmont Road NE, Atlanta, 404-495-1660, www.consulfrance-atlanta.org
- **Consulate General of Germany**, 285 Peachtree Center Avenue NE, Atlanta, 404-659-4760, www.germany-info.org/atlanta
- **Consulate General of Great Britain**, 133 Peachtree Street NE, Atlanta, 404-954-7700, www.britainusa.com/atlanta
- **Consulate General of Israel**, 1100 Spring Street, Atlanta, 404-487-6500, http://atlanta.mfa.gov.il
- **Consulate General of Japan**, 3500 Lenox Road, Atlanta, 404-240-4300, www.japanatlanta.org
- **Consulate General of Mexico**, 2600 Apple Valley Road, Atlanta, 404-266-2233, http://consulmexatlanta.org
- **Consulate General of Nigeria**, 8060 Roswell Road, Atlanta, 770-394-6261, www.nigeria-consulate-atl.org
- **Consulate General of Switzerland**, 1275 Peachtree Street NE, Atlanta, 404-870-2000, www.eda.admin.ch/atlanta_cg/e/home

CITIZENSHIP AND IMMIGRATION SERVICES

US Citizenship and Immigration Services (USCIS) for metro Atlanta is located in the Martin Luther King Jr. Federal Building, at 77 Forsyth Street SW, Atlanta, 30303. Contact them at 800-375-5283 or www.uscis.gov for more information.

IMMIGRATION RESOURCES

- **Bureau of Immigration and Customs Enforcement**, www.bice. immigration.gov
- **Customs and Border Protection**, www.cbp.gov
- **Department of Homeland Security**, www.dhs.gov; www.white house.gov/deptofhomeland
- **General Government Questions**, 800-688-9889, www.firstgov.gov
- **Social Security Administration**, 800-772-1213, www.ssa.gov
- **US Bureau of Consular Affairs**, www.travel.state.gov
- **US Department of State, Visa Services**, http://travel.state. gov/visa_services
- **US Immigration Online—Green Cards, Visas, Government Forms**, www.usaimmigrationservice.org

PUBLICATIONS

- *Newcomer's Handbook for Moving to and Living in the USA*, by Mike Livingston (First Books)

- **The Immigration Handbook**, 3rd edition, by Henry Liebman (First Books)

MOVING PETS TO THE USA

- **Cosmopolitan Canine Carriers**, 800-243-9105, www.canine carriers.com, has been shipping dogs and cats all over the world for over 25 years. Contact them directly with questions or concerns regarding air transportation arrangements, vaccinations, and quarantine times.
- **The Pet-Moving Handbook** (First Books) covers domestic and international moves, via car, airplane, ferry, etc. Primary focus is on cats and dogs.

GAY, LESBIAN, BISEXUAL, AND TRANSGENDER LIFE

Atlanta has long been known as a city that embraces its large and diverse gay and lesbian community. In fact, the Atlanta City Council recently passed an ordinance prohibiting companies from discriminating on the basis of sexual orientation or domestic relationship status, this despite the fact that the state of Georgia overwhelmingly approved a constitutional ban on same-sex marriage that also includes civil unions and other partnership benefits. Though this unresolved issue has created conflict between the city government and the state legislature, and will most likely be argued both legally and politically for years to come, the Atlanta ordinance is just one way the city has shown its support for the gay community.

According to the most recent US census, metro Atlanta ranks sixth in US metropolitan areas with the highest percentage of same-sex households. Today most areas of the city are "gay-friendly," though you may still find that some neighborhoods are merely tolerant and choose to employ the "don't ask, don't tell" policy, and a handful of communities may be neither accepting nor tolerant. This seems to be most true of the conservative neighborhoods that are furthest away from the heart of the city.

Metro Atlanta's artsy, intown communities, including Midtown, Decatur, Virginia Highland, and Candler Park tend to be the most accepting of gays and lesbians. And it's here that you'll find a number of gay-owned, -operated, and -friendly businesses. Those residents who choose to live in the outer suburbs of, say, Lawrenceville, Norcross, Roswell, and Marietta, and are looking for a night out, generally travel into the city to enjoy the fabulous bookstores, cafes, and nightclubs the city offers.

Some resources for gays and lesbians in metro Atlanta are:
- **Atlanta Gay and Lesbian Chamber of Commerce**, 404-377-4258, http://atlantagaychamber.org; local organization dedicated to

the development and growth of businesses that support the gay, lesbian, bisexual, and transgender community
- **Atlanta Gay and Lesbian Center**, Atlanta, 404-892-0661, www.aglc.org; offers support, friendship and discussion groups for Atlanta's gay and lesbian community. Founded in 1976, this is one of the oldest gay community centers in the USA.
- **Atlanta Pride Committee**, 404-929-0071, www.atlantapride.org; the official committee of the Atlanta's annual Lesbian, Gay, Bisexual, Transgender Pride celebration
- **Atlanta Prime Timers**, 770-441-5573, http://primetimersww.org/atlanta; a non-political, nonprofit, social group for mature gay and bisexual men and their friends
- **Black and White Men Together**, 404-705-5300, www.bwmtatlanta.org; the Atlanta chapter of the national, gay multi-cultural organization that hosts educational, political, cultural, and social activities
- **Color Bi Numbers**, 678-969-9293, www.geocities.com/westhollywood/park/6927; local social group for bisexual people of color and those who love them
- **Family Pride of the South**, 404-786-9711, www.familypridesouth.org; nonprofit organization dedicated to advancing the well-being of LGBT parents and their children through education, community support, social activities, and advocacy
- **Gay Atlanta Online**, www.gayatlanta.com; online directory of local and regional organizations, businesses, and groups for the gay community
- **Gay Fathers of Atlanta**, 770-339-3981; local support group for gay men who are fathers or who want to be fathers
- **Gay & Lesbian Alliance Against Defamation (GLAAD), Southeastern Region**, 323-634-2016, www.glaad.org; office of the southeastern monitor and response team, organized to monitor representations of the gay community
- **Kashi Atlanta**, 404-687-3353, www.kashiatlanta.org; an interfaith center for yoga, service, and community, offering GLBT-friendly yoga and meditation classes, counseling sessions, workshops, community service opportunities and more
- **LGBLife**, www.emory.edu/Campus_life/LGBToffice; Emory University's Office of Lesbian/Gay/Bisexual/Transgender Life, offering programs and services for the school's LGBT students and employees
- **Northlake Alliance of Gays/Lesbians and Straights**, 404-327-9633, www.nagsatlanta.org; local social organization made up of over 150 gay and straight members, focusing on building friendships and strengthening north DeKalb neighborhoods through social activities and community involvement

- **Out in Atlanta**, www.outinatlanta.com; local, online resource guide with news, chat, personals and more.
- **Outwrite Bookstore & Coffeehouse**, 991 Piedmont Avenue NE, 404-607-0082, www.outwritebooks.com; this bookstore stocks a large number of gay and lesbian books and periodicals, and is also the meeting place for several local gay and lesbian social groups
- **Parents, Families and Friends of Lesbians and Gays (PFLAG)**, 770-662-6475, www.pflagatl.org; local chapter of the national support organization for parents, families, and friends of gays and lesbians
- **Pride Alliance**, 404-894-5849, http://cyberbuzz.gatech.edu/pride; the GLBT student organization of Georgia Tech University
- *Southern Voice*, Atlanta, 404-876-1819, www.southernvoice.com; metro Atlanta's premier gay and lesbian newspaper
- **YouthPride Atlanta**, 404-378-7722, www.youthpride.org; offers confidential help, outreach, and support to young gays, lesbians, bisexuals, and transgenders throughout the metro area

This list is just a sampling of the organizations and groups that are available for metro Atlanta's gay and lesbian community. You may also want to check out *Creative Loafing's* **Gay and Lesbian listings** in their weekly "Happenings" section, www.creativeloafing.com.

WHEN MOVING TO A NEW AREA, ONE OF THE MOST CHALLENGING and important tasks parents face is finding good childcare and/or schools for their kids. The results of this search can be a deciding factor in, among other things, choosing a community in which to purchase a home.

While the process is not an easy one, with time and effort it is possible to find the option that works best for your family, whether it's in-home or on-site daycare, an after-school program, a good public or private school, or even homeschooling. The keys, of course, are research and persistence.

Please note: *Listing in this book is merely informational and is* **not** *an endorsement. When entrusting your child to strangers, always err on the side of safety and caution.*

CHILDCARE

DAYCARE

Metro Atlanta is home to hundreds of daycare facilities, some of which have waiting lists of a year or more. If you anticipate needing childcare, start your search as far in advance as possible. Daycare options in the metro area run the gamut: You can place your child in a privately owned national daycare center chain or a local facility; you can choose a nonprofit center run by a church, community group, or the city; you can bring your child to someone else's home; you can use your business's daycare service; or you can hire a nanny or au pair to come to your house.

Good advice when looking for childcare is to ask friends or co-workers with children if they have any recommendations. Your real estate agent or leasing agent could possibly provide suggestions as well. You may also want to check the Atlanta Yellow Pages under "Childcare Centers,"

"Childcare Service," or "Nanny Service" for daycare centers close to home. For a comprehensive list of daycare facilities in the Atlanta area, contact **Child Care Resource and Referral of Metro Atlanta**, 404-479-4200, a private, nonprofit, telephone referral service. Not only will they locate childcare centers in your area, they will also give you pertinent information such as the school's registration charges, weekly rates, and student-to-teacher ratios. You can also visit them online at www.qualitycarefor children.org, where you will also find information on childcare laws in Georgia, what to look for in a daycare facility, a listing of childcare centers throughout the state, useful links, and more. Gwinnett County parents can call **Parent's Choice**, 770-242-2077, a childcare network and referral service that screens babysitters and childcare professionals.

Following is a list of typical daycare options available in the metro Atlanta area:

- **Family Daycare Homes** are small facilities (up to six children) that operate in the home of the childcare provider. The care here is generally more individualized than what you may find in a larger facility, and prices tend to be much lower. Family daycare homes can be less structured than larger facilities and may not offer a daily curriculum for your child. Talking to the parents of other children that attend the daycare, and/or asking specific questions of the childcare provider regarding her childcare philosophy and daily routine, is a good idea.

- **Group Daycare Homes** are similar to family daycare homes in that, they too, operate in the provider's home. The difference, however, is that group daycare homes are licensed to care for a greater number of children. In Georgia, that number ranges from 7 to 18 children.

- **Childcare Centers** are what most people think of when they hear "daycare." Generally, these centers are larger and more structured than family daycare homes, and because of the number of employees and costly overhead needed to operate these facilities, prices tend to be much higher. Many of these centers are run like schools, with babies in one room, toddlers in another, preschool in yet another, and after-school students in another. A downside of childcare centers is that they often have a high teacher turnover rate, due to low pay. This can be difficult for your child if his/her favorite teacher suddenly leaves to take a more lucrative position elsewhere. When considering a childcare facility, it's important to ask about the teacher turnover rate, what incentives the school offers its employees to keep them on the job, whether or not any of the childcare workers are certified, and what type of curriculum will be offered to your child.

- **Montessori Childcare**, developed by Dr. Maria Montessori, who became Italy's first female physician in the early 1900s, is a method of childcare and teaching based on a child's individual needs and learning style. Creativity is encouraged at these centers, as well as the mixing of older children with younger children. While the overall structure here is loose compared to some other schools, the child's every experience, from water play to choosing a snack to helping to clean up, is embraced as a learning opportunity. There are several Montessori schools in metro Atlanta, some of which accept students from the age of two to twelve years; check the Atlanta Yellow Pages. For more information on the Montessori method, or to find local listings online, visit **Montessori Connections**, www.montessoriconnections.com.

- **Non-Traditional Options** refer to child development centers run out of neighborhood houses of worship as well as employer-provided daycare and co-op daycare. To find a church-sponsored daycare center, your best bet is to call the churches in your area. You'll find many churches offering this service, even if you do not attend that church, though some offer only half-days or after-school programs.

Employer-provided daycare is becoming more prevalent in metro Atlanta, particularly in the intown neighborhoods, though it's still not the norm. Be sure to ask your employer, or potential employer, whether or not it offers this benefit to their employees.

Co-op daycare is also becoming more mainstream, though not highly advertised. This option sells by word of mouth, so ask around to see if any of your friends or co-workers can recommend a co-op, or call the referral services listed above. Co-op daycare is an especially good option for parents who work part time, or have flexible schedules, and can contribute the time necessary to make the co-op work. Though co-ops are run differently and according to the needs of each particular group, in a co-op situation you can expect to work a specified number of hours each week providing daycare at the center in exchange for daycare time for your own children. Such a scenario provides for greatly reduced daycare costs and the added perk of milling about with a bunch of little ones. If you have a job that requires you to work 50 hours a week or your employer won't give you time off to participate at the co-op, this option may not be for you.

WHAT TO LOOK FOR IN DAYCARE

When visiting a prospective childcare center, ask the staff for the names and phone numbers of other parents using the center, and give them a call. Later, if you're still interested, make at least one unannounced visit to the facility. Also, make sure that the center is licensed by the state. Earning a state license involves strict health and safety requirements. The **Georgia Department of Human Resources, State Office of Regulatory Services**, 404-657-5700, www2.state.ga.us/departments/dhr/ors, can tell you whether a facility is licensed and whether complaints have been filed against the center. They can also assist you with any questions you may have about the over 650 daycare centers in metro Atlanta.

When viewing daycare centers, you may want to consider the following:

- How long has the school been in operation?
- Is the school licensed?
- Does the school receive funding from the state's "Georgia Lottery Pre-K" fund? (In some cases, facilities that receive state funds are held to stricter requirements than schools that do not.)
- Determine how many students are currently enrolled in the school and in your child's class, and what the student-to-teacher ratio is.
- Are any of the teachers degreed or currently enrolled in child development classes?
- Does the school provide incentive for the teachers to become degreed or certified?
- Does the school run background checks on new employees to ensure that none has a criminal record?
- What is the school's pupil and daycare provider turnover rate?
- How many of the teachers are currently child-CPR certified? (The state of Georgia requires that 50% of a facility's staff have up-to-date CPR certification.)
- What are the school's hours of operation?
- Are children provided with a hot, nutritious lunch each day? Ask for a sample week's lunch menu.
- How does the staff handle discipline?
- Will your child's teacher provide age-appropriate projects and activities throughout the day? Is there a set schedule or routine?
- How often are the children allowed to play outside?
- Is the outside play area safe? Be sure to investigate.
- Is your child's classroom child-proofed? Are dangerous items (like scissors or cleaning supplies) locked away or kept out of reach?
- How often are the classrooms cleaned? How often are the toys sanitized?
- What is the school's policy on sick children?

Once the questions have been asked, make sure you take your child to the school and let him/her meet the teacher and spend some time with you in the classroom. Often your child's impression of the daycare center is a great indication of whether or not it will be the right fit for your family.

NANNIES

Hiring a nanny can be the most expensive daycare option, but it may also be the most rewarding for your family, if you can find the right person.

The going rate for nannies in metro Atlanta is anywhere from $15,000 to $25,000 annually, depending on the nanny's experience and whether or not she will be receiving room and board.

To find a good match, nanny referral agencies are available and offer the benefit of prescreening applicants for you, but they will cost more than if you locate one yourself. If you are hiring a nanny without the help of an agency (see below), you'll want to do a background check, which can be done online. Go to any search engine and type in "employment screening." A host of companies are available to research criminal records, driving records, and credit information for you. Locally, you can check with **Investigative Solutions, Inc.**, 770-220-1912, 800-398-2775, www.invsol.com, an Atlanta-based, full-service, private investigation agency specializing in background checks and detailed, pre-employment screenings.

To find a nanny, check the *Atlanta Journal-Constitution*'s classified ads, especially the Sunday edition, or the monthly *Atlanta Parent* magazine (see below).

When talking to a nanny's former employer, you may want to ask questions like:
- How did they come to hire the nanny in the first place?
- How long was the nanny in their service?
- How many children did the nanny care for at one time?
- What were the nanny's responsibilities?
- Did they ever have any problems with the nanny?
- Why did the nanny leave that job?
- Would they hire this person again?

NANNY PLACEMENT SERVICES

If you'd rather hire a professional nanny placement service, you may want to consider the companies listed below. These companies usually do a thorough background and criminal check on nannies they represent. However, it's still important to do your own thorough interview of the potential candidates and ask for verification from the agency that all references and background checks came out clean.

The following companies offer a range of domestic care providers. For a full listing check the Atlanta Yellow Pages under "Nanny Service" (inclusion here does not imply endorsement by First Books):
- **All-American Nanny**, 800-3-NANNYS, www.allamericannanny.com
- **A Friend of the Family**, 770-725-2748, 770-333-3407, www.afriend.com
- **Childcare Resources**, 770-619-0377, www.childcareresources.com
- **The Hazel Agency**, 770-643-2034, www.thehazelagency.com
- **Nannies and Sitters International**, 404-885-6644, www.nasint.com

- **Nanny Solutions**, 404-607-7709, www.hometown.aol.com/ amy4686/nannysolutions.html

NANNY TAXES

For those hiring a nanny directly (not using a nanny agency) there are certain taxes you will be responsible for paying, specifically social security and Medicare, and possibly unemployment. For help with such issues, check the **Nanitax** web site, www.4nannytaxes.com, or call 800-626-4829. Nanitax provides household payroll and employment tax preparation services. You can also check with The **Nanny Tax Company**, 800-747-9826, www.nanny taxprep.com, or the **IRS's** household employer page, www.irs.gov/ taxtopics/tc756.html, which discusses taxes for household employees.

AU PAIRS

If you land the right applicant, an au pair (typically, a young woman—18 to 25—from abroad who will take care of your child and do light house-keeping in exchange for room, board, and a weekly stipend) may be a better alternative than a nanny. However, an au pair is not likely to have the extended experience of a professional nanny, usually works for only one year, and is required to enroll in an accredited post-secondary insti-tution for not less than six semester hours of academic credit. The **US Department of State's Bureau of Educational and Cultural Affairs**, 202-647-4000, http://exchanges.state.gov, oversees and approves the organizations that offer this service in the USA. To find out more about hosting an au pair, or to begin the hiring process, you may want to contact the following national agencies. Any of them can con-nect you with a local coordinator who will answer your questions and/or match up your family with the right au pair.

- **Au PairCare Inc.**, 800-4AUPAIR, www.aupaircare.com
- **Au Pair in America**, 800-928-7247, www.aupairinamerica.com
- **Au Pair USA InterExchange**, 800-AU-PAIRS, www.interexchange. org/aupair
- **Cultural Care Au Pair**, 800-333-6056, www.culturalcare.com
- **EurAupair Intercultural Child Care Programs**, 949-494-5500, www.euraupair.com
- **Go Au Pair**, 888-AUPAIR1, www.goaupair.com

BABYSITTING

Finding a dependable babysitter can be a daunting task, especially if you are new to a city. Once again, referrals from co-workers or friends are usually the best way to go, but if you don't know anyone with children, there are other options. Local **YMCA**s and **YWCA**s often have a list of teenage members who have either gone through their CPR program or who have volunteered as counselors for the Ys for after-school or summer camp programs. (Some locations may require you to become a Y member before being granted access to the list.) Contact the metro Atlanta **YMCA**, 404-588-9622, www.ymcaatlanta.org, and **YWCA**, 404-527-7575, www.ywcaatlanta.org, for further details. Other organizations that can assist you in locating a babysitter are nanny placement services (see above), your local house of worship, college job referral services, or campus employment offices.

At this writing, high school and college-age sitters can expect to earn between $8 and $15 per hour. Some of the more savvy ones may even charge you a minimum (e.g., $10 per hour with a three-hour minimum). If you use a nanny placement service, you should expect to pay more than you would for a neighborhood teenager.

ONLINE RESOURCES—CHILDCARE

If you'd like to use the Internet to find childcare services in the metro Atlanta area, whether it's a facility or an au pair you're looking for, the following sites may be of some use:

- **www.cremechildcare.com**, offers comprehensive information about Crème de la Crème childcare centers.
- **www.georgiadaycare.com**, is a searchable database of over 2,000 daycare centers.
- **www.goddardpreschool.com**, offers information about the Goddard School daycare centers, as well as a listing of its three locations throughout Cobb County.
- **www.kehillatchaim.org/preschool.html**, offers information about Roswell's Temple Kehillat Chaim childcare facility.
- **www.primroseschools.com**, offers information about Primrose childcare centers, as well as a listing of all metro Atlanta locations.
- **www.qualitycareforchildren.org**, a childcare solutions referral service.

PARENTING PUBLICATIONS

Metro Atlanta is home to *Atlanta Parent*, 770-454-7599, www.atlanta parent.com, an award-winning parenting magazine that provides information on raising children in Atlanta. In addition to its helpful articles, each issue of *Atlanta Parent* also offers a comprehensive list of area schools, daycares, party planners, fun things to do around town with the family, and a monthly special events calendar. This free magazine is published monthly and can be picked up at area bookstores, toy stores, and childcare centers.

CHILD SAFETY

In metro Atlanta, the **Georgia Division of Public Health**, 404-657-2700, http://health.state.ga.us, works to ensure the safety, health, and welfare of children and families across the state. Additionally, each county's **Board of Health** has established programs that work to distribute information on child safety issues such as detecting lead paint levels in older homes; immunization; and common childhood illnesses. Several metro Atlanta counties are listed below. (To find the Board of Health office in counties other than those listed here, check the county government listings in the blue pages of your Atlanta phone book or contact the county offices listed in the **Neighborhoods** chapter of this book.)

- **Cobb & Douglas County Public Health**, 770-514-2300, www.cobb countypublichealth.org
- **DeKalb County Board of Health**, 404-294-3700, www.dekalb health.net
- **Fulton County Department of Health and Wellness**, 404-730-1211, www.co.fulton.ga.us/departments/health.html
- **Gwinnett County Department of Health and Human Services**, 770-822-8000, www.co.gwinnett.ga.us

Other child safety resources worth taking a look at are **Children's Healthcare of Atlanta: Wellness and Safety**, 404-250-KIDS, www.choa.org/wellnessandsafety.asp, an informative online newsletter with information on child safety, wellness basics, and injury prevention; **DeKalb County's Board of Health, Safe Kids Program**, 404-294-3700, www.dekalbhealth.net, which offers useful information on topics such as injury prevention, swimming pool safety, and carbon monoxide, as well as a downloadable home safety checklist; and the **National Safe Kids Campaign**, 202-662-0600, www.safekids.org, which offers valuable child safety information as well as an online, searchable listing of each state's child safety laws.

If you are interested in taking emergency training classes, including infant and child CPR, contact the hospitals in your area, as most of them offer these classes periodically throughout the year. You may also want to consider your local YMCA, since they too offer CPR classes from time to time.

LEAD POISONING

According to the EPA, lead is one of the most pervasive toxic substances in the country today. Lead in paint, which children ingest by eating paint chips or inhaling paint dust, can result in serious and permanent damage to the brain, kidneys, bones, nervous system, and red blood cells. Unfortunately, about 75% of houses and apartments built before 1978 in the USA contain lead paint. And houses built before 1960 may contain old lead paint with concentrations up to 50 percent lead by weight.

In Georgia, landlords, sellers, and renovators are required to provide information on lead-based paint and lead-based paint hazards before the sale or lease of a private home or apartment built before 1978. Properties not included in the law are zero bedroom dwellings (such as lofts and efficiencies), short-term or vacation rentals, housing for the elderly and the handicapped (unless children live there), and foreclosure sales. The **Georgia Department of Natural Resources, Environmental Protection Division**, 404-657-5947, www.dnr.state.ga.us/dnr/environ, is the office in charge of creating and enforcing environmental safety rules based on Georgia statutes, including those dealing with lead-based paint hazards and their abatement (through containment, replacement, or removal). They are also in charge of providing certification and licensing for all state lead inspectors and assessors, and anyone conducting lead training programs. If you have questions or complaints regarding a home lead inspection, or if you would like to find a certified inspector in your area, this is the office to contact.

For additional information about lead poisoning and prevention, including screening guidelines for children, contact the **Georgia Division of Public Health, Lead Poisoning Prevention Program**, 404-463-3754, http://health.state.ga.us/programs/lead, or the **National Lead Information Center**, 800-424-LEAD, www.epa.gov/lead/nlic.htm.

SCHOOLS

The following information may be useful as you search for the best schooling option for your children.

PARENT RESOURCES

There are a number of resources available for parents, both locally and nationally. If you want to find out more about education or schools in the metro Atlanta area, you may want to consider the following:

- **American Association for Gifted Children**, 919-783-6152, www.aagc.org; information on gifted children and their education

- **Educational Resources Information Center**, 800-538-3742, www.eric.ed.gov; federally funded, national information system that provides information about a broad range of education issues
- **The Association of Boarding Schools**, 202-966-8705, 800-541-5908, www.schools.com; comprehensive directory of boarding schools
- *Atlanta Parent Magazine*, 770-454-7599, www.atlantaparent.com; a city parenting magazine that often lists private schools, highlights the top public schools, and features editorials on local education issues
- **Coordinated Campaign for Learning Disabilities**, www.ld online.org; information on all types of learning disabilities
- **Georgia State School Report Card**, 404-256-4050, www. gppf.org; provides the Georgia Public Policy Foundation's statewide report card for public schools
- **The National Association of Independent Schools (NAIS)**, 202-973-9700, www.nais-schools.org; a detailed guide to selecting a non-public school, also provides a nationwide database of schools and parenting resources
- **National PTA (Parent Teacher Association)**, 800-307-4782, www.pta.org
- **School Match**, 614-890-1573, www.schoolmatch.com; a private organization offering one-page summary statistics on area high schools or lists of the top 15 schools (public or private) in your area that best meet your requirements
- **US Department of Education**, 800-872-5327, www.ed.gov, provides a wide variety of education information pertaining to both public and private schools

PUBLIC SCHOOLS

Metro Atlanta is home to a number of nationally recognized public schools. Whether you live within the city limits, or in one of Atlanta's growing suburbs, you are bound to find an elementary, middle, or high school in your district that can provide a safe, educationally stimulating environment for your child. The key is to do your research ahead of time, find out as much as you can about your county's individual schools, and try to find one that would be the best fit for your family. Following is some basic information on the various school districts around Atlanta.

All of the school districts in metro Atlanta are experiencing record growth as more and more newcomers move to the area. This increase in population has led to overcrowding in many classrooms. School boards have tried to keep up with the boom by adding mobile classrooms (i.e., trailers) to area schools; to help with the school travel crunch, "staggered" or "varying" schedules have been suggested (where some students attend school from 8 a.m. to 3 p.m., while others attend from 8:45 a.m. to 3:45 p.m.); and by offering parents the option of sending their children to other, less-crowded, schools within their county, when space is available. State and local school superintendents are also working to ensure that metro Atlanta schools are staffed accordingly. Today, the average student-to-teacher ratio in each Atlanta area district is about 26:1.

In addition to the overcrowding issue, Atlanta-area parents are also dealing with changes to the school schedules in each county. Instead of operating on the typical September through June schedule, metro Atlanta schools now begin the school year by mid-August. Despite some complaining from parents that the early start dates interfere with vacation plans, not to mention the complaints from children, education officials at both state and local levels believe the early start dates are necessary in order to ensure that students have enough time to prepare for their annual standardized tests.

Families moving to Georgia and planning to enroll children in the public school system should contact the school superintendent in the county or city school system where they will be residing for registration specifics. Typically, registration is held in the spring, and procedures vary from school system to school system. Regardless of your county of residence, you will be required to show the following:

- records or transcripts from your child's previous school (if applicable)
- your child's social security number (or a signed statement from the parent declining to provide the number)
- proof of residency
- an official document (like a birth certificate) showing proof of the child's age (Georgia requires that all children between the ages of 6 and 16 be enrolled in a public, private, or homeschool program)
- certification of eye, ear, and dental examinations
- a current certificate of immunization for measles, rubella, tetanus, diphtheria, polio, mumps, whooping cough, and hepatitis B (or a signed medical exemption authorized by a medical doctor; or a sworn affidavit from the parents stating that immunization conflicts with their religious beliefs)

For more detailed information on education in Georgia, visit the **Georgia Department of Education** web site at www.doe.k12.ga.us. Or contact metro Atlanta's city and county school districts directly. Phone numbers and web addresses for some are listed below; others can be found in the Government Blue Pages of the Atlanta Business phone book.

ATLANTA CITY SCHOOLS

Public school students living within the Atlanta city limits, regardless of county, will attend an **Atlanta City School**. District maps can help you figure out which schools serve each neighborhood, and can be found online at www.atlanta.k12.ga.us. Though the **Atlanta City Schools** do not always garner as much praise as their suburban counterparts, they continue to make great strides toward achieving academic excellence. In fact, the Atlanta City School Board is so intent on educating students, they've made two major changes in the last decade—first implementing a year-round schedule at three of its elementary schools, and, in order to give students an extra half hour a day in the classroom, cutting recess time. Cutting recess has been controversial, with some parents and child advocates worried about student burnout, but, if test scores are the measure of success, then the school board's focus seems to be working. Almost 50% of Atlanta City students in grades one through eight scored at or above the national norm in reading on the Iowa Test of Basic Skills, and a full 53% of them scored at or above the national norm in mathematics. That's several percentage points higher than in previous years.

There are currently over 51,000 students enrolled in Atlanta's 59 elementary, 16 middle, 7 charter, and 10 high schools. A few of the system's standout schools include **Mary Lin Elementary School**, located in Candler Park, **Willis Sutton Middle School**, located in Buckhead, and **Grady High School**, located near downtown. Mary Lin boasts strong parental involvement, a curriculum that combines core skills with arts-based education, and a diverse student body, all of which makes it one of the most popular neighborhood elementary schools in the city. Willis Sutton offers excellent academic and extracurricular opportunities, including a respected jazz band and concert orchestra program, national and international field trips, and math and science clubs. Willis Sutton also allows students to earn up to three high school credits while attending the school. Grady High School is home to *The Southerner,* an award-winning student newspaper, recently named one of the best high school papers in the country. Grady is also home to several state and nationally recognized academic teams, including a winning Mock Trial Team and Debate Team.

In addition, the City of Atlanta school system is home to seven not-for-profit charter schools, including **Charles R. Drew Charter School**, the **Neighborhood Charter School, Inc.**, and **Tech High School**. Each boasts strong parental involvement, academic excellence, and innovative educational ideas. Charles R. Drew students, for example, attend an extra hour of school each day, and an extra 20 days of school each year. And, under Drew's technology program, all students receive a computer for their home beginning in third grade. For more information on Atlanta City Schools, contact the **Atlanta City School Board**, 404-827-8599, www.atlanta.k12.ga.us.

COBB COUNTY SCHOOLS

The **Cobb County** school system is the second largest in Georgia and is among the 30 largest in the USA. It is also one of the fastest growing districts in the state, with an annual student population of more than 100,000, and approximately 2,500 new students enrolling each year. Because of this tremendous growth, Cobb County residents pay a 1% sales tax for education. The money collected provides funding to build new schools and renovate nearly all of the other school facilities in the county.

In Cobb County, there are 69 elementary schools, 21 middle schools, and 14 high schools; all of which operate on a semester schedule, meaning that the 180-day school year is divided into two 90-day segments, with a break in between, rather than the typical three, 60-day quarter system. Proponents believe this allows for more uninterrupted instructional time for students, leading to better retention of the subjects that are covered.

Parental involvement is well documented in the Cobb County School System, which may account for the students' high test scores and numerous honors. For instance, several of the district's high school marching bands have been invited to play at prestigious events such as the Rose Bowl, Orange Bowl, and Cotton Bowl parades, and almost 90% of all Cobb County graduates go on to colleges or universities.

Despite the accolades, the Cobb County School System is probably best known for its controversial stance on evolution. In 2002, school officials placed disclaimers in the school systems' science textbooks, stating: "This textbook contains material on evolution. Evolution is a theory, not a fact, regarding the origin of living things. This material should be approached with an open mind, studied carefully, and critically considered." The move brought national criticism from educators, scientists, the ACLU, and even former President Jimmy Carter. The Cobb County school board defended the warning as a show of religious tolerance, rather than religious activism, and noted that prior to adding the disclaimer, they had received several thousand calls from Cobb County parents complaining about the textbooks' presentation of evolution as fact, without offering alternative theories. Other area parents, however, felt the stickers went too far, blurring the line between church and state. Four Cobb County families went so far as to file suit against the school system, and in 2004, a federal judge ruled in their favor, stating that Cobb's warning stickers were unconstitutional. The school system was then ordered to remove the disclaimers from all textbooks. Though the brouhaha has since died down, vocal proponents on both sides of the issue continue to debate the subject of evolution, and how it should be taught in local schools. For more information on Cobb County schools, contact the **Cobb County Board of Education**, 770-426-3300, www.cobb.k12.ga.us.

DEKALB COUNTY SCHOOLS

The **DeKalb County** school system, with over 100,000 students enrolled annually, is one of Georgia's best and brightest. The 84 elementary, 19 middle, and 21 high schools here have received more state and national honors than any other district in Georgia. A few shining examples follow: **Austin Elementary School** in Dunwoody consistently ranks among the top ten highest-scoring elementary schools in the state on nationally standardized tests. This school also offers foreign language classes, a chess club, and more. **Avondale High School** has boasted two Governor's Honors students, an MLK Essay Award winner, and winners of National Council of Teachers of English Achievement awards and numerous state and national literary awards. It was also one of seven schools in the USA, and the only Georgia school selected to represent the USA at the International GLOBE Conference in Helsinki, Finland. **Chamblee High School** perennially scores among the highest SAT scores at public schools in the state, boasts an award-winning band, choir, student newspaper, and yearbook, and has been awarded the Siemens Award for Science, Math and Technology. In 2003, Chamblee High boasted 15 National Achievement Finalists, 10 National Merit Finalists, and one National Hispanic Scholar. A consistent 90% of the school's graduating class qualifies for the HOPE Scholarship each year.

While these examples of student achievement clearly point to a strong school system, DeKalb County schools also offer something else: diversity. As mentioned in previous chapters, DeKalb County is one of the most diverse counties in the USA, with residents from across the country and from around the world settling here. **Cross Keys High School** in North Druid Hills has the most culturally diverse student population in the state, with students from 65 countries, who speak over 75 different languages, currently enrolled. For more information on DeKalb County schools, contact the **DeKalb County Board of Education**, 678-676-1200, www.dekalb.k12.ga.us.

FULTON COUNTY SCHOOLS

The **Fulton County** school system serves all of Fulton County outside of the Atlanta City limits. Like DeKalb County schools, Fulton County schools have also received a fair amount of local and national recognition over the last decade, with students scoring above 1000 combined on the Verbal and Math SATs. Five Fulton County schools are currently Georgia Schools of Excellence, and one is a National Blue Ribbon School. More than 80 percent of Fulton County graduates go on to some form of higher education. And this school district was one of four in the USA to receive a Gold Medallion from the National School Public Relations Association in the late 1990s.

Top schools here include **Alpharetta Elementary School**, which offers students both a mentoring program, and "The Eagles Nest," an outdoor classroom featuring an amphitheater, pond, and certified wildlife habitat; **Camp Creek Middle School**, the birthplace of the school system's After Three Club, an after-school program offering a variety of free activities to Fulton County middle school students, and home to several enrichment programs including The Writers Workshop, Math Club, Chess Club, and Junior Beta Club; and **North Springs High School**, which boasts the only Arts & Science Magnet Program in Georgia. The program allows students to participate in either one or both of the components, through a variety of challenging opportunities focusing on the areas of math, science, drama, dance, technology, and visual art.

All 52 elementary, 18 middle, and 12 high schools that make up Fulton County's schools currently operate on a semester school calendar rather than the typical three, 60-day quarter system. Student population in Fulton County schools is lower than the populations of other area school systems, with just over 75,000 enrolled annually. For more information on Fulton County schools, contact the **Fulton County Board of Education**, 404-768-3600, www.fultonschools.org.

GWINNETT COUNTY SCHOOLS

The **Gwinnett County** school system is the most heavily populated in metro Atlanta and is one of the fastest growing in the USA. Approximately 140,000 students are enrolled annually, with an increase of approximately 6,000 new students per year. To keep up with this rapid growth, Gwinnett County opened 10 new schools in 2004 and is planning to build at least that many more by the end of the decade. Currently, there are 63 elementary schools, 20 middle schools, and 16 high schools serving the district.

Gwinnett County public school educators are consistently recognized for outstanding achievements by national organizations including the President's Award for Excellence in Math and Science Teaching, the National School Library of the Year award, and National Middle School Teaching Team awards. Gwinnett County boasts both Georgia Schools of Excellence and National Schools of Excellence, and, over the last ten years, the school system's academic teams have won regional and state academic competitions in science, math, and problem solving. About 85% of Gwinnett County high school students continue their education after graduation. Innovative schools here include **Peachtree Elementary**, which offers a variety of fun events for students and their families throughout the year, including an "International Block Party," celebrating diversity through traditional dances, songs, stories and food from around the world, and "The Queen Visits Peachtree," a Great Britain unit-study tie-in featuring tea, crumpets, and conversation with "the Queen"; and **Central Gwinnett High School**, which offers college level classes in Language Composition, Literature, Calculus, Statistics, World History, Economics, Chemistry, and more. In addition, Central Gwinnett High is home to the *Troubadour,* a student-run literary magazine, and at least 40 more extracurricular clubs and programs, including athletic teams, a Drama Club, and Thespian Society. If you'd like to find out more about Gwinnett County schools, contact the **Gwinnett County Board of Education**, 770-963-8651, www.gwinnett.k12.ga.us.

PRIVATE AND PAROCHIAL SCHOOLS

Despite the glowing reviews garnered by many of metro Atlanta's public schools, some parents still choose to send their children to private or parochial school. If this is an option you'd like to pursue, you may want to research the following schools and organizations (for a complete list, check the Atlanta Yellow Pages under "Schools—Private"):

- **The Atlanta Girls' School**, 3254 Northside Parkway, Atlanta, 404-845-0900, www.atlantagirlsschool.org; offers instruction for girls in grades 6–11
- **Atlanta New Century School**, 300 Luckie Street, Atlanta, 404-525-1909, www.atlantancs.com; provides a customized curriculum designed to challenge students
- **Atlanta International School**, 2890 North Fulton Drive, 404-841-3840, www.aischool.org; serves children in grades pre-K–12
- **Catholic Archdiocese of Atlanta, Department of Education**, 404-888-7802, www.archatl.com; can provide you with information on local Catholic schools and requirements
- **Children's School**, 345 10th Street, NE, Atlanta, 404-873-6985, www.thechildrensschool.com; accepts children from 3 years old through 6th grade
- **Brandon Hall School**, 1701 Brandon Hall Drive, Atlanta, 770-394-8177, www.brandonhall.org; boys' college preparatory boarding school accepting students in grades 4–12. Brandon Hall offers coeducational classes during the day.

- **First Montessori School of Atlanta**, 5750 Long Island Drive NW, Atlanta, 404-252-3910, www.firstmontessori.org; offers individualized instruction for ages 2 1/2 to 12
- **IMHOTEP Center of Education**, 541 Harwell Road NW, Atlanta, 404-696-8777, www.imhotep.com; accepts students in K–12th grade, and offers extensive curriculum including African-American Studies
- **Lovett School**, 4075 Paces Ferry Road, NW, Atlanta, 404-262-3032, www.lovett.org; enrolls children in grades pre-K–12
- **Lullwater School**, 705 South Candler Street, Decatur, 404-378-6643, www.lullwaterschool.org; accepts students between the ages of 5 and 15 years
- **Montessori School at Emory**, 1677 Scott Boulevard, 404-634-5777, http://yp.bellsouth.com/sites/montessorischoolemory; accepts students from 18 months to 12 years
- **Noble World Montessori**, 2676 East Piedmont Road, Marietta, 770-509-1775, www.moteaco.com/members/nobleworld.htm; accepts students from 18 months to 9 years
- **Northwoods Montessori**, locations in Doraville and Decatur, 770-457-7261, www.northwoodsmontessori.com; accepts students from 2 1/2 to 12 years old
- **Pace Academy**, 966 West Paces Ferry Road, NW, Atlanta, 404-262-1345, www.paceacademy.org; accepts students in grades 1–12
- **Trinity School**, 4301 Northside Drive, NW, Atlanta, 404-231-8100, www.trinityatl.org; a coeducational school serving preschool and elementary age children
- **Westminster School**, 1424 West Paces Ferry Road, NW, Atlanta, 404-355-8673, www.westminster.net; accepts students in grades 1–12

HOMESCHOOLING

Georgia's state laws regarding homeschooling are relatively simple and easy to follow. Basically, all Georgia children between the ages of 6 and 16 are required to enroll in a public, private, or homeschool program. Therefore, homeschoolers must submit a Letter of Intent to their county school system each September (or no later than 30 days after beginning a homeschool program), for each child. They must also submit monthly attendance forms for each child, showing that they are receiving a home education equal to four and a half hours per day for 180 days during a 12-month period. Official forms can be found at the **Georgia Home Education Information Resource (HEIR)** web site, www.heir.org. There, you will also find more detailed information on Georgia homeschool laws, current updates on proposed changes to Georgia's homeschool legislation, and links to various homeschool groups and organizations around the state. Many metro Atlanta parents have now chosen homeschooling as a viable educational option for their families. And many more are considering it. While exact numbers aren't available, it's believed that homeschooling families in metro Atlanta number in the high hundreds. Because of this increasing interest in home education, a handful of excellent support groups are now in place, offering information for new homeschoolers, parent support, social opportunities, homeschool classes, and more.

A few to consider are (some may be of a religious affiliation):

- **Atlanta Alternative Education Network**, www.aaengroup.com; local homeschooling group serving metro Atlanta through classes, park days, field trips, and more
- **Atlanta Homeschool Happenings**, http://groups.yahoo.com/ group/atlantahshappenings; an email list for posting any and all metro Atlanta events for, about, or of interest to area homeschoolers
- **Communities of Home Educators for Christ**, www.chec-ga.org; Christian-based homeschooling group serving Cobb and Paulding counties
- **Gifted Home Educated**, http://groups.yahoo.com/group/GHE; an online group for metro Atlanta parents who are homeschooling their gifted children
- **Georgia Home Education Association**, 770-461-3657, www.ghea.org; great online resource for homeschooling in Georgia, including lists of homeschool activities and local groups, information on state laws, tips for new homeschoolers, and more
- **Georgia Homeschool**, http://groups.yahoo.com/group/georgia homeschool; an online e-mail list for homeschoolers (or those considering homeschooling) in Georgia
- **Georgia Unschoolers**, http://groups.yahoo.com/group/ga unschoolers; an all-inclusive support group for families unschooling in Georgia
- **Harvest Home Educators**, www.harvesthomeeducators.com; homeschooling group that arranges homeschooling events and activities at various zoos, theme parks, and museums around the state
- **HomeSchool FISH (Families in Support of Homeschooling)**, 770-202-7802, http://homeschoolfish.com; a local, nonprofit, founded to support Christian homeschooling families
- **LEADhomeschool**, http://groups.yahoo.com/group/LEADhome school; an all-inclusive, Decatur-based homeschooling group serving Atlanta area homeschoolers through weekly park days and classes, monthly parent support meetings, and field trips

- **North Fulton Home Educators Encouragers** (**NFHEE**), www. nfhee.com; a network of homeschool families from North Fulton, East Cobb, Cherokee, and Forsyth counties
- **West Metro Home Educators**, http://westmetrohe.tripod.com; an all-inclusive group of home educating families from the Douglas, Paulding, and South Cobb county areas

T YPICAL OF OTHER LARGE METROPOLITAN AREAS, ATLANTA IS A land of malls, superstores, and shopping districts. It is likely that wherever you choose to live in metro Atlanta, you will be an easy drive from at least one shopping mall or district.

SHOPPING DISTRICTS

If you prefer to avoid chain stores and mammoth parking lots, there are several shopping districts around the city where you can walk in the open air and browse to your heart's content.

If Atlanta has a quintessential shopping district, **Buckhead** is it. This is where you'll find two of the city's most popular malls—Lenox Square Mall and Phipps Plaza, as well as an assortment of galleries, tony clothing stores, and several upscale boutiques. Prices here seem astronomical, compared to what you'll find in other areas of the city; however, this is most likely the only place you'll be able to find that breathtaking Versace gown or locally designed fine jewelry. Don't be intimidated by Buckhead's high-class reputation; shopping here can be a great adventure, and bargains can be had, particularly during the changing seasons' clearance sales. Numerous Buckhead boutiques can be found by driving up Peachtree Road until it forks with Roswell Road. Stores are also situated off of Peachtree. And don't forget Pharr Road or Buckhead Avenue; these two side streets often boast some of the most interesting and affordable of Buckhead's retail establishments, such as **Work of Our Hands**, 404-504-9912, www.workofhands.com, and **Sweet Repeats**, 404-261-7519.

Virginia Highland offers stylish clothing, antiques, cards, flowers, and other delights in one-of-a-kind boutiques that mix funky with upscale. Shops in Virginia Highland line three non-consecutive blocks along North Highland Avenue. Start your tour just before the intersection of North

Highland and Virginia Avenue, and head south. On weekends especially, you may have to pay $5 to $10 to park in one of the pay lots located throughout the neighborhood (or you can try parking on one of the side streets radiating off of North Highland—watching for the posted no parking zones). Top off the day with a visit to **Murphy's** (at the intersection of North Highland and Virginia Avenue), 404-872-0904, www.murphys vh.com, a popular neighborhood restaurant offering brunch, lunch and dinner, as well as a full dessert menu, specialty coffee, and wine.

The **Little Five Points** (**L5P**) area is for the young and cool. Come here to rifle through vintage clothing, buy a kite, get your navel pierced, or browse some of Atlanta's best music stores. Shopping starts on Moreland Avenue with the **Junkman's Daughter**, 404-577-3188 (a popular L5P destination offering funky clothing, kitschy household items, and more), and **The Vortex Bar and Grill**, 404-688-1828, www.thevortexbarand grill.com, and continues around the bend on Euclid Avenue and beyond.

The city of **Decatur**, like Virginia Highland, abounds with small, independently owned boutiques, cafés and restaurants, and more. Because downtown Decatur is a true town square, you'll want to park your car and head out on foot. (Your best bet for parking is to find one of the metered spaces along East Ponce de Leon, or one of the side streets, which can be a challenge on weekends.) Popular shops include the **Squash Blossom** clothing boutique, 404-373-1864, www.squashblossomboutique.com, on East Court Street, **The Inner Child** toy store, 404-377-7775, on West Ponce de Leon, and **Mingei World Arts**, 404-371-0101, www.mingei worldarts.com, on Church Street. And, if you find yourself hungry, nothing beats an inexpensive, gourmet taco from **Taqueria del Sol**, 404-377-7668, www.taqueriadelsol.com.

SHOPPING MALLS

Malls here run the gamut in size and quality—Phipps Plaza, for example, is modeled after an elegant, Georgian mansion, with its interior boasting brass fixtures, fine woodwork, and marble floors. The delight of mall shopping for many is the efficiency and comfort it offers; a shopper can bring a list of diverse items and find them all at one convenient (and air conditioned) location. (For a list of anchor stores for Atlanta's malls, see below under **Department Stores**.)

- **Cumberland Mall**, I-75 at Cobb Parkway, Atlanta, 770-435-2206, www.cumberlandmall.com
- **Discover Mills**, 5900 Sugarloaf Parkway, Lawrenceville, 678-847-5000, www.discovermills.com
- **Galleria Specialty Mall**, One Galleria Parkway NW, Marietta, 770-989-5100, www.galleriaspecialtymall.com

- **Greenbriar Mall**, I-285 at Lakewood Freeway, Atlanta, 404-344-6611, www.shopgreenbriar.com
- **Gwinnett Place Mall**, 2100 Pleasant Hill Road, Duluth, 770-476-5160, www.simon.com
- **Lenox Square**, 3393 Peachtree Road NE, Atlanta, 404-233-6767, www.simon.com
- **Mall at Stonecrest**, 2929 Turner Hill Road, Lithonia, 678-526-8955, www.mallatstonecrest.com
- **Mall of Georgia**, 3333 Buford Drive, Buford, 678-482-8788, www.simon.com
- **North DeKalb Mall**, 2050 Lawrenceville Highway, Decatur, 404-320-7960, www.northdekalbmall.com
- **Northlake Mall**, 4800 Briarcliff Road NE, Tucker, 770-938-3564, www.simon.com
- **North Point Mall**, GA 400 at Haynes Bridge Road exit, Alpharetta, 770-740-9273, www.northpointmall.com
- **Perimeter Mall**, Ashford-Dunwoody Road, Atlanta, 770-394-4270, www.perimetermall.com
- **Phipps Plaza**, 3500 Peachtree Road NE, Atlanta, 404-262-0992, www.simon.com
- **South DeKalb Mall**, 2801 Candler Road, Decatur, 404-241-2431, www.southdekalbmall.com
- **Southlake Mall**, 1000 Southlake Mall Drive, Morrow, 770-961-1050, www.southlakemall.com
- **Town Center Mall**, 400 Ernest W. Barrett Parkway, Kennesaw, 770-424-9486, www.simon.com
- **Underground Atlanta**, 50 Alabama Street SW, Atlanta, 404-523-2311, www.underground-atlanta.com

OUTLET MALLS

- **North Georgia Premium Outlets**, Dawsonville, 706-216-3609, www.premiumoutlets.com; this outlet mall is located about 45 minutes north of Atlanta, up Georgia 400, and is enormous, making it impossible to visit all of the stores in one day. Shops here include Off Fifth (the Sak's Fifth Avenue outlet store), a Williams-Sonoma Outlet, Crate and Barrel Outlet, Gap Outlet, Banana Republic Outlet; various shoe stores and toy stores, and more. The mall also offers designer specialty shops—from Calvin Klein to BCBG to Adrienne Vittadini—for shoppers who want designer fashion at discount prices.
- **Tanger Factory Outlets**, I-85 North to exit 52, Commerce, 706-335-3354, www.tangeroutlet.com; located about an hour north of Atlanta on Interstate 85. Shops here include a Polo Ralph Lauren Factory

Outlet, a Brooks Brothers Outlet, J Crew, Tommy Hilfiger Outlet, Alexander Furniture, and the very popular Nike Factory Store.

DEPARTMENT STORES

- **Bloomingdales**, 404-495-2800, 770-901-5200, www.blooming dales.com; located at Lenox Square and Perimeter Mall; an upscale national department store chain that got its start in New York's Lower East Side in the 1860s. Personal shoppers or interior designers are available.
- **J.C. Penney**, 800-322-1189, www.jcpenney.com; multiple locations throughout metro Atlanta, chock full of all the usual department store stuff for your home and you.
- **Neiman Marcus**, 404-266-8200, 800-555-5077, www.neiman marcus.com; located at Lenox Square; this posh department store offers an elegant collection of home goods, clothing, shoes, beauty items, gifts, shoes, etc., from the best designers. Come here for Manolo Blahnik shoes, Prada bags, Dolce & Gabbana dresses, and more.
- **Parisian**, 800-424-8185, www.parisian.com; six locations in metro Atlanta, including Phipps Plaza, Northlake, Northpoint, and Gwinnett Place Mall. This mid-priced department store prides itself on its attention to customer service. Shoppers here can expect to find a wide selection of items for the home, gifts, clothing, makeup, and more.
- **Rich's-Macy's**, 404-231-2800, 770-434-2611, www.richsmacys.com; eight locations in metro Atlanta, including Lenox Square, South DeKalb, Greenbriar, and Cumberland Mall. Rich's-Macy's is a solid, mid-range store with a large variety of items for the home, gifts, clothing, makeup, perfume, shoes, wedding registry, etc.
- **Saks Fifth Avenue**, 404-261-7234; www.saksincorporated.com; located at Phipps Plaza. Another of the nation's finest department stores, Saks has a large selection of upscale goods.
- **Sears**, 800-349-4358, www.sears.com; several locations throughout metro Atlanta, including Southlake, Cumberland, and Northlake Mall. The original department store, Sears is the place for refrigerators, lawn-mowers, toolkits, washers and dryers, etc. And don't forget the automotive centers.

DISCOUNT DEPARTMENT STORES

- **Kmart**, 866-562-7848, www.kmart.com; eight locations throughout the metro Atlanta area
- **Loehmann's**, 404-633-4156, www.loehmanns.com; located at 2480 Briarcliff Road, Atlanta

- **Marshall's**, 888-MARSHALLS, www.marshallsonline.com; five locations throughout metro Atlanta, including Buckhead, Sandy Springs, and Smyrna
- **Target**, 800-440-0680, www.target.com; many in metro Atlanta, including several Super Target and Target Greatland stores
- **Wal-Mart**, 800-925-6278, www.walmart.com; throughout metro Atlanta, including Dunwoody, Tucker, Marietta, and Roswell

HOUSEHOLD SHOPPING

Once you've found your dream home, furnishings may be in order. From appliances to rugs, lamps, beds and bedding, or wallpaper, the following resources will get you started.

APPLIANCES/ELECTRONICS/CAMERAS/COMPUTERS

The Atlanta Yellow Pages lists numerous authorized appliance and electronics dealers and stores. In the Sunday edition of the *Atlanta Journal-Constitution* you can find pullout advertisements for all the major stores in the city; for computer dealers in particular, check the "Personal Technology" section.

- **Apex Supply Company**, 404-262-0562, www.apexsupply.com; three showrooms in metro Atlanta, including Buckhead, Marietta, and Alpharetta
- **Atlanta Computer Systems**, Colton Drive, Atlanta, 404-256-4661, www.atlantacomputersystems.com; specializes in buying and reselling used computer systems and hardware
- **Best Buy**, 888-237-8289, www.bestbuy.com; throughout metro Atlanta
- **Bob Carroll Appliance Co.**, 2122 North Decatur Road, Decatur, 404-634-2411, http://bobcarroll.homeappliances.com; neighborhood appliance store located in Decatur
- **Circuit City**, 800-843-2489, www.circuitcity.com; throughout metro Atlanta
- **CompUSA**, 800-266-7872,www.compusa.com; metro Atlanta
- **Home Depot Expo**, 404-442-1600; www.expo.com; three locations in Metro Atlanta, including Buckhead, Alpharetta, and Perimeter Mall
- **Home Depot**, 800-553-3199, www.homedepot.com; locations throughout metro Atlanta
- **Howard Payne Company**, 3583-D Chamblee Tucker Road, Chamblee, 770-451-0136, www.howardpayne.com; family-owned and -operated kitchen appliance store
- **Lowe's**, 800-445-6937, www.lowes.com; throughout metro Atlanta

- **MicroSeconds**, Sandy Springs, 404-252-7221; Duluth, 770-232-1011, www.microseconds.com; specializing in buying and selling of slightly used computer equipment
- **Office Depot**, 800-GO-DEPOT, www.officedepot.com; locations throughout metro Atlanta
- **Radio Shack**, 800-843-7422, www.radioshack.com; throughout metro Atlanta
- **Staples**, 800-3-STAPLE, www.staples.com; locations throughout metro Atlanta
- **Tippens Appliance & Furniture**, 229 Moreland Avenue SE, Atlanta, 404-521-1676, www.tippensappl-furn.com

BEDS, BEDDING & BATH

- **Bed, Bath and Beyond**, 800-462-3966; www.bedbathandbeyond.com; ten locations in metro Atlanta
- **Bed Down**, 504 Amsterdam Avenue NE, Atlanta, 404-872-3696, www.beddown.com; specializes in luxurious designer linens, beds, and gorgeous bedroom collections
- **The Great Futon Port**, 6576 Dawson Boulevard, Norcross, 770-448-9200, www.thegreatfutonport.com; sells futons, frames, and other home furnishings
- **Home Concepts Futon Superstore**, 404-885-1505, Atlanta; 770-448-8425, Norcross, www.atlantafutons.com; sells futons of varying sizes, as well a wide selection of frames and other home furnishings
- **The Home Store Futon Gallery**, 404-586-9647, Little Five Points; 770-973-1474, Kennesaw, http://thsfutongallery.com; hip futon store specializing in futons of varying sizes and styles as well as contemporary home furnishings
- **Mattress Firm**, 800-MAT-FIRM; www.mattressfirm.com; several locations in metro Atlanta
- **National Mattress & Furniture Warehouse**, 1240 Old Chattahoochee Avenue, Atlanta, 404-351-6760
- **Linens and Things**, 866-568-7378, www.lnt.com; several locations throughout metro Atlanta
- **Linen Supermarket**, Cheshire Bridge Road, Atlanta, 404-636-9157; Memorial Drive, Stone Mountain, 404-508-8535; offers a wide selection of linens at discount prices
- **Waterbed Concepts**, 770-427-3382, Marietta; 770-993-0708, Roswell, www.waterbedconcepts.com

CARPETS & RUGS

- **Allan Arthur Oriental Rugs**, 25 Bennett Street, Atlanta, 404-350-9560, 800-686-7030, www.cyberrug.com
- **Alpha Rug Expo**, 4820 Atlanta Highway, Alpharetta, 770-753-9878, www.alpharugexpo.com
- **Atlanta Carpet Center**, 1105 Parkside Lane, Woodstock, 770-517-5255, www.atlantacarpetcenter.com
- **Atlanta Carpet Center Outlet**, 2673 Canton Road, Marietta, 678-594-4774, www.atlantacarpetcenter.com
- **Bell Carpet Galleries**, 6223 Roswell Road, Atlanta, 404-255-2431, www.bellcarpetgalleries.com
- **Buckhead Yamin's Oriental Rugs**, 3252 Peachtree Road, Atlanta, 404-231-1727, http://yamins.com
- **Carpet Depot**, 770-987-2099, Decatur; 770-736-7361, Snellville; 770-889-9753, Cumming; www.carpet-depot.com
- **Dalton Carpets**, 770-457-7223, Chamblee; 770-643-8236, Roswell; www.daltoncarpets.com
- **Dalton Rug**, 5900 Sugarloaf Parkway, Atlanta, 678-847-5150, www.daltonrug.com
- **Oriental Designer Rugs**, 560-A Amsterdam Avenue, Atlanta, 404-881-8979, www.orientaldesignerrug.com

FURNITURE

To view a lot of furniture in a short time, take I-85 to the Jimmy Carter Boulevard exit. On Dawson Boulevard (the service road on the east side of I-85) is a long row of giant furniture showrooms showcasing a variety of styles of furniture in a wide range of prices. Here are a few other options:

- **By Design**, 404-607-9098, Midtown; 770-840-8832, Norcross; www.bydesignfurniture.com
- **Crate and Barrel**, 800-967-6696, www.crateandbarrel.com; four locations in metro Atlanta
- **Ethan Allen**, 888-EAHELP1; www.ethanallen.com; three locations in metro Atlanta
- **Home Concepts Futon Superstore**, 404-885-1505, Atlanta; 770-448-8425, Norcross, www.atlantafutons.com
- **The Home Store Futon Gallery**, 404-586-9647, Little Five Points; 770-973-1474, Kennesaw, http://thsfutongallery.com
- **House of Denmark**, 6248 Dawson Boulevard NW, Norcross, 770-449-5740; www.houseofdenmark.com

- **Huff Furniture**, 3178 Peachtree Road, Atlanta, 404-261-7636; www.hufffurniture.com
- **Jennifer Convertibles**, 404-351-2919, Atlanta; 770-425-2207, Kennesaw; 770-640-6966, Roswell; 770-469-7939, Stone Mountain; www.jenniferfurniture.com
- **Rooms To Go**, 888-709-5380, www.roomstogo.com; locations throughout metro Atlanta
- **Storehouse**, 888-786-7346, www.storehouse.com; locations throughout metro Atlanta, including clearance centers in Buckhead and Norcross

HOUSEWARES

- **Bed, Bath and Beyond**, 800-462-3966, www.bedbathandbeyond. com; locations throughout metro Atlanta
- **Crate and Barrel**, 800-967-6696, www.crateandbarrel.com; four locations in metro Atlanta
- **Linens and Things**, 866-568-7378, www.lnt.com; locations throughout metro Atlanta
- **Linen Supermarket**, Cheshire Bridge Road, Atlanta, 404-636-9157; Memorial Drive, Stone Mountain, 404-508-8535
- **Pier One Imports**, 800-245-4595, www.pier1.com; throughout metro Atlanta
- **Pottery Barn**, 888-779-5176, www.potterybarn.com; six locations in metro Atlanta, including Lenox Square, Northpoint Mall, and the Mall of Georgia
- **Williams-Sonoma**, 877-812-6235, www.williamssonoma.com; eight locations in metro Atlanta, including a Williams-Sonoma Clearance Center at the North Georgia Premium Outlet Mall

LAMPS & LIGHTING

- **Aaron's Lamp & Shade Center**, 3529 Northside Parkway, Atlanta, 404-231-2160
- **Georgia Lighting**, 530 Fourteenth Street, Atlanta, 404-875-4754, www.georgialighting.com
- **Lamp Arts, Inc.**, 1465-A Howell Mill Road, Atlanta, 404-352-5211, www.lampartsinc.com
- **Lamps N' Things**, 1205 Johnson Ferry Road NE, Marietta, 770-971-0874
- **Lux Lighting**, 5900 State Bridge Road, Alpharetta, 770-476-4028, www.lampsbylux.com

- **Sunlighting Lamp and Shade Center**, 4990 Roswell Road NE, Atlanta, 404-257-0043
- **Vinings Lighting**, 2810 Paces Ferry Road, Atlanta, 770-801-9600, www.viningslighting.com

HARDWARE/PAINTS/WALLPAPER/GARDEN CENTERS

Atlanta is the corporate headquarters of **Home Depot**, a national chain of home improvement warehouses ready to supply you with just about anything you would ever need to fix up your home or apartment. Bring your imagination and a comfortable pair of shoes; you might spend all day there. Below is contact information for Home Depot, **Lowe's**, and local **Ace** and **True Value** stores:

- **Home Depot**, 800-553-3199, www.homedepot.com; over ten locations in metro Atlanta including several in Decatur, Marietta Roswell and the city of Atlanta
- **Home Depot Expo**, 404-442-1600; www.expo.com; located in Buckhead, Alpharetta, and Perimeter Mall
- **Lowe's Home Improvement Warehouse**, 800-445-6937, www.lowes.com; 15 locations in metro Atlanta, including Alpharetta, Chamblee, Lilburn, and Marietta
- **ACE Hardware**: 866-290-5334; over 30 neighborhood locations throughout metro Atlanta. Some are listed here, others can be found online at www.acehardware.com.
- **Bates Ace Hardware**, 1709 Howell Mill Road NW, Atlanta, 404-351-4240
- **Community Ace Hardware**, 1316 Dunwoody Village Parkway, Dunwoody, 770-394-6938
- **East Atlanta Ace Hardware**, 1231 Glenwood Avenue SE, 404-627-5757
- **Gwinnett Ace Hardware**, 4624 Jimmy Carter Boulevard, Norcross, 770-934-0200
- **Intown Ace Hardware**, 854 North Highland Avenue NE, Atlanta, 404-874-5619
- **Mid-Town Ace Hardware**, 626 Glen Iris Drive, Atlanta, 404-872-6651
- **Smith Ace Hardware**, 601 East College Avenue, Decatur, 404-373-3335
- **The Workbench Ace Hardware**, 2983 North Druid Hills Road, Atlanta, 404-325-8000
- **Workbench Ace Hardware**, 2365 Peachtree Road NE, Atlanta, 404-841-9525
- **True Value**, 773-695-5000; locations throughout the metro Atlanta area. Some are listed here, others can be found online at www.truevalue.com.
- **B & C True Value Hardware**, 2389 Lawrenceville Highway, Lawrenceville, 770-963-5556

- **Howard's True Value Hardware**, 6884 Buford Highway NE, Doraville, 770-449-1819
- **Glazes True Value Hardware**, 3054 Peeler Road, Atlanta, 770-396-4826
- **Greer-Ivy Hardware**, 81 South Peachtree Street, Norcross, 770-448-3934
- **Sandy Springs True Value Hardware**, 6125 Roswell Road NE, Sandy Springs, 404-255-2151
- **Shallowford True Value Hardware**, 2510 Shallowford Road, Marietta, 770-926-0700
- **Stone Mountain True Value Hardware**, 6204 Memorial Drive, Stone Mountain, 770-469-2628

SECOND-HAND SHOPPING

If you're someone who enjoys rack-rummaging at thrift stores and looking for treasures at various flea markets and antique shops, then you'll like metro Atlanta—home to hundreds of second-hand stores, antique centers, and indoor flea markets. And because of the mild weather here throughout most of year, outdoor flea markets are abundant as well.

ANTIQUE STORES & AUCTIONS

The undeniable antique capital of metro Atlanta (and some say the South) is **Antique Row**, 404-606-3367, www.antiquerow.com, in Chamblee, located along Peachtree Road, between Chamblee-Dunwoody Road and North Peachtree. Dealers here sell crafts, toys, jewelry, furniture, and a wide variety of collectibles. And with over 15 stores, comprising 500,000 square feet of antiques and collectibles, Antique Row attracts shoppers from all over the state. Well-known establishments, such as **Biggar Antiques**, 770-451-2541, a cool and kitschy shop selling everything from antique signs and furniture to 1950s kitchenware; **China and Crystal Matchers, Inc.**, 800-286-1107, www.chinaandcrystal.com, a company specializing in helping people replace missing or broken items in their discontinued china and crystal patterns; and **Eugenia's**, 770-458-1677, www.eugeniaantique hardware.com, a family-owned, hardware store, carrying authentic antique hardware for the home—no reproductions—are located here. When visiting Antique Row, your best bet is to park and walk. A walking map is available online at the Antique Row web site.

If it's southern antiques and country furniture you're looking for, try **Stone Mountain Village**, 770-938-1200, www.stonemountainvillage. com, located just outside of Georgia's Stone Mountain Park. Many of the stores here are housed in charming historic buildings and feature everything from collectibles and furniture to jewelry and hand-made gifts by Georgia artisans. Some of the more popular spots here are **Stone Mountain Relics**, 770-469-1425, www.stonemountainrelics.com, a Civil War museum and memorabilia shop; **Swan Galleries**, 770-498-9696, specializing in collectible, antique figurines; and the **Stone Mountain General Store**, 770-469-9331, which offers household and kitchen gadgets, garden accessories, bird feeders, souvenirs, and more.

If upscale, high-design antiques are more your taste, and you've got the budget to support that, you will probably want to check out the shops at **Miami Circle**, www.buckhead.org/miamicircle, in Buckhead. Located just off Piedmont Road, a few blocks north of the Lindbergh MARTA station, this little antique and design district is now home to over 80 shops including **Across the Pond Antiques & Interiors**, 404-262-9516, www.acrossthepondantiques.com, specializing in European antiques and furnishings; **Mandarin Antiques**, 404-467-1727, the largest Chinese antiques importer in the southeast; and **Frances Aronson Fine Art**, 404-949-9975, www.francesaronsonfineart.com, a gallery specializing in 19th and early 20th century French and American fine art. Miami Circle is also home to **Eclipse di Luna**, 404-846-0449, www.eclipsediluna.com, a deliciously funky restaurant and tapas bar, perfect for a quick lunch when you've had enough shopping.

In Marietta, the **Historic Shopping Square**, www.marietta square.com, features beautifully restored buildings and warehouses that are now home to nearly 20 collectibles and antiques shops. While here, be sure to visit **Mountain Mercantile**, 770-429-1663, a cozy shop that sells everything from Primitive, Victorian, and American Country art to books, albums, and gift items. You'll also want to check out **King's Row Antiques**, 770-919-7877, a 3,200-square-foot shop featuring quality, solid-wood, antique furniture and home accessories; and the **Church Street Market**, 770-499-9393, a gourmet shop specializing in native Georgia food products, herb baskets, fresh cut garden flowers, heirloom vegetable and flower seeds, and more. To get to the square, take I-75 North from Atlanta to GA 120 West and exit on Marietta Parkway.

To find other antique shops in your neighborhood, check out the Atlanta Yellow Pages under "Antiques." For more information on local and national antique sales and auctions, check out *Maine Antiques Digest*, www.maine antiquesdigest.com. Or visit **Antique Info**, www.antiqueinfo.com.

FLEA MARKETS

Regardless of where you live in metro Atlanta, there is bound to be a flea market of some sort nearby. Most are fairly large and offer just about anything you can imagine. Others are smaller and may specialize in things like antiques and home furnishings. Some of the larger flea markets are listed below, but be sure to check the Atlanta Yellow Pages for more comprehensive listings, and *Creative Loafing* and the *AJC* for weekly updates.

- **Buford Highway Flea Market**, 5000 Buford Highway, Chamblee; open weekends
- **Finders Keepers Antique and Flea Market**, 253 Scenic Highway, Lawrenceville, 770-962-8008; open seven days a week
- **Flatcreek Flea Market**, 3084 Highway 78, Atlanta, 770-466-4223; call for hours
- **Flea Emporium**, 9740 Main Street, Woodstock, 770-592-1177; open daily
- **Georgia Antique Center & Market**, 6624 Dawson Boulevard NE Expressway, Norcross, 404-446-9292; open weekends
- **Glenwood Flea Market**, 3900 Glenwood Road, Decatur, 404-284-9139; call for hours
- **Highway 41 Flea Market**, 3352 Cobb Parkway NW, Acworth, 770-975-0100; open weekends
- **Lakewood Antiques Market**, 404-622-4488, www.lakewood antiques.com; open the second weekend of every month
- **My Favorite Place Flea Market**, 5596 Peachtree Industrial Boulevard, Chamblee, 770-452-8397; open daily
- **New South Atlanta Flea Market**, 8160 Tara Boulevard, Jonesboro, 770-603-9944; call for hours
- **Peachtree Peddler's Flea Market**, 155 Mill Road, McDonough, 770-914-2269, www.peachtreepeddlers.com; open weekends
- **Pride of Dixie Antique Market**, North Atlanta Trade Center, Norcross, 770-279-9899; open 4th weekend of every month
- **Roswell Antique Mall and Flea Market**, 700 Holcomb Bridge Road, Roswell, 770-993-7200; open seven days a week
- **Scott Antiques Market**, Atlanta Expo Center, Atlanta, 770-569-4112; open the second weekend of every month
- **Village Flea Market**, 1216 Columbia Drive, Decatur, 404-289-8959; call for hours

THRIFT & VINTAGE SHOPS

Not only can you find some really cool, inexpensive stuff at thrift stores, but local charities and organizations often benefit from the proceeds. What could be better than shopping for a cause, and saving a little money? The following are some of the most popular and well-stocked thrift stores in metro Atlanta. Keep in mind, they're all generally busiest on the weekends, and most put out their new items on Tuesdays. Knowing the store's schedule can help you get a jump on other shoppers who may be looking for the same special item you are.

- **America's Thrift Store**, 3344 Canton Highway, Marietta, 770-423-0094; 7055-C Highway 85, Riverdale, 770-996-5900; 3870 Lawrenceville Highway, Lawrenceville, 770-279-1717; www.americas thrift.com
- **Amvets Thrift Store**, 3651 Memorial Drive, Decatur, 404-286-1083
- **Another Man's Treasure Thrift Store & Flea Market**, 707 East Lake Drive, Decatur, 404-373-8950
- **Budget Helper Shop**, 2524 Caldwell Road NE, Atlanta, 404-237-8481, www.stmartins.org/budget.htm
- **Goodwill Thrift Stores**, 2201 Glenwood Avenue SE, Atlanta, 404-373-5815; 888 Ralph David Abernathy Boulevard SW, Atlanta, 404-755-6440; www.ging.org
- **Last Chance Thrift Store**, 1977 S. Cobb Drive, Marietta, 770-433-3322; 201 Norcross Tucker Road, Norcross, 770-662-5616; 1709 Church Street, Decatur, 404-296-1711; www.lastchancethriftstore.com
- **St. Vincent de Paul Thrift Store**, 2050 Chamblee Tucker Road, Chamblee, 770-576-4082; 3256 Buford Highway, Duluth, 770-622-9533; 4687 Rockbridge Road, Stone Mountain, 404-292-4102, www.svdpatl.org
- **Second Chance Thrift Shop**, 205 Hilderbrand Drive NE, Atlanta, 404-303-0364
- **Cathedral Thrift House**, 2581 Piedmont Road, Suite A-700, Atlanta, 404-233-8652
- **Value Village**, 1320 Moreland Avenue, Atlanta, 770-840-7283, www.valuevillage.com

FOOD

Metro Atlanta is home to a healthy offering of supermarkets, warehouse shopping, farmers' markets, and health food and specialty stores. Have fun stocking your kitchen with all your favorites!

SUPERMARKETS

The major grocery store chains in the Atlanta area are **Kroger**, **Publix**, and **Whole Foods**.
- **Kroger**, 866-221-4141, www.kroger.com; known as a 24-hour, one-stop shop in Atlanta, with most of its 50+ locations providing pharmacy services, film developing, banking, cafés, and health food departments in addition to grocery items. Some stores even have gas stations in the parking lot, offering lower gas prices to Kroger Plus members.

- **Publix**, 800-242-1227, www.publix.com; offers a wide selection of produce and grocery items, banking and pharmacy services at most locations, and publishes a free monthly health-food guide, *Greenwise*. Their Publix Apron's program, designed to inspire customers to discover the joys of cooking, through in-store demonstrations and cooking classes, recipe cards, and meal-planning assistance, is popular.
- **Whole Foods**, www.wholefoods.com; this Texas-based natural foods supermarket debuted in Atlanta in the late 1990s in the Emory area, and two more were quickly added in Midtown and Sandy Springs. Whole Foods then went on to purchase the popular Atlanta-based Harry's Farmers Markets. Today, there are six Whole Foods/Harry's locations throughout the metro Atlanta area, offering organic meats, produce, and dairy items, fresh food cafés, kosher bakeries, sushi, and more.

WAREHOUSE SHOPPING

If you have a huge crowd to feed, then buying in bulk may be for you. In metro Atlanta, there are two chain stores (each with several locations) that offer residents the warehouse shopping experience for a membership fee. Whether you are in the market for jumbo cans of corn or cases of paper towels, these stores are sure to meet all your bulk shopping needs.

- **Costco Wholesale**, 800-220-6000, www.costco.com; four locations throughout metro Atlanta
- **Sam's Club**, 888-746-7726, www.samsclub.com; over ten locations throughout metro Atlanta

FARMERS' MARKETS

A favorite shopping place of many Atlantans is the **DeKalb Farmers' Market**, an immense indoor market with an amazing and often inexpensive array of produce, not to mention cheeses, meats, seafood, coffee, and other exotic foods from around the world. **Whole Foods Harry's Farmers Markets** tend to attract an upscale clientele, with beautiful produce, cheeses, and organic meats, with prices to match.

Other popular markets include the **Atlanta State Farmers' Market** in Forest Park, and the many outdoor, neighborhood "tailgate" markets scattered throughout the city, particularly between June and October. Following is a listing of the best-known and established markets in and around metro Atlanta:

- **Atlanta State Farmers' Market**, 16 Forest Parkway, Forest Park, 404-675-1782, www.agr.state.ga.us/html/atlanta_farmers_market. html; 150-acre, open-air market, open year-round

- **Covington Square Market**, 1169 Washington Street, Covington, 770-784-1718, www.squaremarket.com; open-air market, located on the square in Covington, open Fridays 4 p.m. to dusk, through October
- **DeKalb Farmers' Market**, 3000 East Ponce De Leon Avenue, Decatur, 404-377-6400, www.dekalbfarmersmarket.com; open daily, year round from 9 a.m. to 9 p.m.
- **Downtown Decatur Market**, Decatur Square, behind the old courthouse, 404-377-0894, www.decaturfarmersmarket.com; weekly, outdoor farmers' market, open Wednesdays 10:30 a.m. to 1:30 p.m., through December
- **Farmers' Market at Spruill Gallery**, 4681 Ashford-Dunwoody Road, Dunwoody, 770-394-4019, www.spruillarts.org; outdoor market, open Wednesdays, 8 a.m. to 1 p.m., through December
- **Green Market at Piedmont Park**, 1071 Piedmont Avenue, Atlanta, 404-875-7275, www.piedmontpark.org; open-air market, open Saturdays, 8 a.m. to noon, through October
- **Harry's Farmers Market**, Roswell, 770-664-6300; Marietta, 770-578-4400; www.wholefoods.com; local market, owned and operated by Whole Foods. Open daily, year round. Call each location for hours and specials.
- **International Farmers' Market**, 770-455-1777, Chamblee; 770-840-7660, Norcross; http://internationalfarmersmarket.com; both locations open daily, year-round
- **Morningside Farmers' Market**, 1393 North Highland Avenue, Atlanta, 404-444-9902, www.morningsidemarket.com; outdoor market, located in the parking lot next to Horizon Restaurant, open Saturdays 8 a.m. to 11:30 a.m., April through December
- **North Fulton Tailgate Market**, 11913 Wills Road, Alpharetta, 770-551-7670; outdoor market, located in the parking lot next to Wills Park Service Center, open Saturdays 7 a.m. until "sold out," through September

HEALTH FOOD STORES

There is no shortage of health food stores, natural food grocers, and vegetarian cafés in metro Atlanta. For a complete list, check the Atlanta Yellow Pages under "Health and Diet Food Products." Some of the most popular include:
- **ABC Natural Food Outlet**, 4003 Memorial Drive, Decatur, 404-299-1191; natural foods, health and book store
- **Figs & Twigs Health Shop**, 1475 Holcomb Bridge Road, Roswell, 770-642-4534, ww.figsandtwigs.com; health food, vitamin, and nutritional supplement shop

- **The Good Earth**, 211 Pharr Road, Atlanta, 404-266-2929; natural foods store and café
- **Life Grocery**, 1453 Roswell Road, Marietta, 770-977-9583, www.life grocery.com; natural foods co-op, open to the public
- **Mother Nature's Market**, 3853 Lawrenceville Highway, Tucker, 770-491-0970; natural foods market and health shop
- **Nuts 'N Berries**, 4274 Peachtree Road, Atlanta, 404-237-6829; natural foods and supplement store with deli and juice bar
- **Peachtree Natural Foods**, 227 Sandy Springs Place NW, Atlanta, 404-843-2233; 1630 Scenic Highway, Snellville, 770-982-4989; 1000 Peachtree Industrial Boulevard, Suwanee, 770-614-5117; www.peachtreenaturalfoods.com; health food store and co-op, with three locations in metro Atlanta
- **Rainbow Grocery**, 2118 North Decatur Road, Decatur, 404-636-5553; all-vegetarian, health food market
- **Return to Eden**, 2335 Cheshire Bridge Road, Atlanta, 404-320-EDEN, www.return2eden.com; family-owned, all vegetarian, health food supermarket
- **Sevananda Food Co-Op**, 467 Moreland Avenue NE, Atlanta, 404-681-2831, www.sevananda.com; organic food co-op, open to the public
- **Whole Foods**, Atlanta, 404-634-7800; www.wholefoods.com; natural foods supermarket, with six locations in metro Atlanta

ETHNIC DISTRICTS

Metro Atlanta's diverse ethnic populations are generally concentrated in specific areas throughout the city, and it's in these communities that you will find the largest number of ethnic specialty stores. For example, those in the market for Asian products should head over to Buford Highway and New Peachtree Road, near DeKalb Peachtree Airport in Chamblee. Here, you'll find authentic Asian restaurants, strip malls, and grocery stores, as well as the **Chinese Community Center**, 770-454-9167. Some of the most popular spots for dining, shopping, and socializing in this part of town include **Chinatown Square**, 770-458-6660, www.atlantachina town.com; **Hae Woon Dae Korean BBQ**, 770-458-6999; the **Oriental Food Mart**, 770-457-5666; and the **Hong Kong Supermarket**, 404-325-3999 to name just a few. You'll also find that many of the ethnic grocers in this area carry hard-to-find Indian, Mexican, and Japanese ingredients as well. To find out more about Asian shopping and dining, check out **Asian Business Community in Atlanta** online, www. abcatl.com.

The North Druid Hills and Toco Hills communities are both home to a large Indian and Pakistani population. In these neighborhoods, where North Druid Hills intersects with Briarcliff Road, LaVista Road, Clairmont Road, and then Lawrenceville Highway, you'll find a great selection of Indian clothing stores, food markets, and restaurants. Some of the most popular shops and restaurants here include **Madras Saravana Bhavan**, 404-636-4400, www.madrassaravanabhavan.net, considered by many to be the best South Indian restaurant in town; **Texas Sari Sapne**, 404-633-7274; and **Al-Huda Groceries**, 678-205-5252. For more information about Indian shopping and dining in Atlanta, visit **India in Atlanta**, www.indiainatlanta.com.

Though the intown neighborhoods, particularly in DeKalb County, boast the largest international population, it's not uncommon to find authentic ethnic restaurants, shops, and grocery stores scattered throughout metro Atlanta. In recent years, Gwinnett County, in particular, has attracted a large number of Asian and Indian residents, many of whom have opened businesses along Jimmy Carter Boulevard, including **Ladlee Sarees**, 678-357-8812; **Spices House**, 678-969-9797; and **Amrutha Indian Restaurant**, 770-246-0093, www.amrutha-atlanta.com. Jimmy Carter Boulevard is also home to the **Global Mall**, www.amsglobalmall.com, a 220,000-square-foot shopping center full of Indian and Asian restaurants, movie rental stores, clothing boutiques, and more.

Back along Buford Highway, towards the intersection of Buford Highway and Clairmont Road, many from the Hispanic community shop at the **Plaza Fiesta**, 404-982-9138, www.plazafiesta.net, a 380,000-square-foot shopping center, billing itself as *"the* shopping center for the Latin family."* Plaza Fiesta prides itself on offering warm and friendly service, authentic Mexican- and Latin-American restaurants, and nearly 200 shops and kiosks, selling "a great variety of items not easily found anywhere else in the US." For more information about the Hispanic community in metro Atlanta, go online to **Atlanta Latino**, www.atlantalatino.com.

WELCOME TO THE ARTS! WHETHER IT'S HIGH-CALIBER performances in music, dance, or theater, or a tour of the visual arts you're wanting, it's all here. As the center for culture and arts in the southeast, Atlanta is particularly proud of the Woodruff Arts Center, which houses several of the area's fine arts institutions, including the internationally acclaimed Atlanta Symphony Orchestra, the Alliance Theatre Company, and the High Museum of Art. Theatrical performances, from touring Broadway shows and Shakespearean drama to traditional ballet performances and classical opera, are readily available in the metro region. And, if your taste is more suited toward student lab productions, puppet shows, or off-the-beaten-path theater productions, such as "Hamlet, The Musical," you will be certain to find a venue that suits you. Local museums exhibit a wide assortment of visual arts—African-American, ancient, folk, and high Renaissance, to name a few, and area galleries are a great place to browse for funky local talent. Local music establishments host a variety of touring and local acts, from jazz, blues, acoustic, and punk to big band and reggae. And, finally, Atlanta has a thriving literary and intellectual community, which hosts lecture series, author readings, and book signings.

To take advantage and enjoy metro Atlanta's diverse cultural offerings, refer to the *AJC*, which publishes a "Weekend" section every Friday alerting readers to the goings-on about town. In addition, the weekly *Creative Loafing* is an excellent source of information on artistic endeavors of all kinds: Check its articles, reviews, and event listings in the "Happenings" section. Also, the following contacts can point you in the right direction for art events:

- **Arts at Emory**, 404-727-5050, www.emory.edu/arts; information on current and upcoming art, theater, and musical events sponsored by Emory University

- **Arts Hotline**, 404-853-3ART; provides updated information on current and upcoming cultural events throughout metro Atlanta
- **Atlanta Symphony Orchestra Recorded Information**, 404-733-4949; updated information on current and upcoming ASO concerts and events

TICKETS

Tickets for most major events and performances can be purchased at the venue box office or at any **Ticketmaster** location. You can also charge by phone with Ticketmaster at 404-249-6400 or visit www.ticketmaster.com. **Empire Tickets** (formerly Ticketline) specializes in hard-to-get tickets. Contact them at 404-255-2020, www.empiretickets.com, for more information. It's usually a good idea to get tickets as far in advance as possible, as many shows, concerts, exhibits, and events sell out quickly. When calling ahead, make sure you have your credit card ready and be prepared to pay service charges, usually between $5 and $10 per ticket. If you prefer to avoid the service charges, buy your tickets directly from the box office (cash or credit card only).

PERFORMANCE VENUES:
CONCERT HALLS, STADIUMS, AND ARENAS

The following concert venues are the largest in metro Atlanta. They play host to a variety of concerts each year—from rock, to country, to classical, and everything in between. When big-named acts and national and international performers come to town, these are the places they play, though you may also catch some of the better-known local bands here as well. For information about upcoming shows, ticket prices, and seating, contact each venue directly.

- **Atlanta Civic Center**, 395 Piedmont Avenue, 404-523-6275, www.atlantaciviccenter.com
- **Chastain Park Amphitheater**, 4469 Stella Drive NW, Atlanta, 404-233-2227, www.atlantaconcerts.com/chastain.html
- **Coca-Cola Roxy**, 3110 Roswell Road, Atlanta, 404-233-7699, www.atlantaconcerts.com/roxy.html
- **Earthlink Live**, 1374 West Peachtree Street, 404-885-1365, www.earthlinklive.com
- **The Fox Theatre**, 660 Peachtree Street, Atlanta, 404-881-2100, www.foxtheatre.org
- **The Georgia Dome**, One Georgia Dome Drive, Atlanta, 404-223-9200, www.gadome.com

- **Georgia State University Concert Hall**, 404-651-4636, or www. music.gsu.edu/events.aspx
- **The Gwinnett Civic Center Arena**, 6400 Sugarloaf Parkway, Duluth, 770-813-7500, www.gwinnettciviccenter.com
- **HiFi Buys Lakewood Amphitheater**, 2002 Lakewood Way, Atlanta, 404-443-5090, www.hob.com/venues/concerts/hifibuys
- **Philips Arena**, One Philips Drive, Atlanta 404-878-3000, www.philips arena.com
- **Rialto Center for the Performing Arts**, 80 Forsyth Street at Luckie Street, Atlanta, 404-651-1234, www.rialtocenter.org
- **Spivey Hall**, 5900 North Lee Street, Clayton State College, 770-961-3683, www.spiveyhall.org
- **Variety Playhouse**, 1099 Euclid Avenue, Atlanta, 404-524-7354, www.variety-playhouse.com
- **Woodruff Arts Center** at 1293 Peachtree Street, Atlanta, 404-733-5000, www.woodruffcenter.org.

PERFORMING ARTS

PROFESSIONAL MUSIC–SYMPHONIC, CHORAL, OPERA, CHAMBER

ATLANTA SYMPHONY ORCHESTRA

Debuting in 1945 as the Atlanta Youth Symphony, and then changing its name in 1947, the Atlanta Symphony Orchestra (ASO), www.atlanta symphony.org, is one of the youngest American orchestras to achieve international prominence. The ASO is also part of the Robert W. Woodruff Arts Center, which includes the **Alliance Theatre Company**, the **High Museum of Art**, and the **Atlanta College of Art**. The ASO is particularly proud of its 15 Grammy Awards, earned from over 40 recordings. The ASO plays its regular season in Symphony Hall, located in the **Woodruff Arts Center** at 1293 Peachtree Street NE, Atlanta, 404-733-5000, www.woodruffcenter.org.

The regular symphony season runs from September through May, but the ASO stays busy throughout the year, giving over 200 performances in all. During the regular season, you can choose from 24 Classical Master Season programs, a Saturday Matinee Series entitled "Four @ 2:00," a Family Concert Series, or a series of Champagne and Coffee concerts featuring popular classics. During the summer months the ASO offers SummerFest, a casual series of concerts centered on a particular composer or theme, which take place in Symphony Hall. You can also attend the ASO's Classic Chastain and Country Chastain summer concerts, which are held at the **Chastain Park Amphitheatre**, 4469 Stella Drive NW in Atlanta. (Visit www.classicchastain.org for more information.) In addition, the symphony puts on a series of free outdoor concerts in Atlanta's city parks, which attract thousands of people with blankets and picnics.

You can purchase **ASO tickets** several ways:

- **By phone**: To charge tickets by phone call 404-733-4800 for full or partial season subscriptions, 404-733-5000 for individual tickets, or 404-733-4848 for group rates. There is an additional fee for this service.
- **In person**: Purchase tickets at the High Museum Store in Perimeter Mall, but they will charge you the same additional fee as you would pay by charging them over the phone. If you purchase tickets at the box office at the Woodruff Arts Center, you will save yourself the cost of the fee. Box office hours are 10 a.m. to 8 p.m., Monday–Friday, and noon to 8 p.m. Saturday and Sunday.
- **Rush tickets** are available for every Thursday night performance of the Master Season Program. You can pay $15 at the box office for whatever remaining seats they have. They sell the tickets starting at 5 p.m. the afternoon of the performance.
- **Sneak preview open rehearsals**: For a few season concerts each year you can see the program for only $10 general admission. These rehearsals typically occur in the mornings. Call the box office, 404-733-5000, for information.

ATLANTA SYMPHONY ORCHESTRA CHORUS AND CHAMBER CHORUS

The ASO Chorus was established under the musical direction of Robert Shaw during the 1967-68 orchestra season. Today, the ASO Chorus is made up of 200 singers that perform with the Atlanta Symphony Orchestra, and the Chamber Chorus is made up of a select group of approximately 60 vocalists that perform both with the Atlanta Symphony Orchestra and independently.

For more information on the ASO Chorus and Chamber Chorus, call 404-733-4876, or visit them online at www.asochorus.org.

ATLANTA BRASS QUINTET

This quintet is the oldest chamber ensemble in Atlanta, and has developed an international reputation by touring Denmark and Norway and playing for such dignitaries as Prince Charles of England. The Atlanta Brass Quintet offers a varied repertoire, from Baroque music to theatrical pieces, performing regularly at Georgia State University's Recital Hall and throughout the USA. Call 404-875-TUBA for more information.

ATLANTA LYRIC THEATRE

The Atlanta Lyric Theatre (formerly the Savoyards Light Opera) performs several fully staged, professional light operas and a handful of smaller, alternative musical theatre productions each year. For more information, contact them at 2221 Peachtree Road NE, Atlanta, 404-377-9948, www.atlantalyrictheatre.com.

ATLANTA OPERA

Since the late 19th century, the City of Atlanta has been home to an assortment of opera companies. The present-day Atlanta Opera has been in existence since 1985, when it changed its name from the Atlanta Civic Opera and appointed William Fred Scott as Artistic Director. Today this nationally acclaimed company offers four main stage productions each season. Recent shows have included Beethoven's *Fidelio, La Boheme, Aida,* and Gershwin's *Porgy and Bess.* Opera performances take place at the Atlanta Civic Center. For ticket information or to be added to the Atlanta Opera's mailing list, call 404-881-8801, or go online to www.atlantaopera.org.

COMMUNITY MUSIC—SYMPHONIC, CHAMBER

Many local musicians are keeping the community-based orchestra tradition alive in metro Atlanta. The following list is just a sampling of local community orchestras.

ALPHARETTA CITY BAND

The Alpharetta City Band is a traditional community band made up of amateur adult and high school–aged musicians. They play a variety of music ranging from marches to big band jazz. Performances are held at various locations throughout north metro Atlanta. Contact them at 770-475-9684, for more details.

ATLANTA CONCERT BAND

The Atlanta Concert Band performs free to the general public at various locations throughout metro Atlanta or at special events. Funded by donations and the Fulton County Board of Commissioners, this North Atlanta community band provides an outlet for adult musicians to maintain and improve their musical skills and talents. Contact them at 404-237-9711 for more information.

ATLANTA WIND SYMPHONY

The Atlanta Wind Symphony was established in 1979 and is composed of adult musicians ranging in experience from professional to hobbyist. The AWS Master Concert Series is made up of five core events and is performed annually at the **Roswell Cultural Arts Center**, 770-594-6232, www.ci.roswell.ga.us. They also play various outdoor venues and special events throughout the year. Call 770-641-1260, or visit them online at www.atlantawindsymphony.org for more information.

EMORY COMMUNITY BRASS ENSEMBLE

The Emory Community Brass Ensemble is a 20-piece community ensemble composed of students, semi-professionals, and amateur adult musicians. Rehearsals are held weekly in White Hall on the Emory University Campus, and concerts are held in Emory University's **Glenn Memorial Auditorium**, 1652 North Decatur Road, http://arts.emory.edu. The musical director is Michael Moore, Principal Tuba of the Atlanta Symphony Orchestra and Brass Lecturer at Emory University. Call 404-875-TUBA for more information.

DANCE PERFORMANCES—BALLET, JAZZ, MODERN

ATLANTA BALLET

The Atlanta Ballet started in 1929 at the Fox Theatre, where they still present their production of "The Nutcracker" each Christmas season. The ballet's regular season shows are held at the **Atlanta Civic Center**, www.atlantaciviccenter.com, located at the corner of Piedmont Avenue and Ralph McGill Boulevard. Here, this internationally acclaimed company performs five or six ballets each season, including classical productions like *Romeo and Juliet* and *Swan Lake,* alongside modern and innovative pieces such as *Shed Your Skin/The Indigo Girls Project* and *Dracula.* The Atlanta Ballet also travels internationally, performing for audiences around the world. The Atlanta Ballet box office is located at 1400 West Peachtree Street NW, Atlanta. For schedule and season ticket information, contact the box office at 404-892-3303, or visit the Atlanta Ballet online at www.atlantaballet.com. Individual tickets can be purchased through TicketMaster, 404-249-6400, www.ticketmaster.com.

BALLETHNIC DANCE COMPANY

The Ballethnic Dance Company, 2587 Cheney Street, East Point, 404-762-1416, http://ballethnic.org, which celebrated its 15th season in 2005, is metro Atlanta's premier dance company, renowned for its mixing of rhythms of African dance with the precise techniques of classical ballet. The company performs various original pieces throughout the year, including their annual *Urban Nutcracker.*

BEACON DANCE COMPANY

The Beacon Dance Company, headquartered in the **Beacon Hill Arts Center**, 410 West Trinity Place, Decatur, is a contemporary dance troupe that regularly performs at various venues throughout metro Atlanta. For more information, call 404-377-2929 or go online to www.beacondance.org.

DANCERS' COLLECTIVE OF ATLANTA

While this innovative dance company does not yet have a permanent home, it still manages to put on amazing performances at various venues around town, including the **Rialto Center**, www.rialtocenter.org. It also plays host to numerous visiting contemporary companies and choreographers, emerging artists, and established national troupes. For more information contact the collective at 404-233-7600.

THEATER—PROFESSIONAL AND COMMUNITY

Metro Atlanta doesn't technically have a theater district, but it does have a theater scene. Forty theaters throughout the Atlanta metro area form the **Atlanta Coalition of Performing Arts**, 404-873-1185, www.atlantaperforms.com, which produces a wide variety of shows in various neighborhood locales. Though you will find expensive visiting Broadway productions in a few theaters, for the most part, Atlanta's theater scene offers a variety of smaller, more affordable productions.

- **Actor's Express**, 887 West Marietta Street NW, Atlanta, 404-875-1606, www.actors-express.com; box office 404-607-7469
- **Alliance Theatre Company**, Woodruff Arts Center, 1280 Peachtree Street NE, Atlanta, 404-733-5000, www.alliancetheatre.org
- **Atlanta Shakespeare Company**, 499 Peachtree Street NE, Atlanta, 404-874-9219, www.shakespearetavern.com

- **Aurora Theatre Company**, 3087 Main Street, Duluth, 770-476-7926, http://auroratheatre.com
- **Class Act Theatre**, 25 Powder Springs Street, Marietta, 770-579-3156, www.classacttheatre.com
- **Georgia Ensemble Theatre**, Roswell Cultural Arts Center, 770-641-1260, www.get.org
- **Georgia Tech Theatre for the Arts**, 349 Ferst Drive NW, Atlanta, 404-894-9600, www.ferstcenter.gatech.edu
- **Horizon Theatre Company**, 1083 Austin Avenue NE, Atlanta, 404-584-7450, www.horizontheatre.com
- **Neighborhood Playhouse**, 430 West Trinity Place, Decatur, 404-373-5311, www.nplayhouse.org
- **Onstage Atlanta**, 420 Courtland Street NE, Atlanta, 404-872-8427, www.onstageatlanta.com; box office 404-897-1802
- **Push Push Theater**, 121 New Street, Decatur, 404-377-6332, www.pushpushtheater.com
- **Seven Stages**, 1105 Euclid Avenue NE, Atlanta, 404-523-7647, www.7stages.org
- **Stage Door Players**, 5339 Chamblee-Dunwoody Road, Dunwoody, 770-396-1726, www.mindspring.com/~stagedoorplayers
- **Theater Emory**, Emory University, Atlanta, 404-727-6187, www.theater.emory.edu
- **Theatre Gael**, 173 Fourteenth Street NE, Atlanta, 404-733-4750, www.theatregael.com
- **Theatrical Outfit**, 84 Luckie Street, Atlanta, 678-528-1500, www.theatricaloutfit.org
- **Whole World Theatre**, 1214 Spring Street, Atlanta, 404-817-0880, www.wholeworldtheatre.com

FILM

Metro Atlanta is home to a few good, alternative movie houses. If you are interested in foreign films, art house flicks, documentaries, or classic B-movies, the theaters below will probably have what you are looking for. If you're looking for mainstream, Hollywood movies, refer to the Atlanta Yellow Pages under "Theaters" for general multi-screen movie complexes.

- **Garden Hills Cinema**, 2835 Peachtree Street, Atlanta, 404-266-2202, www.lefonttheaters.com
- **Plaza Theater**, 1049 Ponce de Leon Avenue, Atlanta, 404-873-1939, www.lefonttheaters.com

- **Tara Cinema**, 2345 Cheshire Bridge Road NE, 404-634-6288
- **Fernbank Museum of Natural History IMAX Theatre**, 767 Clifton Road NE, Atlanta, 404-370-0019, www.fernbank.edu
- **IMAGE Film and Video Center**, 535 Means Street, Atlanta, 404-352-4225, www.imagefv.org
- Various departments at **Emory University** regularly sponsor film series at White Hall and the Harland Cinema that are open to the public. Contact 404-727-5050, http://arts.emory.edu, for more information.
- The **High Museum** hosts film series in the Hill Auditorium throughout the year. Contact them at 404-733-4570 or www.high.org for details.
- **Cinefest** at Georgia State University is well known for bringing wacky, obscure, and arty films to Atlanta film buffs. To contact Cinefest, call 404-651-2463, or visit them online at www.cinefest.org.

FILM FESTIVALS

- **Atlanta Film and Video Festival**, various locations throughout Atlanta, 404-352-4225, www.imagefv.org; showcases the innovative animation, documentary, experimental, and student works by local, national, and international video and filmmakers. Highlights include screenings of work, educational seminars, guest speakers, and contests.
- **Summer Film Series**, Fox Theatre, Atlanta, 404-881-2100, www.fox theatre.org; each summer the Fox Theatre hosts a series of films, which may include recently released movies, family-oriented movies, and classic films. The schedule changes annually, so be sure to contact the theater for more information.
- **Peachtree International Film Festival**, Phipps Plaza, 770-729-8487, www.peachtreefilm.org; this film festival, showcasing some of the best movies from around the world, is a must for true film lovers.

MUSIC—CONTEMPORARY

Metro Atlanta has a thriving and diverse local music scene, helped out by the success stories of local bands gone big—the Black Crowes, TLC, R.E.M., and The Indigo Girls—and popular R&B artists Usher and Toni Braxton. Atlanta definitely gets its share of major stadium acts, but for an inexpensive night on the town, try out local bands at smaller clubs. *Creative Loafing*, www.creativeloafing.com, publishes a weekly schedule of performances as well as reviews of local talent. The following list of venues is a good place to start your music search, but keep in mind that many of the clubs present different styles of music depending on the night.

BARS AND NIGHTCLUBS

There are a number of really good bars and nightclubs in and around Atlanta, but, without a doubt, the undisputed mecca of Atlanta nightlife and entertainment is the intown community of **Buckhead**. Here you'll find some of the hottest clubs in town, and plenty of them. As mentioned in the **Neighborhoods** chapter, along the two and a half blocks dubbed the "Buckhead Village" area, there are over 100 restaurants and nightspots, including a piano bar, British pub, and other bars ranging from trendy posh to sand-floor dives. People drive in from all over the metro Atlanta area to party here—which doesn't come without a hitch: Buckhead's weekend nightlife is notorious for its rowdiness and its lack of parking, so be prepared to walk. For more information on the bars and clubs in Buckhead, go online to www.buckhead.org/bars.

If the Buckhead scene's a little much for your taste, you may want to check out some of the other well-known establishments in Midtown, Little Five Points, Virginia Highland, and East Atlanta. The following list includes some of the city's best and brightest hotspots:

ALTERNATIVE, ROCK, HIP-HOP
- **Darkhorse Tavern**, 816 North Highland Avenue, Atlanta, 404-873-3607, www.darkhorseatlanta.com
- **Echo Lounge**, 551 Flat Shoals Avenue SE, Atlanta, 404-681-3600, www.echostatic.com/echolounge
- **Masquerade**, 695 North Avenue NE, Atlanta, 404-577-8178, www.masq.com
- **Smith's Olde Bar**, 1578 Piedmont Avenue, Atlanta, 404-875-1522, www.smithsoldebar.com
- **The Tabernacle**, 152 Luckie Street, 404-659-9022, www.atlanta musicguide.com/tabernacle.htm

BLUES
- **Blind Willie's**, 828 North Highland Avenue, Atlanta, 404-873-2583, www.blindwilliesblues.com
- **Blues in the Alley**, 50 Upper Alabama Street, Atlanta, 404-584-7557, www.bluesinthealley.net
- **Darwin's**, 1598 Roswell Road, Marietta, 770-578-6872, www.darwins blues.com

FOLK, COUNTRY, ACOUSTIC
- **Buckhead Saloon**, 3107 Peachtree Road NE, Atlanta, 404-261-7922
- **Eddie's Attic**, 515 North McDonough Street, Decatur, 404-377-4976, www.eddiesattic.com

- **Trackside Tavern**, 313 East College Avenue, Decatur, 404-378-0504, www.tracksidetavern.com

IRISH
- **Fado Atlanta**, 3035 Peachtree Road, Atlanta, 404-841-0066, http://fadoirishpub.com
- **The County Cork Irish Pub**, 56 East Andrews NW, Atlanta, 404-262-2227
- **Limerick Junction**, 824 North Highland Avenue, Atlanta, 404-874-7147, www.limerickjunctionpub.com

NIGHTCLUBS
- **Club Uranus**, 3049 Bolling Way NE, Atlanta, 404-816-9931, www.cluburanusatlanta.com
- **Eleven50**, 1150 Peachtree Road, Atlanta, 404-874-0428, www.eleven50.com
- **Masquerade**, 695 North Avenue NE, Atlanta, 404-577-8178, www.masq.com
- **Sanctuary**, 3209 Paces Ferry Road, Atlanta, 404-262-1377, www.sanctuarynightclub.com
- **Tongue & Groove**, 3055 Peachtree Road NE, Atlanta, 404-261-2325, www.tongueandgrooveonline.com

R&B, JAZZ
- **Dante's Down the Hatch**, 3380 Peachtree Road NE, Atlanta, 404-266-1600, www.dantesdownthehatch.com
- **High Note Jazz Club at The Vault**, 3259 Roswell Road, 404-239-0202
- **Sambuca Jazz Café**, 3102 Piedmont Road, 404-237-5299, www.sambucarestaurant.com

REGGAE
- **Jamaica Jamaica,** 50 Upper Alabama Street SW, Underground Atlanta, 404-526-6467
- **The Royal Peacock**, 186 Auburn Avenue, Atlanta, 404-584-2522, http://theroyalpeacock.com

VISUAL ARTS AND SCIENCES

ART MUSEUMS

- **The High Museum of Art**, 1280 Peachtree Street NE, Atlanta, 404-733-4400, www.high.org; designed by Richard Meier, this museum houses an extensive permanent collection of decorative art, 19th-century American paintings, and modern art. Admission is free for the permanent exhibits, but a donation is appreciated.

- **Atlanta International Museum of Art and Design,** Peachtree Center, Marquis Two, 285 Peachtree Center Avenue, Atlanta, 404-688-2467, www.museumofdesign.org; hosts multicultural folk art, ethnographic, and design exhibitions. Free admission, but a donation is appreciated.
- **Hammonds House Galleries and Resource Center of African American Art,** 503 Peeples Street, Atlanta, 404-752-8730, www.hammondshouse.org; showcases African-American art, including works by Romare Bearden, and an extensive Haitian art collection.
- **High Museum of Art at Georgia Pacific Center,** 30 John Wesley Dobbs Avenue NE, Atlanta, 404-577-6940, www.high.org; hosts folk art, photography, and traveling exhibitions. Admission is free, but a donation is appreciated.
- **Michael C. Carlos Museum,** Emory University, 571 South Kilgo Street, Atlanta, 404-727-4282, http://carlos.emory.edu; hosts a large collection of ancient art of the Mediterranean and Americas. Free admission, but $3 donation is appreciated.
- **Oglethorpe University Museum,** 4484 Peachtree Road NE, 404-364-8555, http://museum.oglethorpe.edu; hosts original exhibits of mythological art. Free admission.

If you want to get out of the museum setting and see some art in its natural habitat, consider Reverend Howard Finster's **Paradise Gardens** in Pennville, GA, about an hour-and-a-half drive north of Atlanta. Finster is famous for his album covers (Talking Heads and R.E.M. among others), painted Coca-Cola bottles, and his preaching. Though Reverend Finster passed away in 2001, the trip to Paradise Gardens is worth the drive, and you can buy a Finster without the exorbitant gallery mark-up. For more information, call 706-857-5791, or check out www.finster.com.

To find out more about Atlanta's fine and decorative art scene, check out **Art Atlanta,** www.artatlanta.com. This site includes a calendar of exhibit openings, maps, and more.

HISTORY AND CULTURAL MUSEUMS

- **African-American Panoramic Experience-APEX,** 135 Auburn Avenue NE, Atlanta, 404-523-2739, www.apexmuseum.org; presents American history from an African-American perspective
- **Atlanta Cyclorama,** Grant Park, Georgia Avenue and Cherokee Avenue SE, Atlanta, 404-658-7625, www.webguide.com/cyclorama.html; 360 degree diorama depicting Civil War battles in Atlanta

- **Atlanta History Center**, 130 West Paces Ferry Road NW, Atlanta, 404-814-4000, www.atlhist.org; both permanent and temporary exhibits highlighting various aspects of Atlanta's history
- **BellSouth Telephone Museum**, Plaza Level, BellSouth Center, 675 West Peachtree Street NE, Atlanta, 404-529-0971, www.bellsouthga pioneers.org/museumtemp.htm; open Monday-Friday, 11 a.m. to 1 p.m.; free admission
- **Herndon Home**, 587 University Plaza NW, Atlanta, 404-581-9813, www.herndonhome.org; the historic home of Alonzo Herndon, an ex-slave who became one of the foremost African-American businessmen of his era. The museum offers tours, exhibits, special events and more. Admission is free, but donations are appreciated.
- **Jimmy Carter Library and Museum**, 441 Freedom Parkway, Atlanta, 404-865-7100, www.jimmycarterlibrary.org; the Presidential Library of former US President Jimmy Carter. The Carter Center (as it's known) offers museum tours, lectures, special events, and more. Admission is $7 for adults and free for children under 16 years old.
- **The Margaret Mitchell House**, 990 Peachtree Street, Atlanta, 404-249-7015, www.gwtw.org; the historic home of "Gone With the Wind" author Margaret Mitchell, and birthplace of this classic American novel. The museum highlights Mitchell's life both before and after the book, as well as the making of the movie, which premiered in Atlanta in 1939.
- **The Martin Luther King, Jr., Birth Home Museum**, 450 Auburn Avenue NE, Atlanta, 404-331-5190, www.nps.gov/malu; admission is free to this birthplace of civil rights activist, Dr. Martin Luther King, Jr.
- **The Martin Luther King, Jr., Center for Nonviolent Social Change**, 449 Auburn Avenue NE, Atlanta, 404-526-8900, http://the kingcenter.org; admission is free, though a donation is appreciated
- **Omenala-Griot Afrocentric Teaching Museum**, 337 Dargan Place, Atlanta, 404-755-8403; general admission is free
- **Road to Tara Museum**, 104 North Main Street, Jonesboro, 770-478-4800, www.visitscarlett.com; another "Gone With the Wind" museum, featuring original film props, costume reproductions, a foreign edition library, photo gallery, and more. The museum is open Monday through Saturday.
- **Southeastern Railway Museum**, 3966 Buford Highway, Duluth, 770-476-2013, www.srmduluth.org; Georgia's official transportation history museum featuring Pullman cars, classic steam locomotives, and more. During spring, summer, and fall, the museum is open Thursdays, Fridays and Saturdays. During the winter, they're open on Saturdays only. Call for times and admission prices.
- **The William Breman Jewish Heritage Museum**, 1440 Spring Street, Atlanta, 678-222-3700, www.thebreman.org; a museum dedi-

cated to collecting, preserving, interpreting and teaching about Jewish history, particularly the Holocaust and the experience of Jews in Georgia

SCIENCE MUSEUMS

- **The Fernbank Museum of Natural History**, 767 Clifton Road NE, Atlanta, 404-929-6300, www.fernbank.edu; a beautiful, natural history museum featuring permanent exhibits such as "A Walk Through Time in Georgia" and traveling exhibits such as "Frogs: A Chorus of Colors," "DNA," and "Chimpanzees." Fernbank is also home to an interactive science room, an IMAX theatre, café, and more. This is a popular destination for adults and children. Call for admission prices.
- **Fernbank Science Center**, 156 Heaton Park Drive NE, Atlanta, 678-874-7102, www.fernbank.edu; features an observatory, planetarium, library, and exhibit hall. Admission to the Library and Exhibit Hall is free, and visitors will see a variety of floor exhibits, interactive models, and a real Apollo space capsule. The Observatory is also free, but is only open on Thursday and Friday nights from 8 p.m. to 10:30 p.m. when the weather is clear. Admission to the planetarium is $4 for adults and $3 for students and seniors.

CULTURE FOR KIDS

Cultural opportunities for children abound in metro Atlanta. From children's museums and nature centers to a world-class zoo, you'll find it all here. In addition, many of the regular museums and theatres offer children's programs on a monthly basis. Be sure to check out museum web sites, or look in the weekend edition of the *Atlanta Journal-Constitution* for event announcements and schedules.

MUSEUMS

Most of the above listed museums are as good for youngsters as for adults. Some even offer special kid-friendly events or shows geared toward children. Contact the above museums for details. A few specialty museums, many designed with the child in mind, include:
- **The Fernbank Museum of Natural History**, 767 Clifton Road NE, Atlanta, 404-929-6300, www.fernbank.edu; children love this museum's permanent exhibit, "A Walk Through Time in Georgia," as well as its many traveling exhibits including "Frogs: A Chorus of Colors." Other popular parts of the museum include the interactive science room, the two Children's Discovery Rooms, the giant-sized dinosaur models, and the IMAX theatre.

- **Fernbank Science Center**, 156 Heaton Park Drive NE, Atlanta, 678-874-7102, www.fernbank.edu; admission to the Exhibit Hall is free and features a real Apollo space capsule, interactive models, and more. Children may also enjoy visiting the Science Center's Observatory, and checking out the kid-friendly shows in the planetarium.
- **Georgia Aquarium**, www.georgiaaquarium.org; opening late 2005 in downtown Atlanta, across from Centennial Olympic Park and the Georgia World Congress Center. Visit them online for additional information.
- **Imagine It! The Children's Museum of Atlanta**, 275 Centennial Olympic Park Drive NW, Atlanta, 404-659-5437, www.childrensmuseum atl.org; recommended for children aged two through eight, and their accompanying adults.
- **Southeastern Railway Museum**, 3966 Buford Highway, Duluth, 770-476-2013, www.srmduluth.org; for railroad lovers of all ages. Admission is $5 for adults, $3 for children, and includes a train ride.
- **The World of Coca-Cola**, 55 Martin Luther King Jr. Drive, Atlanta, 404-676-5151, www.woccatlanta.com; learn the history of Coca-Cola and sample different flavors of Coke from around the world.

OUTDOOR

- **The Atlanta Botanical Garden**, 1345 Piedmont Avenue NE, Atlanta, 404-876-5859, www.atlantabotanicalgarden.org; in addition to the regular gardens (which are often a draw for children of all ages), the Atlanta Botanical Garden also offers a fantastic, whimsical children's garden. The Children's Garden features a variety of plants, flowers, and trees, an open fountain perfect for playing in during Atlanta's hottest months, slides, waterfalls and more.
- **Chattahoochee Nature Center**, 9135 Willeo Road, Roswell, 770-992-2055, www.chattnaturecenter.com; popular nature center offers a variety of fun programs for children of all ages. There are also gardens, picnic areas, an aviary, a Discovery Center, and more . . . all alongside the Chattahoochee River.
- **Dunwoody Nature Center**, 5343 Roberts Drive, Dunwoody, 770-394-3322, www.dunwoodynature.org; kids can enjoy up close animal encounters, an annual Butterfly Festival, a wetlands boardwalk, and more. Dunwoody Nature Center also offers spring break and summer Day Camps, as well as weekly tours and hikes along their main trail, which leads past a meadow, to peaceful Wildcat Creek.
- **Six Flags Over Georgia,** 7561 Six Flags Parkway, Austell, 770-948-9290, www.sixflags.com/parks/overgeorgia; this world-class amusement park features over 100 family rides and thrill rides, as well as Skull

Island, a one-acre family water play area with six water slides and a gigantic water play structure. In addition to its regular shows, the park also hosts numerous special events, such as a Christian music festival, a kids' festival, and a Halloween-themed fright festival.

- **Stone Mountain Park**, Highway 78, Stone Mountain, 770-498-5702, www.stonemountainpark.com; part outdoor getaway and part theme park. Kids will probably be most drawn to the theme park aspect. Here you'll find the Great Barn, an 1870s era barn that's been renovated and filled with four floors of rope nets for climbing, mazes to explore, and super slides that whisk you from the ceiling to the floor. The park is also home to a skylift, which takes visitors to the top of the mountain, an antebellum plantation and farmyard, two three-story-high tree houses (one for boys, one for girls) with over three dozen interactive activities, numerous restaurants and gift shops, and much, much more.
- **Zoo Atlanta**, Grant Park, 800 Cherokee Avenue SE, Atlanta, 404-624-5000, www.zooatlanta.com; home to a variety of animals, housed in outdoor, natural habitats. It's also home to a train, which takes you on a short tour of the zoo, a carousel, a playground, a petting zoo and more.

THEATER

- **Alliance Theatre Children's Theatre**, 1280 Peachtree Street, Atlanta, 404-733-4660, www.alliancetheatre.org
- **ART Station**, 5384 Manor Drive, Stone Mountain, 770-469-1105, www.artstation.org; contemporary arts center and theatre, located in downtown Stone Mountain
- **Aurora Theatre, Leaps and Bounds**, 3087-B Main Street, Duluth, 770-476-7926, www.auroratheatre.com
- **Center for Puppetry Art**, 1404 Spring Street, Atlanta, 404-873-3391, www.puppet.org
- **Dad's Garage**, 280 Elizabeth Street, Atlanta, 404-523-3141, www.dadsgarage.com; theater company and improv group
- **Georgia Ensemble Theatre**, Roswell Cultural Arts Center, 950 Forrest Street, Roswell, 770-641-1260, www.get.org
- **Horizon Theatre Company**, 1083 Austin Avenue, Atlanta, 404-523-1477, www.horizontheatre.com
- **Kudzu Playhouse**, 608 Holcomb Bridge Road, Roswell, 770-594-1020, www.kudzuplayhouse.com
- **Little General Playhouse**, 4857 North Main Street, Acworth, 770-565-3995; admission is $8 for shows by the Little General and Little General Junior Players; $12 to $16 for shows by Barnbuster Musicals and Cobb Players

- **Neighborhood Playhouse**, 430 West Trinity Place, Decatur, 404-373-5311, www.nplayhouse.org
- **Stage Door Players**, 5339 Chamblee-Dunwoody Road, Dunwoody, 770-396-1726
- **Theatre in the Square**, 11 Whitlock Avenue, Marietta, 770-422-8369, www.theatreinthesquare.com

OTHER

- **Hobbit Hall Children's Bookstore–Story and Crafts**, 120 Bulloch Avenue, Roswell, 770-587-0907, www.hobbithall.com; special events, story time, arts and crafts, and more; check online for current schedule. Admission is free.
- **Plaster Palace Art Studio**, 5075 Abbotts Bridge Road, Alpharetta, 770-569-7755, www.plasterpalace.com; for ages 3 and up. No appointments necessary, no studio fees—you just pay for what you make.
- **Redwall Art Studio**, 1428 Ponce de Leon Avenue NE, Atlanta, 404-371-9383, www.redwallstudio.net; ongoing hands-on art classes for children and adults of all ages
- **Spruill Center for the Arts, Education Center**, 5339 Chamblee-Dunwoody Road, Atlanta, 770-394-3447, www.spruillarts.org/education_center.htm; call for class and events schedule, and pricing

LITERARY LIFE AND HIGHER EDUCATION

BOOKSTORES

Metro Atlanta is home to a wide selection of bookstores. Whether you prefer an independent bookseller or a large chain store, you're sure to find what you're looking for somewhere in the city. Below is a listing of some of your options, including literary workshops and groups.

CHAIN BOOKSELLERS

- **Barnes & Noble**, 800-843-2665, www.barnesandnoble.com; several locations throughout metro Atlanta
- **Books-A-Million**, 205-942-3737, www.booksamillioninc.com, several locations throughout metro Atlanta
- **Borders Books and Music**, 888-81-BOOKS, www.bordersstores.com; multiple locations throughout metro Atlanta
- **Chapter 11 Discount Bookstore**, www.chapter11books.com; 15 locations throughout metro Atlanta

INDEPENDENT BOOKSELLERS

- **A Capella Books**, 1133 Euclid Avenue, Atlanta, 404-681-5128; two-room shop specializing in out-of-print titles, first editions, fine literature, and books on culture and the arts
- **The Book Nook**, 3073 North Druid Hills, Atlanta, 404-633-1342; 595 Roswell Street SE, Marietta, 770-499-9914; popular local bookstore, with two locations selling new and used books, CDs, videos/DVDs and more
- **CHARIS Books and More, Feminist Bookstore**, 1189 Euclid Avenue NE, 404-524-0304, http://charis.booksense.com; the South's oldest, independent feminist bookstore
- **Engineer's Bookstore**, 748 Marietta Street NW, Atlanta, 404-221-1669, www.engrbookstore.com; the largest technical bookstore in the southeast
- **Hoot Owl Attic Metaphysical Bookstore**, 185 Allen Road NE, Sandy Springs, 404-303-1030, www.hootowlattic.com; popular metaphysical shop specializing in books, candles, and more
- **Outwrite Bookstore**, 991 Piedmont Avenue, Atlanta, 404-607-0082, www.outwritebooks.com; Atlanta's premier gay and lesbian community bookstore
- **Phoenix & Dragon Bookstore**, 5531 Roswell Road, Sandy Springs, 404-255-5207, www.phoenixanddragon.com; Atlanta's largest, oldest and most well-known metaphysical bookstore
- **St. Mary's Bookstore and Church Supply**, 2140 Peachtree Road, Atlanta, 404-351-2865; Christian book and supply shop
- **Shepherd's Staff Christian Bookstore**, 1425 Market Boulevard, Roswell, 770-998-6009; specializing in new Christian releases and bibles
- **Tall Tales Book Shop**, 2105 LaVista Road, Atlanta, 404-636-2498; small shop specializing in both wide-release titles and smaller market books, including a nice-sized children's section
- **Wordsworth Booksellers**, 2112 North Decatur Road, Decatur, 404-633-4275; offers books in all areas of interest as well as rare and out-of-print books

LITERARY WORKSHOPS AND GROUPS

There are several literary groups in metro Atlanta. Whether you're interested in joining a book club, or would like to workshop with other struggling writers, you're bound to find a group to fit your needs. Below you'll find just a sampling of what's out there. For more options, check out *Creative Loafing*'s "Happenings" section, under "Literature."

- **First World Writers**, 770-981-3076, local black poets and writers group
- **Georgia Writers, Inc.**, 770-943-5699, meets monthly at the Sandy Springs Public Library
- **Murder, Inc. Book Club**, 404-237-0707, meets the fourth Wednesday of every month at Borders Books and Music in Buckhead, to discuss their mystery of the month.
- **Poetry Discussion Forum**, 404-237-0707, meets the last Thursday of each month at Borders Books and Music in Buckhead.
- **Village Writers Group**, 404-296-6391, meets the first Tuesday of each month (except July and August) at the Decatur library. The group is open to anyone interested in writing.
- **Women's Book Club**, 404-237-0707, meets the fourth Thursday of every month to discuss books that address the issues and concerns of modern women.

LIBRARIES

Metro Atlanta is home to a number of excellent libraries—from your neighborhood's city or county branches, to the handful of historical libraries, to the many college and university libraries around town. Below is contact information for many of the main branches of metro Atlanta's public libraries as well as information on other libraries open to the public. Most of them offer monthly book clubs, special literary events, family activities and more.

PUBLIC LIBRARIES

- **Fulton County Central Library**, One Margaret Mitchell Square, NW, 404-730-1700, www.af.public.lib.ga.us
- **DeKalb County Central Library**, 215 Sycamore Street, Decatur, 404-370-3070, www.dekalb.public.lib.ga.us
- **Cobb County Central Library**, 266 Roswell Street, Marietta, 770-528-2320, www.cobbcat.org
- **Gwinnett County Central Library**, 1001 Lawrenceville Highway, 770-822-4522, www.gwinnettpl.org
- **City of Smyrna Public Library**, 100 Village Green Circle, Smyrna, 770-431-2860, www.smyrna-library.com

HISTORICAL LIBRARIES

- **Atlanta History Center (Archives)**, 130 West Paces Ferry Road NE, Atlanta, 404-814-4000, www.atlantahistorycenter.com; one of the Southeast's largest history museums, with a full research library and archives that serve more than 10,000 patrons each year

- **Auburn Avenue Research Library of African American Culture and History**, 101 Auburn Avenue NE, Atlanta, 404-730-4001, www.af.public.lib.ga.us; part of the Atlanta Fulton County library system, this research branch specializes in texts and events highlighting African-American culture and history
- **City of Roswell Archives and Research Library**, 770-594-6405, www.ci.roswell.ga.us; this research library, housed in the Roswell Cultural Arts Center, is open Monday-Thursday, from 1 p.m. to 4:30 p.m., and features text and archives highlighting local history and preservation efforts
- **Jimmy Carter Library and Museum**, 441 Freedom Parkway NE, Atlanta, 404-865-7100, www.jimmycarterlibrary.org; presidential library of former US President Jimmy Carter

COLLEGE AND UNIVERSITY LIBRARIES

- **Agnes Scott College Campus Library**, 141 East College Avenue, Decatur, 404-471-6339, http://library.agnesscott.edu
- **Clark Atlanta University Campus Library**, James P. Brawley Drive and Fair Street, Atlanta, 404-880-8697, www.auctr.edu
- **Emory University Libraries**, 540 Asbury Circle, Atlanta, 404-727-6873, www.emory.edu/libraries
- **Georgia Institute of Technology Campus Library**, 225 North Avenue NW, Atlanta, 404-894-4529, www.library.gatech.edu
- **Georgia Perimeter College**, **Decatur Campus Library**, 3251 Panthersville Road, Decatur, 404-244-5026; **Dunwoody Campus Library**, 2101 Womack Road, Dunwoody, 770-551-3046; **Lawrenceville Campus Library**, 1301 Atkinson Road, Lawrenceville, 770-339-2279; www.gpc.edu/library
- **Georgia State University**, **Pullen Library**, 100 Decatur Street, Atlanta, 404-651-2422; **Law Library**, 100 Decatur Street, Atlanta, 404-651-2767; www.gsu.edu
- **Mercer University Campus Library**, 3001 Mercer University Drive, Atlanta, 770-986-3282, www2.mercer.edu

LECTURES

Many Atlanta area universities and colleges sponsor lecture series, as do public libraries, bookstores, and churches. **Emory University**, 404-727-6397, www.emory.edu; **Georgia State University**, 404-651-1777, www.gsu.edu; and **Georgia Tech**, 404-894-2000, www.gatech.edu, are good places to start. The best place to learn about the weekly lecture scene is to consult *Creative Loafing;* under the "Happenings" section is a

"Lectures and Seminars" column, which will direct you to lectures on everything from Jungian philosophy to personal charisma. Popular hosts to visiting lecturers include:

- **Fernbank Science Center**, 404-378-4311, www.fernbank.edu; offers various lecture series on scientific topics, such as astronomy, geology, and biology
- **Atlanta Botanical Garden**, 404-876-5859, www.atlantabotanical garden.org; provides interested participants with an ongoing series of workshops, seminars, and lectures about gardening and horticulture
- **High Museum**, 404-733-4400, www.high.org; sponsors numerous lectures in the Hill Auditorium by artists and scholars specializing in the visual arts
- **The Buckhead Library**, 404-814-3500, www.afplweb.com; often hosts lectures on a wide variety of subjects
- **The Art Institute of Atlanta**, 770-394-8300, www.aia.artinstitutes. edu; offers art seminars and courses
- **Theosophical Society**, 404-943-9469, www.theosophical.org; holds public lectures every Sunday at 3 p.m. (except holidays) at 126 Johnson Ferry Road, Atlanta

HIGHER EDUCATION

Metro Atlanta is home to nearly 30 universities, trade schools, and technical institutes, providing more than 350 programs of study to more than 120,000 students. Many of the local colleges and universities offer concerts, plays, lectures, and numerous other cultural opportunities for the general public throughout the year. Call the schools' information lines, check campus kiosks, or pick up Atlanta's weekly *Creative Loafing* newspaper for information about upcoming events. The following are Atlanta's largest and most prominent institutions of higher education. For further listings, be sure to check the Atlanta Yellow Pages under "Schools."

- **Agnes Scott College**, 141 East College Avenue, Decatur, 404-471-6000, 800-868-8602, www.agnesscott.edu, is an independent national liberal arts college for women, located in a national Historic District in Decatur. Founded in 1889, Agnes Scott is affiliated with the Presbyterian Church (USA) and is consistently ranked one of the best women's colleges in the nation by publications such as *The Princeton Review, Kaplan/Newsweek College Catalogue,* and *The Fiske Guide to Colleges.* Approximately 1,000 students are enrolled each year, with more than 90% residing in college residence halls or apartments.
- **Atlanta College of Art**, Woodruff Arts Center, 1280 Peachtree Street NE, Atlanta, 404-733-5001, www.aca.edu, is the only accredited four-year art college in the USA to share a campus with a noted museum,

theater company, and symphony orchestra. Founded in 1905, Atlanta College of Art currently instructs 350 full-time students seeking a Bachelor of Fine Arts degree in one of 13 areas, and offers a 10:1 student-to-faculty ratio.

- **Emory University**, 1380 South Oxford Road NE, Atlanta, 404-727-6123, www.emory.edu, is noted nationally for its many fine programs and departments, as well as its most prominent lecturer and faculty member, former President Jimmy Carter. Emory University offers nine major academic divisions, numerous centers for advanced study, and a host of affiliated institutions including Oxford College, a two-year undergraduate division located in Oxford, Georgia. There are currently over 11,000 students enrolled at Emory, representing all regions of the USA and 100 foreign nations.
- **Georgia Institute of Technology**, 225 North Avenue NW, 404-894-2000, www.gatech.edu, founded in 1888, Georgia Tech is consistently ranked among the top ten universities in the USA by *US News & World Report* and *Money* magazine. Known for its schools of engineering, science, business management, and architecture, this university enrolls approximately 16,000 students each year. Georgia Tech's placement center is also one of the nation's most successful: At each graduation, over 50% of students receiving their diplomas have already been hired for a job or accepted into graduate school.
- **Georgia Perimeter College, Decatur Campus**, 3251 Panthersville Road, 404-244-5090; **Dunwoody Campus**, 2101 Womack Road, 770-551-3000; **Lawrenceville Campus**, 1000 University Center Lane, 678-407-5000; **Clarkston Campus**, 555 North Indian Creek Drive, 404-299-4000; www.gpc.edu; is a non-residential, multi-campus unit of the University System of Georgia. Established in 1964, the school now offers 38 undergraduate credit and non-credit programs, specializing in liberal arts and professional preparation. The 22,000 students enrolled each year are seeking to complete associate's degrees, transfer to senior colleges or universities, or prepare for entry into careers.
- **Georgia State University**, 33 Gilmore Street, SE, Atlanta, 404-651-2000, www.gsu.edu, features six academic colleges including a respected law department, and is the second largest institution in the University System of Georgia. Georgia State, nicknamed the "concrete campus" because of its location in downtown Atlanta, offers 52 undergraduate and graduate degree programs in more than 250 fields of study to approximately 40,000 students annually. About 30% of the student body is made up of graduate students.
- **Mercer University**, Cecil B. Davis Campus, 3001 University Drive, Atlanta, 678-547-6000, www.mercer.edu, offers programs in nine diverse fields of study including liberal arts, business, and medicine.

Founded in 1833 in Penfield, Georgia, and later moved to Macon (where the school's main campus is located), Mercer University is home to approximately 7,200 students, 2,600 of which attend the Cecil B. Davis Campus in Atlanta. The Cecil B. Davis Campus is home to the Graduate and Professional Center as well as its newest academic unit, the James and Carolyn McAfee School of Theology.

- **Oglethorpe University**, 4484 Peachtree Road NE, Atlanta, 404-261-1441, 800-428-4484, www.oglethorpe.edu, is an independent, coeducational liberal arts institution of approximately 1,200 students. Chartered by the state in 1835, Oglethorpe opened in 1838 and then closed again in 1862 due to the Civil War. The school was rechartered in 1913 and opened at its current location in Brookhaven in 1915. Oglethorpe University is home to the Georgia Shakespeare Festival, a not-for-profit repertory theatre that offers Shakespearean productions throughout the year. Call 404-264-0020 or visit www.gashakespeare.org for tickets/show information.

Atlanta University Center is a consortium of six individual institutions, making it the largest predominantly African-American educational complex in the world. Members of the AUC are:

- **Clark Atlanta University**, 223 James P. Brawley Drive, Atlanta, 404-880-8000, www.cau.edu; a comprehensive, urban coeducational institution offering both undergraduate and graduate courses. Founded in 1988 by the merging of Atlanta University, one of the oldest African-American universities in the nation, and Clark College, a respected liberal arts college, Clark Atlanta University is now home to approximately 5,000 students representing more than 50 different countries and nearly every state in the US.
- **The Interdenominational Theological Center**, 700 Martin Luther King Jr. Drive, Atlanta, 404-527-7700, www.itc.edu; an ecumenical, graduate professional school of theology. Chartered in 1958, the ITC now consists of six seminaries including the Gammon Theological Seminary, the Turner Theological Seminary, the Johnson C. Smith Theological Seminary, the Morehouse School of Religion, the Phillips School of Theology, and the Charles H. Mason Theological Seminary.
- **Morehouse College**, 830 Westview Drive SW, Atlanta, 404-681-2800, www.morehouse.edu; the nation's only historically black private liberal arts college for men. Founded in 1867, Morehouse College now enrolls approximately 3,000 students each year and confers Bachelor Degrees on more African-American men than any other school in the USA.
- **Morehouse School of Medicine**, 720 Westview Drive SW, Atlanta, 404-752-1500, www.msm.edu; a four-year, degree-granting medical institution, established in 1975. Originally a two-year educational

program in basic medical sciences at Morehouse College, Morehouse School of Medicine became an independent institution in 1981. The first class of M.D.'s trained at Morehouse graduated in May 1985. Today there are approximately 145 medical students enrolled at the school.

- **Morris Brown College**, 643 Martin Luther King Jr. Drive NW, Atlanta, 404-739-1000, www.morrisbrown.edu; a coeducational, private liberal arts college, founded in 1885 by members of the African Methodist Episcopal Church. Today, Morris Brown is home to approximately 2,700 students per year, seeking degrees in everything from business science to chemistry.
- **Spelman College**, 350 Spelman Lane SW, Atlanta, 404-681-3643, www.spelman.edu; a predominantly residential, private, liberal arts college for women. Founded in 1881, Spelman consistently ranks among the best liberal arts colleges according to *US News & World Report*, and is home to more than 2,100 students from 41 states and 15 foreign countries.

HOST OF THE 1994 AND 1999 SUPER BOWLS AND THE 1996 OLYMPIC Games, Atlanta has made a name for itself as an international sports center. Warm weather, beautiful parks with winding trails, and state-of-the-art sports facilities make the city an ideal place to engage in sporting activities, and it is home to five professional sports teams, abundant college athletics, and countless participant sports. So, if you're looking to work up a sweat yourself or watch others do it, metro Atlanta offers plenty of opportunities.

To find out more about metro Atlanta area health clubs, exercise trends, and sports teams, check out *Atlanta Sports and Fitness* magazine, 404-870-0123, www.atlantasportsmag.com. This publication features news and information on what's hot in Atlanta sports and fitness.

PROFESSIONAL SPORTS

AUTO RACING

The **Atlanta Motor Speedway**, located 30 miles south of Atlanta off I-75 in Hampton, is home to yearly NASCAR races. For more information, call 770-946-4211, or check them out online at www.atlantamotorspeedway.com.

For additional racing events, try **Road Atlanta**, 404-881-8233, www.roadatlanta.com, in Braselton off I-85 North.

BASEBALL

Atlanta is a city that loves baseball, thanks in part to the superb efforts of its hometown team, the **Atlanta Braves**. With an amazing record of 13 Division titles, five trips to the World Series, and a 1995 World Series victory, over the last 15 years, the Braves are considered by many to be one of the top teams in the history of professional baseball. The Braves play at

Turner Field, situated near the intersection of I-20 and the Downtown Connector, next to where the old Atlanta–Fulton County Stadium once stood. Built for the opening ceremonies and track and field events of the 1996 Olympic Games, Turner Field is the latest in a wave of boutique ballparks that offer fans gourmet food, arcade games, and children's areas. Turner Field, named for former Braves' owner Ted Turner, even has a Braves' museum showcasing memorabilia from the team. Baseball season runs from April to early October though, by now, Atlanta fans expect to see some post-season activity as well.

You can charge individual tickets by contacting **TicketMaster**, 404-249-6400, www.ticketmaster.com, or by visiting any TicketMaster location. Use VISA, MasterCard, American Express, or Discover card over the phone or online, and/or cash when you buy tickets in person. Be advised that TicketMaster does charge a minimal service charge (typically $3.25 per ticket) for each transaction. If you prefer to forgo the service charge, you can buy tickets directly from the Braves through: **at the stadium box office**, Turner Field's North Gate at Ralph David Abernathy Boulevard (box office hours are 8:30 a.m. to 6 p.m., Monday–Friday; 9 a.m. to 5 p.m. on Saturdays; and 1 p.m. to 5 p.m. on Sundays); **by mail**, Atlanta Braves Ticket Office, Turner Field, 755 Hank Aaron Drive, Atlanta, GA 30315; or **online**, www.atlantabraves.com. Ticket prices range from $5 to $50 and are usually available, particularly at the beginning of the season. For information on season tickets, call 404-577-9100. For information on Turner Field tours, call 404-614-2311. For general information about the Atlanta Braves, or Turner Field, go to www.atlantabraves.com.

Parking downtown is always a hassle, even in the best of circumstances, and a sporting event does not offer optimal parking conditions. The best way to get to the stadium is by MARTA, which offers a stadium shuttle service from both the West End and Five Points stations (see the **Transportation** chapter for specifics). The stadium is also located a relatively short walk away from the Georgia State station.

BASKETBALL

Philips Arena, 404-878-3000, www.philipsarena.com, located downtown at One Philips Drive, across from the World Congress Center and CNN Center, is home to the NBA's **Atlanta Hawks**. Basketball season starts in November and lasts until the end of April. Individual tickets are available online or by phone from TicketMaster, 404-249-6400, www.ticketmaster.com, and at TicketMaster locations throughout metro Atlanta. For general information and season tickets, contact the Hawks at 404-827-DUNK (3865), www.nba.com/hawks. Tickets go for anywhere from $10 (upper level bleachers) to $400 (courtside and center).

Parking near Philips Arena is limited, so your best bet may be MARTA: The Georgia Dome/World Congress Center station will take you right to the door of the arena.

FOOTBALL

The **Atlanta Falcons** fight it out at the **Georgia Dome**, 404-223-4636, www.gadome.com, located at One Georgia Dome Drive, next to the World Congress Center, on the side opposite Philips Arena. At capacity the dome holds 71,500 spectators, and fans are fond of saying there's not a bad seat in the house.

Individual tickets are available starting in August. Purchase them at the Dome ticket office or through TicketMaster, 404-249-6400, www.ticket master.com. You can also order them by mail by writing the Atlanta Falcons Ticket Office, One Georgia Dome Drive, Atlanta, GA 30313. For more information about the Atlanta Falcons, check out www.nfl.com/ falcons. For general information and season tickets, call 404-223-8000. Dome seats go for $25 to $50 each, depending on seat location. Football season runs from August through December.

Catching a MARTA train is your best bet for a relatively hassle-free trip to the Dome. Parking nearby is almost a guaranteed nightmare. Both the Georgia Dome/World Congress station and the Vine City station are located conveniently near the stadium. Also, you can take a MARTA shuttle from downtown parking lots and from the Garnett station as well.

GOLF

The **BellSouth Classic**, 770-951-8777, www.bellsouthclassic.com, takes place every spring at the **Atlanta Country Club**, 770-953-3008, located in Marietta at Atlanta Country Club Drive SE. Tickets for this PGA tour event are available from TicketMaster, 404-249-6400, www.ticket master.com, or by contacting BellSouth Classic directly.

Also, in nearby Augusta, just two hours east of Atlanta, you can attend the annual **Masters Tournament,** which is held at the **Augusta National Golf Club** every April. For more information, including ticket prices and availability, visit them online at www.masters.org, or call 706-667-6000.

HOCKEY

From October through April, the NHL **Atlanta Thrashers** compete in **Philips Arena**. Tickets range from $10 to $70 and can be purchased from TicketMaster, 404-249-6400, www.ticketmaster.com, or by calling the Thrashers directly at 404-584-PUCK. If you want to learn more about this team, check them out online at www.atlantathrashers.com. For more information about Philips Arena, including details on party suites, premium seating for events, or arena tours, call 404-878-CLUB, or visit www.philipsarena.com.

Parking near the Philips Arena is limited, so the best transportation method may be MARTA. Fortunately, the Georgia Dome/World Congress Center station will take you right to the door of the arena.

TENNIS

Atlanta is home to the clay court **AT&T Tennis Challenge**. This annual event (late April or early May) is held at the tennis center of Duluth's **Atlanta Athletic Club**, 770-448-2166, www.atlantaathleticclub.org, located at 1930 Bobby Jones Drive. You can purchase tournament tickets, which range between $10 and $40, from TicketMaster, 404-249-6400, www.ticketmaster.com.

COLLEGE SPORTS

College sports often incite as much enthusiasm as professional tournaments. Rowdy fans of the Georgia Tech Yellow Jackets frequently crowd bars to cheer on their team, especially when archrivals the Georgia Bulldogs are the opponent. If you follow the college sports scene, here is some information about Atlanta area college athletic programs:

- **Georgia State** has a 17-sport, Division One athletics program, including a baseball team, men's and women's basketball teams, softball team, and more. Contact 404-651-3166, www.gsu.edu, for schedule and ticket information.
- **Georgia Tech's** basketball and football teams attract many devoted supporters, and garner most of the attention for this school's athletic department. But Tech is also home to a baseball team, softball team, swim teams, and more. For information call 404-894-5447, http://ramblin wreck.collegesports.com.
- **Emory University** and **Oglethorpe University** teams compete in Division Three sports. Call 404-727-6547 or visit www.emory.edu for details about Emory's athletic department; and 404-364-8422, www.oglethorpe.edu for information on sports at Oglethorpe.
- **Clark Atlanta University**, 404-880-8126, www.cau.edu; **Morehouse College**, 404-215-2669, www.morehouse.edu; and **Morris Brown College**, 404-220-0270, www.morrisbrown.edu, also compete against each other in most of the major sports.

In addition, the Georgia Dome hosts the **Peach Bowl** college football game annually. Contact 404-586-8500, www.peachbowl.com, for more information. The Dome also plays host to the **Heritage Bowl**, a match-up of two football teams from historically African-American colleges. Contact 404-223-8427, www.gadome.com, for more information.

OTHER SPECTATOR SPORTING EVENTS

Every Fourth of July, hordes of metro Atlanta spectators line the sidewalks of Peachtree Street early in the morning to watch runners participate in the **Peachtree Road Race**. Cocktails and jam boxes in hand, supporters yell, play the theme from "Chariots of Fire," and offer spirited high-fives while they cheer on the thousands of runners in this gargantuan 10K race. **The Atlanta Track Club**, 404-231-9064, www.atlantatrack club.org, sponsors the event, and all you have to do to watch is find your spot along the course and join in the merriment.

The **Atlanta Steeplechase** takes place each spring in Cumming, Georgia, complete with candelabras, strawberries, and champagne. To buy tickets for this equestrian racing event, contact 404-237-7436, www.atlantasteeplechase.org, or write to the Atlanta Steeplechase, 3160 Northside Parkway NW, Atlanta, GA 30327.

PARTICIPANT SPORTS AND ACTIVITIES

PARKS AND RECREATION DEPARTMENTS

Joining an amateur sports team is an effective and fun way to meet new friends and get a workout at the same time. Neighborhood parks and recreation departments offer adult and child leagues in many sports, including baseball, softball, and basketball. Contact the one nearest you to investigate your options:

- **Atlanta City Parks and Recreation**, 404-817-6766, www. atlantaga.gov
- **Alpharetta Parks and Recreation**, 678-297-6100, www. alpharetta.ga.us
- **Chamblee Parks and Recreation**, 770-986-5016, www.chamblee ga.com
- **Cherokee County Recreation and Parks Authority**, 770-924-7768, www.crpa.net
- **Cobb County Parks and Recreation**, 770-528-8800, www.cobb county.org
- **Decatur Recreation Department**, 404-377-0494, www.decatur-ga. com

- **DeKalb County Parks and Recreation**, 404-371-2631, www.co. dekalb.ga.us/parks
- **Duluth Parks and Recreation**, 770-623-2781, 770-814-6981, www.duluth-ga.com
- **Fulton County Parks and Recreation**, 404-730-6200, www.co.fulton. ga.us/departments
- **Gwinnett County Parks and Recreation**, 770-822-8840, www.co. gwinnett.ga.us
- **Marietta Parks and Recreation**, 770-794-5601, www.city.marietta. ga.us/parks_rec
- **Roswell Recreation and Parks**, 770-641-3705, www.roswell gov.com
- **Smyrna Parks and Recreation**, 770-431-2842, www.ci.smyrna. ga.us
- **Stone Mountain Recreation Department**, 770-498-2414, www.stonemountaincity.org

Another way to join an amateur team is through your place of work. Corporate sponsorship of amateur sports teams is a popular metro Atlanta practice. Check with your employer about current team sponsorship or organize one yourself if no team exists. Many businesses don't mind footing the bill when team playing on the field translates into professional team playing in the office.

BASEBALL/SOFTBALL

If you're looking to join a team and play scheduled games throughout the season, call the **Atlanta Men's Senior Baseball League**, 770-785-2588, www.atlantamsbl.com. They will be able to give you detailed information on trying out, practices, games, and more. You can also call the **parks and recreation department** in your community (see phone numbers above) for a complete listing of adult and youth baseball and softball teams. Or pick up your glove and head to **Piedmont Park**, 404-875-7275, www.piedmontpark.org, with some friends—you'll probably meet others who are there for the same reason and you'll have a game going in no time.

BASKETBALL

Run N' Shoot Athletic Center, 1959 Metropolitan Parkway, 404-762-6222, offers seven indoor basketball courts with freshly painted hardwood floors, and computers that keep track of play time, so those in line for a court know exactly how long they'll have to wait. The center is open 24 hours a day. Admission is $6 per person per day, with no membership fees.

Another popular indoor basketball spot is the **YMCA** gymnasium (several locations throughout metro Atlanta, contact 404-588-9622, www.ymcaatlanta.org, for the location nearest you). Most Ys offer open court time periodically throughout the day and may require a membership fee, so be sure to call first for schedules and pricing.

BICYCLING

The **Southern Bicycle League (SBL)**, 770-594-8350, www.bikesbl.org, is a volunteer organization designed to support recreational cycling. The SBL sponsors monthly rides throughout Atlanta, as well as a magazine called *Freewheelin'*—available at your local bike shop. The magazine includes a calendar of ride events and a schedule of club member gatherings. The SBL also organizes rides of different lengths throughout Chastain Park.

One of the most popular locales for bicycling is **Piedmont Park**, 404-875-7275, www.piedmontpark.org, where you will share the paths with runners and rollerbladers. You can rent bikes across from the park at **Skate Escape**, 404-892-1292, www.skateescape.com. The **Freedom Parkway**, a road that connects the Downtown Connector to Ponce de Leon and Moreland Avenue, has bike paths that wind around the Carter Presidential Center and through Candler Park.

Bike rentals are also available at **Stone Mountain Park**, 770-498-5690, www.stonemountainpark.com. Robert E. Lee Boulevard makes a five-mile circle around the park and is very popular with cyclists.

A few other bicycling clubs to consider are:

- **Bicycle Club of Atlanta**, 770-496-1908, www.oldbike.com
- **Cherokee Velo Club**, www.cherokeebikeshop.com
- **Gwinnett Touring Club**, 770-476-7975, www.gtcbike.org
- **North Atlanta Riding Club**, 770-977-9696
- **North Georgia Cycling Association**, www.cycleworksinc.com
- **Southern Off-Road Bicycle Association**, 770-565-1795, www.sorba.org

Even though metro Atlanta does not enforce a strict helmet law, it's always a good idea to wear one when you ride.

BOATING/SAILING/WINDSURFING

Pools are not the only way to escape the Atlanta summer heat. You can pass a splendid lazy summer afternoon cooling off while floating down the Chattahoochee River. Rent a raft, canoe, or inner tube anytime between Memorial Day weekend and Labor Day weekend, and enjoy the ride. The Johnson Ferry Unit of the **Chattahoochee River National**

Recreation Area, www.nps.gov/chat (located across from the intersection of Riverside Drive and Johnson Ferry Road), is the most popular put-in point on the river. Be sure to contact the Recreation Area's **Visitor Station**, 1978 Island Ford Parkway, 678-538-1200, for raft rental information and more. Or contact the **City of Roswell Recreation Department**, 770-641-3705, www.roswellgov.com.

A great spot for sailing, boating, and water fun is **Lake Lanier**, www.lakelanierislands.com, less than an hour's drive northeast of Atlanta. You can sun on a human-made beach, ride down the rapids in the water park, swim in the lake, or rent a boat from Lake Lanier's **Harbor Landing**, 770-932-7255. Sailing enthusiasts can join the **Lake Lanier Sailing Club**, 770-967-6441, www.llsc.com, to meet other sailors and take advantage of charter cruises and boat rentals. The club also offers sailing lessons for adults and juniors.

If boating interests you, contact one of the following organizations. This may be a great way to meet people with similar interests, and get your feet wet!

- **Atlanta Yacht Club**, www.atlantayachtclub.org, in Lake Allatoona, sponsors sailing and sailboat racing activities for adults and families
- **Atlanta Rowing Club**, 770-993-1879, www.atlantarow.org
- **Atlanta Boardsailing Club**, 404-237-1431, http://windsurf atlanta.org
- **Atlanta Whitewater Club**, 800-231-6058, www.atlantawhite water.com
- **Georgia Canoeing Association**, 770-421-9729, www.georgia canoe.org
- **Lanier Canoe and Kayak Club**, 770-287-7888, www.lckc.org

BOWLING

If you're looking for a sport you can practice year round, bowling may be it. There are several popular bowling alleys in the metro Atlanta area, and most of them offer bowling league play if you're interested in joining a team. A few to consider are:

- **AMF Bowling Centers**: Chamblee Lanes, 2175 Savoy Drive, Chamblee, 770-451-8605; Stone Mountain Lanes, 720 Hambrick Road, Stone Mountain, 404-296-2400; Village Lanes, 2692 Sandy Plains Road NE, Marietta, 770-973-2695; Gwinnett Lanes, 4990 Jimmy Carter Boulevard NW, Norcross, 770-923-5080; www.amfcenters.com
- **Brunswick Bowling Centers**: Azalea Lanes, 2750 Austell Road SW, Marietta, 770-435-2120; Cedar Creek Lanes, 2749 Delk Road, Marietta, 770-988-8813; Gwinnett Lanes, 3835 Highway 29, Lawrenceville, 770-

925-2000; Roswell Lanes, 785 Old Roswell Road, Roswell, 770-998-9437; http://bbb.brunswickbowling.com
- **Express Bowling Lanes**, 1936 Piedmont Circle NE, Atlanta, 404-874-5703
- **Northeast Plaza Lanes**, 3285 Buford Highway NE, Atlanta, 404-636-7548, www.fun-bowl.com
- **Suburban Lanes**, 2619 North Decatur Road, Decatur, 404-373-2514, www.suburbanlanes.com
- **Tucker Bowling Center**, 4365 Cowan Road, Tucker, 770-938-7171

CHESS

There are several good chess clubs and centers in metro Atlanta. For a complete listing, and for more information on chess in Georgia, check out the **Georgia Chess Association**, www.georgiachess.org. You may also want to consider the following:
- **Atlanta Chess and Game Center**, 3155 East Ponce de Leon Avenue, Scottdale, 404-377-4400; offers rated tournaments and a large selection of chess books and equipment
- **Championship Chess**, 3565 Evans Road, Doraville, 770-939-4596
- **Cobb County Chess Club**, 770-977-3951; all-ages group that meets at the East Cobb Borders Books location, 4475 Roswell Road, on Tuesdays (adults) and Thursdays (kids)
- **Emory Chess Association**, 106 Bishops Hall, Emory, 404-778-4121, www.emorychess.org; meets weekly, open to the public; call for day and time

DANCE

If you'd like to learn a new dance, join a dance club, or be invited to members-only social dances, the following resources may be useful:
- **Atlanta Ballroom Dance Club**, www.atlantaballroomdance.org, holds monthly dances at the Knights of Columbus Hall, 2620 Buford Highway; also offers Wednesday night dance lessons for beginning and intermediate dancers of all ages
- **Atlanta Swing Era Dance Association**, www.aseda.org, is a non-profit organization that sponsors monthly community dances, workshops, dance events, lessons, and more
- **Atlanta Tango**, www.atlantatango.com, offers weekly classes, events and community dances at various locations around town
- **Atlanta Waltz Society**, 770-499-0142, www.splittree.org/atlantawaltzsociety.htm, offers lessons followed by an open-to-the-public

dance on Sundays at Several Dancers Core on the square in downtown Decatur; call for times and prices

- **Awalim Dance Company**, 404-297-9343, www.tribalbellydance. com, offers traditional, Middle-Eastern dance classes at Studioplex on Auburn Avenue, and performances at various locations throughout metro Atlanta
- **Metro Atlanta Square Dancers Association**, 770-445-7035, www. masda.net, is a network of square dancers across the state. The association can provide you with a schedule of upcoming events and classes, as well as offer an introduction to other folks interested in this art form.
- **The Royal Scottish Country Dance Society**, 770-242-3889, www. mindspring.com/~atlbrnch, is the Atlanta branch of this national organization

Many of the local **YMCA**, 404-588-9622, www.ymcaatlanta.org, and **YWCA**, 404-527-7575, www.ywcaatlanta.org, branches also offer dance classes for adults and children. Contact your neighborhood branch directly for schedule and pricing information.

FENCING

For information on fencing in metro Atlanta, including locations for classes, summer camps, and local tournaments, contact the **Atlanta Fencers Club**, 404-762-7666, www.atlantafencersclub.com.

FISHING

It's fairly simple to get a fishing license in metro Atlanta. All you need is a photo ID, proof of residency (such as a signed lease or recent utility bill), and $9. Once you have those things, just head over to the fishing section of your local sporting goods or discount department store. There, you'll be able to purchase a license in less time than it takes to bait a hook. A few stores to consider for fishing equipment and licenses are listed below.

- **Dick's Sporting Goods**, 877-846-9997, www.dickssporting goods.com; formerly Galyans, three locations in metro Atlanta
- **REI—Recreational Equipment**, 800-426-4840, www.rei.com; three locations in metro Atlanta
- **The Sports Authority**, www.sportsauthority.com; ten locations throughout metro Atlanta
- **Kmart**, 866-562-7848, www.kmart.com; ten locations throughout metro Atlanta
- **Wal-Mart**, 800-925-6278 www.walmart.com; ten locations through-out metro Atlanta

It's also possible to purchase your fishing license directly from the **Department of Natural Resources, License Unit**, over the phone by calling 888-748-6887, or online at http://georgiawildlife.dnr.state.ga.us. There is, however, an additional service charge of $3.95 per license for either of those options. For more information on obtaining a fishing license in Georgia, call the **Fishing License Information Line**, 770-414-3333.

Once you have your license, you'll probably want to know where to go for good fishing. Some of the small lakes in metro Atlanta's parks are open for fishing. To find out if there's one close to you, call the **Parks and Recreation Department** in your neighborhood (see numbers above). For statewide fishing information, contact the **Georgia State National Resources Department, Fishing Information Line**, 770-918-6418, http://georgiawildlife.dnr.state.ga.us.

FRISBEE

Though some may think a Frisbee is just something to toss around the park after they've finished their picnic lunch, many people consider disc golf to be a serious (yet fun!) sport. If you'd like to learn more or just find out where you can go to be a spectator or to participate, contact the **Atlanta Disc Golf Organization**, http://discgolfatlanta.com; or the **Atlanta Flying Disc Club**, 404-351-0914, www.afdc.com.

GOLF

Local parks and recreation departments operate a number of golf courses. Call the one convenient to your neighborhood for fees and reservations. For a list of additional public golf courses and private golf clubs, consult your Yellow Pages.

- **City of Atlanta**: **9-Hole Golf Course**: Candler Park Golf Course–Candler Park, 585 Candler Park Drive NE, 404-371-1260, www.candlerparkgolf.com; **18-Hole Golf Courses**: Alfred Tup Holmes Golf Course, 2300 Wilson Drive SW, 404-753-6158; Bobby Jones Golf Course, 384 Woodward Way NW, 404-355-1009; Browns Mill Golf Course, 480 Cleveland Avenue SE, 404-366-3573; North Fulton Golf Course, 216 West Wieuca Road NE, 404-255-0723; www.atlantaga.gov
- **DeKalb County**: Mystery Valley Golf Course, 6100 Shadow Rock Drive, Lithonia, 770-469-6913; Sugar Creek Golf Course, 2706 Bouldercrest Road SE, Atlanta, 404-241-7671; www.co.dekalb.ga.us/parks/gt.htm
- **Cobb County**: Cobblestone Golf Course, 4200 Nance Road, Acworth, 770-917-5151, www.cobblestonegolf.com; Legacy Links Golf Course,

1825 Windy Hill Road, Marietta, 770-434-6331, www.legacy foxcreek.com

- **Cherokee County**: BridgeMill Athletic Club, 1190 BridgeMill Avenue, Canton, 770-345-5500, www.bridgemillgc.com; Woodmont Golf Club, 3105 Gaddis Road, Canton, 770-345-9260, www.woodmont golfclub.com; Cherokee Golf Center, Highway 92 and I-575, Woodstock, 770-924-2062; Eagle Watch Golf Course, 3055 Eagle Watch Drive, Woodstock, 770-591-1000; Towne Lake Hills Golf Club, 1003 Towne Lake Hills East, Woodstock, 770-592-9969; www.cherokee ga.com
- **Gwinnett County**: Bear's Best, 5342 Aldeburgh Drive, Suwanee, 678-714-2582; Heritage Golf Club, 4445 Britt Road, Norcross, 770-493-4653; St. Marlo Golf Club, 7755 St. Marlo Country Club Parkway, Duluth, 770-495-7725; Collins Hill Golf Club, 585 Camp Perrin Road, Lawrenceville, 770-822-5400; http://gcvb.org/golf.asp

There are also several **golf clubs and organizations** (both amateur and professional) in the metro Atlanta area. A few to consider:

- **Amateur Golf League of Atlanta**, 404-467-4853
- **Atlanta Junior Golf Association**, 770-850-9040, www.atljrga.org
- **American Singles Golf Association**, Atlanta chapter, 770-785-2669, www.atlantasinglesgolf.com
- **Executive Women's Golf League**, Atlanta, 770-984-7617, www.ew gatlanta.com
- **Georgia State Golf Association**, 770-955-4272, www.gsga.org

HIKING

Aside from the many miles of trails in area parks, there are countless scenic places to hike within a ninety-minute drive of the city. Especially enticing to many Atlantans are the **North Georgia Mountains**, home to quaint southern towns and various state parks. In the **Chattahoochee National Forest**, Springer Mountain is the southern starting point of the Appalachian Trail, which winds for 2,050 miles through the eastern United States. An eight-mile trail meanders through **Amicalola Falls State Park,** located 50 miles north of Atlanta; its falls are some of the highest in the United States. The **Tallulah Gorge State Park** offers hiking and wildflower trails leading to the spectacular gorge that measures 1000 feet in depth. For more information about hiking trails in and around metro Atlanta, see the **Greenspace** and **Quick Getaways** chapters of this book. To learn more about Georgia's State Parks, contact the **State Parks and Historic Sites Information Office**, 404-656-3530, www.gastateparks.org.

If you'd like to meet others interested in hiking, or learn more information about area trails, consider the following organizations:

- **Benton MacKaye Trail Association**, www.bmta.org
- **Dog Hikers of Georgia**, 770-992-2002
- **Kennesaw Outdoors Activities Club**, http://home.earthlink. net/~koac/index.htm
- **Pine Mountain Trail Association**, 706-663-4858, www.pine mountaintrail.org
- **Sierra Club**, 404-607-7819, www.sierraclub.org/chapters/ga/outings

HOCKEY

The **Atlanta Amateur Hockey League**, 770-650-RINK, www.atlanta hockey.org, organizes matches for metro Atlanta's league teams, which play at **The Marietta Ice Center**, 4880 Lower Roswell Road, 770-509-5067, www.themicice.com. The Ice Center also offers hockey lessons for children and adults, as does the **Alpharetta Family Skate Center**, 770-649-6600, www.cooler.com. Call for schedule and pricing. You may also want to contact the **Atlanta Coed Hockey League**, 770-414-8950; the **Georgia Amateur Hockey Association**, 404-816-3303; and the **Metro Atlanta Street Hockey Association**, 770-840-6952, www.mashahockey.com, for more information on teams, leagues, classes, and events for all ages in your area.

HORSEBACK RIDING

Numerous metro Atlanta stables offer horseback riding lessons, rent and sell horses, and board horses. Here are just a few:

- **Chastain Horse Park**, 4371 Powers Ferry Road NW, Atlanta, 404-252-4244, www.chastainhorsepark.org
- **East Cobb Stables**, 1649 Johnson Ferry Road, Marietta, 678-560-9154, www.eastcobbstables.com
- **Happy Horse Farm**, 4539 North Arnold Mill Road, Woodstock, 770-367-9894, www.happyhorsefarm.com
- **Vogt Riding Academy**, 1084 Houston Mill Road NE, Atlanta, 404-321-9506
- **Wills Park Equestrian Center**, Alpharetta, 678-297-6120, http://alpharetta.ga.us

ICE SKATING

Though Atlanta's temperatures are pretty moderate year round, you can still hone your ice skating skills on the city's few indoor rinks. The **Atlanta**

Iceforum, 2300 Satellite Boulevard, Duluth, 770-813-1010, and the **IceForum at Town Center**, 3061 Busbee Parkway, Kennesaw, 770-218-1010, www.iceforum.com, offer public skating, birthday packages, private lessons, rentals, and more. **The Marietta Ice Center**, 4880 Lower Roswell Road NE, Marietta, 770-509-5067, www.themicice.com, offers hockey leagues, lessons, private parties, public skating, and more. All three rinks provide a full-service pro shop and day care packages.

For a limited time each winter (usually just December and January), skaters can enjoy an outdoor rink hosted by either Centennial Olympic Park or The World of Coca-Cola (the facilities alternate each year). For additional information on hours of operation, admission prices, skate rentals, and more, contact **Centennial Olympic Park** at 404-223-4412, www.centennialpark.com, or **The World of Coca-Cola** at 404-676-5151, www.woccatlanta.com.

IN-LINE/ROLLER SKATING/SKATEBOARDING

If in-line skating is your thing, you will find many fellow enthusiasts in metro Atlanta. One of the most popular spots to show off your skills and whiz down paved trails is **Piedmont Park**, 404-875-7275, www.piedmontpark.org. You can rent or buy blades right across the park at **Skate Escape**, 1086 Piedmont Avenue NE, 404-892-1292, www.skateescape.com.

If you'd like to skate with others, participate in races, or just get more information on the best places to skate, contact the **Atlanta Peachtree Road Rollers**, 404-806-7251, www.aprr.org, or the **Cobb County Cruisers**, 770-421-1247.

If a few lessons are needed before heading out on your own, you may want to consider **Bohemian Skate School**, 404-377-5811, www.bohemian skateschool.com; or the **Starlite Skating Center**, 770-474-7655, www.starliteskatingcenter.com. Both places have certified instructors that can help get you rolling.

And if you're a skateboarder, check out the ESPN X Games Skateboard Park at Discover Mills in Lawrenceville, 678-847-5727, www.xgames skatepark.com/atlanta.html, with facilities for all levels and ages.

LACROSSE

There are several local amateur lacrosse clubs and associations. To find out more about the sport, local teams, and events, contact any of the following organizations:

- **Atlanta Youth Lacrosse Association**, www.atlantayouthlacrosse. com
- **Bagataway Lacrosse**, 770-777-9331, www.bagatawaylacrosse.com

- **East Cobb Lacrosse**, http://eteamz.active.com/eclax
- **Georgia Lacrosse Foundation**, www.lacrossegeorgia.com
- **Southeastern Lacrosse Conference**, www.selc.org

RACQUET SPORTS—TENNIS AND SQUASH

The **Atlanta Lawn Tennis Association** (**ALTA**), with over 70,000 members, is the largest organization of its kind in the United States. It offers league matches for men, women, juniors, and wheelchair players; leagues are divided according to levels of expertise. Contact 770-399-5788, www.altatennis.org, for more information.

The **parks and recreation department** in your area operates a multitude of public tennis centers where you can play without paying a fee. Here's a list of the major tennis centers:

CITY OF ATLANTA
- **Bitsy Grant Tennis Cente**r, 2125 Northside Drive NW, 404-351-2774
- **Chastain Park Tennis Center**, 110 West Wieuca Road NE, 404-255-1993
- **Piedmont Park Tennis Center**, Park Drive NE, 404-872-1507

FULTON COUNTY
- **North Fulton Tennis Center**, 500 Abernathy Road NE, Sandy Springs, 404-303-6182
- **South Fulton Tennis Center**, 5645 Mason Road, College Park, 770-306-3059

DEKALB COUNTY
- **Blackburn Tennis Center**, 3501 Ashford-Dunwoody Road NE, Atlanta, 770-451-1061
- **DeKalb Tennis Center**, 1400 McConnell Drive, Decatur, 404-325-2520
- **Sugar Creek Tennis Center**, 2706 Bouldercrest Road SE, Atlanta, 404-243-7149

COBB COUNTY
- **Fair Oaks Tennis Center**, 1460 Brandon Drive SW, Marietta, 770-528-8483
- **Harrison Tennis Center**, 2650 Shallowford Road NE, Marietta, 770-591-3150
- **Kennworth Tennis Center**, 4100 Highway 293 NE, Acworth, 770-917-5161
- **Sweetwater Tennis Center**, 2447 Clay Road SW, Austell, 770-819-3221

GWINNETT COUNTY

- **Hudlow Tennis Center**, 2051 Old Rockbridge Road, Norcross, 770-417-2210
- **Mountain Park Tennis Center**, 5050 Five Forks Trickum Road, Lilburn, 770-564-4651
- **Pleasant Hill Tennis Center**, 3620 Pleasant Hill Road NW, Duluth, 770-417-2210
- **Rhodes Jordan Park**, 100 E. Crogan Street, Norcross, 770-417-2210

ROCK CLIMBING

If you're interested in rock climbing and backpacking courses, try the **Providence Outdoor Recreation Center**, 13440 Providence Park Drive, Alpharetta, 770-740-2419, www.co.fulton.ga.us. All-day and overnight courses introduce participants to the basics. **Atlanta Rocks**, www.atlantarocks.com, offers indoor rock climbing classes, camps, and more at two locations: **Intown**, 1019-A Collier Road, Atlanta, 404-351-3009, and **Perimeter**, 4411-A Bankers Circle, Atlanta, 770-242-7625. You can also practice on the big rock wall at **Dick's Sporting Goods** (formerly Galyans) in Buckhead, 3535 Peachtree Road, 404-267-0200, www.dicks sportinggoods.com.

If you'd like to learn more about rock climbing in Georgia, or if you'd like to meet other enthusiasts, contact the **Atlanta Climbing Club**, 404-237-4021, www.atlantaclimbingclub.org.

RUGBY

Diehard rugby enthusiasts can scrum with the **Atlanta Renegades Rugby Club**, 770-483-6793, www.atlantarenegades.com; the **High Country Rugby and Social Club**, www.highcountryrugby.com; or the **Atlanta Harlequins Women's Rugby Club**, 770-908-1526, www.atlantaharlequins.com.

RUNNING

Because the weather is rarely cold here, runners hit the paths year round. On any given day, at most hours of the day or night, you can find at least one or two joggers huffing and puffing down the road; on a sunny spring or fall weekend afternoon, runners are out in force on neighborhood streets and in parks all over the city. There are countless opportunities in the greater Atlanta area to run in various races or just for fun.

The **Atlanta Track Club**, 404-231-9064, www.atlantatrackclub.org, one of the largest running clubs in the country, sponsors over 20 races a year, including the popular Thanksgiving morning marathon and half-marathon. Its biggest event is the Peachtree Road Race, an incredibly well attended 10K on the Fourth of July. It attracts 50,000 amateur and professional runners and wheelchair racers each year. Watch for entry blanks in the paper and act fast. For such a large race, it fills up quickly. The ATC also operates the **Atlanta Race Hotline**, 404-262-RACE (7223), which provides callers with recorded information about weekly racing events.

A few neighborhood running clubs to consider are: **Buckhead Road Runners**, 404-816-6299; the **Chattahoochee Road Runners**, 770-984-0451, www.crrclub.com; the **Greater Gwinnett Road Runners**, 770-979-6336, www.ggrr.org; and the **Roswell Runners Club**, 770-451-5500, www.roswellrunners.com. For more information about running clubs in Georgia, contact **Run Georgia** at 770-704-9057, www.rungeorgia. com. Remember, it's not always safe to run alone, even in the daytime, so you may want to contact the organizations above to find running partners and a list of safe routes in your area.

SKIING

There are no slopes nearby, but there is an **Atlanta Ski Club** that sponsors local activities as well as ski trips around the world. For more information, call 404-303-1460, or visit www.atlantaskiclub.org.

SOCCER

If soccer is your game, consider contacting the **Georgia State Soccer Association**, 770-452-0505, www.gasoccer.org; or the **Atlanta Youth Soccer Association**, 404-248-9333, www.aysa.net, for information about the numerous leagues, teams, and soccer programs in the metro Atlanta area. Or you may want to contact the organizations listed below:
- **The Atlanta Cup (Youth Tournament)**, 770-452-0505, www. atlantacup.com
- **Cobb Futbol Club**, 678-594-5041, www.cobbfc.org
- **Georgia Adult Co-ed Soccer League**, 770-428-0364, www. gacsl.addr.com
- **Greater Atlanta Women's Soccer Association**, www. piercing.org/gawsa
- **Gwinnett Soccer Association**, 770-925-4106, www.gsasoccer.com
- **Lightning Soccer Club**, 770-486-8070, www.fcysl.org

SWIMMING

Alas, the nearest ocean is about a three-hour drive, but during those hot summer months, you can still cool off in one of metro Atlanta's many public pool facilities. Whether you want to tan at an outdoor pool or swim laps year round in an indoor natatorium, there is an opportunity to make a splash in every county.

The **City of Atlanta**, www.atlantaga.gov, offers 18 outdoor aquatics facilities that operate only in the summertime. For a complete listing, see the blue pages Atlanta City Government section of your phone book. Here are a few of the more popular **outdoor pools**:

- **Candler Park Pool**, 1500 McLendon Avenue NE, 404-373-4349
- **Chastain Park Pool**, 235 West Wieuca Road NW, 404-255-0863
- **Garden Hills Pool**, 4058 East Brookhaven Drive NE, 404-848-7220
- **Grant Park Pool**, 625 Park Avenue SE, 404-622-3041
- **Piedmont Park Pool**, 1085 Piedmont Avenue NE, 404-892-0117

Atlanta also operates three **indoor aquatic facilities**:

- **M.L. King**, 90 Boulevard NE, 404-658-1149, 404-658-7330
- **J.F. Kennedy**, 225 James P. Brawley Drive SW, 404-215-2823, 404-215-2855
- **Southeast Atlanta**, 365 Cleveland Avenue SE, 404-624-0772, 404-624-0774

COBB COUNTY, www.cobbcounty.org:

- **Aquatic Center at Larry Bell Park**, 520 Fairground Street SE, Marietta, 770-528-8465
- **Mountain View Aquatic Center**, 2650 Gordy Parkway, Marietta, 770-509-4925
- **West Cobb Aquatic Center**, 3675 Macland Road, Powder Springs, 770-222-6700

DEKALB COUNTY

- **DeKalb County Aquatics Department,** 678-937-8925, www.co.dekalb.ga.us/parks/aqua.htm

GWINNETT COUNTY, www.co.gwinnett.ga.us:

- **Best Friend Park Pool**, 6224 Jimmy Carter Boulevard, Norcross, 770-417-2202
- **Collins Hill Aquatic Center**, 2200 Collins Hill Road, Lawrenceville, 770-237-5647
- **Dacula Park Pool**, 205 Dacula Road, Dacula, 770-822-5410

- **Mountain Park Pool**, 5050 Five Forks Trickum Road, Lilburn, 770-564-4650
- **Rhodes Jordan Park Pool**, 100 East Crogan Street, Lawrenceville, 770-822-5143

SOUTH FULTON COUNTY
- **Welcome All Park Pool**, 4255 Will Lee Road, College Park, 404-762-4058, www.co.fulton.ga.us

There are also several metro Atlanta **swim clubs** to consider, including:
- **Swim Atlanta Masters**: Roswell, 770-992-1778; and Lawrenceville, 678-442-7946; www.swimatlantamasters.com
- **Dynamo Swim Club**, 770-772-6789, www.dynamoswimclub.com
- **Dynamo Masters Swim Club**, 770-457-7946, www.dynamomasters.com
- **Chattahoochee Gold Masters**, 770-928-1506, www.goldswim.com

And finally, **White Water Park**, 250 North Marietta Parkway, Marietta, 770-948-9290, www.sixflags.com/parks/whitewater, offers 40 acres of water activities, including water slides, wave pools, and a toddler pool, so it's fun for the whole family. For those who don't mind a short drive to Buford, Georgia—about 40 miles north of Atlanta—there's always **Lake Lanier Islands**, 6950 Holiday Road, Buford, 770-932-7200, www.lakelanierislands.com, which offers a man-made beach, boat and jet-ski rentals, resort, and a water park.

VOLLEYBALL

For information on volleyball in metro Atlanta, including teams, schedules, workshops, open play, and more, contact **Volleyball Atlanta**, www.volleyballatlanta.org. You may also want to check out **Atlanta Area Volleyball**, www.volleyball.org/atlanta, for a listing of local adult and junior leagues, college teams and more.

YOGA

Yoga has become increasingly popular in metro Atlanta over the last decade, though several schools and organizations have been here since the 1970s. Keep in mind, there are several different styles of yoga, though they all share a common lineage. No style is better than another; it's simply a matter of personal preference. **Ashtanga Yoga** (also called Power Yoga) is very rigorous; participants jump from one posture to another, building strength, flexibility, and stamina. If you are a beginner, or haven't worked out in a while, you may want to steer clear of this one. **Kripalu Yoga** is a gentle form of yoga that emphasizes pranayama (proper breathing), alignment, coordinating breath and movement, and working within the limits of each individual's flexibility and strength. It's very popular with beginning students. **Iyengar Yoga** (named for legendary teacher B.K.S. Iyengar) is one of the most popular styles of yoga in the world. Iyengar teachers stress the importance of the precise alignment of postures. Props are often used to assist beginners who may not be able to complete an asana (pose). **Viniyoga**, in the tradition of renowned yoga teacher T.K.V. Desikachar, is a form of flow yoga that can be gentle for beginners yet becomes more strenuous as you advance. Teachers of this yoga style will generally adapt the asanas to fit each practitioner, so you can work at your own pace. And, finally, **Classical Yoga**, a system based in ancient yogic philosophy, incorporates varying degrees of breathwork, asana, meditation, mudra, and mantras, and emphasizes *seva,* or selfless service as an integral part of one's personal practice.

For more complete information on yoga and its various branches, try *Yoga Journal*, www.yogajournal.com, and *Yoga International*, www.yimag.org, two bimonthly publications that can be found at any of the major bookstores. You should also talk to someone at the school or schools you are interested in attending to find out more about the type of yoga they teach before signing up. Yoga can be a wonderful physical and mental workout, if you find the style that works best for you.

Today, there are a number of really good schools in the area, and yoga classes can even be found at your local **YMCA**. A few established schools to consider are:

- **Atlanta Yoga**, 660 Ninth Street, Studio B, Atlanta, 404-892-7797, www.atlantayoga.com; offers classes in Ashtanga yoga
- **Decatur Hot Yoga**, 431 West Ponce de Leon Avenue, 404-377-4899, www.decaturhotyoga.com; Bikram-style classes and more
- **Kashi Atlanta**, 1681 McLendon Avenue, Atlanta, 404-687-3353, www.kashiatlanta.org; classical yoga, meditation and more
- **Metamorphosis Yoga Center**, 2931A North Druid Hills Road NE, Atlanta, 404-633-8484, www.metamorphosisyoga.com; Kripalu-style yoga and Phoenix Rising Yoga Therapy
- **Peachtree Yoga Center**, 6050 Sandy Springs Circle, Sandy Springs, 404-847-9642, www.realpagessites.com/peachtreeyoga; offers a variety of classes, including Kripalu and Ashtanga
- **The Pierce Program**, 1164 North Highland Avenue NE, Atlanta, 404-875-7110, www.pierceyoga.com; offers Viniyoga classes in the tradition of T.K.V. Desikachar
- **Stillwater Yoga Studio**, 931 Monroe Drive, Atlanta, 404-874-7813, www.stillyoga.com; offers classes in Iyengar yoga

- **YMCA**, 404-588-9622, www.ymcaatlanta.org; various locations throughout metro Atlanta

HEALTH CLUBS, GYMS, AND YMCAS

Health clubs are a way of life in metro Atlanta among the young and fitness-minded. Deciding which one to join can be rather overwhelming, but many clubs offer free or inexpensive introductory memberships as an incentive to try them out. The following is only a partial list of your many options. Consult the Atlanta Yellow Pages for more.

- **Bally's Holiday Fitness Centers**, www.ballyfitness.com; multiple locations throughout metro Atlanta
- **Buckhead Athletic Club**, 3353 Peachtree Road NE, Atlanta, 404-364-2222
- **Curves**, www.curvesinternational.com; several locations throughout metro Atlanta
- **DeKalb Medical Center**, 2665 North Decatur Road, Decatur, 404-501-2222, www.dekalbmedicalcenter.org/wellnesscenter.asp
- **Gold's Gym**, www.goldsgym.com; over 20 locations throughout metro Atlanta
- **HFC Health Fitness Center Midtown**, 725 West Peachtree Street, 404-892-4348, www.midtown.hfitcenter.com
- **LA Fitness**, www.lafitness.com; several locations throughout metro Atlanta
- **Lee Haney World Class Fitness**, 675 Ponce de Leon Avenue NE, Atlanta, 404-892-6737, www.leehaney.com/center.htm
- **Northpark 400 Health Club**, 1000 Abernathy Road NE, Sandy Springs, 770-668-2220
- **Peachtree Center Athletic Club**, 227 Courtland Street NE, Atlanta, 404-523-3833, www.wellbridge.com/peachtree
- **The Sporting Club at Windy Hill**, 135 Interstate North Parkway, Atlanta, 770-953-1100, www.sportingclubwindyhill.com
- **YMCA**, 404-588-9622, www.ymcaatlanta.com; several locations throughout metro Atlanta

SPORT AND SOCIAL CLUBS

In addition to the many social organizations specific to a particular sport (see listings above), metro Atlanta is also home to several clubs geared towards fitness-minded people in general. Two to consider are **Atlanta Club Sport**, 404-257-3355, www.usclubsport.com, and the **Adventure Club**, www.adventureclub.com. Contacting these organizations may be a great way to meet people who share similar interests and learn more about sports and fitness opportunities throughout the city. Newcomers may also want to try the **Newcomer Women's Club of North Fulton and Gwinnett**, P.O. Box 3097, Duluth, GA 30096-9998, 678-714-5464; the **Alpharetta Roswell Newcomer's Club**, 678-318-1442; or the **Black Newcomers Network**, 770-438-4600, www.black newcomersnetwork.org. All of these clubs offer regular socials and events for those new to the city.

ATLANTA IS A CITY RENOWNED FOR ITS BEAUTIFUL TREES AND LUSH urban landscape. It's a city that takes pride in its parks and reveres its trees, so much so that in 1984 a group of residents formed **Trees Atlanta**, 404-522-4097, www.treesatlanta.org, a volunteer organization dedicated to planting and preserving trees throughout the city. Every spring, when the dogwood trees bloom and colorful azaleas blanket the roadsides, metro Atlanta feels like a garden paradise. As a resident of this blooming oasis, you too can enjoy the wide variety of indigenous and non-native trees and flowers in the numerous parks and gardens that blanket the city.

All of metro Atlanta's neighborhoods boast their own small green gems—modest but beautiful parks that welcome nearby residents. There are so many, in fact, throughout the metro Atlanta area, it's impossible to list them all here. However, one such Atlanta park, known as the **Duck Pond**, is a lovely expanse of green space located in the middle of Buckhead's Garden Hills district. Picnickers have been coming here for years, spreading out on the lawn, and saving their breadcrusts to share with the pond's year-round population of ducks. Another beloved neighborhood park is **Murphy-Candler Park** in Dunwoody, a sprawling, 135-acre park featuring nature trails, a beautiful lake (with ducks and fish), a playground, picnic tables, and more.

Regardless of which part of town you're in, be sure to take time to explore your new community and its area greenspaces and pocket parks; you may discover an unexpected jewel of your own and get to know some of your new neighbors in the process.

While most of the suburban parks offer a number of amenities including picnic tables, playgrounds, and acres of greenspace, it's the impressive City of Atlanta parks that draw the largest crowds. Intowners and suburbanites alike frequent these intown parks regularly throughout the warm weather months, enjoying the sunshine and open space, as well as the many festivals that are held in Atlanta's parks each year.

Below you'll find an overview of and contact information for metro Atlanta's largest and most popular greenspaces. For a listing of parks in your community, check the Parks and Recreation Department of the county in which you reside.

CITY PARKS

Atlanta's largest and best-known park is **Piedmont Park**, 404-875-7275, www.piedmontpark.org, located in Midtown at Piedmont Avenue and 14th Street. Originally part of the Gentleman's Riding Club, the land was purchased by the city government in 1904 for use as a public park. A four-mile jogging trail snakes through the grounds, which house a tennis center, athletic fields, and Playscapes (an unusual children's playground designed by sculptor Isamu Noguchi). The park is a favorite locale for joggers, rollerbladers, cyclists, families, and picnickers who enjoy exploring the trails around lovely Lake Clara Meer.

Numerous events take place in Piedmont Park throughout the year, including the **Arts Festival of Atlanta**, which attracts artists from all over the state; **The Peachtree Road Race**, which begins and ends at the park every July 4th; and free Sunday evening, summertime concerts by the **Atlanta Symphony Orchestra**. Piedmont Park also plays host to the always-popular **Dogwood Festival**, 404-329-0501, www.dogwood.org, every April, and its well-tended fields are the locale of choice for several local softball leagues. Contact the park to learn more about upcoming events and field use.

Piedmont Park is also home to the **Atlanta Botanical Garden (ABG)**, 404-876-5859, www.atlantabotanicalgarden.org, a private, non-profit facility designed to educate the public, support horticulture research, and display a wide variety of plant life. The entrance to the Atlanta Botanical Garden is located at the north end of the park on Piedmont Avenue, and it includes the Storza Woods, a 15-acre hardwood forest with trails, the Dorothy Chapman Fuqua Conservatory, and landscaped gardens that spread across 15 acres. In the 16,000-square-foot glass-covered Conservatory is a fabulous array of tropical, desert, and endangered species; the outdoor gardens display over 3,000 plants, including a rose garden, vegetable and herb gardens, a fragrance garden for the blind, and a Japanese garden. Green-thumb enthusiasts can take advantage of the ABG's extensive **Sheffield Botanical Library** and can also call the **Garden's Plant Hotline**, 404-888-GROW, with any gardening questions. In more recent years, the botanical garden has expanded to include a $3 million dollar orchid house and a whimsical children's garden replete with fountains, a butterfly pavilion, a treehouse, and a number of hands-on exhibits and activities.

At Atlanta Avenue and Boulevard, in the heart of the neighborhood that shares its name, lies Atlanta's oldest park, **Grant Park**, home to lofty shade trees, numerous pavilions, and enticing paved paths. In addition, Grant Park is home to **Zoo Atlanta**, 404-624-5600, www.zooatlanta.com, and the **Atlanta Cyclorama**, 404-658-7625, a fifty-foot circular painting of the Battle of Atlanta. And amateur sports teams utilize its athletic facilities throughout the year. Annual events include September's **Grant Park Tour of Homes**, 404-215-9955, www.grantpark.org, through the surrounding Victorian neighborhood, as well as the **Christmas Candlelight Tour**, which takes place in December.

In the heart of the Emory University campus, just off the main entrance at Clifton Road, lies **Lullwater Estate Park**, the beautifully maintained, residential grounds belonging to the university's president. A hidden treasure, this 185-acre park features a paved trail leading around the Tudor Revival style house and several miles of dirt trails winding around the lake. Lullwater is a popular destination with Emory students and faculty and with local residents.

Six miles east of the downtown area, in the stately Druid Hills neighborhood, it is a real treat to wander through **Fernbank Forest**, a 65-acre old growth forest. A two-mile-long trail winds through the dense woods, and signs marking the area's vegetation educate the interested observer. If you want to relax in the midst of the forest, you can take a seat at one of several rest areas; mobility-impaired visitors can enjoy the forest's wonders by using the paved "easy effort" trail located near the gatehouse. The forest is located on the grounds of the **Fernbank Science Center**, 678-874-7102, www.fernbank.edu, which houses a planetarium, an observatory, and an exhibition hall. Visitors may also view a greenhouse and the Cator Woolford Memorial Gardens. Finally, the **Fernbank Museum of Natural History**, 404-929-6300, www.fernbank.edu, with its IMAX theater and science exhibits, is situated on adjoining land.

Chastain Park, 404-237-2177, eight miles north of downtown, just off of Roswell Road, is a city-run, 320-acre park that's home to a tennis center, swimming pool, riding stables, public golf course, art gallery, and much more. The park is really an all-purpose sporting and recreation extravaganza. Joggers, walkers, and rollerbladers crowd the 3½-mile jogging trail, and cyclists can join in organized rides throughout the park. Amateur sports enthusiasts play year round on Chastain's many athletic fields, while families and kids make use of the playground and many picnic areas. In addition, the park's **Chastain Amphitheater**, 404-233-2227, www.atlantaconcerts.com/chastain.html, accommodates over 6,000 people, and hosts various outdoor concerts and performances throughout the year.

For more information on Atlanta's many city parks, contact the **Bureau of Parks** for Atlanta, 404-817-6744, www.atlantaga.gov.
For more information on parks in your community, contact your local **Parks and Recreation Department**:

- **Alpharetta Parks and Recreation**, 678-297-6100, www.alpharetta.ga.us
- **Chamblee Parks and Recreation**, 770-986-5016, www.chamblee ga.com
- **Cobb County Parks and Recreation**, 770-528-8800, www.cobb county.org
- **Decatur Recreation Department**, 404-377-0494, www.decatur-ga.com
- **DeKalb County Parks and Recreation**, 404-371-2631, www.co.dekalb.ga.us
- **Duluth Parks and Recreation**, 770-623-2781, www.duluth-ga.com
- **Fulton County Parks and Recreation**, 404-730-6200, www.co.fulton.ga.us
- **Gwinnett County Parks and Recreation**, 770-822-8840, www.co.gwinnett.ga.us
- **Marietta Parks and Recreation**, 770-794-5601, www.city.marietta.ga.us
- **Roswell Recreation and Parks**, 770-641-3705, www.roswell gov.com
- **Smyrna Parks and Recreation**, 770-431-2842, www.ci.smyrna.ga.us
- **Stone Mountain Recreation Department**, 770-498-2414, www.stonemountaincity.org

CHATTAHOOCHEE NATURE CENTER

In addition to the city parks mentioned above, the privately owned, not-for-profit **Chattahoochee Nature Center**, 770-992-2055, www.chatt naturecenter.com, is also one of metro Atlanta's most popular green-space destinations. Located about 17 miles north of downtown, it is a wonderful place to hike, explore, and be environmentally educated. The center contains two nature trails, which allow hikers to experience the Chattahoochee's ecosystem firsthand. The Woodland Trails lead past Kingfisher Pond into forestland populated by indigenous birds and animals. One branch of the trail passes the remains of a pioneer cabin and a cemetery, while another offers an assortment of seasonal wildflowers.

The Wetland Trail meanders through the Redwing Marshland on the banks of the Chattahoochee River, where beavers and other marsh creatures make their homes. The center also hosts a wide variety of educational programs for visitors of all ages.

STATE PARKS

If you want to bicycle or jog along scenic paved roads, all in sight of the world's largest chunk of exposed granite, visit Georgia's **Stone Mountain Park**, 770-498-5600, just 16 miles due east of Atlanta. A must for hikers, this 2,300-acre park contains numerous trails that twist and turn around three picturesque lakes and up the mountain itself. Whether you're looking for a five-mile hike around the mountain or an easy stroll through the woods, you'll find it here. Many choose to walk up the mountain and ride the skylift back down, but you can reverse the trip. Either way, take time to relish the mountain's man-made miracle— the world's largest statue, a 90-foot-tall carving of Robert E. Lee, Stonewall Jackson, and Jefferson Davis on horseback—as well as its natural wonders. Trail maps are available at park information desks. The park also features lakefront beaches, a golf course, a scenic railroad, restaurants, a paddlewheel riverboat, a petting zoo, family-friendly attractions, including an indoor playground called "The Great Barn," and a reconstructed antebellum plantation. A small fee is charged per car to enter the park and access the public picnic areas, nature trails, and playgrounds. And there are additional charges for guests who want full access to the park's attractions. One-day passes can be purchased at the front gate. Annual parking and visitor passes are available as well.

Like nearby Stone Mountain, Panola Mountain is a mass of exposed granite. But unlike Stone Mountain Park, a definite tourist mecca, **Panola Mountain State Conservation Park**, 770-389-7801, www.gastate parks.org/info/panolamt, is 600 acres of virtually untouched hilly forestland. Situated 18 miles southeast of the city, this day-use park is a Registered National Landmark, designed to preserve and showcase the mountain environs in their natural state. Guided tours of the mountain take place each weekend, and visitors can explore the area adjacent to the mountain on two marked trails. The park also offers wildflower walks in the spring and fall as well as other educational programs.

For a more comprehensive list of Georgia's state parks, see the **Quick Getaways** chapter of this book, or contact **Georgia State Parks and Historic Sites**, 404-656-2770, 800-864-7275, www.georgiastate parks.org.

NATIONAL PARKS

The **Chattahoochee River National Recreation Area**, 678-538-1200, www.nps.gov/chat, which contains over 70 miles of trails along the banks of the river north of Atlanta, extending from Standing Peachtree Creek all the way to Lake Lanier, should not be missed. Established in 1978 as part of the National Parks system, the Recreation Area is made up of several wilderness land units where visitors can fish, hike, and raft. The Johnson Ferry Unit provides a put-in point for commercial rafting and canoe trips as well as guided tours of the its numerous trails. Along the river's shores in the Palisades West Unit, people flock to fish and to view the rafters floating by. At the Cochran Shoals Unit, fitness buffs take to the 3.1-mile fitness trail. Cochran Shoals is also a popular haunt for cyclists and joggers. The Recreation Area is home to a spectacular array of landscapes, including zones of pristine Appalachian old-growth forests, steep outcroppings of rock, river channels and creeks, and flood plains. Hiking, whether you want an easy jaunt or a strenuous trek, is especially recommended in the fall, when temperatures cool and the leaves offer striking color contrasts.

If you'd like to combine your back-to-nature activities with an educational exploration of a Civil War battlefield, just head 19 miles northwest of downtown Atlanta on I-75 to the **Kennesaw Mountain National Battlefield Park**, 770-427-4686, www.nps.gov/kemo. Designed to commemorate and tell the story of the Atlanta Campaign and the Battle of Kennesaw Mountain, this 2,884-acre National Battlefield Park has over 16 miles of hiking trails that snake through the countryside. Whether you choose to make the entire 16-mile loop around the mountain or take an abbreviated hike, you can see remains of Confederate fortifications and some exquisite scenery along the way. There is no entrance fee.

For more information on Georgia's National Parks, see the **Quick Getaways** chapter of this book, or contact the **National Park Service**, 800-365-2267, www.nps.gov.

FOR THOSE MOVING TO ATLANTA FROM THE NORTH, THE OBVIOUS good news is that the area boasts relatively mild weather most of the year, allowing for nearly 12 months of outdoor recreation.

Springtime temperatures in metro Atlanta generally hover in the mid-60s to mid-70s from March to May, but don't be surprised if you wake up one April morning to find the mercury has dropped to 40 degrees. In spring, Atlanta temperatures can fluctuate wildly, from frosty one day to the mid-80s the next, so it's probably a good idea to wait until the middle of May to pack away your winter wardrobe. The fluctuating springtime temperatures sometimes cause severe weather situations to develop. Thunderstorms and tornadoes usually occur during this time of year, and while devastating funnel clouds rarely touch down in the metro Atlanta area, tornado activity here is a real possibility. In 1998, for instance, tornadoes plowed through several parts of the city, causing severe damage to homes and businesses in the north Atlanta suburb of Dunwoody, as well as several communities in Gwinnett County.

In addition to the threat of tornadoes and thunderstorms, springtime in metro Atlanta also brings **pollen**. Lots of pollen. And you'll find it everywhere. The pollen can be so heavy that it covers everything in sight—cars, outdoor furniture, the ground—and many Atlanta residents get regular allergy shots or take antihistamines rather than face a month or two of sneezing and watery eyes. For pollen count updates, watch your local news; area weather forecasters devote a significant chunk of their on-air time to pollen counts and lists of other allergens affecting the city. These reports can help you decide whether to limit your outdoor time on days when the pollen counts are highest.

While tornadoes and pollen counts seem to get the most media coverage, Atlanta's biggest weather story may actually be the sweltering heat and unbearable humidity of **summer**. Because the north Georgia mountains block cooler air from the north and hold in moisture from the Gulf Coast, not to mention the heat and pollution generated by urban environs, summer temperatures often soar to the upper 90s or even higher, with a whopping 90% humidity. Most Atlanta homes and apartments now offer central air conditioning (or, at the very least, window units), though some hearty souls still manage to survive the sticky heat with nothing more than a few good electric fans. Fortunately, the stifling summer spells are often interrupted by cooling, afternoon thundershowers, so Atlanta residents are given some relief as the temperatures drop to the lower 90s.

Fall is probably Atlanta's most predictable season weather-wise. Temperatures this time of year are normally in the upper 60s, though the mercury has been known to hit 80 degrees throughout the month of September. The first freeze generally doesn't occur until early November. Autumn is an especially pleasant season in Atlanta, since mild temperatures allow residents to spend more time outside enjoying the changing colors.

Temperatures during the winter months are more variable. Often, stretches of mild, cool weather (or "sweater weather" as many locals call it) will alternate with winter cold spells. The high humidity in Atlanta during the summer months contributes to a damp cold winter from December to February, with at least one day of snow or ice. Atlanta's snowfall is generally less than 4 inches (see statistics below), but, unfortunately, that's usually enough to throw the city into chaos. When snow falls in Atlanta, the schools and most businesses close, while news reports warn people to stay off the roads. All this hoopla over an inch or two of the white stuff usually makes transplanted northerners groan with disbelief, though many are happy to have an extra day off work.

Metro Atlanta records significant **rainfall** on about 120 days each year, with an annual rainfall average of about 50 inches. The wettest months are December through April; October is normally the driest. Despite the accumulation of rainfall in winter and early spring, metro Atlanta residents are still faced with permanent outdoor water restrictions. The current city-wide restriction policy states that people with even numbered or unnumbered addresses can water outside on Mondays, Wednesdays, and Saturdays. Residents with odd numbered addresses may water on Tuesdays, Thursdays, and Sundays. Outdoor watering on Fridays is prohibited. The exceptions to the rule are commercial operations such as car washes and landscaping companies that require water to stay in business. This permanent ban can be an annoyance for people who are used to watering their lawns or washing their cars whenever they want, but most residents take it in stride. Besides, the alternative is being fined up to $1,000 if you're caught violating the restriction.

METRO ATLANTA WEATHER STATISTICS

According to the National Weather Service, on average, Atlanta experiences clear skies 28% of the time; partly cloudy 33% of the time; and cloudy skies 39% of the time, with an annual average rainfall of 48–50 inches, and snowfall of 2–4 inches.

The following represent average daily low and high temperatures for each month, but don't let these averages fool you—as mentioned above, summertime temperatures can soar to the upper 90s, while winter temperatures often drop below freezing: **January** 35–51° F; **February** 36–54° F; **March** 43–62° F; **April** 51–71° F; **May** 60–79° F; **June** 67–86° F; **July** 70–87° F; **August** 69–86° F; **September** 64–82° F; **October** 54–72° F; **November** 43–61° F; **December** 37–52° F.

If you'd like more information on Atlanta's weather, including current conditions and weekly forecasts, visit the **National Weather Service** web site, www.nws.noaa.gov, or **The Weather Channel**, www.weather.com.

AIR POLLUTION

In Atlanta, air pollution is one of the city's biggest challenges. During the hot summer months (May to September), emissions from cars and other sources mix with sunlight and the city's heat to form ground level ozone, or smog. This toxic gas is a serious public health problem that causes respiratory problems, chest pain, shortness of breath, and sore throats. It may even lead to permanent lung damage. The Atlanta Regional Commission reports that the Environmental Protection Agency (EPA) has categorized metro Atlanta as a "Serious Non-Attainment" area for ground level ozone, meaning that Atlanta and its surrounding communities consistently exceed the federal air quality standard of 0.12 parts per million. In fact, metro Atlanta has not met federal standards for ground level ozone since it began monitoring ozone levels in the early 1980s. And, as daily commute times continue to grow longer and more cars hit Atlanta's streets, the problem could get significantly worse.

Atlanta's air quality problem gets a lot of media attention during peak months, so residents are kept informed. Local newspapers, television, and radio stations report air quality levels daily as part of their weather reports, and do an excellent job of explaining what these levels mean. There are also several "clean air" organizations in metro Atlanta that lobby for stricter emissions testing, help to educate the public on ground level ozone, and offer helpful tips on improving Atlanta's air quality. To find out more, contact **Georgia's Clean Air Force**, www.cleanairforce.com, 800-449-2471; the **Metro Atlanta Clean Air Campaign**, www.cleanaircampaign.com,

877-CLEANAIR; and the **Atlanta Regional Commission**, www.atlanta regional.com, 404-463-3100. If you'd like up-to-the-minute ozone reports, the EPA provides real-time data at their **AIRNOW** web site, www.epa. gov/airnow.

INSECTS

Though not as serious as Atlanta's air pollution problem, insects are still a major issue here in the south. Mosquitoes are the most prevalent flying pest in the metro area, and are particularly bothersome after an especially wet winter. Those venturing outside from April through October may find themselves besieged by these blood-sucking creatures. Your best bet is to invest in a good insect repellent and wear it faithfully if you plan on enjoying Atlanta's beautiful weather.

Aside from being plain pesky, mosquitoes are a health issue because of **West Nile virus**, which causes an infection similar to encephalitis. Although the virus most commonly plagues birds and horses, it is possible for a person bitten by a mosquito carrying West Nile to become infected. According to the Centers for Disease Control, approximately 80% of people who are infected with WNV will not show any symptoms. For the other 20%, the most common symptoms are fever, headache, muscle weakness, body aches, swollen lymph glands, and rashes. Those suffering a more severe case may also have a high fever, neck stiffness, stupor, disorientation, coma, tremors, convulsions, paralysis, and encephalitis. Between 3% and 15% of those with visible infection may die, particularly young children, the elderly, and those with compromised immune systems. Unfortunately, there's not yet a vaccine or specific treatment for the virus. The best prevention is to avoid going out for prolonged periods at night, particularly to woodsy or swampy areas, to wear bug spray, and to make sure you have screens on your windows. For more information on this issue, contact the **Centers for Disease Control**, 404-639-3311, www.cdc.gov.

In addition to mosquitoes, bees and ticks can pose challenges to the city's nature lovers. Bees are attracted to metro Atlanta's many flowers, and can be a major nuisance to anyone trying to enjoy a picnic or a day in the park. Ticks, on the other hand, aren't as troublesome unless you live (or play) in heavily wooded areas, or own pets that run around outside. With regard to ticks, your best bet is to slather on the insect repellent when you plan on spending time in the woods, and then do a tick check on yourself and your pet once you head back inside.

GIVING BACK TO THE COMMUNITY IS A REWARDING EXPERIENCE. Whether you are skilled at building houses, caring for the elderly, tutoring underprivileged children, or canvassing neighborhoods (having bilingual skills in any of these areas can be particularly useful), you can find a volunteer project that suits your talents and beliefs. Helping out in your new community is also a great way to meet people, and it can make the transition to an unfamiliar place less stressful.

HOW YOU CAN HELP

THE HUNGRY AND THE HOMELESS

Scores of volunteers concern themselves with shelter for Atlanta's homeless. Jobs include monitoring and organizing the shelters, providing legal help, ministering to psychiatric, medical, and social needs, raising money, manning phones, and caring for children in the shelters. Many people solicit, organize, cook, and serve food to the destitute at sites throughout Atlanta. Still others deliver meals to the homeless and the homebound.

CHILDREN

If involvement with children is especially appealing, you can tutor in and out of schools, be a big brother or sister, teach music and sports in shelters or at local community centers, run activities in the parks, entertain children in hospitals, and accompany kids on weekend outings. Schools, libraries, community associations, hospitals, and other facilities providing activities and guidance for children are all worth exploring.

HOSPITALS

The need for volunteers in hospitals is manifold: From interpreters to admitting and nursing aides, many volunteers are required. Assistants in crisis medical areas—emergency rooms, intensive care units, and the like—may be an option if you have the skills, as are volunteers to work with victims of sexual abuse. If you just want to be helpful, you might assist in food delivery or work in the gift shop.

THE DISABLED AND THE ELDERLY

You can read to the blind, help teach the deaf, work to prevent birth defects, and help the retarded and developmentally disabled, among others. You can also make regular visits to the homebound elderly, bring hot meals to their homes, and teach everything from nutrition to arts and crafts in senior centers and nursing homes.

EXTREME CARE SITUATIONS

Helping with suicide prevention, Alzheimer's and AIDS patients, rape victims, and abused children is a special category demanding a high level of commitment—not to mention emotional reserves and in many cases, special skills.

THE CULTURE SCENE

Museums and cultural centers are always in need of volunteers to lead tours or lend a hand in any number of ways. Libraries, theater groups, and ballet companies have plenty of tasks that need to be done. Fundraising efforts also require many volunteers to stuff envelopes and/or make phone calls. The Public Broadcasting Service (PBS) is a good example. Its large volunteer staff raises money for its stations through extensive on-air fundraising campaigns that include collecting pledges.

THE COMMUNITY

Work in your neighborhood. You can help out at the local school, neighborhood block association, nursing home, settlement house, or animal shelter.

VOLUNTEER PLACEMENT SERVICES

The following organizations coordinate much of metro Atlanta's volunteer activity. Contact them directly if you want to volunteer but aren't sure where. They'll send you where help is needed most. Or contact **Volunteer Match**, www.volunteermatch.org, a national volunteer placement service.

- **Hands on Atlanta**, 600 Means Street, Atlanta, 404-979-2800, www.handsonatlanta.com
- **The United Way of Metropolitan Atlanta**, 100 Edgewood Avenue NE, Atlanta, 404-614-1000, www.unitedwayatlanta.org

OTHER CONNECTIONS
- **Check bulletin boards** at your office, church, neighborhood grocery store, laundries, and school.
- Walk into local **places of worship**, **community organizations**, and/or **libraries**.

AREA CAUSES

If you were involved in a volunteer effort before you moved, or if you already know the specific cause that sparks your interest, you can call the following organizations and inquire about donating your time.

AIDS

- **AID Atlanta**, 1438 West Peachtree Street, Suite 100, Atlanta, 404-870-7700, www.aidatlanta.org
- **AIDS Education/Services for Minorities**, 2140 Martin Luther King Drive, Atlanta, 404-691-8880, www.naesmonline.org
- **Atlanta Interfaith AIDS Network**, 1053 Juniper Street NE, Atlanta, 404-874-8686, http://aian.home.mindspring.com
- **Haven House Hospice**, 5411 Northland Drive NE, Atlanta, 404-874-8313, www.havenhousehospice.com
- **Project Open Hand Atlanta**, 176 Ottley Drive NE, Atlanta, 404-872-8089, www.projectopenhand.org

ALCOHOL AND DRUGS

- **Alcohol and Drug Resource Center**, 2921 Piedmont Road NE, Atlanta, 404-239-0044

- **Atlanta Harm Reduction Center**, 1561 McLendon Avenue NE, Atlanta, 404-526-9222, www.atlantaharmreduction.org
- **Council on Alcohol and Drugs**, 6045 Atlantic Boulevard, Norcross, 770-239-7442, www.livedrugfree.org
- **Phoenix Alliance, Inc.**, 3735 Memorial Drive, Atlanta, 404-288-2280, www.phoenixallianceinc.org

ANIMALS

- **Atlanta Humane Society**, 981 Howell Mill Road, Atlanta, 404-875-5331, www.atlantahumane.org
- **Cherokee County Humane Society**, 770-928-5115, www.cc humanesociety.org
- **Cobb County Humane Society**, 770-428-5678, www.humane cobb.org
- **Gwinnett County Humane Society**, 770-798-7711, www.gwinnett humane.com
- **PAWS Atlanta** (the **DeKalb County Humane Society**), 5287 Covington Highway, Decatur, 770-593-1155, www.pawsatlanta.org
- **Zoo Atlanta**, 800 Cherokee Avenue, Atlanta, 404-624-5600, www.zooatlanta.org

CHILDREN

- **Big Brothers—Big Sisters of Metro Atlanta**, 100 Edgewood Avenue, Suite 710, Atlanta, 404-601-7000, www.bbbsatl.org
- **Boys and Girls Club of Metro Atlanta**, 100 Edgewood Avenue, Suite 700, Atlanta, 404-527-7100, www.bgcma.org
- **Children's Wish Foundation**, 8615 Roswell Road, Atlanta, 770-393-9474, www.childrenswish.org
- **Children's Rights Council of Georgia**, 110 Aaronwood Court, Alpharetta, 678-643-5924 www.gocrc.com
- **Center for Children and Young Adults Center/Open Gate**, 2221 Austell Road, Marietta, 770-803-3500
- **Families First**, 1105 West Peachtree Street NE, Atlanta, 404-853-2800, www.familiesfirst.org
- **Georgia Council of Child Abuse**, 1375 Peachtree Street, Atlanta, 404-870-6565, www.preventchildabusega.org
- **Quality Care for Children**, 50 Executive Park South, Suite 5015, Atlanta, 404-479-4200, www.qualitycareforchildren.org

CULTURE AND THE ARTS

- **African-American Panoramic Experience-APEX**, 135 Auburn Avenue NE, Atlanta, 404-523-2739, www.apexmuseum.org
- **Atlanta Ballet**, 1400 West Peachtree Street NW, Atlanta, 404-873-5811, www.atlantaballet.com
- **Atlanta Cyclorama**, 800 Cherokee Avenue SE, Atlanta, 404-658-7625, www.webguide.com/cyclorama.html
- **Atlanta History Center**, 130 West Paces Ferry Road NW, Atlanta, 404-814-4000, www.atlhist.org
- **Atlanta Symphony Orchestra Volunteer Ushers**, 404-733-4899, www.atlantasymphony.org
- **Fernbank Museum of Natural History**, 767 Clifton Road NE, Atlanta, 404-929-6300, www.fernbank.edu
- **The Fox Theatre**, 660 Peachtree Street, Atlanta, 404-881-2100, www.foxtheatre.org
- **Hammonds House Galleries/Resource Center of African American Art**, 503 Peeples Street, Atlanta, 404-752-8730, www.hammondshouse.org
- **High Museum of Art**, 1280 Peachtree Street NE, Atlanta, 404-733-4400, www.high.org
- **Historic Rhodes Hall**, 1516 Peachtree Street NW, Atlanta, 404-885-7800, www.georgiatrust.org
- **Jimmy Carter Library and Museum**, 441 Freedom Parkway, Atlanta, 404-865-7100, www.jimmycarterlibrary.org
- **Margaret Mitchell House**, 990 Peachtree Street NE, Atlanta, 404-249-7015, www.gwtw.org
- **Martin Luther King Historical Site**, 449 Auburn Avenue NE, Atlanta, 404-526-8900, www.thekingcenter.org
- **Rialto Center for the Performing Arts**, 80 Forsyth Street at Luckie Street, Atlanta, 404-651-1234, www.rialtocenter.org
- **The William Breman Jewish Heritage Museum**, 1440 Spring Street, Atlanta, 678-222-3700, www.thebreman.org

DISABLED ASSISTANCE

- **American Foundation for the Blind, National Literacy Center**, 100 Peachtree Street, Atlanta, 404-525-2303, www.afb.org
- **Center for the Visually Impaired**, 739 West Peachtree Street NW, Atlanta, 404-875-9011, www.cviatlanta.org
- **Compeer Atlanta**, 1903 North Druid Hills Road, Atlanta, 678-686-5918, www.compeeratlanta.org

- **Creative Community Services**, 1543 Lilburn-Stone Mountain Road, Stone Mountain, 770-469-6226, www.ccsgeorgia.org
- **The Disability Action Center of Georgia**, 755 Commerce Drive, Decatur, 404-687-8890, www.disabilitylink.org
- **Georgia Council for the Hearing Impaired**, 4151 Memorial Drive, Decatur, 404-292-5312, www.gachi.org

ENVIRONMENT

- **Earthshare for Georgia**, 1447 Peachtree Street, Atlanta, 404-873-3173, www.earthsharega.org
- **Environmental Community Action**, 44 Broad Street NW, Atlanta, 404-584-6499, www.eco-act.org
- **Georgia Conservancy**, 817 West Peachtree Street, Atlanta, 404-876-2900, www.gaconservancy.org
- **Georgia Forest Watch**, 706-635-TREE, www.gafw.org
- **Georgia Public Interest Research Group**, 1447 Peachtree Street NE, Atlanta, 404-892-3573, www.georgiapirg.org
- **Georgia Sierra Club**, metro Atlanta, 404-607-1262, http://georgia.sierraclub.org
- **Southern Environmental Law Center**, 127 Peachtree Street, Atlanta, 404-521-9909, www.selcga.org

GAY & LESBIAN

- **Atlanta Gay and Lesbian Center**, 170 Eleventh Street NE, Atlanta, 404-874-9890
- **Atlanta Lambda Community Center**, 828 West Peachtree Street NW, Atlanta, 404-881-1985
- **Atlanta Pride Committee**, 20 Executive Park West, Atlanta, 404-929-0071, www.atlantapride.org
- **YouthPride Atlanta**, 302 East Howard Avenue, Decatur, 404-378-7722, www.youthpride.org

HEALTH & HOSPITALS

- **American Cancer Society**, 2200 Century Parkway, Atlanta, 404-315-1123, www.cancer.org
- **American Lung Association of Georgia**, 2452 Spring Road, Smyrna, 770-434-5864, www.lungusa2.org/georgia
- **DeKalb Medical Center**, 2701 North Decatur Road, Decatur, 404-501-1000, www.dekalbmedicalcenter.org

- **Northside Hospital**, 1000 Johnson Ferry Road NE, 404-851-8000, www.northside.com
- **Peachtree Hospice**, 15 Dunwoody Park, Atlanta, 770-698-8785
- **Piedmont Hospital**, 1968 Peachtree Road NW, Atlanta, 404-605-5000, www.piedmonthospital.org
- **South Fulton Medical Center**, 1170 Cleveland Avenue, East Point, 404-466-1170, www.southfultonmedicalcenter.com
- **United Cerebral Palsy of Greater Atlanta**, 3300 Northeast Expressway, Atlanta, 770-676-2000, www.ucpga.org

HISTORICAL RESTORATION

- **Historic Oakland Foundation**, 248 Oakland Avenue SE, Atlanta, 404-688-2107, www.oaklandcemetery.com

HOMELESS

- **Atlanta Union Mission**, 2353 Bolton Road NW, Atlanta, 404-367-2244, www.aumcares.org
- **Homeless Task Force**, 363 Georgia Avenue SE, Atlanta, 404-589-9495
- **Legal Clinic for the Homeless**, 60 Walton Street NW, Atlanta, 404-681-0680, www.galawcenter.org
- **Samaritan House of Atlanta**, 458 Edgewood Avenue, Atlanta, 404-523-1239, www.samhouse.org

HUMAN SERVICES

- **American Red Cross**, 1955 Monroe Drive NE, Atlanta, 404-876-3302, www.redcrossatlanta.org
- **Atlanta Urban League**, 100 Edgewood Avenue NE, Atlanta, 404-659-1150, www.atlul.org
- **Catholic Social Service**, 680 West Peachtree Street NW, Atlanta, 404-881-6571, www.cssatlanta.com
- **Compeer Atlanta**, 1903 North Druid Hills Road, Atlanta, 678-686-5918, www.compeeratlanta.org
- **Creative Community Services**, 1543 Lilburn-Stone Mountain Road, Stone Mountain, 770-469-6226, www.ccsgeorgia.org
- **Families First**, 1105 West Peachtree Street NE, Atlanta, 404-853-2800, www.familiesfirst.org
- **Habitat for Humanity**, 519 Memorial Drive SE, Atlanta, 404-223-5180, www.habitat.org

• **Jewish Family Services**, 4549 Chamblee-Dunwoody Road, Atlanta, 770-677-9300, www.jfcs-atlanta.org

HUNGER

• **Atlanta Community Food Bank**, 732 Joseph E. Lowery Boulevard, Atlanta, 404-892-3333, www.acfb.org
• **Atlanta Union Mission**, 2353 Bolton Road NW, Atlanta, 404-367-2244, www.aumcares.org
• **Food Not Bombs**, 770 Ormewood Avenue SE, Atlanta, 404-622-5859, www.foodnotbombs.net
• **Kashi Atlanta**, 1681 McLendon Avenue, Atlanta, 404-687-3353, www.kashiatlanta.org/service.htm

INTERNATIONAL

• **Amnesty International USA**, 730 Peachtree Street NE, Suite 1060, Atlanta, 404-876-5661, www.amnestyusa.org
• **American Red Cross**, 1955 Monroe Drive NE, Atlanta, 404-876-3302, www.redcrossatlanta.org
• **Georgia Peace Coalition**, P.O. Box 133016, Atlanta, 30333, 404-522-4500, www.georgiapeace.org

LEGAL—CIVIL RIGHTS

• **American Civil Liberties Union of Georgia**, 70 Fairlie Street, Suite 340, Atlanta, 404-523-5398, www.acluga.org
• **Martin Luther King Jr. Center for Nonviolent Social Change**, 449 Auburn Avenue NE, Atlanta, 404-526-8900, www.theking center.org
• **The Southern Center for Human Rights**, 83 Poplar Street NW, Atlanta, 404-688-1202, www.schr.org

LITERACY

• **Literacy Volunteers of America**, 246 Sycamore Street, Decatur, 404-377-READ, www.lvama.org

POLITICS—ELECTORAL

• **The Democratic Party of Georgia**, 404-870-8201, www.georgia party.com

- **The Georgia Green Party**, 404-806-0480, www.greens.org/georgia
- **The League of Women Voters (Georgia)**, State Office, 678-547-0755, www.lwvga.org; Fulton County, 404-577-8683; DeKalb County, 404-321-0913; Cobb County/Marietta, 770-592-0625
- **The Libertarian Party of Georgia**, 404-888-9468, www.lpgeorgia.com
- **North Fulton Young Republicans**, www.nfyr.org
- **The Republican Party of Georgia**, 404-257-5559, www.gagop.org
- **Young Democrats of Georgia**, www.georgiayds.org

SENIOR SERVICES

- **American Association of Retired Persons**, 999 Peachtree Street NE, Atlanta, 404-881-0292, www.aarp.org/ga
- **Central Fulton Senior Services**, 236 Forsyth Street SW, Suite 201, Atlanta, 404-818-8001
- **Compeer Atlanta**, 1903 North Druid Hills Road, Atlanta, 678-686-5918, www.compeeratlanta.org
- **Creative Community Services**, 1543 Lilburn-Stone Mountain Road, Stone Mountain, 770-469-6226, www.ccsgeorgia.org
- **Georgia Association of Homes and Services for the Aging**, 607 Peachtree Street NE, Atlanta, 404-872-9191, www.gahsa.org
- **I Care, Atlanta**, 404-681-2552
- **National Caucus & Center On Black Aged**, 1514 East Cleveland Avenue, Atlanta, 404-762-9500, www.ncba-aged.org
- **Senior Citizens Law Project**, 151 Spring Street, Atlanta, 404-524-5811, www.atlantalegalaid.org
- **Senior Citizen Services**, 1705 Commerce Drive NW, Atlanta, 404-351-3889, www.scsatl.org

WOMEN'S SERVICES

- **Aid to Children of Imprisoned Mothers**, 906 Ralph David Abernathy Boulevard, Atlanta, 404-755-3262, www.takingaim.net
- **Atlanta Women's Foundation**, The Hurt Building, Suite 401, Atlanta, 404-577-5000, www.atlantawomen.org
- **Battered Women Shelter**, 1475 Peachtree Street NE, Atlanta, 404-873-1766
- **DeKalb Rape Crisis Center**, 204 Church Street, Decatur, 404-377-1429, www.dekalbrapecrisiscenter.org
- **Feminist Women's Health Center**, 1924 Cliff Valley Way NE, Atlanta, 404-728-7900, www.atlfwhc.org

- **Georgia Abortion Rights Action League**, P.O. Box 5589, Atlanta, 404-875-6338, www.garal.org
- **Georgia Advocates for Battered Women & Children**, 250 Georgia Avenue SE, Suite 308, Atlanta, 404-524-3847
- **Georgians for Choice**, 743 Virginia Avenue, Atlanta, 404-532-0022, www.georgiansforchoice.org
- **Grady Hospital Rape Crisis Center**, 80 Jesse Hill Jr. Drive SE, Atlanta, 404-616-4861, www.gradyhealthsystem.org
- **Healthy Mothers Healthy Babies of Georgia**, 3562 Habersham Road, Tucker, 770-451-0020, www.hmhbga.org

YOUTH

- **Asian American Youth Alliance**, www.aayouth.org
- **Big Brothers–Big Sisters of Metro Atlanta**, 100 Edgewood Avenue, Suite 710, Atlanta, 404-601-7000, www.bbbsatl.org
- **Boys and Girls Club of Metro Atlanta**, 100 Edgewood Avenue, Suite 700, Atlanta, 404-527-7100, www.bgcma.org
- **Center for Children and Young Adults/Open Gate**, 2221 Austell Road, Marietta, 770-803-3500
- **Southwest YMCA Youth Outreach**, 2220 Campbellton Road SW, Atlanta, 404-753-4169, www.ymcaatlanta.org

A RECENT VISITOR TO ATLANTA REMARKED THAT THERE SEEMED TO be a church on every street corner. While this may be a slight exaggeration, metro Atlanta does offer a multitude of opportunities for prayer, spiritual retreats, and religious communities of all kinds. The city's diverse racial and ethnic population is echoed in a wide assortment of houses of worship. For a more complete listing of the over 2,000 organized places of worship in Atlanta, check the Yellow Pages.

BAHÁ'Í

Although Bahá'í houses of worship may differ from one another in architectural styles, they are often stunning and are recognizable by their nine sides and central dome, which symbolize "the diversity of the human race and its essential oneness." To find out more about the Bahá'í religion, visit its main web site, www.bahai.org. To find out more about Atlanta's Bahá'í community, check out www.atlantabahai.org.

- **Atlanta Bahá'í Center**, 379 Edgewood Avenue SE, Atlanta, 404-688-0208
- **The Bahá'í Center of Alpharetta**, 10690 Jones Bridge Road, Alpharetta, 770-619-0945
- **Bahá'í Unity Center**, 2370 Wesley Chapel Road, Decatur, 770-981-0097
- **North Gwinnett Bahá'í House**, 5621 Little Mill Road, Buford, 770-932-8399

BUDDHIST

Buddhism dates back over two millennia, and today over 350 million around the world consider themselves Buddhists. There are many different sub-traditions, including **Zen**, **Tibetan**, **Tantric** (**Vajrayana**), and

Mahayana. An informative online resource for Buddhism is www. buddhanet.net; for more information on the Buddhist community in Atlanta, visit the Atlanta Buddhist Directory, www.well.com/user/ tomcarr/atlanta_buddhism.htm.

- **Atlanta Soto Zen Center**, 1167 C/D Zonolite Place, Atlanta, 404-532-0040, www.aszc.org
- **Dorje Ling Buddhist Center**, 3253 Shallowford Road, Chamblee, 770-451-7715, www.jonang.org
- **Drepung Loseling Institute**, 2531 Briarcliff Road NE, Atlanta, 404-982-0051, www.drepung.org
- **Georgia Buddhist Vihara**, 1683 South Deshon Road, Lithonia, 770-482-9913, www.gbvihara.org
- **Rameshori Buddhist Center**, 260 Howard Street NE, Atlanta; 130 Allen Road, Unit B, Sandy Springs; 404-378-8599, www.rameshori.com

CHRISTIAN

AFRICAN METHODIST EPISCOPAL AND EPISCOPAL ZION

If you'd like to find out more about the AME or Episcopal Zion church, visit www.ame-today.com. To find an AME church in your neighborhood, check out the AME links page at www.ame-today.com/links/index.shtml, or visit www.amechurch.com. You may also want to investigate the following:

- **Allen Temple AME Church**, 1625 Simpson Road NW, Atlanta, 404-794-3316
- **Big Bethel AME Church**, 220 Auburn Avenue NE, Atlanta, 404-659-0248
- **St**. **Paul AME Church**, 821 Third Street, Stone Mountain, 770-469-4995
- **St**. **Philip AME Church**, 240 Candler Road SE, Atlanta, 404-371-0749
- **Turner Monumental**, 66 Howard Street NE, Atlanta, 404-378-5970

ANGLICAN/EPISCOPAL

The Episcopal and Anglican churches are both descended from the Church of England. The Episcopal Church took root in America as early as 1607, with the first permanent English settlement in Jamestown, Virginia. There are plenty of Episcopal and Anglican churches in metro Atlanta. To find one in your neighborhood, check the Atlanta Yellow Pages, or consider the listings below. To learn more about the **Episcopal Church of the US**, visit them online at www.episcopalchurch.org; for information on the **Anglican Church** worldwide, go to http://anglicansonline.org.

- **All Saints Episcopal Church**, 634 West Peachtree Street NW, Atlanta, 404-881-0835, www.allsaintsatlanta.org
- **Holy Comforter Episcopal Church**, 737 Woodland Avenue, Atlanta, 404-627-6510, www.holycomforter-atlanta.org
- **The Church of Our Savior**, 1068 North Highland Avenue, Atlanta, 404-872-4169, www.oursavioratlanta.org

APOSTOLIC

The Apostolic Church of America consists of approximately 90 congregations throughout the United States, Japan, Mexico, and Canada. The church also conducts services on many college campuses, and is in engaged in missionary and humanitarian work throughout the world. For more information about the Apostolic Church, visit their web site, www.apostolicchristian.org. To find a church in your neighborhood, check the Atlanta Yellow Pages, or consider the following:

- **Apostolic Christian Church of Atlanta**, 6225 Campbellton Road, Fairburn, 770-306-1113
- **Apostolic Faith Church**, 629 James P. Brawley Drive NW, Atlanta, 404-524-1861
- **Greater Christ Temple Holiness Church**, 914 Cherokee Avenue SE, Atlanta, 404-622-9723

ASSEMBLY OF GOD

Assemblies of God are the largest Pentecostal denomination of the Protestant church in the USA. Their homepage, http://ag.org/top, is informative and provides a complete directory of its churches nationwide. A few to consider in metro Atlanta are:

- **Bridge of Hope Assembly of God**, 6204 East Ponce de Leon Avenue, Stone Mountain, 770-469-9745
- **Cavalry Assembly of God**, 5067 Chamblee-Dunwoody Road, Dunwoody, 770-393-2197
- **Celebration Church**, 7373 Covington Highway, Lithonia, 770-482-7770
- **Roswell Assembly of God**, 11440 Crabapple Road, Roswell, 770-993-6586

BAPTIST

American, Free Will, and **Southern Baptists** are all found throughout metro Atlanta. To find out more about Southern Baptists, visit www.sbc.net; for more on Free Will Baptists, go to www.nafwb.org; and for American Baptists, check out http://abc-usa.org. Some Baptist churches in the metro Atlanta area include:

- **Avondale Estates First Baptist Church**, 17 Covington Road, Avondale Estates, 404-294-5284
- **Briarcliff Baptist Church**, 3039 Briarcliff Road NE, Atlanta, 404-633-6103
- **Clairmont Hills Baptist Church**, 1995 Clairmont Road, Decatur, 404-634-6231
- **Druid Hills Baptist Church**, 1085 Ponce de Leon Avenue NE, Atlanta, 404-874-5721
- **Ebenezer Baptist Church**, 407 Auburn Avenue NE, Atlanta, 404-688-7263
- **First Baptist Church of Atlanta**, 4400 North Peachtree Road, Atlanta, 770-234-8300
- **Gwinnett Baptist Tabernacle**, 6690 Buford Highway NE, Atlanta, 770-448-2656
- **Northside Drive Baptist Church**, 3100 Northside Drive NW, Atlanta, 404-237-8621
- **Pleasant Hill Baptist Church**, 4278 Chamblee Tucker Road, Doraville, 770-939-1255
- **Second-Ponce de Leon Baptist Church**, 2715 Peachtree Road NE, Atlanta, 404-266-8111
- **Wright Street Baptist Church**, 395 Wright Street NE, Marietta, 770-422-5851

CHRISTIAN SCIENCE

The Church of Christian Science was established by Mary Baker Eddy in 1879. Today the Mother Church is headquartered in Boston, with 2,000 branch churches in 80 countries around the world, including eight in metro Atlanta. For more information on the Mother Church or Christian Science in general, visit www.tfccs.com. To learn more about Christian Science in Georgia, visit www.christiansciencega.com.

- **First Church of Christ Scientist Atlanta**, 150 Fifteenth Street NE, Atlanta, 404-892-7838
- **First Church of Christ Scientist Decatur**, 446 Clairmont Avenue, Decatur, 404-373-8383
- **First Church of Christ Scientist Lilburn**, 1627 Hewatt Road, Lilburn, 770-985-0562
- **First Church of Christ Scientist Marietta**, 2641 Old Sewell Road, Marietta, 770-565-7271
- **Second Church of Christ Scientist Atlanta**, 3372 Peachtree Road NE, Atlanta, 404-233-4582

CHURCH OF CHRIST

There are several Churches of Christ in metro Atlanta. To find one near you, check the Atlanta Yellow Pages, or consider the churches listed below. To find out more about the Church of Christ, visit http://church-of-christ.org, or the United Church of Christ web site, www.ucc.org.

- **Atlanta Virginia Highland Church UCC**, 743 Virginia Avenue NE, Atlanta, 404-873-1355, www.vhchurch.net
- **Hillcrest Church of Christ Decatur**, 1939 Snapfinger Road, Decatur, 404-289-4573, http://hillcrestchurchofchrist.net
- **North Atlanta Church of Christ**, 5676 Roberts Drive, Dunwoody, 770-399-5222, http://nacofc.org

CHURCH OF GOD

The **Worldwide Church of God** has about 64,000 members in 860 congregations around the world, including metro Atlanta. To find out more or to locate congregations in your area, visit them online at www.wcg.org. The **United Church of God** is also represented in metro Atlanta and around the world. For more information, visit www.ucg.org, or www.ucgatlanta.org. And, finally, information on **The Church of God** can be found at their homepage, www.thechurchofgod.org.

- **Mount Paran Church of God**, 2055 Mount Paran Road NW, Atlanta, 404-923-8700, www.mountparan.com
- **Living Hope Christian Fellowship**, 3181 Hogan Road, Atlanta, 770-994-8828, http://churches.wcg.org/atlanta-ga/atlanta.htm
- **Pleasantdale Church of God**, 3434 Pleasantdale Road, Doraville, 770-491-7071

CHURCH OF GOD IN CHRIST

For more information about the Church of God in Christ, including churches throughout metro Atlanta, visit www.cogic.org. A few local Church of God in Christ congregations to consider are:

- **Greater Community Church of God in Christ**, 406 Roswell Street, Marietta, 770-590-8510, www.greatercommunitycogic.com
- **Holy Fellowship Church of God in Christ**, 3691 Centerville Highway, Snellville, 770-736-0207, www.holyfellowship.org
- **Victory Church of God in Christ**, 3704 Campbellton Road, Atlanta, 404-349-0400, http://cogicdir.home.att.net/viccogic.htm

CHURCH OF THE NAZARENE

For information about the Church of the Nazarene and a church locator service, try the main web site for the Church of the Nazarene, www. nazarene.org. Area churches include:
- **Atlanta First Church of the Nazarene**, 1600 Agape Way, Decatur, 404-284-2900
- **Church of the Nazarene**, 170 Plaza Drive SE, Smyrna, 770-436-6784
- **East Point Church of the Nazarene**, 2736 Cheney Street, East Point, 404-762-6417

EVANGELICAL

A few of metro Atlanta's Evangelical churches are listed below. For a more complete listing, be sure to check the Atlanta Yellow Pages.
- **New Covenant Community Church**, 3147 Chamblee Tucker Road, Atlanta, 770-451-2038, www.atlantanccc.org
- **Northside Community Church**, 5185 Peachtree-Dunwoody Road NE, Atlanta, 404-256-5700, www.northsidecommunity.org
- **Slavic Evangelic Christian Church**, 4577 Roswell Road NE, Atlanta, 404-255-5758

FRIENDS (QUAKERS)

Members of the **Society of Friends**, a.k.a. **Quakers**, can trace their church's roots back to some of the first European settlers. Persecuted in England for their beliefs, and then again in Massachusetts by the Puritans, many Friends fled the Boston area to settle in other colonies along the eastern United States. Today, Friends churches can be found throughout the world. To learn more about the Friends church, visit www.quaker.org. Local Friends Meetinghouses include:
- **Atlanta Friends Meeting**, 701 West Howard Avenue, Decatur, 404-377-2474, http://atlanta.quaker.org
- **North Atlanta Worship Group**, 1085 David Trace, Suwanee, 770-886-3411

INDEPENDENT/INTERDENOMINATIONAL/ NONDENOMINATIONAL

The following churches are just a few in metro Atlanta that identify themselves as independent, interdenominational, or nondenominational:

- **Cumberland Community Church**, 3110 Sports Avenue, Smyrna, 404-952-8834, www.cumberlandchurch.org
- **Free Gospel Interdenominational Church**, 957 Wylie Street SE, Atlanta, 404-584-7874
- **Green Pastures Christian Ministries**, 5455 Flat Shoals Parkway, Decatur, 770-987-8121, www.gpcm.org
- **Martin Street Church of God**, 148 Glenwood Avenue, Atlanta, 404-688-8545, www.mstcog.org
- **Midtown Church**, 3202 Paces Ferry Place NW, Atlanta, 404-261-7100
- **New Life Family Church**, 320 Austin Avenue NE, Marietta, 770-425-2811, http://members.aol.com/newlifefc
- **Northwest Community Church**, 40 Whitlock Place SW, Marietta, 770-218-6129, www.nwcchurch.com
- **Smyrna Christian Church**, 910 Concord Road SE, Smyrna, 770-435-1723, www.smyrnachristianchurch.org

JEHOVAH'S WITNESS

For information about Jehovah's Witness or to find a kingdom hall near you, visit www.watchtower.org or www.jw-media.org.
- **Chamblee, Dunwoody English and Korean Congregations**, 2300 Dunwoody Club Drive, Atlanta, 770-396-7171
- **College Park Congregation**, 4474 Scarborough Road, Atlanta, 30349, 404-684-1492
- **Woodstock Congregation**, 2369 Cherokee Lane, Atlanta, 770-926-0639

LATTER DAY SAINTS/MORMON

If you'd like to find out more about the Church of Jesus Christ of Latter-Day Saints, or search for a ward in your neighborhood, visit www.lds.org. A few metro Atlanta locations to consider are:
- **Atlanta Temple**, 6450 Barfield Road, Sandy Springs, 770-393-3698
- **Church of Jesus Christ of Latter-Day Saints**, **Atlanta Stake**, 1450 Ponce de Leon Avenue NE, 404-378-0488
- **Church of Jesus Christ of Latter-Day Saints**, **Glenridge Ward**, 6449 Glenridge Drive NE, Atlanta, 404-256-2092

LUTHERAN

Lutheranism came to the New World with the immigrants of the northern European countries, including Norway, Sweden, Denmark, Finland, and

Germany. Today about two thirds of American Lutherans belong to the Evangelical Lutheran Church in America, www.elca.org, the largest conference of Lutherans in this country. Missouri Synod is the more conservative branch of the Lutheran church. Metro Atlanta Lutheran churches include:

- **All Saints Lutheran Church**, 722 Rockbridge Road SW, Lilburn, 770-923-7283, www.aslc.org
- **Lord of Life Lutheran Church ELCA**, 5390 McGinnis Ferry Road, Alpharetta, 770-740-1279, www.lord-life.org
- **Lutheran Church of the Messiah**, 465 Clairmont Avenue, Decatur, 404-373-1682, www.lmessiah.org
- **Lutheran Church of the Redeemer**, 731 Peachtree Street NE, Atlanta, 404-874-8664, www.redeemer.org
- **Rivercliff Lutheran Church**, 8750 Roswell Road, Atlanta, 770-993-4316, www.rivercliff.org

MENNONITE

Until the 19th century, most Mennonites were concentrated in rural farming communities, speaking German, and spurning much of the secular world. Since the 1800s, there have been divisions in the church, yielding the **Old Mennonite Church**, the **General Conference Mennonite Church**, the **Mennonite Brethren**, and the **Old Order Amish**. For more information about the Mennonite Church of the USA, visit http://mcusa.mennonite.net, or www.mennoniteusa.org. For more information about the Mennonite Church in metro Atlanta, contact the **Atlanta Mennonite Fellowship**, 404-627-5013, http://atlanta.ga.us. mennonite.net.

METHODIST (UNITED)

For more information on the United Methodist Church, visit their web site, www.umc.org. If you'd like a complete listing of Methodist Churches in the metro Atlanta area, check the Atlanta Yellow Pages. A few local churches to consider are:

- **Atlanta First United Methodist Church**, 360 Peachtree Street NE, 404-524-6614, www.atlantafumc.org
- **Brookhaven United Methodist Church**, 1336 North Druid Hills Road NE, Atlanta, 404-237-7506, www.brookhavenumc.org
- **Druid Hills United Methodist Church**, 1200 Ponce de Leon Avenue NE, Atlanta, 404-377-6481
- **North Springs United Methodist Church**, 7770 Roswell Road NW, Atlanta, 770-396-0844, www.northspringsumc.org

- **Northside United Methodist Church**, 2799 Northside Drive NW, Atlanta, 404-355-6475, www.northsideumc.org
- **Sandy Springs United Methodist Church**, 86 Mount Vernon Highway NE, Atlanta, 404-255-1181, www.ssumc.org

ORTHODOX (COPTIC, EASTERN, GREEK, ALBANIAN, RUSSIAN)

For information on the **Orthodox Church in America**, visit www.oca.org, or try the **Greek Orthodox Archdiocese of America** at www.goarch.org/en/archdiocese. Two beautiful Orthodox churches in Atlanta are:
- **Greek Orthodox Cathedral of the Annunciation,** 2500 Clairmont Road NE, Atlanta, 404-633-5870, www.atlgoc.org
- **St. Elias Antiochian Orthodox Church**, 2045 Ponce de Leon Avenue NE, Atlanta, 404-378-8191, www.steliasofatlanta.org

PENTECOSTAL/CHARISMATIC

If you'd like to learn more about the **Pentecostal/Charismatic Churches of North America**, or to find a local church, go to www.pccna.org. For more about the **International Communion of the Charismatic Episcopal Church**, check out www.iccec.org. Or try the **Pentecostal-Charismatic Theology Inquiry International** at www.pctii.org. A few Pentecostal churches in metro Atlanta to consider are:
- **Locust Grove Pentecostal Church**, 244 Beershuba Road, Atlanta, 678-432-4477
- **Mableton Pentecostal Church**, 1000 Old Powder Springs Road, Mableton, 770-941-6502
- **Rehoboth Community Church**, 1423 Akridge Street NW, Atlanta, 404-758-2009
- **Seal of Life Ministry**, 6991 Peachtree Industrial Boulevard, Norcross, 770-417-1928

PRESBYTERIAN (USA)

A Protestant Church with its roots in 17th-century England, it was the Scottish and Irish who brought Presbyterianism to the USA in the late 1600s. The largest US Presbyterian branch is the **Presbyterian Church (USA)**; find them online at www.pcusa.org. Area Presbyterian churches include:
- **Church of St. Andrew Presbyterian Church**, 5855 Riverside Drive, Atlanta, 404-252-5287, www.churchofstandrew.org
- **Druid Hills Presbyterian Church**, 1026 Ponce de Leon Avenue NE, Atlanta, 404-875-7591, www.dhpc.org

- **Emory Presbyterian Church**, 1886 North Decatur Road NE, Atlanta, 404-325-4551, www.emorypresbyterian.org
- **First Presbyterian Church-Marietta**, 189 Church Street, Marietta, 770-427-0293, www.fpcmarietta.org
- **Korean Central Presbyterian Church**, 4011 Chamblee-Dunwoody Road, Chamblee, 770-457-1998
- **Mount Vernon Presbyterian Church**, 471 Mount Vernon Highway NE, Atlanta, 404-255-2211, www.mvpchurch.org

ROMAN CATHOLIC

In 2000, the Vatican reported that approximately 21% of the American population is Roman Catholic. That's about 60 million people in the USA. Here in Atlanta, there are over 100,000 Roman Catholic families, in over 100 parishes, in counties throughout the entire metro area. For more information about the Roman Catholic religion in Atlanta, or to search for local parishes, visit the Archdiocese of Atlanta online at www.archatl.com. For a complete listing of Catholic churches in your community, check the Atlanta Yellow Pages. A few to consider are:

- **Cathedral of Christ the King**, 2699 Peachtree Road NE, Atlanta, 404-233-2145, www.christtheking-atl.org
- **Immaculate Heart of Mary**, 2855 Briarcliff Road NE, Atlanta, 404-636-1418, www.ihmatlanta.org
- **St. John Vianney Catholic Church**, 1920 Skyview Drive, Lithia Springs, 770-941-2807
- **St. Jude Catholic Church,** 7171 Glenridge Drive NE, Atlanta, 404-394-3896, www.stjudeatlanta.net
- **St. Paul of the Cross Roman Catholic Church**, 551 Harwell Road NW, Atlanta, 404-696-6704, www.spcatl.catholicweb.com
- **Shrine of Immaculate Conception**, 48 Martin Luther King Jr. Drive, Atlanta, 404-521-1866, www.catholicshrineatlanta.org

SEVENTH-DAY ADVENTIST

For information about the Seventh-Day Adventist Church, check out www.adventist.org. For a comprehensive list of churches in metro Atlanta and around the world, visit Adventist Churches Online at http://mcdonald.southern.edu. A few local churches to consider are:

- **Alpharetta Seventh-Day Adventist Church**, 3315 Francis Road, Alpharetta, www.alpharettasda.com
- **Cherokee Seventh-Day Adventist Church**, 101 Rope Mill Road, Woodstock, 770-591-7304, www.tagnet.org/cherokee

- **Decatur Seventh-Day Adventist Church**, 2365 Candler Road, Decatur, 404-284-6908, http://decatursda.faithweb.com
- **Marietta Adventist Church**, 1330 North Cobb Parkway, Marietta, 770-427-7668, www.tagnet.org/marietta_adventist

UNITY

For information about the Unity Church, or to find local congregations throughout metro Atlanta, visit the Association of Unity Churches' web site, www.unity.org. You may also want to consider the following:
- **Atlanta Unity Church**, 4146 Chamblee-Dunwoody Road, Chamblee, 770-455-8920, www.atlantaunity.org
- **Unity Midtown Church**, 875 West Peachtree Street NE, Atlanta, 404-874-1937
- **Unity North Atlanta Church**, 4255 Sandy Plains Road, Marietta, 678-819-9101, www.unitynorth.org

WESLEYAN

For more information about the Wesleyan Church, visit the Wesleyan Church online at www.wesleyan.org. A few local Wesleyan churches to consider are:
- **Atlanta First Wesleyan Church**, 3220 Bouldercrest Road, Atlanta, 404-243-1900
- **Decatur Wesleyan Church**, 3840 Kensington Road, Decatur, 404-294-4402
- **Northside Wesleyan Church**, 2397 Beaver Ruin Road, Norcross, 770-448-8861

HINDUISM

Nearly 13% of the world's population is Hindu. Although most still live in India and parts of Southeast Asia, there are now roughly one million Hindus in the United States, including a large population in metro Atlanta. To learn more, call the Atlanta Hindu Society, 770-248-9599, or contact the following Hindu temples:
- **BSS Hindu Temple**, 3518 Clarkston Industrial Boulevard, Clarkston, 404-297-0501
- **Hindu Temple of Atlanta**, 5851 Georgia Highway 85, Riverdale, 770-907-7102, www.hindutempleofatlanta.org
- **Shiv Mandir of Atlanta**, Global Mall, 5675 Jimmy Carter Boulevard, Norcross, 770-271-5398, www.shivmandiratlanta.org

ISLAM

To learn more about the Islamic community in metro Atlanta, contact the Sahebozzaman Islamic Center of Atlanta at 770-642-9411, online at www.sicoa.org, or contact the Islamic centers and mosques below (for a complete listing, check the Atlanta Yellow Pages):

- **Al-Farooq Masjid of Atlanta**, 442 14th Street NW, Atlanta, 404-874-7521, www.alfarooqmasjid.org
- **Atlanta Masjid of Al-Islam**, 560 Fayetteville Road, Atlanta, 404-378-1600, www.atlantamasjid.com
- **Islamic Center of North Fulton**, 1265 Rucker Road, Alpharetta, 678-297-0019
- **Islamic Community of Bosnians Atlanta**, 803 Jolly Avenue, Clarkston, 404-508-0280
- **Masjid Omar bin Abdul Aziz**, 955 Harbins Road NW, Norcross, 770-279-8606, www.masjidomar.org

JEWISH

To learn more about the Jewish community in metro Atlanta, check out the *Atlanta Jewish Times*, 404-252-1600, www.atljewishtimes.com, a weekly paper (and accompanying web site) covering news and events for Atlanta's Jewish residents. Or visit the **Jewish Federation of Greater Atlanta** homepage, www.shalomatlanta.org. Below are a few local congregations to consider (for a complete listing of area synagogues check the Atlanta Yellow Pages).

CHABAD

- **Chabad Enrichment Center of Gwinnett**, 3855 Holcomb Bridge Road, Norcross, 678-595-0196, www.chabadenrichment.org
- **Chabad of Alpharetta**, 10180 Jones Bridge Road, Alpharetta, 770-410-9000, www.chabadalpharetta.org
- **Chabad of Cobb**, 4450 Lower Roswell Road, Marietta, 770-565-4412, www.chabadofcobb.com

CONSERVATIVE

- **Ahavath Achim Congregation**, 600 Peachtree Battle Avenue NW, Atlanta, 404-355-5222, www.aasynagogue.org
- **Congregation Beth Shalom**, 5303 Winters Chapel Road, Atlanta, 770-399-5300, www.bshalom.net

- **Congregation Etz Chaim**, 1190 Indian Hills Parkway, Marietta, 770-973-0137, www.etzchaim.net

ORTHODOX

- **Congregation Ariel**, 5237 Tilly Mill Road, Atlanta, 770-390-9071, www.congariel.org
- **Congregation Beth Jacob**, 1855 LaVista Road NE, Atlanta, 404-633-0551
- **Congregation Beth Tefillah**, 5065 Highpoint Road, Atlanta, 404-843-2464, www.bethtefillah.org

RECONSTRUCTIONIST

- **Congregation Bet Haverim**, Atlanta, 404-315-6445, www.congregationbethaverim.org
- **Havurat Levshalem**, P.O. Box 40968, Atlanta, 404-434-0122, www.levshalem.org

REFORM

- **Temple Beth David**, 1885 McGee Road SW, Snellville, 770-978-3916, www.gwinnetttemple.com
- **Temple Beth Tikvah**, 9955 Coleman Road, Roswell, 770-642-0434, www.bethtikva.com
- **Temple Kehillat Chaim**, 1145 Green Street, Roswell, 770-641-8630, www.kehillatchaim.org
- **Temple Kol Emeth**, 1415 Old Canton Road, Marietta, 770-973-3533, www.kolemeth.net
- **The Temple, Hebrew Benevolent Congregation**, 1589 Peachtree Street NE, Atlanta, 404-873-1731, www.the-temple.org

TRADITIONAL/CONSERVATIVE

- **Congregation B'nai Torah**, 700 Mt. Vernon Highway, Atlanta, 404-257-0537, www.bnaitorah.org
- **Congregation Shaarei Shamayim**, 1810 Briarcliff Road, Atlanta, 404-417-0472, www.shaareishamayim.com
- **Congregation Shearith Israel**, 1180 University Drive NE, Atlanta, 404-873-1743, www.shearithisrael.com

NEW AGE/ALTERNATIVE SPIRITUALITY

Metro Atlanta is home to a variety of alternative religions and "new age" spirituality practices. Here you'll find everything from Wicca and Paganism to Kabbalah and meditation study. For more detailed listings of new age and spiritual happenings around town, be sure to check out the bulletin boards at local herb shops, health food stores, and metaphysical bookstores, or visit www.aquarius-atlanta.com.

KABBALAH

If you're interested in finding out more about Kabbalah, be sure to visit www.kabbalah.com. For more information on Kabbalah study in Atlanta, contact the **Karin Kabalah Center of Atlanta**, 2531 Briarcliff Road NE, Atlanta, 404-320-1038, www.karinkabalahcenter.com.

MEDITATION CENTERS

The following meditation centers offer classes in meditation, guided meditation workshops, and more. In addition, the Siddha Yoga Meditation Center offers teachings in the lineage of their guru, Gurumayi Chidvilasananda, as well as weekly chanting and satsang. And Kashi Atlanta offers a weekly interfaith darshan (holy teaching) with Jaya Devi Bhagavati, chanting, and kirtan, and an annual weekend intensive with spiritual teacher and guru, Ma Jaya Sati Bhagavati.

- **Siddha Yoga Meditation Center of Atlanta**, 52 Executive Park Drive South NE, Atlanta, 404-633-0044, www.symca.org
- **The InnerSpace—Atlantian Temple Meditation**, 185 Allen Road, Atlanta, 404-252-4540, www.theinnerspace.com
- **Kashi Atlanta Center for Yoga, Service and Community**, 1681 McLendon Avenue, 404-687-3353, www.kashiatlanta.org
- **Shambhala Meditation Center of Atlanta**, 1447 Church Street, Decatur, 404-370-9650, www.atlantashambhalacenter.org

PAGANISM/WICCA/WITCHCRAFT

If you'd like more information about Paganism, Wicca, or Witchcraft (and the various branches therein), go online to www.religioustolerance.org and www.beliefnet.com.

SIKH

Founded just over 500 years ago, the Sikh faith now has a following of over 20 million people worldwide, and is ranked as the world's fifth largest religion. Though only 220,000 Sikhs live in the United States, there is a large enough Sikh population here in metro Atlanta for two gurdwaras: **Gurdwara Sikh Study Circle, Inc. (SSCI)**, 1821 South Hairston Road, Stone Mountain, 770-808-6320, www.sikh-atlanta.org; and the **Guru Ram Das Ashram**, 112 Millbrook Circle, Roswell, 770-993-6633. If you'd like to learn more about Sikhism, contact the gurdwaras directly, or visit www.sikhs.org.

UNITARIAN UNIVERSALIST

The Unitarian Universalist Association (UUA) dates back to 1961, when the Universalism and Unitarianism movements officially merged. For more information about UUA, or to find a congregation near you, visit their web site, http://uua.org. UUA churches in metro Atlanta include:

- **Emerson Unitarian Universalist Fellowship**, 2799 Holly Springs Road, Marietta, 770-578-1533, www.emersonuu.org
- **First Existentialist Congregation of Atlanta**, 470 Candler Park Drive, Atlanta, 404-378-1327, www.firstexistentialist.org
- **Unitarian Universalist Congregation of Atlanta**, 1911 Cliff Valley Way NE, Atlanta, 404-634-5134, www.uuca.org
- **Unitarian Universalist Congregation of Gwinnett**, 12 Bethesda Church Road, Lawrenceville, 770-717-7913, www.uucg.org
- **UU Metro Atlanta North Congregation**, 11420 Crabtree Road, Roswell, 770-992-3949, www.uuman.org

TODAY'S ATLANTA METROPOLITAN AREA ENCOMPASSES 28 COUNTIES and over six thousand square miles, and, even if you live right in the center of things, having access to a car will most likely be necessary at some point. In fact, travel to and from Atlanta's many outer suburbs requires a personal vehicle, as MARTA, the city's public transit system, covers only Fulton and DeKalb counties. Encouraging, however, has been the advent of Xpress commuter service, which offers express bus service into Atlanta from Henry, Clayton, Rockdale, Coweta, and Douglas counties, and operates as part of the Cobb and Gwinnett county transit systems as well. Although public transportation options are not comprehensive, they are improving.

What follows are specifics about how to get around metro Atlanta by car and by public transportation, as well as tips for getting in and out of the city by Greyhound, Amtrak, and Southeast Stages, and contact information for Hartsfield-Jackson International Airport and the numerous airlines that fly in and out of there. Also covered here: what to expect from Atlanta traffic, and tips for getting around on area roads and highways.

GETTING AROUND

To get started, we repeat here a few basic tips to keep in mind as you prepare to make your way around the city:

- Atlanta is divided roughly into four quadrants. Peachtree Street is the east-west dividing line, and the north-south dividing line is Martin Luther King Jr. Drive, on the southern edge of downtown. Therefore, if NW follows an address, this means that your destination is somewhere downtown or north of the downtown area and west of Peachtree.
- I-285 makes a loop around the perimeter of the city. If someone says that a place is located "outside the perimeter," what they mean is that you must travel beyond I-285 to find it.

- Remember the locations of malls. These are major landmarks in the city, and often people give directions based on a locale's proximity to the nearest mall.
- Don't assume that just because two streets run parallel to each other they will stay that way. For example, Peachtree and Piedmont Road, the two major north-south routes, intersect in north Buckhead. Oxford Road crosses Briarcliff twice, effectively paralleling itself.
- Remember that Atlanta streets wind unpredictably. Even if you are convinced that the route you are taking leads you in a straight line, you may very well not end up where you think you should. Keep your sense of humor. Atlanta is a lovely city to get lost in.

BY CAR

Because metro Atlanta is so spread out, owning a car is pretty much a necessity. Depending on your point of view, or the day, cruising around the metro area can be an adventure or a headache. Unlike cities designed with easy-to-follow grid patterns, in Atlanta, streets that you believe to be parallel may eventually cross each other! Streets often change names with little or no warning; many roads that serve as major traffic routes are only two lanes wide; and, as you may have heard, there are over fifty streets with "Peachtree" somewhere in the name. Have patience. Major thoroughfares and highways serve as landmarks and can get you where you want to go. As in all major metropolitan areas, Atlanta drivers tend to be aggressive and may even be confrontational. Though road rage altercations are generally limited to horn honking and angry gestures, you should drive defensively and avoid drivers and situations that could be dangerous. Many savvy metro Atlanta drivers find elaborate short cuts and use back roads to avoid dealing with boiling tempers on interstates and main thoroughfares. Use your map and experiment.

Here is an overview of some of the major highways and byways:

- **I-85** runs northeast through Gwinnett County toward Greenville, South Carolina, and southwest to the airport and Montgomery, Alabama. North of the downtown area it merges with I-75 to become the **Downtown Connector** (75-85). The Downtown Connector cuts directly through the downtown commercial sector, and I-75 and I-85 split again just south of the Lakewood Freeway.
- **I-75** extends north into Cobb and Cherokee counties, heading toward Knoxville, Tennessee, and south to Henry County and eventually Florida.
- **I-20** runs east/west and joins Atlanta to Columbia, South Carolina, and Birmingham, Alabama. It crosses the Downtown Connector just north of Turner Field. It is the road to take to both Zoo Atlanta and Six Flags Over Georgia.

- **I-285**, better known as "The Perimeter," circles around the city, crossing all the major highways at least once. The best known (and best avoided, if possible) interchange is "Spaghetti Junction," where I-285 crosses I-85 in a complex tangle of roadway.
- **Georgia 400** is an excellent commuter road that connects the Lenox Mall area and the financial district to the northern suburbs such as Roswell and Alpharetta. It meets I-85 near Lindbergh Drive and becomes a toll road just north of the Buckhead exit. If you travel GA 400 often, you may want to consider purchasing a GA 400 Cruise Card, which enables you to drive through the toll lanes without stopping. Contact the **State Road and Tollway Authority**, 404-365-7790, www.georgiatolls.com, for more information.
- **Peachtree Street** is the major thoroughfare cutting through downtown, Midtown, and the heart of the Buckhead commercial district. It continues on to Lenox Mall and Phipps Plaza, eventually reaching I-285.
- **Piedmont Road** runs parallel to Peachtree between downtown and Buckhead, although it crosses Peachtree in the northern section of Buckhead.
- **Ponce de Leon Avenue** travels east/west and links the downtown area to the city of Decatur and Stone Mountain.
- **Northside Drive** (which becomes **Cobb Parkway**) winds through Buckhead and Peachtree Battle, continuing on to Marietta.

TRAFFIC

For many years, Atlanta was often called the "New York of the South," due, in part, to its bustling downtown and burgeoning arts scene. These days, however, metro Atlanta is more like Los Angeles than New York City thanks to increasingly long commute times and the huge number of cars on the road. Since 1990, over 800,000 out-of-staters have come to the metro area, raising the population to an astounding 4.1 million. Suburban sprawl has inched its way out to so many surrounding counties that metro Atlanta now encompasses over 6,000 square miles of land. By some estimates, if growth continues at current rates, the North Georgia Mountains could actually become part of metro Atlanta by 2010! This amazing growth in population, especially in suburban neighborhoods outside the I-285 perimeter, combined with the large number of corporations and offices located inside the perimeter, has made for the longest commute in the USA: an average of 36.5 miles roundtrip daily, according to the Atlanta Regional Commission. But even those who live and work intown are feeling the effects of commuting. With so many cars clogging the streets and interstates, commute time during peak hours now averages about an hour and half for a 30-mile drive, or 30 minutes for a mere 10-mile drive, even within the city limits!

In general, I-285 seems to be the most consistently congested during any given rush hour, with I-75 and I-85 southbound close behind. Georgia 400 is usually the least congested, except where it meets I-285 and I-85. None of this is set in stone though, since Atlanta's traffic problems are still evolving. Your best bet is to stay informed of the traffic situation whenever you plan to drive during heavy traffic times (generally 6 a.m. to 9 a.m. and 4 p.m. to 7 p.m., Monday-Friday). For up-to-the-minute traffic information to help you navigate metro Atlanta's streets and interstates, you may want to check out the web sites offered by the **Georgia Department of Transportation**, www.georgia-navigator.com, and the *Atlanta Journal-Constitution's* metro traffic maps at www.ajc.com/metro/content/metro/traffic. If you're not near a computer, you can call the Department of Transportation, 404-635-6800, for traffic information and road conditions. Radio station **WSB-AM 750** offers traffic updates throughout the day, and all of the other local radio stations offer traffic reports during morning and evening rush hours.

Commuting congestion leads to short tempers, high stress levels, and more aggressive driving tactics, and it's made Atlanta a much more dangerous place for pedestrians. According to the **Centers for Disease Control (CDC)** and the **Georgia Department of Human Resources**, over 50 pedestrians are killed here every year, making metro Atlanta the twelfth most dangerous city for pedestrians. One third of the fatalities typically occur on state or county roads that generally do not provide sidewalks for pedestrians. The other two thirds tend to occur intown, on some of Atlanta's busiest streets, including Buford Highway, Peachtree Street, Ponce de Leon Avenue, and Roswell Road. In almost all pedestrian fatality cases, the drivers are exceeding the posted speed limit. If you'd like more information on pedestrians in Atlanta, including helpful safety tips, or if you'd like to read the CDC's most current report, contact **Pedestrians Educating Drivers on Safety (PEDS)** Atlanta, 1447 Peachtree Street, Atlanta, 404-873-5667, www.peds.org.

CARPOOLING

There are approximately 90 miles of High Occupancy Vehicle (HOV) lanes in the metro Atlanta area, running north and south along interstates 75 and 85, and east and west along I-20 from downtown to 285 east. All HOV lanes, which are available to vehicles carrying two or more occupants, and to all motorcycles and emergency vehicles, are strictly enforced. Single-passenger cars using the HOV lanes are ticketed. Many Atlantans take advantage of these lanes to decrease commute time to and from downtown by about 10 or 15 minutes, but finding someone to carpool with is not always easy. Your best bet is to check with co-workers to see if you can find anyone who lives close to you and would like to share a ride to work. If you don't have much luck there, you can contact the **Atlanta Regional Commission's Ride Find**, 1-87-RIDEFIND, www.187ridefind.com. This organization may be able to put you in touch with others close to you who would like to share your commute. For more information on HOV lanes, including planned extensions, contact the **Department of Transportation**, 404-624-1300, www.dot.state.ga.us.

CAR RENTAL

There are hundreds of car rental companies to choose from in metro Atlanta. For a complete listing, check the Atlanta Yellow Pages under "Automobile Renting." To help you get started, you may want to consider the following:

- **Accent Rent-A-Car**, 404-264-1773, www.accentrentacar
- **Alamo Rent-A-Car**, 800-462-5266, www.alamo.com
- **Atlanta Rent-A-Car**, 404-344-1060, 800-542-8278, www.atlantarac.com
- **Auto Save Car Rentals**, 770-497-9076, www.autosavecarrentals.com
- **Avis Rent-A-Car**, 800-230-4898, www.avis.com
- **Budget Car and Truck Rental**, 800-527-0700, www.budget.com
- **Enterprise Rent-A-Car**, 800-261-7331, www.enterprise.com
- **Hotlanta Exotic Car Rentals**, 678-461-2220, www.hotlantarentals.com
- **Hertz Car Rental**, 800-654-3131, www.hertz.com
- **Thrifty Car Rental**, 800-847-4389, www.thrifty.com

TAXIS

Although taxis are not as common in metro Atlanta as they are in other major cities (especially outside of the downtown area), there are still many companies providing service in the city. But keep in mind, it's impossible to flag down a cab in Atlanta; instead you have to call the dispatcher and have one sent to you. So, if you think you'll need a cab, it's a good idea to keep the phone numbers handy.

In the mid 1990s (just in time for the 1996 Olympic Games), Atlanta's city government began to crack down on "gypsy" cabs in order to regulate cab service in the area. For the most part, this has worked, and the majority of taxis you see throughout the city belong to licensed cab companies, though you can still find independent cab drivers out and about, particularly around Hartsfield International Airport. For a complete listing, check out the Atlanta Yellow Pages under "Taxicabs." Here is a list of the city's largest cab companies:

- **Atlanta Yellow Cab Company**, 404-521-0200; serving the city of Atlanta and surrounding communities
- **Buckhead Safety Cab**, 404-875-3777; serving Buckhead, Lenox, and north Atlanta
- **Checker Cab Company**, 404-351-1111, www.atlantacheckercab. com; serving metro Atlanta
- **Norcross/Gwinnett Cab Company**, 770-458-1600; serving Norcross and other parts of Gwinnett County
- **Style Taxi**, 404-522-8294, www.styletaxi.com; serving north metro Atlanta

BY BIKE

Despite increasing traffic (or perhaps because of it), many Atlantans make their commute via bicycle. Of course, this only works for those not traveling into the city from an outer suburb. Biking is becoming a popular alternative, although sometimes a dangerous one, for those who live and work in the same area. In Atlanta, bicycles are considered vehicles and, in the absence of a bicycle lane, must be ridden in traffic, often on busy, four-lane thoroughfares. The problem: Most metro Atlanta roads do not offer bike lanes, and when bike lanes are added, they are generally on low-traffic streets like Fifth Street at West Peachtree, where many cyclists find they are not needed. However, there is a growing movement among bike enthusiasts and bike activists who are lobbying to make Atlanta streets safe for non-motorized vehicles. The **Southern Bicycle League**, 770-594-8350, www.bikesbl.org, recently petitioned the state to include bicycles as an alternative form of transportation in an effort to reduce automobile congestion and improve the city's air quality. **Bicycle Georgia**, http://bicyclegeorgia.com, offers information on bicycle-related news stories, ride calendars, personals, discussion groups, bicycle advocacy organizations, and more. The **Atlanta Bicycle Campaign**, 404-881-1112, www.atlantabike.org, is an advocacy/social group committed to educating the public on bike safety. They even offer "Effective Cycling" classes to those who want to learn safe methods of riding in Atlanta traffic.

You can also combine your bike commute with a ride on MARTA. Bicycles are welcome on trains, and every MARTA bus can accommodate two bikes on its front rack.

If you'd like to learn more about Georgia's bike laws, get the latest information on proposed bike lanes in Atlanta, or lodge a complaint with officials, contact the **Georgia Bicyclist and Pedestrian Coordinator**, 404-657-6692, www.dot.state.ga.us; the **Governor's Highway Safety Representative**, 404-656-6996, http://gohs.georgia.gov; or the **Atlanta Regional Commission**, 404-463-3100, www.atlantaregional.com.

Remember: Even though metro Atlanta does not enforce a helmet law, it's always a good idea to wear one when you ride.

BY PUBLIC TRANSPORTATION

MARTA

The **Metropolitan Atlanta Rapid Transit Authority (MARTA)** is the public transportation system of Atlanta. It operates three train lines and the bus system. The MARTA north/south train line splits at the Lindbergh Center station to become the north/south and northeast/south lines. The north line continues to the Buckhead, Medical Center, Dunwoody, Sandy Springs and North Springs stations; the northeast line continues to the Lenox, Brookhaven, Chamblee, and Doraville stations. Regardless of where you choose to board the train, keep in mind the northeast/north/south rail line offers travelers a hassle-free ride to the airport.

Riding MARTA costs $1.75 for a one-way fare on the train and/or bus. For those who use MARTA regularly, it's a good idea to buy a roll of 20 tokens for $30 or, purchase a weekly TransCard (with unlimited rides during that week) for $13, or a monthly TransCard (with unlimited rides during that month) for $52.50. TransCards can be purchased at any of MARTA's RideStores, located inside the Five Points, Lenox, and Airport stations, as well as at the Lindbergh Headquarters building. Senior citizens (above 65) and the disabled (either mentally or physically) can pick up half-fare permits ($.85) at the Five Points or Lindbergh stations. The catch, if you use the permit, you'll have to pay your half of the fare in cash. No TransCards are available for this discount. For primary and secondary students attending Fulton or DeKalb county schools, a weekly student pass is available for $10. This TransCard can be used from 6 a.m. to 7 p.m., Monday-Friday, and can be purchased through your child's school. For out-of-town visitors (especially tour groups and conventioneers), MARTA offers a special discount program with passes valid only for the duration of their stay. The visitor pass allows unlimited travel on MARTA trains and buses for groups of 15 or more. A minimum of 20 days notice is required to book passes. Call 404-848-5501 for more information on this program.

MARTA schedules and maps are available at the Five Points Station and other MARTA information booths. For schedule information call 404-848-4711 or go online to www.itsmarta.com.

TRAIN

MARTA's two train lines, the north/south (orange) line, which also contains the northeast/south line, and the east/west (blue) line intersect at only one point, the Downtown Five Points station. For a single fare you can ride one line, transfer to the other line at Five Points, and transfer again to a bus for your final destination.

At the moment, the north/south line starts in North Springs, heads down to Buckhead, shoots through downtown, and ends up finally at the airport. The northeast/south line starts in Doraville, heads down to Brookhaven and Lenox Mall, and connects with the north/south line at Lindbergh, then travels the same route down to the airport. The east/west line extends from Hamilton E. Holmes (formerly Hightower) and proceeds through downtown and toward Decatur and beyond. A map of MARTA's train lines is available at www.itsmarta.com and is also provided at the back of this book. Maps are clearly posted at all train stations and inside each train car.

The two northernmost stations are particularly useful for commuters from North Fulton County who wish to avoid a downtown (or Buckhead) trek by taking the train. The Sandy Springs station, just one mile northwest of the Dunwoody station, is located at the intersection of Mt. Vernon Highway and Perimeter Center West. The North Springs station, located to the east of Georgia 400 and to the west of Peachtree-Dunwoody Road, approximately one mile north of Abernathy Road, serves as a commuter station for people living along the northern Georgia 400 corridor. This station features a multi-level parking deck for approximately 2,200 cars with access from Georgia 400 and a second surface lot for approximately 300 vehicles, accessible from Peachtree-Dunwoody Road.

Each MARTA rail station is 100% accessible to senior citizens and the disabled, with wide gates, escalators, and elevators. All of the trains offer special wheelchair spaces at the end of each rail car. MARTA also welcomes guide dogs on all of its trains and buses. No other pets are allowed.

Riding MARTA is an affordable and easy way to get around the city and is a great choice for downtown sporting events and trips to the airport. The rail system operates from 5 a.m. to 1 a.m., Monday-Friday, and from 6 a.m. to 12:20 a.m. on weekends and holidays. Trains are scheduled to run every 8 minutes on weekdays, every 10 minutes on Saturdays, and every 15 minutes on Sundays and holidays.

BUS

MARTA runs 150 bus routes throughout the city. Many bus routes connect the train stations to nearby neighborhoods or attractions. All buses accept the weekly and monthly TransCard passes, the visitor pass, tokens, or exact change (bills or coins). If you need a transfer card, ask the driver as you pay your fare. The driver can also assist riders who may have questions about identifying their stops.

Though some bus routes now offer 24-hour service, buses generally run from 5 a.m. to 1 a.m., Monday-Friday, and from 6 a.m. to 12:30 a.m. on weekends and holidays. To find out which routes run through your neighborhood, check out the **Neighborhoods** chapter of this book. For a complete listing of bus routes and schedules, contact MARTA's Customer Information, 404-848-4711, or check www.itsmarta.com.

In a continuing effort to make mass transit accessible to everyone, MARTA now offers buses equipped with wheelchair lifts on more than 100 of the 150 routes. They also provide designated priority seating at the front of every bus for senior citizens and the disabled. To find out when the wheelchair-accessible buses operate, call **Paratransit Information** at 404-848-5389. To request a lift-equipped bus to stop along your route, call 404-848-5826.

EXPRESS SHUTTLES

During the summer, MARTA operates several express shuttles to help people reach local events and attractions without the hassle of traffic jams. These shuttles leave from designated stations and operate up to 90 minutes before the event. They will also bring passengers back to the station when the event ends. For instance, if you are heading out to a Braves game at **Turner Field**, you simply take a bus or drive to a convenient MARTA station, pay your fare, then take the train to the Five Points Station. Once you exit the train at Five Points, just follow the signs leading to the shuttle, and there you are. There is no additional charge for the shuttle service as long as you are transferring from a MARTA bus or train. For those not using MARTA to get to the Five Points station, shuttle service is $1.75.

Besides the Braves shuttle, MARTA also operates a **HiFi Buys Amphitheater Shuttle**, which departs from the Lakewood/Ft. McPherson station, and a **Six Flags Over Georgia Shuttle**, which departs from the Hamilton E. Holmes station.

For more information on MARTA's summer shuttle service, call 404-848-4711.

MARTA PHONE NUMBERS AND WEB SITE
- **Web Site**, www.itsmarta.com
- **Schedule Information**, 404-848-4711
- **General Information**, 404-848-5000
- **Customer Service**, 404-848-4800
- **Bus Services for Disabled**, 404-848-5389
- **TTY Service**, 404-848-5665

XPRESS COMMUTER SERVICE

The most exciting new option for metro area commuters is **Xpress Commuter Service**. Xpress offers luxury commuter buses from the outer-ring counties to downtown Atlanta locations as well as to outlying MARTA stations, making the commute from Henry, Clayton, Rockdale, Coweta, and Douglas counties, as well as Cobb, Cherokee, Forsyth, and north Fulton counties, much more convenient. Tickets are available individually for one-way ($3) or round-trip ($5) excursions, or as 31-day ($80) and 20-ride ($45) passes. For information on current and future routes, schedules, and ticket purchase, contact Xpress at 404-463-4782 or www.xpressga.com.

COBB COMMUNITY TRANSIT

Cobb County has its own bus system, which runs in and around Cobb County along 15 routes from 5 a.m. to midnight, Monday–Saturday (though not all buses run on Saturday). There is no bus service on Sunday. Fares are $1.25 for adults 18 and over, $.80 for children under 18, free for children under 42 inches (with a paying adult), and $.60 for senior citizens and the disabled. Along with its bus service throughout Cobb County, **Cobb Community Transit (CCT)** also offers limited express service to Atlanta, connecting with MARTA in Buckhead (Lenox Station), Midtown (Arts Center Station), and downtown (Five Points Station). Transfers to and from the trains and buses are free between both systems. For schedule information, or for further details on the CCT/MARTA connection, call 770-427-4444. Hearing-impaired customers can use the TDD line at 770-419-9183. Online, go to www.cobbdot.org.

GWINNETT COUNTY TRANSIT

Gwinnett County now has its own bus system, which runs local and express buses throughout Norcross and Lawrenceville, and to Gwinnett Place Mall and the Mall of Georgia along 12 routes. Buses run from about 5 a.m. to midnight, Monday-Saturday, except for express routes, which operate Monday-Friday. There is no bus service on Sunday. Fares are $1.75 for regular routes and $3 for express routes. Ten-ride ticket books can be purchased for $14 and $27. An express monthly pass costs $100. For complete schedule information and more, contact the **Gwinnett County Transit** at 770-822-5010, www.gctransit.com.

NATIONAL/REGIONAL TRAIN & BUS SERVICE

AMTRAK

Atlanta's **Amtrak** passenger train station is located at 1688 Peachtree Street NW. If you're looking to take a vacation, but prefer not to fly or drive, riding the rails may be for you. Amtrak offers competitive pricing and special saver fares for passengers throughout the year, traveling to many destinations in the USA. For the best rates, including internet-only discounts, check out www.amtrak.com. You can research Amtrak's train accommodations, plan your route, and even make your reservations online, sometimes at great savings. If you'd rather use the phone, you can get the same information (though not the same discounts) by calling 800-USA-RAIL (872-7245).

GREYHOUND

You can find the **Greyhound Bus Terminal** in downtown Atlanta at 232 Forsyth Street SW. To make reservations, or get schedule information, you have three choices: you can call the station directly at 404-584-1731, call Greyhound's National Reservation Line at 800-231-2222, or log onto Greyhound's web site, www.greyhound.com.

SOUTHEASTERN STAGES

Southeastern Stages, 232 Forsyth Street, 800-596-0462, www.south easternstages.com, offers nationwide connecting motorcoach service with daily schedules from Atlanta and Decatur to several cities throughout Georgia and the southeast, including Athens, Augusta, Savannah, Charleston, and Columbia.

BY AIRPLANE

HARTSFIELD–JACKSON INTERNATIONAL AIRPORT

According to Airports Council International, **Hartsfield-Jackson International Airport**, www.atlanta-airport.com, has been the busiest airport in the world since 1998, running about 72 million passengers each year—that's one million more than the previous record-holder, Chicago/O'Hare. In the 1990s, Hartsfield-Jackson was also named "Best Airport in North America" by the readers of *Business Traveler International,* and is consistently ranked in the top five of all US airports.

Hartsfield-Jackson International Airport is conveniently located about ten miles south of the city off of I-85, and unless it is rush hour, you shouldn't have much trouble driving to the airport. However, as smooth as the drive may be, parking can still be a hassle, especially during peak travel times (during the summer months and around holidays). If you're up to the challenge and choose to take a chance on finding a space, there are a few things to keep in mind. First, Hartsfield offers more than 30,000 public parking spaces, including approximately 14,500 deck spaces, 8,000 in Econo-lots, and 8,500 in Park & Ride lots, but all of these spaces can fill up fast. To stay on top of the parking situation at the airport, call the **Hartsfield-Jackson Parking InfoLine**, 404-530-5010. You'll hear a recorded message telling you which lots are full and which have spaces still available. This is a valuable service if you're on your way to the airport, but be sure to call as close to your departure time as possible, since the information changes throughout the day. You can also get updated parking information by tuning in to the airport's radio station, **WQO-AM 830**, or by going online to www.atlanta-airport.com.

Once you know that there are spaces available, it's time to figure out which lot you want to use. The length of time you'll need the space should determine where you park. For instance, if you are just running in to see someone off or pick someone up, you can take advantage of the hourly parking located near the front of the airport. Rates are $1 per hour for the first and second hours; $2 per hour for the third and fourth hours; up to $48 per day for anything over six hours. Designated long-term parking spaces are located in the Econo-lots or covered parking decks. One way to save time if you're traveling during peak travel season, and the inner lots are filling up, is to use one of the airport's Park & Ride lots (with shuttle service) located around the outer perimeter of the airport; the shuttles run on a fairly tight schedule, so the wait usually isn't very long. In fact, it generally takes less time to use the shuttle at these lots than to drive in and out of parking decks looking for a closer space. Rates for Park & Ride lots start at $1 per hour, or a maximum $9 per day.

By far the easiest way to get to Hartsfield-Jackson is to use MARTA and avoid parking nightmares altogether. Most MARTA stations offer long-term parking for riders, and it only costs $1.75—the price of your fare. If this sounds like the choice for you, simply catch one of MARTA's southbound trains (on the north/south or northeast/south lines) and take it all the way to the end. MARTA will actually drop you off inside the airport. For more information on parking at the airport, including various rates and parking options, call 404-209-1700. For more information on taking MARTA to the airport, call 404-848-5000 or visit www.itsmarta.com.

Finally, if you just don't want to drive and you're carrying too many bags to take the train, you may want to consider taking an airport shuttle or hiring a car or limousine. The following services offer transportation to and from the airport (for a more complete listing, check www.atlanta-air port.com, under "Ground Transportation"):

- **AAA Airport Express**, 404-767-2000, www.aaaairportexpress.com
- **A & M Limo Corporation,** 770-955-4565, aandmlimo.com
- **Airport Metro Limo and Shuttle Service**, 404-766-6666, www.airportmetro.com
- **Atlanta Corporate Limo**, 404-344-1903, www.atlantacorporate limo.com
- **London Livery, Ltd.**, 404-231-9800, www.londonlivery.com

Hartsfield-Jackson is home to both **Delta Airlines** and **AirTran**, and almost every other major airline offers service here as well. Following is a list of airlines that fly into Hartsfield-Jackson. When making reservations or checking flight schedules, you should call the airlines directly. For general airport information and flight delays, call Hartsfield-Jackson at 404-530-7300.

- **Aero Mexico**, 800-237-6639, www.aeromexico.com
- **Air Canada**, 888-247-2262, www.aircanada.ca
- **Air France**, 800-237-2747, www.airfrance.com
- **Air Jamaica**, 800-523-5585, www.airjamaica.com
- **AirTran**, 800-247-8726, www.airtran.com
- **American Airlines**, 800-433-7300, www.aa.com
- **America West**, 800-327-7810, www.americawest.com
- **Atlantic Southeast Airlines (Delta Connection)**, 800-325-1999, www.delta.com
- **British Airways**, 800-247-9297, www.britishairways.com
- **Comair (Delta Connection)**, 800-325-1999, www.comair.com
- **Continental**, 800-231-0856, www.flycontinental.com
- **Delta Air Lines**, 800-325-1999, www.delta.com
- **Frontier Airlines**, 800-432-1359, www.flyfrontier.com
- **Hooters Air**, 888-359-4668, www.hootersair.com
- **Independence Air**, 800-359-3594, www.flyi.com
- **Korean Air**, 800-438-5000, www.koreanair.com
- **Lufthansa**, 800-645-3880, www.lufthansa-usa.com
- **Midwest**, 800-452-2022, www.midwestexpress.com
- **Northwest Airlines**, 800-225-2525, www.nwa.com
- **South African Airways**, 800-722-9675, www.flysaa.com
- **United**, 800-241-6522, www.ual.com
- **US Airways**, 800-428-4322, www.usairways.com

DEKALB PEACHTREE AIRPORT

DeKalb Peachtree Airport, 2000 Airport Road, Chamblee, 770-936-5440, www.pdkairport.org, is the second busiest airport in Georgia (behind Hartsfield-Jackson) in the number of take-offs and landings each year: an average of approximately 230,000 per year over the last 30 years. What started as the site of Camp Gordon, a World War I Army training base, is now a 765-acre home to 570 aircraft (including 50 corporate jets), 4 runways, 25 large hangars, and 90 T-hangars. There is no regularly scheduled passenger or cargo service at DeKalb Peachtree; instead the airport is used for corporate aircraft, charter service, pilot training, and recreational flights. Several large aviation service companies (**Epps Air Service**, 770-458-9851, www.eppsaviation.com; **Mercury Air Group**, 770-454-5000, www.mercuryaviators.com; and **Signature Flight Support**, 770-452-0010, www.bba-aviation.com/flightsupport) operate out of DeKalb Peachtree, offering arrival/departure terminals, fuel sales, charter flights, hangar rentals, maintenance, and more. **Biplane Rides Over Atlanta**, 770-393-3937, http://biplaneridesoveratlanta.com, offers rides, sightseeing tours, and aerobatic flights. **American Air Flight Training**, 770-455-4203, www.fly-aaft.com; **Aviation Atlanta**, 770-458-8034, www.aviationatlanta.com; **PDK Flight Academy**, 770-457-1270; and **Quality Aviation**, 770-457-6215, www.qualityaviation.net, provide flight lessons by certified, experienced instructors, from the airport daily. DeKalb Peachtree Airport has also built a small picnic/visitor area complete with big wooden swings, picnic tables, and view stands for people who may not want to fly, but want to watch people who do. It doesn't cost anything to sit and watch the planes take off, so if you like airplanes, it's a great place to spend an afternoon.

FLIGHT DELAYS

Information about flight delays can be checked online on your airline's web site, or at www.fly.faa.gov. Similarly, the site www.flightarrivals.com offers real-time arrival, departure, and delay details for commercial flights.

CONSUMER COMPLAINTS—AIRLINES

To register a complaint against an airline, call or write the Department of Transportation: 202-366-2220, Aviation Consumer Protection Division, C-75 Room 4107, 400 7th Street SW, Washington, DC 20590.

I F YOU NEED TEMPORARY QUARTERS WHILE SEARCHING FOR YOUR house or apartment, metro Atlanta offers a variety of options, from inexpensive to those fit for royalty. There are even a growing number of special needs accommodations available at hotels throughout the city. In fact, all of the major hotels and motels listed below now offer rooms and services for the physically disabled, though services vary from location to location; if this is an issue, be very clear about specific needs when making a reservation. Whether a hotel, hostel, bed and breakfast, or short-term rental suits you, this section should give you a good start. Keep in mind that the prices listed below are per night and pre-tax. The current lodging tax in Atlanta is 14%, on top of a local sales tax of 4% to 7%, depending on the county.

ROOM RESERVATION SERVICES

There are hundreds of hotels and motels throughout metro Atlanta, offering everything from the bare bones room-with-a-bed to opulent hotel suites with fresh-cut flowers, a separate bedroom suite, and thick, white robes. With so many options to choose from, it's often difficult to know where to start. Fortunately there are several reservation services and online travel agents that can help you find the hotel or motel that is right for you. Here are just a few to get you started:

- **Central Reservation Services**, 800-555-7555, www.reservation-services.com
- **Expedia**, 800-397-3342, www.expedia.com
- **Hotel Reservations Network**, 800-715-7666, www.hotel discount.com
- **Hotels.com**, 800-246-8357, www.hotels.com
- **Orbitz**, 888-656-4546, www.orbitz.com

- **Priceline**, www.priceline.com
- **Quikbook**, 800-789-9887, www.quikbook.com

When making reservations through any discount site, it's important to ask about their cancellation policy and whether or not the rates they quote include hotel tax or any other charges. Most reservation services require a credit card for booking. A few may even require payment in full when making the reservation, though usually, payment for the room will be made directly to the hotel when you check out.

INEXPENSIVE LODGINGS

If budget is more important than luxury, the following listings may be of interest. Most are chain hotels, with locations here and there throughout the city. All of them offer standard accommodations—bed, bath, towels, TV. Some may also offer additional amenities, so it might be a good idea to check around before making a decision on where to stay. Prices generally range between $60 and $150 per night, though you will want to confirm the rate with the hotel when making your reservation:

- **Best Western**, 800-780-7234, www.bestwestern.com; over 40 locations in the metro Atlanta area
- **Cheshire Motor Inn**, 1865 Cheshire Bridge Road, NE, 404-872-9628
- **Days Inn**, 800-329-7466, www.daysinn.com; over 30 locations throughout metro Atlanta
- **The Highland Inn**, 644 North Highland Avenue NE, Atlanta, 404-874-5756; located in the heart of Virginia Highland
- **Holiday Inn**, 800-465-4329, www.holiday-inn.com; over 30 locations throughout metro Atlanta
- **Red Roof Inn**, 800-733-7663, www.redroof.com; several locations throughout metro Atlanta
- **Sierra Suites**, 888-695-7608, www.sierrasuites.com; 4 locations in metro Atlanta
- **Suburban Lodge Hotel**, 800-265-0363, www.suburbanlodge.com; 11 locations in metro Atlanta
- **Travelodge**, 800-578-7878, www.travelodge.com; 4 locations in metro Atlanta
- **Wyndham Garden Hotel**, 800-999-3223, www.wyndham.com; 5 locations in metro Atlanta

MEDIUM-PRICED LODGINGS

The following hotels range in price between $100 and $200 per night. Here you can expect rooms that are a little larger than what you'd find in the inexpensive hotels. You may also find additional amenities such as room service, internet access, and in-room mini-bars. Most are national chains, with several convenient locations thoughout the metro Atlanta area:

- **Embassy Suites Hotel**, 800-EMBASSY, www.embassysuites.com; several locations in metro Atlanta
- **Homewood Suites**, 800-445-8667, www.homewoodsuites.com; 4 locations in metro Atlanta
- **The Omni Hotel at CNN Center**, 404-659-0000, 800-843-6664, www.omnihotels.com; located inside the CNN Center in downtown Atlanta
- **Raddison Inn**, 800-333-3333, www.radisson.com; several locations in metro Atlanta
- **The Sheraton**, 800-325-3535, www.sheraton.com; 10 locations in metro Atlanta
- **Summerfield Suites by Wyndham**, 800-WYNDHAM, www.wyndham.com; 2 locations in metro Atlanta
- **W Hotel Atlanta**, 111 Perimeter Center West, NE, 770-396-6800, www.whotels.com; one Atlanta location; the W is a chain hotel, and is actually on the cusp between mid-priced lodging and luxury. While not as expensive as some of the higher-priced hotels in the area, it does offer upscale ambiance and incredible customer service that guests may not find at the other mid-priced hotels.

LUXURY LODGINGS

The following luxury hotels offer a wide variety of services and comforts for their guests. Rates begin at about $200 per night and go up from there, based on season and availability.

- **The Four Seasons Hotel**, 75 Fourteenth Street, Atlanta, 800-819-5053, www.fourseasons.com; first-class accommodations contained within a stunning neo-classical tower of rose and marble granite, over-looking both midtown and downtown Atlanta, the Four Seasons is arguably Atlanta's most upscale hotel.
- **Grand Hyatt Atlanta**, 3300 Peachtree Road NE, Atlanta, 404-365-8100, 800-633-7313, www.grandatlanta.hyatt.com; first-class accom-modations located in Buckhead, at the intersection of Peachtree Road and Piedmont Road, convenient to Lenox Mall and Phipps Plaza, as well as Buckhead's popular bar and nightclub scene.
- **The Ritz Carlton**, 181 Peachtree Street NE, Atlanta, 404-659-0400; 3434 Peachtree Road, Buckhead, 404-237-2700; 800-241-3333, www.ritzcarlton.com; both the downtown and Buckhead locations

offer the first-class accommodations you'd expect from the Ritz.

- **Westin Atlanta North at Perimeter**, 7 Concourse Parkway, 770-395-3900, 888 625-5144, www.starwood.com/westin; offers first-class accommodations north of the city, at Perimeter Mall. The Westin Atlanta North is a sleek, contemporary hotel located alongside a private lake.
- **Westin Buckhead**, 3391 Peachtree Road NE, 404-365-0065, 888-625-5144, www.starwood.com/westin; (formerly the Swissôtel) first-class accommodations located in the heart of Buckhead, adjacent to Lenox Mall. This location is conviently located in Atlanta's most popular shopping and entertainment district.
- **Westin Peachtree Plaza**, 210 Peachtree Street NW, Atlanta, 404-659-1400, 888-625-5144, www.starwood.com/westin; a downtown Atlanta landmark offering first-class accommodations and phenomenal views of the city.

BED & BREAKFASTS

To reserve a space in one of metro Atlanta's many bed and breakfast establishments, you may want to consider using a reservation service. Two to consider are **Bed and Breakfast Atlanta**, 404-875-0525, www.bedand breakfastatlanta.com; and **Bed and Breakfast Inns Online**, www.bb online.com/ga. However, if you'd rather make your reservations directly with the bed and breakfast facility, you may want to try the following. Rates typically range between $100 and $300 per night:

- **Ansley Inn**, 253 Fifteenth Street NE, Atlanta, 404-872-9000, 800-446-5416, www.ansleyinn.com; historic Tudor mansion located in midtown Atlanta
- **Gaslight Inn Bed and Breakfast**, 1001 St. Charles Avenue NE, Atlanta, 404-875-1001, www.gaslightinn.com; Craftsman-style home located in the Virginia Highland community. Much of the Inn is lit by flickering gaslight fixtures (hence the name). A two-night minimum stay is preferred.
- **King-Keith House Bed and Breakfast**, 889 Edgewood Avenue, Atlanta, 404-688-7330, 800-728-3879, www.kingkeith.com; this 1890 Queen Anne-style home located in historic Inman Park boasts 12-foot ceilings and beautifully carved fireplaces. Two-night minimum.
- **Sixty Polk Street Bed and Breakfast**, 60 Polk Street, Marietta, 770-419-1688, 800-845-7266, www.sixtypolkstreet.com; historic Victorian home located near the Marietta Square, approximately 30 minutes from downtown Atlanta.
- **The Village Inn Bed and Breakfast**, 992 Ridge Avenue, Stone Mountain, 770-469-3459, 800-214-8385, www.villageinnbb.com; this historic 1820s inn is the oldest structure in Stone Mountain Village.

HOSTELS/YMCA

Hostels and YMCAs are excellent low-budget options for travelers. Unfortunately, metro Atlanta doesn't offer many options. At the moment, there is only one hostel and one YMCA location offering lodging in the city. Contact information for both are listed below:

- **Atlanta International Hostel**, 223 Ponce de Leon Avenue, 404-875-9449, 800-473-9449, www.hostel-atlanta.com; prices start at $19 per night.
- **YMCA**, 22 Butler Street NE, 404-659-8085, www.ymca.net; rooms are for men only, age 21 and up.

SHORT-TERM LEASES

A short-term lease or corporate apartment may be a good bet if you plan on using temporary lodging for more than just a few weeks. Accommodations typically range from furnished studios to one- or two-bedroom apartments. And prices can range from $300 a week to $3,000 per month, depending on the establishment. A few to consider are:

- **Apartment Selector**, 770-552-9255, 866-494-3329, www.apt selector.com/atlanta; free service that can assist you in finding a corporate or short-term apartment that meets your needs.
- **Extended Stay America**, 800-804-3724, www.extendedstay america.com; seven locations throughout metro Atlanta, offering fully furnished studios with full kitchens, cable TV, and free voicemail service.
- **Post Corporate Apartments**, 770-434-6494, 800-643-POST, www.postproperties.com; tastefully furnished and fully equipped apartment homes include housewares, linens, washer and dryer, all utilities and weekly housekeeping. Post has several locations throughout metro Atlanta, so call for more information.
- **Residence Inn by Marriott**, 800-331-3131, www.marriott.com/residenceinn; fourteen locations throughout metro Atlanta, offering suites that include a full-size kitchen, TV, linens, dishes and utensils, and daily maid service.
- **Studio Plus**, 800-804-3724, www.studioplus.com; four locations throughout metro Atlanta, offering deluxe studios that include a TV, kitchen, sofa sleeper, separate bedroom, fitness center, and weekly housekeeping.
- **Windsor Communities**, 800-888-RENT, www.windsorcommunities. com; four locations in metro Atlanta, offering tastefully furnished and fully equipped apartment homes ranging in size from studios to three-bedroom townhomes.

G EORGIA IS A BEAUTIFUL STATE THAT OFFERS RESIDENTS AND VISI-
tors a variety of landscapes. From the golden beaches of Georgia's
coast to the beautiful mountains in the north, there are enough
quick getaway destinations here to please any weekend wanderer.

Most of the following locales can be reached by car, though if you're
planning to spend time on the islands dotting the coastline, you'll have
about a six-hour drive and may have to ferry across once you reach the
water. These island trips are generally not day trips from metro Atlanta, but
are perfect for overnight, weekend, or even weeklong stays. Trips to the
North Georgia Mountains can be done in a day, but with such magnificent
views, many opt to stay longer.

GEORGIA'S COAST

- **Cumberland Island**, off the coast of Georgia near St. Mary's, is 17
  miles long and 1.5 to 3 miles wide. It is accessible by a ferry, which
  operates year-round from St. Mary's. There is a small ferry fee and reservations are required. Cumberland Island is a great place to visit if you
  are interested in walking tours and want to escape the typical tourist
  destinations. There are no restaurants or shops here, but you will find
  plenty of salt and freshwater marshes, white sand beaches, and live oak
  forests. Swimming and camping are available daily, though camp
  spaces must be reserved in advance. Most of the structures on the
  island date back to the pre–Civil War plantation era, though there are a
  few turn-of-the-century buildings that were erected by the Thomas
  Carnegie family. For more information on visiting Cumberland Island,
  or to make reservations, contact the Superintendent at P.O. Box 806,
  St. Mary's, GA 31558, 912-882-4335, 888-817-3421, www.nps.gov.
- **Jekyll Island**, off the coast of Georgia near Brunswick, is the smallest
  of Georgia's coastal islands, with 5,600 acres of highlands and 10,000

acres of marshlands. In 1886, a group of wealthy businessmen bought the island and formed the Jekyll Island Club. Members of the club, including J.P. Morgan and William Rockefeller, vacationed here each winter in fabulous cottages, some of which are still standing. In 1947, the club was abandoned for economic reasons and the island was sold to the state. Today, the Jekyll Island Authority maintains the island as a year-round resort, offering visitors a number of hotels, restaurants, and activities, including golf, water skiing, swimming, shopping, tennis, bicycling, and fishing. For more information on Jekyll Island, including lodging, dining, and entertainment options, contact the Jekyll Island Convention & Visitors Bureau, One Beachview Drive, Jekyll Island, GA 31527, 877-4-JEKYLL, www.jekyllisland.com.

- **St. Simons Island**, off the coast of Georgia near Brunswick, is another of Georgia's famous coastal islands. Originally home to several planta- tions in the pre–Civil War era, St. Simons flourished until Union troops, led by General Sherman, razed the estates, leaving only the slave quar- ters standing. Today, St. Simons Island is home to numerous museums, art galleries, family attractions, hotels, shops and restaurants, as well as the fully inclusive Sea Palms Golf and Tennis Resort, 912-638-3351, www.seapalms.com. Besides golf and tennis, the resort offers three swimming pools, a private beach, a fitness center, a playground, out- door buffets, and more. Rates vary depending on room size and the time of year. For more information on St. Simons Island, including a complete listing of hotels, restaurants, and entertainment options, con- tact the St. Simons Visitors' Center, 912-638-9014, 800-933-2627; or visit St. Simons Online, www.saintsimons.com.
- **Savannah**, located on Georgia's Atlantic coast approximately 250 miles from Atlanta, has an abundance of history and architecture that few American cities can match. Having preserved its colonial grace and charm through the restoration of more than 1,400 historically significant buildings, Savannah has become one of the largest urban historic land- mark districts in the USA, and also one of the state's most popular tourist destinations. In fact, an estimated 6.5 million visitors travel to this city each year. In addition to its historical relevance, Savannah also boasts several museums, a number of fine restaurants and cafés, and over 8,000 rooms in properties ranging from luxury hotels to small bed and breakfasts. Several airlines fly directly into Savannah International Airport, including AirTran, Comair, Continental Express, Delta Airlines, United, and US Airways. For more information on Savannah, contact the Savannah Area Convention and Visitors' Bureau, 101 East Bay Street, Savannah, GA 31401, 877-SAVANNAH, www.savannah-visit.com.
- **Tybee Island**, located off the coast of Savannah, is one of the most popular of Georgia's coastal islands, due to its many beachside attrac-

tions including a boardwalk, fishing pier, amusements, hotels, and vacation cottages. Tybee Island's beach runs the entire length of the island—with nearly four miles of Atlantic Ocean on one side and two miles of the Savannah River on the other. The northern tip of Tybee boasts the Fort Pulaski National Monument, 912-786-5787, www.nps.gov/fopu; and the Tybee Museum and Lighthouse, 912-786-5801, www.tybeeisland.com. The island can be reached by a causeway from Savannah and US 80. For more information, contact the Savannah Area Convention and Visitors' Bureau, 101 East Bay Street, Savannah, GA 31401, www.savannah-visit.com.

GEORGIA'S HEARTLAND

- **Athens**, approximately 65 miles northeast of Atlanta on the Atlanta Highway/GA-8, is home to the University of Georgia, 706-542-3000, www.uga.edu, the Georgia Museum of Art, 706-542-4662, www.uga.edu/gamuseum, and the State Botanical Garden, 706-542-1244, www.uga.edu/botgarden. Many Atlanta residents head over to Athens on weekends to see great college sports (UGA's football team, the Bulldogs are a big draw), or to hear some of the up-and-coming, local rock bands that frequent the clubs surrounding the university. An added bonus for some Athens visitors is that members of R.E.M. and the B-52's (who both got their start here) can occasionally be seen around town. If you'd like more information on Athens, including where to stay or what to do while you're in town, contact the Athens Convention and Visitors' Bureau, 300 North Thomas Street, Athens, GA 30601, 800-653-0603, www.visitathensga.com.
- **Macon**, about three hours south of Atlanta, is the largest city in Georgia's historic heartland. It is home to several popular tourist attractions including the Ocmulgee National Monument, 478-752-8257, www.nps.gov/ocmu, which traces the area's Native American heritage back 12,000 years, and the Tubman African-American Museum, 478-743-8544, www.tubmanmuseum.com, a showcase of African-American art, history, and culture. Macon also boasts the Georgia Sports Hall of Fame, 478-752-1585, www.georgiasportshalloffame.com, and the Georgia Music Hall of Fame, 478-750-8555, 888-GA-ROCKS, www.gamusichall.com, which honors the many Georgia natives who changed the face of rock, rhythm and blues, jazz, gospel, and country music. For more information on Macon, including lodging, dining, and entertainment options, contact the Macon Convention/Visitors' Bureau and Welcome Center, P.O. Box 6354, Macon, GA 31208-6354, 478-743-3401, 800-768-3401, www.maconga.org.

GEORGIA'S MOUNTAINS & STATE PARKS

- The **City of Dahlonega**, located approximately 63 miles northwest of Atlanta, was the site of the first major gold rush in the USA in 1828—20 years before gold fever hit California. Today, Dahlonega offers ways to experience glimpses of the past with a visit to the **Gold Museum**, 706-864-2257, www.gastateparks.org/info/dahlonega, for gold panning and underground tours of the area's three major mines; many opt to visit during the annual Gold Rush Days celebration, the third weekend in October. Thousands of residents and visitors congregate on the town square to view over 300 arts and crafts exhibits, run a 5K race, listen to bluegrass music, and eat. A hog calling contest, king and queen coronation, and a number of children's activities add to the festivities. Dahlonega also plays host to several other non-gold-related festivals throughout the year, including the Bear on the Square Festival, held the third weekend in April, commemorating the bear that came to the square in the spring of 1996; the Fourth of July Family Day celebration, named one of the "Top Twenty Events in the Southeast" by the Southeast Tourism Society; and the Wildflower Festival of Arts, held the third weekend in May, showcasing the work of hundreds of local artists. For more information, contact the Dahlonega-Lumpkin County Chamber of Commerce, 706-864-3711, 800-231-5543, www.dahlonega.org.
- **Helen, Georgia**, approximately 80 miles north of Atlanta, is unlike any other community in Georgia. Originally a small, run-of-the-mill mountain town, Helen began a transformation process in 1968. Led by a group of area businessmen and local artist, John Kollak, they turned the town into the Alpine village replica that it is today. Kollak, inspired by the time he had spent in Bavaria, presented the Alpine village idea, and Helen residents immediately began renovations. Today this quaint town offers over 150 import shops, 30 factory outlets, and a cobble-stone alley of small boutiques and restaurants, with an array of old-world shopping, dining, and lodging opportunities. One of Helen's most popular annual events is the annual Oktoberfest celebration, which runs from mid-September through early November. German bands perform nightly, dancers in traditional Bavarian garb dance the polka and waltz, and visitors are invited to enjoy a selection of imported German wines and beers, warm pretzels, and specialty foods such as Bavarian wurst and sauerkraut. Contact the Helen Welcome Center, 706-878-1619, 800-858-8027, or the Helen Convention and Visitors Bureau, 706-878-2747, www.helenga.org, for more information.

- **Amicalola Falls**, located approximately 66 miles northwest of North Fulton County, offers visitors the chance to see the highest waterfalls (729 feet) in the state. Amicalola is also home to 17 tent and trailer sites, a 57-room lodge with restaurant, rental cottages, playgrounds, picnic shelters, and more set on 1,020 acres of lushly wooded land. Amicalola is a great place to visit if you want to fish, camp, hike, or just relax. Call 706-265-4703, 800-864-7275 or visit www.gastateparks.org/info/amicalola for additional information.

- **Black Rock Mountain State Park**, located astride the eastern Continental Divide in northeast Georgia, near the North Carolina border, is the highest state park in Georgia. Named for its sheer cliffs of dark-colored rock, Black Rock Mountain encompasses some of the most amazing scenery in all of Georgia's Blue Ridge Mountains—including a spectacular 80-mile view of the Southern Appalachians. The 1,502-acre park area is home to 52 tent and trailer sites, 10 rental cottages, 11 walk-in campsites, 2 picnic shelters, a visitor's center, and a 17-acre lake. Hiking, fishing, and primitive camping trips are available for visitors. For more information, call 706-746-2141, 800-864-7275, or visit www.gastateparks.org/info/blackrock.

- **Cloudland Canyon State Park**, located on the western edge of Lookout Mountain in northwest Georgia, near the Alabama border, attracts visitors with its 2,219 acres of rugged geology and beautiful scenery. The park straddles a deep gorge cut into the mountain by Sitton Gulch Creek, and visitors are invited to hike its 4.5-mile waterfalls trail, or 6.5-mile backcountry trail. If hiking isn't your thing, the park also offers 75 tent and trailer sites, a 40-bed group camp, rental cottages, picnic shelters, tennis courts, and swimming pools. Call 706-657-4050, 800-864-7275, or visit www.gastateparks.org/info/cloudland for more information.

- **Fort Mountain State Park**, located 8 miles east of Chatsworth, Georgia, along Highway 52, near the Tennessee border, derives its name from the 855-foot long wall of rock, which stands along the mountain's highest point. The theory is that early Native Americans built the wall as protection against hostile invaders or for ancient ceremonies. Today the 3,428-acre park offers a variety of outdoor activities including 14 miles of hiking trails, a lake with a swimming beach, boat rentals and fishing, 74 tent and trailer sites, cottage rentals, and picnic sites. For more information, call 706-695-2621, 800-864-7275, or visit www.gastateparks.org/info/fortmt.

- **Hart State Park**, located in northeast Georgia at the South Carolina border, offers visitors several water-related outdoor activities including boating, water skiing, bass fishing, and swimming on Lake Hartwell.

Large mouth bass, black crappie, rainbow trout, and walleyed pike can be found in the park's 5,590-acre reservoir. Boat ramps and docks offer easy access, and a small man-made beach is designated for swimmers. There are also 76 tent and trailer sites, two rental cottages, three picnic shelters, and a 1.5-mile multi-use trail. For more information, call 706-376-8756, 800-864-7275, or visit www.gastateparks.org/info/hart.

- **Moccasin Creek State Park**, located approximately 20 miles north of Clarksville near the North Carolina border, is often referred to as the park "where spring spends the summer." Nestled in the Blue Ridge Mountains on the shores of Lake Burton, a Georgia Power Company reservoir, Moccasin Creek is a great starting point for high country exploration. Visitors are invited to tour the adjacent Lake Burton Fish Hatchery, operated by the Department of Natural Resources, which raises rainbow trout for lakes and streams across the Georgia Blue Ridge, or hike the 1-mile looping nature trail, or the 1.5-mile trail up Moccasin Creek. Other activities include volleyball, basketball, horseshoes, camping, fishing, and boating. There are 54 tent and trailer sites with water and electrical hookups, wheelchair accessible fishing piers, a public boat ramp, and boat rentals. If you'd like to find out more about Moccasin Creek State Park, including registering for a campsite, call 706-947-3194, 800-864-7275, or visit www.gastateparks.org/info/moccasin.

- **Tallulah Gorge State Park**, located approximately 80 miles northeast of Atlanta, is Georgia's newest state park. One of the most spectacular gorges in the eastern USA, at 2 miles long and nearly 1,000 feet deep, this park is a favorite destination for Atlantans and North Georgians. The park was created through a partnership between the Georgia Department of Natural Resources and Georgia Power Company, and offers 50 tent and trailer sites, two lighted tennis courts, a picnic area, a 63-acre lake with beach, a visitors center, and more than 20 miles of trails. For more information, call 706-754-7970, 800-864-7275, or visit www.gastateparks.org/info/tallulah. For reservations, call 706-754-7979.

- **Tugaloo State Park** is located on a rugged peninsula that juts into the Lake Hartwell reservoir in northeast Georgia, near the South Carolina border. Named by Indians for the river that once flowed near the park, Tugaloo offers year-round bass fishing, camping, volleyball, horseshoes, water skiing, swimming, and hiking. There are 120 tent and trailer sites and 20 rental cottages on 393 acres of land. For more information, call 706-356-4362, 800-864-7275, or visit www.gastateparks.org/info/tugaloo.

- **Unicoi State Park and Lodge**, located just two miles from the faux Alpine village of Helen in northeast Georgia, is a popular and comfortable destination with its 100-room lodge and year-round schedule of activities. This 1,081-acre site hosts over 80 tent and trailer sites, 30 rental cottages, lighted tennis courts, the lodge, a buffet-style restaurant, a craft shop, and a 53-acre lake. Visitors can enjoy a wide range of activities including hiking, camping, picnicking, swimming, boating, and an informative mountain culture and environmental program. Special Friday and Saturday night programs are scheduled throughout the year. For more information, call 706-878-2201, 800-864-7275, or visit www.gastateparks.org/info/unicoi.

- **Vogel State Park**, about 11 miles south of Blairsville within the Chattahoochee National Forest, is one of Georgia's oldest and most popular state parks. Despite being one of the state's smallest parks, a mere 280 acres, it offers 110 tent and trailer sites, 36 rental cabins, 4 picnic shelters, and a 20-acre lake. Visitors are invited to enjoy the park's many family-oriented activities, including miniature golf, swimming, pioneer camping, pedal boats, and hiking along 17 miles of lush trails. For more information, call 706-745-2628, 800-864-7275, or visit http://gastateparks.org/info/vogel.

For those considering a visit to one of Georgia's State Parks, keep in mind that a Georgia Park Pass is required for all parked vehicles. Visitors may pay a daily parking fee of $2 to $4, or purchase an annual pass for $25, which is valid at all state parks. If you'd like to avoid the parking fee, Wednesdays are free for all day-use visitors. For more information on parking passes, contact any of the state parks at the numbers listed above.

NATIONAL PARKS

- **Chattahoochee River National Recreation Area**, located on Island Ford Parkway in Atlanta, consists of 16 land units along a 48-mile stretch of the Chattahoochee River. The park offers visitors a variety of recreational activities including fishing, hiking, picnicking, and boating, as well as the chance to view a wide selection of natural flora and fauna, and Native American archeological sites. Restrooms, a bookstore, and wheelchair-accessible trails are open to the public, and picnic tables are offered on a first-come basis. Camping is not allowed in the park. There are no entrance fees, though a daily parking fee of $2 for all park units has been instituted. For more information, call 678-538-1200, or visit www.nps.gov/chat.
- **Chickamauga and Chattanooga National Military Park**, located in north Georgia along the Tennessee border, was the first established National Military Park in the USA, back in 1890. The park honors the Civil War soldiers who fought at the Battle of Chickamauga in September 1863 and the Battles for Chattanooga in November 1863.

Today, the park, which consists of over 8,200 acres spread over Georgia and Tennessee, houses a Visitor Center with exhibits on the battles, as well as a Civil War timeline. Several trails are available for walking or hiking, as well as audio tour tapes of the Chickamauga battlefield and seasonal tours of the Cravens House, which was a strategic location in the Battle of Lookout Mountain. For more information, call 706-866-9241, or visit www.nps.gov/chch.

- **Fort Frederica National Monument**, on St. Simons Island off the coast of Brunswick, was established in 1736 as the southernmost post of the British colonies in North America. The fort served as protection for Georgia and South Carolina from the Spanish, who had settled in Florida. Today the park is known for its exceptional beauty. Stately oak trees, well established and trailing grapevines, and Spanish moss give it an air of antiquity. Visitors are invited to view exhibits on the history of Frederica, as well as the ruins of the fort's barracks. There are a number of special tours and activities offered throughout the year for both adults and children, including the Fort Frederica Festival in March, the Fort Frederica 5K Easter Race, and the Holiday Open House in December. The park gift shop sells souvenirs, soft drinks, insect repellent (a must), and film. Lodging is not available in the park. For more information, call 912-638-3639 or visit www.nps.gov/fofr.

- **Fort Pulaski National Monument**, on Tybee Island, contains 5,365 acres of land, including some of the most pristine marshland on the Georgia coast. Named for Revolutionary War hero Count Casimir Pulaski, Fort Pulaski took 18 years to build and was the first military assignment for Robert E. Lee. Today, this remarkably intact fort affords visitors the chance to tour the grounds and surrounding park and check out the fort's Civil War–era cannons, damaged walls, and parade grounds. There is also a quarter-mile trail for walking or hiking, a visitors center and museum, fishing and picnicking areas, and a boat-launching ramp that is open to the public. For more information, call 912-786-5787 or visit www.nps.gov/fopu.

- **Ocmulgee National Monument**, in Macon, is a memorial to the estimated 12,000 years of human habitation in this corner of North America. From Ice Age hunters, to Creek Indians, to the Mississippian culture that settled here from 900 to 1100 AD, Ocmulgee preserves a continuous record of human life in the Southeast. Today, the monument consists of two land units separated by three miles of wetlands along the Ocmulgee River. The park is open daily from 9 a.m. to 5 p.m., except for Christmas and New Years Day. For more information call 912-752-8257, or visit www.nps.gov/ocmu.

For those considering a visit to a national park, either in Georgia or elsewhere in the USA, the **National Park Service** offers a camping and tour-reservation system. Check out http://reservations.nps.gov, or call 800-365-2267. A basic map and free brochures of national park locations can be obtained by calling 202-208-4747.

NATIONAL FOREST SERVICE

If you're considering a camping trip, you may want to call the **National Forest Service's** toll-free reservation line, 877-444-6777, TDD 877-833-6777. There are nearly 40,000 nationwide campsites on national land, and you can make your reservations up to 240 days in advance. For more information, visit www.reserveusa.com.

NUMEROUS ORGANIZATIONS IN ATLANTA AND IN THE SURROUND-
ing communities sponsor festivals, fairs, and feasts that draw crowds
of enthusiastic participants every year. Because the area has such a
mild climate, many of these events take place outdoors. *Creative Loafing* and
the *Atlanta Journal-Constitution* often highlight annual celebrations, so keep
your eyes peeled for information each month. For a complete list of annual
events, contact the **Georgia Department of Trade & Tourism**, 404-
656-3590, www.georgiaonmymind.org, or your county's visitors bureau.

JANUARY

- **Dr. Martin Luther King Jr. Celebration**, metro Atlanta, 404-526-
8900, http://thekingcenter.org; Atlanta honors the birthday of the Civil
Rights leader with three days of activities and events throughout the city.
- **Resolution Run 2K/5K/10K**, Technology Park, Norcross, 404-231-
9064, www.atlantatrackclub.org; good for beginners wanting to start
out with a 2K race or experienced athletes interested in the 10K.

FEBRUARY

- **Black History Month Celebration**; Atlanta and surrounding communities play host to a wide variety of events celebrating African-
American heritage and culture. For complete listings of scheduled
activities, check the local newspapers during February, or contact your
county's convention and visitors bureau.
- **Groundhog Day**, Yellow River Game Ranch, Lilburn, 770-972-6643,
www.yellowrivergameranch.com; will he or won't he? Each year,
Atlanta residents wait to find out whether or not General Lee (Atlanta's
favorite groundhog) will see his shadow. Many visitors make a day of it,
enjoying the ranch's picnic and play areas, and the 24-acre indigenous
animal preserve.

- **Southeastern Flower Show**, Georgia World Congress Center, Atlanta, 404-351-1074, www.flowershow.org; this five-day festival of gardening inspiration, education, and fun for the entire family is one of the top three flower and gardening events in the USA. Highlights include guest speakers, a black-tie dinner, the annual Flower Power Party for young adults, and a silent auction. Local experts are on hand to demonstrate the latest in garden design and landscaping, the Daffodil Diner food court serves lunch and refreshments throughout the festival, and the Flower Show Marketplace sells garden supplies as well as arts and crafts. Proceeds benefit the Atlanta Botanical Garden.

MARCH

- **Conyers Cherry Blossom Festival**, Conyers, 770-602-2606, 800-CONYERS, www.conyerscherryblossom.com; celebrate the arrival of spring and the flowering of the cherry blossoms with food, music, and activities for the entire family.
- **Cracker Barrel 500**, Atlanta Motor Speedway, 770-946-4211, www.atlantamotorspeedway.com; the name of this annual NASCAR Winston Cup race says it all. "Gentlemen, start your engines . . ."
- **St. Patrick's Day Parades**, Downtown and Buckhead, www.stpats paradeatlanta.com; a celebration of the popular Irish holiday, through the streets of downtown and Buckhead. Many area bars offer green beer for the occasion.
- **Walking Tours of Historic Atlanta** (through November), 404-688-3350, www.preserveatlanta.com; tours, conducted by the Atlanta Preservation Center, showcase the rich historical tapestry of Atlanta, from the Civil War to the Civil Rights Movement.

APRIL

- **AJC Atlanta International Car Show**, Georgia World Congress Center, 770-916-1741, www.ajcautoshow.com; annual event, sponsored by the AJC, showcases over 500 new import and domestic vehicles being introduced to the public, with factory and dealer representatives on hand to answer questions. Highlights of the show include the concept car presentation, where the cars of tomorrow are unveiled today, and the Motor Sports Pavilion, featuring NASCAR cars and drivers up close and personal.
- **Atlanta Dogwood Festival**, Piedmont Park, 404-329-0501, www.dogwood.org; celebrate springtime in the South—highlighting Atlanta's history, culture, and beauty. Features include artists' booths, a children's area, canine Frisbee, live music, hot air balloons, and food.

- **Easter Sunrise Service**, Stone Mountain Park, 770-498-5690, www.stonemountainpark.com; held at the top of the mountain, this nondenominational Easter service offers breathtaking views as the sun rises over the horizon.
- **Georgia Renaissance Festival** (to June), Fairburn, 770-964-8575, www.garenfest.com; offers visitors the chance to "journey back in time" to the Renaissance period, as they enter an elaborately detailed old-world village. Authentic food, detailed costumes, and activities for all ages help set the scene.
- **Great Bunny Hop**, Zoo Atlanta, 404-624-5600, www.zoo atlanta.com; families are invited to come visit the Easter Bunny, look for Easter eggs, and enjoy a wide array of fun activities at Zoo Atlanta.
- **Inman Park Festival and Tour of Homes**, Inman Park, 770-242-4895, www.inmanpark.org; offers residents and visitors the chance to get to know each other and tour some of the neighborhood's most interesting homes.
- **Jonquil City Jog 5K Run**, Smyrna, 770-518-8002, www.ci.smyrna.ga.us; 5K run through the city of Smyrna.
- **Spring Jonquil Festival**, Village Green, Smyrna, 770-434-6600, www.ci.smyrna.ga.us; residents of Smyrna celebrate spring and the blooming of their city flower, the jonquil, with music, food, activities, arts and crafts, and more.
- **Taste of Marietta**, Glover Park, Marietta, 770-429-1115, www.marietta square.com; a sampling of the wide variety of foods found in Marietta, provided by area restaurants.
- **WalkAmerica**, Centennial Olympic Park, Atlanta, 404-350-9800, www.walkamerica.org; www.marchofdimes.com/georgia; the March of Dimes' largest fundraising event and also one of the oldest fundraising walks in the USA. All proceeds from this 10K walk, held on the last Saturday in April, benefit the March of Dimes.

MAY

- **American Indian Festival**, Gwinnett County Fairgrounds, 770-791-0066, 770-963-6522, www.gwinnettcountyfair.com; a celebration of American Indian heritage and culture, this festival is both fun and educational. Food, music, American Indian performers, arts and crafts, and more are featured. Held every Memorial Day weekend and also the first weekend in October.
- **Atlanta Jazz Festival**, various locations throughout Atlanta, 404-817-6815, www.atlantafestivals.com; one of the country's largest free jazz festivals. Running the entire month of May, the Atlanta Jazz Fest offers music lovers the chance to hear good, live jazz music at various venues

throughout the city. Presented by the City of Atlanta Bureau of Cultural Affairs, performers include local and national jazz musicians.

- **Historic May-retta Arts & Crafts Festival**, Glover Park, Marietta, 770-794-5601, www.mariettaga.gov; arts and crafts by local artists are on display and for sale at this festival held in Glover Park, on the Marietta Square. Music, food, and activities are also featured.
- **Lasershow** (through October), Stone Mountain Park, 770-498-5690, www.stonemountainpark.com; an amazing outdoor light show, set to music ranging from classical to southern rock.
- **Memorial Day Salute to the Troops**, Stone Mountain Park, 770-498-5690, www.stoneountainpark.com; a four-day celebration of American spirit featuring a variety of entertainment and activities, with a special military tribute.
- **Spring Fling—Kirkwood Festival and Tour of Homes**, Bessie Branham Park, 404-377-4253, www.historic-kirkwood.com; a celebration of this historic Atlanta neighborhood, featuring live music, a children's area, food, history exhibits, and arts and crafts. The tour of homes features a variety of architectural styles, with homes ranging from elaborate restorations to works-in-progress.
- **Spring Moon Stroll**, Atlanta Botanical Garden, 404-876-5859, www.atlantabotanicalgarden.org; take a stroll through the Botanical Garden at night, and enjoy the spring air, the moonlight, and the delicate scent of blossoming flowers. Music, children's activities, and snacks are offered.
- **Sweet Auburn SpringFest**, Auburn Avenue, Atlanta, 404-886-4469, www.sweetauburn.com; celebrates the rich history of Atlanta's Auburn Avenue, former home of Martin Luther King, Jr., with food, music, and entertainment along the avenue.
- **Taste of Alpharetta**, 800-294-0923, www.alpharetta.ga.us; a sampling of the wide variety of foods found in Alpharetta, provided by area restaurants.

JUNE

- **Atlanta Fest Christian Music Festival**, Six Flags Over Georgia, 800-783-8839, www.atlantafest.com; features the best in traditional and contemporary Christian music, as well as food, activities and fellowship.
- **Atlanta Film Festival**, various locations throughout Atlanta, 404-352-4225, www.imagefv.org; showcases the innovative animation, documentary, experimental, and student works by local, national, and international video and filmmakers. Highlights include screenings of work, educational seminars, guest speakers, and contests.

- **Atlanta Lesbian and Gay Pride Festival**, Piedmont Park, 404-929-0071, www.atlantapride.org; a celebration of Atlanta's lesbian and gay community, featuring activities, games, music, food, and more. This festival is open to anyone who wants to show support for the gay and lesbian communities, regardless of sexual orientation.
- **Atlanta Symphony Orchestra Summer Concert Series**, Chastain Park Amphitheater, 404-733-5000, www.classicchastain.com; the ASO performs under the stars at Atlanta's Chastain Park. For more information, including the concert schedule and play list, contact the ASO directly.
- **Festival of India**, various locations throughout Atlanta, 336-593-8108, www.festivalofindia.org; three-day event, hosted by ISKON of Atlanta, features cultural shows (including Indian dance and music), seminars, arts and crafts, and authentic Indian food.
- **Georgia Shakespeare Festival**, Oglethorpe University, 404-264-0020, www.gashakespeare.org; popular June–November festival that showcases elaborate productions of some of Shakespeare's best plays, performed by the critically acclaimed Georgia Shakespeare Festival nonprofit repertory theatre company.
- **Georgia Special Olympics Summer Games**, Emory University, 404-521-6600, 866-946-7642, www.specialolympicsga.org; Emory University hosts this statewide Olympiad featuring mentally and physically disabled athletes, competing in a variety of events.
- **Music Midtown Festival**, Midtown, 770-MIDTOWN, www.musicmidtown.com; this annual three-day music festival, encompassing several blocks along Peachtree Street in Midtown, offers festival-goers an unequaled opportunity to hear a variety of bands on nine stages. Local performers, up-and-coming acts, and big-name rock bands alternate throughout the festival. In addition to all the great music, there are also food stands operated by local restaurants, children's activities, and an artists' market.
- **Peachtree Jr. 3K Race**, Piedmont Park, 404-231-9064, www.atlantatrackclub.org; annually held on the first Saturday in June, this event attracts 1500 7- to 12-year-olds. The race takes place entirely inside Piedmont Park.
- **Summer Film Festival**, Fox Theatre, Atlanta, 404-881-2100, www.foxtheatre.org; each June through August the Fox Theatre hosts a series of films, which may include recently released movies, family-oriented movies, and classic films. The schedule changes annually, so be sure to contact the theater for more information.
- **Virginia Highland SummerFest**, Virginia Highland, 404-222-8244, www.vahi.org/summerfest.html; offers residents and visitors the

chance to discover the neighborhood, sample food from local restaurants, visit the numerous galleries and boutiques that line Highland Avenue, meet new people, and listen to great local music.

JULY

- **Fantastic Fourth Celebration**, Stone Mountain Park, 770-498-5690, www.stonemountainpark.com; fireworks, food, music, and games are offered throughout Stone Mountain Park in honor of Independence Day.
- **Fourth in the Park**, Marietta Square, 770-794-5601, www.marietta square.org; Marietta's Independence Day celebration features food, music, activities, and fireworks.
- **Fourth of July**, Lenox Square Mall, Atlanta, 404-233-6767, www.simon.com; this concert and massive fireworks display over Lenox Square in Buckhead is very popular and well attended. In recent years, crowds as large as 200,000 have descended on the mall parking lot to watch the show. Those not wanting to fight the crowds for this Independence Day celebration may opt to stay home and watch the party on TV.
- **July 4th Celebration**, Lake Lanier Islands, 770-932-7200, www.lake-lanierislands.com; Lake Lanier Islands' Independence Day celebration features food, music, activities, and fireworks, as well as the opportunity to watch the sun set over the water.
- **Peachtree Road Race 10K**, Lenox Square Mall to Piedmont Park, 404-231-9064, www.atlantatrackclub.org; the famous race attracts runners and spectators from around the world. The race begins at Lenox Mall and winds down Peachtree to Piedmont Park. Spectators fill the outdoor patios of all of the Buckhead restaurants along Peachtree, and line the sidewalks as well. Runners who participate get a Peachtree Road Race T-shirt and the satisfaction of competing in the largest 10K road race in the world.
- **Pied Piper Parade, Concert, and Fireworks**, Downtown Decatur, 404-371-9583, www.decaturga.com/events.aspx; Fourth of July festival on the square in Decatur, featuring a parade, live music, and spectacular fireworks.
- **Salute 2 America Parade**, Downtown Atlanta, 404-897-7385, www.argonneparades.com; this parade, sponsored by WSB-TV Channel 2, kicks off Atlanta's Independence Day celebrations that culminate in a massive fireworks display when the sun goes down.

AUGUST

- **Cobb County Classic Rodeo**, Miller Park, Marietta, 770-528-8875, www.cobbcounty.org; annual, classic rodeo at Miller Park, begins at 8 p.m. and runs until 10:30 p.m.
- **Decatur BBQ, Blues & Bluegrass Festival**, Downtown Decatur, 404-371-9583, www.decaturga.com/events.aspx; annual BBQ and blues festival on Howard Avenue at the Old Depot.
- **Roswell Heritage Music Festival**, Historic Town Square, Roswell, 770-640-3253, 800-776-7935, www.cvb.roswell.ga.us; weekend-long festival features live music and entertainment, food, and more.
- **Smyrna's Birthday Celebration**, Village Green, Smyrna, 770-434-6600, www.cobbcvb.com; annual festival celebrating the history of Smyrna.

SEPTEMBER

- **Alpharetta Annual Heritage Festival**, Milton High School, Alpharetta, 678-297-6000, www.alpharetta.ga.us; features heritage demonstrations, militia re-enactments, puppeteers, magicians, arts and crafts, an antique car show, food, and live entertainment.
- **Annual Historic Marietta Antique Street Festival**, Marietta Square, 770-429-1115, www.antiquesofmarietta.com; this annual street festival features live entertainment, dining, and a classic car show.
- **Art in the Park**, Marietta Square, 770-429-1115, www.mariettaga.biz; enjoy local arts and crafts on the historic Marietta Square.
- **Arts Festival of Atlanta**, various locations around Atlanta, 404-521-6600, www.atlanta.net/acvb; this week-long arts festival celebrates the work of local artists, jewelers, dancers, and musicians. Bring your checkbook.
- **Atlanta Cup Soccer Tournament**, various locations throughout Atlanta, 770-452-0505, www.atlantacup.com; one of the premier soccer tournaments in the USA. Offers competitive play for boys' and girls' teams, ages 10 through 19. Matches are held over Labor Day weekend, and all proceeds benefit the Georgia Soccer Foundation.
- **ATC Singleton 5 Mile & 10 Mile Race**, Stone Mountain Park, 404-231-9064, www.atlantatrackclub.org; the Atlanta Track Club sponsors this annual five- and ten-mile race through Stone Mountain Park.
- **DragonCon**, various locations throughout Atlanta, 770-909-0115, www.dragoncon.org; the largest sci-fi, fantasy, and comic book convention in the USA, this Labor Day weekend event features presentations, gaming tournaments, contests, auctions, performances, and exhibits.

Many popular artists, actors, and authors of the sci-fi/fantasy/comic book genres attend to answer questions and sign autographs.

- **Grant Park Tour of Homes**, Grant Park, 404-688-7501, www.grant park.org; discover the unique beauty of Grant Park and tour some of the neighborhood's most interesting homes, including recently reno-vated bungalows and restored Victorians.
- **Gwinnett County Fair**, County Fairgrounds, Lawrenceville, 770-963-6522, www.gwinnettcountyfair.com; boasts traditional carnival rides, games of luck and skill, and good old-fashioned fair food.
- **JapanFest**, Stone Mountain Park, 404-842-0736, www.japanfest.org; celebrates Japanese culture by featuring street performers, authentic Japanese cuisine, traditional dance, martial arts and bonsai demonstra-tions, a tea ceremony, and Japanese folk music.
- **North Georgia State Fair**, Miller Park, Marietta, 770-528-8989, www.northgeorgiastatefair.com; this state fair attracts visitors from across metro Atlanta and north Georgia. Traditional carnival rides, games, live entertainment, and food are the big attractions.
- **Sandy Springs Festival**, Sandy Springs, 404-851-1328, www.sandyspringsfestival.com; festival includes food, music, arts and crafts, a 10K road race, and family-oriented activities.
- **Spice of Life**, Village Green, Smyrna, 770-434-6600, www.ci.smyrna.ga.us; offers great food, musical performances, and more.
- **Taste of Atlanta**, Lenox Square Mall, www.tasteofatlanta.org; come for a sampling of the wide variety of foods found throughout Atlanta, provided by local restaurants.
- **US 10K Classic**, Cobb Parkway, Marietta, 770-432-0100 ext. 645, www.us10k.org; annual charity 10K race through Cobb County is open to anyone who wants to participate or watch.
- **Yellow Daisy Festival**, Stone Mountain Park, 770-498-5690, www.stonemountainpark.com; celebrates the blooming of the rare yellow daisy, which can only be found within a 50-mile radius of Stone Mountain Park, by showcasing the work of over 400 local artists and crafters. Live entertainment, a children's corner, music, and food are also featured.

OCTOBER

- **A Haunting in the Hall**, Bulloch Hall, Roswell, 770-992-1731, www.bullochhall.org; storytelling and refreshments are featured at this annual, family-oriented Halloween event. Guests are invited to come in costume, but must RSVP at the number above before attending.
- **AIDS Walk**, Midtown, 404-876-9255, http://walk.aidatlanta.org; annual Walk through Midtown raises awareness and money for AIDS research.

- **Alpharetta Mayor's Challenge 5K Walk/Run**, Wills Park, Alpharetta, 678-297-6078, www.mayorschallenge.com; annual 5K race through Wills Park.
- **American Indian Festival**, Gwinnett County Fairgrounds, 770-791-0066, 770-963-6522, www.gwinnettcountyfair.com; a celebration of American Indian heritage and culture, this festival is both fun and educational. Food, music, American Indian performers, arts and crafts, and more are featured. Held every Memorial Day weekend and also the first weekend in October.
- **Atlanta Greek Festival**, Greek Orthodox Cathedral of the Annunciation, 404-633-5870, www.atlgoc.org/festival; Greek history and culture are honored at the Atlanta Greek Festival. Authentic food, performances, and more are highlights of this popular annual event.
- **Candler Park Fall Fest**, Candler Park, 404-522-8951, www.cpfallfest.com; weekend-long festival held in Candler Park, features live music, arts and crafts from neighborhood artists, food, and games.
- **Candler Park Tour of Homes**, Candler Park, www.candlerpark.org; many take this opportunity to tour some of Candler Park's most interesting and funky houses.
- **Chili Cook-off**, Stone Mountain Park, 770-498-5690, www.stonemountainpark.com; one of Stone Mountain's most popular events. Whether you are interested in competing or just eating, the cook-off is fun for the entire family.
- **Fall Harvest Festival**, Cagle Dairy, Canton, 770-345-5591, www.caglesdairy.com; the dairy offers daily tours of the farm, hayrides, and a cornfield maze to walk through.
- **The Great Atlanta Pot Festival**, Piedmont Park, 404-522-2267, www.millionmarijuanamarch.com; focuses on the movement to legalize marijuana and on hemp education. Festival-goers can learn more about the history of hemp and purchase hemp products including lip balm, paper, and clothing.
- **Great Halloween Caper**, Zoo Atlanta, 404-624-5600, www.zooatlanta.com; Zoo Atlanta offers an interesting alternative to door-to-door trick or treating, with Halloween games, treats, and more. Children (and adults) are invited to attend this Halloween event in costume.
- **Harvest Moon Stroll**, Atlanta Botanical Garden, 404-876-5859, www.atlantabotanicalgarden.org; take a stroll through the Botanical Garden at night, and enjoy the cool autumn air, the bright harvest moon, and the delicate fall foliage.
- **Stone Mountain Highland Games & Scottish Festival**, Stone Mountain Park, 770-521-0228, www.smhg.org; annual festival featuring traditional Scottish games (both spectator and participatory), Scottish food, and music.

NOVEMBER

- **A Southern Christmas**, Stone Mountain Park, 770-498-5690, www. stonemountainpark.com; a celebration of the holiday season, featuring music, food, activities, and gifts market; runs through December.
- **Atlanta Marathon and Half Marathon,** outside Turner Stadium, downtown, 404-231-9064, www.atlantatrackclub.org; the Atlanta Track Club sponsors this annual Thanksgiving morning event, run along the 1996 Olympic marathon course. Half marathon begins at the halfway point of the full marathon.
- **Lighting of the Tree**, Historic Courthouse, Lawrenceville, 770-882-5450, www.co.gwinnett.ga.us; the annual lighting of the Lawrenceville Courthouse, complete with carolers, Christmas tree, and holiday decorations, helps set the mood for the upcoming holiday season.
- **Lighting of Rich's-Macy's Great Tree**, Lenox Square Mall, Atlanta, 404-233-6767, www.simon.com; the annual lighting of this enormous Christmas tree traditionally draws a large crowd, and many Atlanta residents view this as the official start of the holiday season.
- **NAPA 500**, Atlanta Motor Speedway, 770-946-4211, www.atlanta motorspeedway.com; NASCAR Winston Cup Race.
- **Veterans Day Parade**, Buckhead, 404-521-6600, www.atlanta. net/acvb; www.avvba.org; this parade along Peachtree Road in Buckhead pays tribute to the veterans of the armed forces who have served in uniform and risked their lives to keep our country safe.

DECEMBER

- **Atlanta Symphony Orchestra Holiday Concerts**, Symphony Hall, 404-733-4900, www.atlantasymphony.org; feature season-appropriate compositions performed by the Orchestra, the ASO Chorus, and the ASO Opera.
- **Christmas at Bulloch Hall**, Roswell, 770-640-3253, www.cvb. roswell.ga.us; Christmas decorations, music, and more highlight this annual holiday event at Roswell's historic Bulloch Hall.
- **Christmas at Callanwolde**, Callanwolde Fine Arts Center, 404-872-5338, www.callanwolde.org; Christmas decorations, musical performances, and art are part of this annual holiday event.
- **Dropping of the Great Peach**, Underground Atlanta, 404-523-2311, www.peachdrop.com; Atlanta's answer to New York's ball drop on Times Square; revelers at this New Year's Eve celebration count down the minutes to the new year in anticipation of the dropping of the great peach.

- **The Marietta Pilgrimage, Christmas Home Tour**, Historic District, Marietta, 770-429-1115, www.mariettasquare.com; a tour of six private, historic Marietta homes, lovingly restored and decorated for the holidays.
- **The Nutcracker**, Fox Theatre, 404-881-2100, www.foxtheatre.org; 404-873-5811, www.atlantaballet.com; the annual Atlanta Ballet production of this beloved Christmas classic is a favorite among local residents.
- **Peach Bowl**, Georgia Dome, 404-223-4636, www.peachbowl.com; www.gadome.com; this annual college football post-season game is the only guaranteed Bowl match-up between rivals from the Atlantic Coast Conference and the Southeastern Conference.
- **Peach Bowl Parade**, Downtown, 404-586-8537, www.peachbowl. com; this parade heralds the upcoming Peach Bowl, with both of the participating college football teams, their school bands, and their fans partying through downtown.
- **Santa on the Square**, Santa's Workshop, Glover Park, Marietta, 770-429-1115, www.mariettasquare.com; children (and adults) can visit Santa and view his Marietta workshop on weekends throughout December.

THOSE INTERESTED IN LEARNING MORE ABOUT THE HISTORY OF Atlanta, or just getting a feel for the city, may want to consider the following list of books.

CHILDREN/YOUNG ADULTS

- *The Atlanta Braves Baseball Team* by Thomas S. Owens and Tom Owens. A comprehensive history of the Atlanta Braves' organization, from their early days to their championship runs of the 1990s. (ages 9–12)
- *The Atlanta Braves* by John F. Grabowski. (ages 9–12)
- *Competitive Edge (Hardy Boys Casefile #111)* by Franklin W. Dixon. The Hardy Boys must discover who's out to sabotage the 1996 Olympic Games—before it's too late. (young adult)
- *Happy Birthday Martin Luther King* by Jean Marzollo and J. Brian Pinkney. A brief biography (with pictures) for young children. The authors are especially sensitive when it comes to King's death. (ages 4–8)
- *Leaving Atlanta* by Tayari Jones. A novel set in 1979 Atlanta during the infamous Atlanta child murders. The story centers on the relationships of three fifth graders as they struggle with family issues, and the string of murders that has left the city terrified. (young adult)
- *On the Mound With . . . Greg Maddux* by Matt Christopher. A biography of Atlanta Braves' pitcher Greg Maddux, considered by many to be one of the best pitchers in Major League Baseball. (ages 9–12)

NONFICTION

ART/ARCHITECTURE

- *AIA Guide to the Architecture of Atlanta* by Isabelle Gournay. Profiles the various architectural styles of the city.

- *American Paintings at the High Museum of Art* by Judy L. Larson, Donelson Hoopes, and Phyllis Peet. Covers the three centuries of American art on permanent display at the High Museum of Art.
- *Atlanta Architecture—Art Deco to Modern Classic, 1929–1959* by Robert M. Craig and Richard Guy Wilson. A scholarly review of the art deco and modern classic architectural styles in Atlanta.

BIOGRAPHIES

- *The Autobiography of Martin Luther King Jr.* by Martin Luther King Jr., and Clayborne Carson. This autobiography, written by Carson, is based on thousands of King's essays, notes, letters, speeches, and sermons, and offers a glimpse of King's life.
- *Born to Rebel: An Autobiography* by Benjamin E. Mays. Starting life humbly as the son of a sharecropper, he went on to become the President of Morehouse College for almost three decades and the first black president of the Atlanta School Board.
- *Ted Turner: It Ain't As Easy As It Looks: A Biography* by Porter Bibb. An in-depth portrait of the often outspoken, larger-than-life media mogul.

FOOD

- *Atlanta at the Table* by Frances Schultz and Dot Griffith. A look at how Atlanta entertains—from fancy balls to down-home Sunday dinners. Each chapter includes photos and recipes.
- *Cooking Atlanta Style: Delicious Recipes from Atlanta's Best Restaurants, Hotels and Caterers*; and *More Cooking Atlanta Style*, by Margaret E. Norman. A compilation of interesting recipes from some of the best chefs in Atlanta.

GUIDES

- *147 Fun Things to do in Atlanta* by Karen Foulk.
- *Around Atlanta with Children: A Guide for Family Activities* by Denise Black. A look at places to visit and things to do with children in Atlanta.
- *The Atlanta Dog Lovers Companion* by Marilyn Windle and Phil Frank. Highlights places to go and things to do with dogs in Atlanta.
- *Atlanta Walks: A Comprehensive Guide to Walking, Running, and Bicycling Around the Area's Scenic and Historic Locales* by Ren and Helen Davis.

- ***Gardening Around Atlanta*** by Avis Aronovitz. Atlanta as seen through its lush and diverse gardens.
- ***Ponce de Leon: An Intimate Portrait of Atlanta's Most Famous Avenue*** by George Mitchell. A glimpse of Ponce de Leon Avenue some twenty years ago.
- ***Sideways Atlanta: A Field Guide to Offbeat Attractions in the "City Too Busy to Hate"*** by Suzanne Winterberger and Bill Tomey. A look at some of Atlanta's little known, yet memorable, events and places.

HISTORY

- ***Archival Atlanta: Electric Street Dummies, the Great Stonehenge Explosion, Nerve Tonics, and Bovine Laws: Forgotten Facts and Well-Kept Secrets From Our City's Past*** by Perry Buffington and Kim Underwood. An offbeat look at Atlanta's history.
- ***Atlanta: An Illustrated History*** by John Lewis.
- ***Atlanta and Environs, A Chronicle of Its People and Events*** (Volumes I, II, and III) by Franklin M. Garrett. Chronicles the people and events shaping Atlanta from 1820 to 1976, by one of Atlanta's most respected historians.
- ***Atlanta and the War*** by Webb Garrison. A look at the city before, during, and after the Civil War.
- ***Atlanta on My Mind*** by Stanley Skoryna. A 335-page compilation of facts and details about the city.
- ***Atlanta Rising: The Invention of an International City, 1946-1996*** by Frederick Allen. Chronicles 50 years of Atlanta history, concluding with the 1996 Olympic Games.
- ***Atlanta Then and Now*** by Michael Rose. Chronicle of Atlanta's growth and change over the last century
- ***Atlanta—Voices of the Civil War*** by the editors of Time Life Books. An audio presentation through letters, diaries, and personal recollections of the events surrounding the Atlanta campaign.
- ***Black Atlanta in the Roaring Twenties*** by Herman Skip Mason, Jr. A compelling look, through pictures and stories, of Atlanta's black culture during the jazz age.
- ***Emblems of Conduct*** by Donald Windham. A memoir of the author's Depression-era Atlanta youth.
- ***The Legacy of Atlanta: A Short History*** by Webb B. Garrison. An abbreviated paperback history of Atlanta, highlighting important people and events.
- ***Pickin' on Peachtree: A History of Country Music in Atlanta*** by Wayne W. Daniel. Traces the roots and growth of country music, from county fairs to Atlanta radio, to national recording deals.

- **The Temple Bombing** by Melissa Faye Greene. An exploration of the events surrounding the racially motivated bombing of Atlanta's oldest synagogue in 1958.
- **To 'Joy My Freedom: Southern Black Women's Lives and Labors After the Civil War** by Tera W. Hunter. Chronicles African-American working women from slavery to their struggles as free domestic laborers, using Atlanta as a backdrop.
- **Where Peachtree Meets Sweet Auburn** by Gary Pomerantz. Atlanta history as seen through the lives of two families and two mayors, one black and one white.

SPORTS

- **The History of the Atlanta Falcons** by Michael E. Goodman. A look at Atlanta's professional football team.
- **None But the Braves: A Pitcher, A Team, A Champion** by Tom Glavine, Nick Cafardo (with an introduction by Greg Maddux). World Series MVP and Braves' pitcher Tom Glavine tells the inspiring story of how the Braves went from "worst to first."

FICTION

- **The Answer Man** by Roy Johansen. Ken Parker, owner of an Atlanta-based polygraph service, soon finds himself caught up in two high-profile murder cases, and he's the prime suspect. (Mystery)
- **Atlanta** by Sara Orwig. The final book in Orwig's southern Civil War trilogy (which also includes New Orleans and Memphis) begins as Sherman makes his way through Atlanta, and tells the story of Yankee Colonel Fortune O'Brien and southern beauty Claire Dryden. (Romance)
- **Atlanta Graves** by Ruth Birmingham. Debut novel featuring Sunny Childs, an Atlanta private investigator, as she tries to solve an art theft and catch a killer, before her company defaults on its bank loan. (Mystery)
- **Atlanta Heat** by Robert Coram. A rookie detective tries to solve a double homicide with help from one of Atlanta's most famous crime reporters. (Mystery)
- **The Blue Place** by Nicola Griffith. Former cop Aud Torvingen finds herself becoming personally involved, as she investigates a puzzling art theft and murder. (Mystery)
- **The Dog Star** by Donald Windham. Chronicles the life of 15-year-old Blackie Pride as he roams the streets of post-Depression Atlanta. (General Fiction)

- **Down On Ponce** by Fred Willard. Debut novel by Atlanta resident Fred Willard offers a sometimes humorous yet noir-esque look at a handful of interesting characters from one of the seediest parts of town. (Mystery/Suspense)
- **Downtown** by Anne Rivers Siddons. *Downtown* tells the story of a plucky young Irishwoman, Smoky O'Donnell, who arrives in Atlanta in 1966 to find herself working at "Downtown," a small, hip magazine. (General Fiction) Other books by local author Anne Rivers Siddons include: *Outer Banks, Hill Towns, Homeplace, Fox's Earth, Heartbreak Hotel, Low Country, King's Oak,* and *Peachtree Road.*
- **Driving Miss Daisy** by Alfred Uhry. The play, which was adapted into the 1989 Academy Award winning film of the same name. (Fiction/Play)
- **Gone With the Wind** by Margaret Mitchell. The consummate saga of love and struggle during the Civil War. (General Fiction/Literature)
- **The Kidnapping of Aaron Greene** by Terry Kaye. Average "Joe," Aaron Greene, is kidnapped on his way to work and held for $10 million. The catch is that the kidnappers want a powerful Atlanta bank to pay the ransom, not Aaron's parents. When the bank refuses, a storm of controversy erupts. Where is Aaron? And why would anyone want to kidnap him? (Mystery) Other books by local author Terry Kaye include *The Runaway, Shadow Song,* and *To Dance with the White Dog.*
- **The Last Night of Ballyhoo** by Alfred Uhry. A play depicting life in Atlanta's Jewish community of the late 1930s. (Fiction/Play)
- **Looking for Atlanta** by Marilyn Dorn Staats. Margaret Hunter Bridges, an aging Atlanta debutante, tries to find herself and make sense of her life amidst the pain of a messy divorce and the accidental death of her daughter. (General Fiction)
- **A Man in Full** by Tom Wolfe. Set in Atlanta, this 700+ page novel explores (and satirizes) the lives of several interesting southern characters. (General Fiction)
- **Irish Eyes** by Kathy Hogan Trocheck. One of several Callahan Garrity mysteries set in Atlanta. (Mystery)
- **A Plague of Kinfolks** by Celestine Sibley. Atlanta political journalist turned columnist and mystery writer Sibley tells another Kate Mulcay story set in Atlanta and woven around eccentric characters and humorous, down-home situations. (General Fiction)

AMBULANCE

For emergency ambulance service in the greater Atlanta area dial 911. If you are calling DeKalb County from another county in the metropolitan area, dial 404-294-2493.

ALCOHOL & DRUG DEPENDENCY

- **Alcoholics Anonymous**, metro Atlanta Central Office, 404-525-3178, www.atlantaaa.org
- **Alcohol Treatment Center**, 24 Hour Helpline, 800-711-1000
- **Drug HelpLine**, 800-662-HELP, www.drughelp.org
- **Focus Healthcare**, 24 Hour Substance Abuse Helpline, 800-234-0420, www.focushealthcare.com
- **National Substance Abuse HelpLine**, 800-378-4435
- **Narcotics Anonymous**, 800-711-6375, www.grscna.com
- **Northside Hospital Recovery Center**, Alcohol & Drug Services, 404-851-8961, www.northside.com

ANIMALS

- **Animal Bites**, 911
- **Animal Control, Cherokee County**, 678-493-6200, www.cherokeega.com
- **Animal Control, Cobb County**, 770-499-4136, www.cobbanimalcontrol.org
- **Animal Control, DeKalb County**, 404-294-2996, http://dekalbpolice.com/ac
- **Animal Control, Fulton County**, 404-794-0358, www.fultonanimalservices.com

- **Animal Control, Gwinnett County**, 770-339-3200, www.gwinnettanimalcontrol.com
- **Animal Emergency Clinic (Atlanta)**, 1911 Piedmont Circle, Atlanta, 404-252-7881
- **Animal Emergency Clinic (DeKalb-Gwinnett)**, 6430 Lawrenceville Highway, Tucker, 770-491-0661
- **Atlanta Dead Animal Removal**, 404-330-6333, www.atlantaga.gov/government/publicworks.aspx
- **Atlanta Humane Society**, 404-875-5331, www.atlhumane.org
- **Cherokee County Humane Society**, 770-928-5115, www.cc humanesociety.org
- **Cobb County Humane Society**, 770-428-5678, www.humane cobb.org
- **Gwinnett County Humane Society**, 770-798-7711, www.gwinnett humane.com
- **PAWS Atlanta** (the **DeKalb County Humane Society**), 770-593-1155, www.pawsatlanta.org

AUTOMOBILES

- **Abandoned Vehicle Removal**, 404-658-6666, www.atlantapd.org
- **American Automobile Association (AAA)**, 404-222-1134, www.aaa.com
- **Atlanta Police Property** (number to call for impounded cars), 404-853-4330, www.atlantapd.org
- **State Department of Motor Vehicles, Tag, and Title Information**, 404-362-6500, www.dmvs.ga.gov

PARKING VIOLATIONS
- **Parking Collections**, 404-658-6886, www.atlantaga.gov
- **Parking Violations**, 404-658-6935, www.atlantaga.gov
- **Traffic Court—General Ticket Information**, 404-658-6940, www.atlantaga.gov

BIRTH AND DEATH RECORDS

- **State of Georgia, Department of Vital Records**, 404-679-4701, http://health.state.ga.us

CONSUMER COMPLAINTS AND SERVICES

- **Atlanta Bar Association**, 404-521-0781, www.atlantabar.org

- **Atlanta Chamber of Commerce**, 404-880-9000, www.metro atlantachamber.com
- **Better Business Bureau of Metropolitan Atlanta**, 404-766-0875, www.atlanta.bbb.org
- **Consumer Product Safety Commission**, 404-730-2870, 800-638-2772, www.cpsc.gov
- **Federal Trade Commission**, 404-656-1390, 877-382-4357, www.ftc.gov
- **State Attorney General Consumer Affairs Division**, 404-656-3790, http://ganet.org/ago
- **State Insurance Commissioner**, 404-656-2070, 800-656-2298, www.inscomm.state.ga.us
- **State Consumer Affairs Office**, 404-651-8600, 800-869-1123, www2.state.ga.us/gaoca
- **US Attorney General, Northern District of Georgia**, 404-581-6000, www.usdoj.gov/usao/gan
- **US Public Interest Research Group (USPIRG)**, 404-892-3403, http://uspirg.org, www.pirg.org

CRISIS

CHILD ABUSE AND NEGLECT
- **Cherokee County Child Protective Services**, 770-720-3610, www.cherokeega.com
- **Cobb County Child Protective Services**, 770-528-5015, www. cobbdfcs.state.ga.us
- **DeKalb County Child Protective Services**, 404-370-5066, www. co.dekalb.ga.us/dfcs
- **Fulton County Child Protective Services**, 404-699-4399, www. fultondfacs.org
- **Gwinnett County Child Protective Services**, 770-995-2122, www.gwinnettcounty.com
- **State of Georgia Department of Family and Children Services**, 404-463-7291, http://dfcs.dhr.georgia.gov

CRIME
- **Crime in Progress**, 911
- **Crime & Trauma Scene Cleanup Assistance**, 888-979-2272, www.americanbiorecovery.org
- **Atlanta Police Department**, 404-853-3434, www.atlantapd.org
- **Cherokee County Sheriff's Office**, 678-493-4200, www.cherokee ga-sheriff.org

- **Cobb County Police Department**, 770-499-3900, www.cobb countypolice.com
- **Cobb County PD Crime Prevention Unit**, 770-499-3909, www.cobbpolice.com/crime_prevention.htm
- **DeKalb County Police Department**, 404-294-2519, www.dekalbpolice.com;
- **DeKalb County PD Crime Prevention Unit**, 404-294-2610, www.dekalbpolice.com
- **Fulton County Police Department**, 770-495-8738, www.fulton police.org
- **Gwinnett County Police Department**, 770-513-5000, www.gwinnettcounty.com
- **Gwinnett County PD Crime Prevention Unit**, 770-623-2610, www.gwinnettcounty.com
- **State Patrol Office**, 404-624-7000, http://dps.georgia.gov
- **Victim-Witness Assistance Program**, 404-865-8127, www.atlanta-vwap.com

RAPE AND SEXUAL ASSAULT SERVICES
- **Cherokee/Cobb Rape Crisis Center**, **Crisis Line**, 770-427-3390
- **DeKalb Rape Crisis Center**, **Crisis Line**, 404-377-1428
- **Georgia Network to End Sexual Assault**, 678-701-2700, www.gnesa.org
- **Grady Hospital Rape Crisis Center**, **Crisis Line**, 404-616-4861
- **Gwinnett Sexual Assault Center**, **Crisis Line**, 770-476-7407

DISCRIMINATION

- **Atlanta Human Services**, 404-330-6360, www.atlantaga.gov/government/humanresources.aspx
- **Cobb County Community Services Board**, 770-429-5000, www.cobbcsb.com
- **DeKalb County Community Relations Commission**, 404-371-2393, www.co.dekalb.ga.us
- **Fulton County Human Services Department**, 404-730-7944, www.co.fulton.ga.us
- **Georgia Commission on Equal Opportunity (Employment)**, 404-656-1736, http://gceo.state.ga.us
- **Georgia Commission on Equal Opportunity (Housing)**, 404-656-7708, http://gceo.state.ga.us/housing.htm
- **Gwinnett County Community Services Department**, 770-822-8880, www.gwinnettcounty.com

- **State Department of Community Affairs**, 404-679-4840, www.dca.state.ga.us
- **US Government Employment Discrimination Department**, 800-669-4000, www.eeoc.gov
- **US Government Health & Human Services, Office for Civil Rights**, 800-368-1019, www.hhs.gov/ocr/index.html
- **US Government Housing Discrimination Department**, 800-669-9777, www.fairhousinglaw.org

ELECTED OFFICIALS AND GOVERNMENT

BOARD OF ELECTIONS
- **Board of Elections (Cherokee County)**, 770-479-0595, www.cherokeega.com
- **Board of Elections (Cobb County)**, 770-528-2300, www.cobbelections.org
- **Board of Elections (DeKalb County)**, 404-298-4020, http://dklbweb.dekalbga.org/voter
- **Board of Elections (Fulton County)**, 404-730-7072, www.co.fulton.ga.us
- **Board of Elections (Gwinnett County)**, 770-822-8787, www.gwinnettcounty.com
- **Secretary of State, Elections Division**, 404-656-2871, www.sos.state.ga.us

CITY OF ATLANTA
- **Atlanta City Council**, 404-330-6030, www.atlantaga.gov
- **Atlanta Mayor's Office**, 404-330-6100, www.atlantaga.gov/mayor

COUNTY OFFICIALS
- **Cherokee County Government**, 678-493-6000, www.cherokeega.com
- **Cobb County Government**, 770-528-1101, www.co.cobb.ga.us
- **DeKalb County Government**, 404-371-2000, www.dekalb.ga.us
- **Fulton County Government**, 404-730-4000, www.co.fulton.ga.us
- **Gwinnett County Government**, 770-822-8000, www.co.gwinnett.ga.us

STATE GOVERNMENT
- **Georgia State Government Official Web Site**, www.georgia.gov
- **Georgia Secretary of State**, 404-656-2881, www.sos.state.ga.us
- **Georgia Governor's Office**, 404-656-1776, www.gov.state.ga.us

EMERGENCY

For fire, police, or medical emergencies in the greater Atlanta area dial 911. If you are calling DeKalb County from another county in the metropolitan area, dial 404-294-2493.

ENTERTAINMENT

FINE ARTS
- **Alliance Theatre**, 404-733-5000, www.alliancetheatre.org
- **Arts at Emory**, 404-727-6187, www.emory.edu/arts
- **Arts Hotline**, 404-853-3ART
- **Atlanta Ballet**, 404-892-3303, www.atlantaballet.com
- **Atlanta Coalition of Performing Arts**, 404-873-1185, www.atlantaperforms.com
- **Atlanta Entertainment Online**, http://atlantaentertainment.com
- **Atlanta Symphony Orchestra**, 404-733-4949, www.atlantasymphony.org
- **Ballethnic Dance Company**, 404-762-1416, http://ballethnic.org
- **City of Atlanta Bureau of Cultural Affairs**, 404-817-6815, www.bcaatlanta.com
- *Creative Loafing* **Online Happenings Calendar**, www.creativeloafing.com/happenings
- **Fulton County Arts Council**, 404-730-5780, www.fultonarts.org
- **99Xtension Music Line**, 404-364-0997, www.99x.com
- **TicketMaster**, 404-249-6400, www.ticketmaster.com

VENUES
- **Atlanta Civic Center**, 404-523-6275, www.atlantaciviccenter.com
- **Chastain Park Amphitheater**, 404-233-2227, www.atlantaconcerts.com/chastain.html
- **The Coca-Cola Roxy Theatre**, 404-233-7699, www.atlantaconcerts.com/roxy.html
- **Earthlink Live**, 404-885-1365, www.earthlinklive.com
- **The Fox Theatre**, 404-881-2100, www.foxtheatre.org
- **The Georgia Dome**, 404-223-9200, www.gadome.com
- **The Gwinnett Civic Center Arena**, 770-813-7500, www.gwinnettciviccenter.com
- **HiFi Buys Lakewood Amphitheater**, 404-443-5090, www.hob.com/venues/concerts/hifibuys
- **Rialto Center for the Performing Arts**, 404-651-1234, www.rialtocenter.org

- **Philips Arena**, 404-878-3000, www.philipsarena.com
- **Variety Playhouse**, 404-524-7354, www.variety-playhouse.com
- **Woodruff Arts Center**, 404-733-5000, www.woodruffcenter.org

HEALTH AND MEDICAL CARE

- **AIDS Advisory Hotline**, 404-222-0800
- **AIDS Hotline—CDC National**, 800-342-AIDS
- **Alzheimer's Association, Georgia Chapter**, 404-728-1181, www.alzga.org
- **American Cancer Society**, 800-ACS-2345, www.cancer.org
- **American Lung Association of Georgia**, 770-434-5864, www.lungusa.org
- **Board of Health (Cherokee County)**, 770-345-7371, www.cherokeega.com
- **Board of Health (Cobb County)**, 770-514-2300, www.cobbanddouglaspublichealth.org
- **Board of Health (DeKalb County)**, 404-294-3700, www.dekalbhealth.net
- **Board of Health (Fulton County)**, 404-730-1211, www.co.fulton.ga.us/departments/health.html
- **Board of Health (Gwinnett County)**, 770-963-5142, www.gwinnettcounty.com
- **Diabetes Association of Atlanta**, 404-527-7150, www.diabetesatlanta.org
- **Families First**, 404-853-2800, www.familiesfirst.org
- **Poison Control Center** (metro Atlanta), 404-616-9000, 800-222-1222, http://gpc.dhr.georgia.gov

HOUSING

- **Atlanta Housing Authority**, 404-892-4700, www.ahaweb.org
- **Atlanta Neighborhood Development Partnership**, 404-522-2637, www.andpi.org
- **City of Atlanta Housing Code Enforcement**, 404-330-6190, www.atlantaga.gov/government/planning.aspx
- **US Department of Housing and Urban Development, Georgia**, 404-331-5136, www.hud.gov/local/index.cfm?state=ga

IMMIGRATION

- **Bureau of Immigration and Customs Enforcement**, www.bice.immigration.gov

- **Customs and Border Protection**, www.cbp.gov
- **Department of Homeland Security**, www.dhs.gov; www.whitehouse.gov/deptofhomeland
- **General Government Questions**, 800-688-9889, www.first gov.gov
- **Social Security Administration**, 800-772-1213, www.ssa.gov
- **US Bureau of Consular Affairs**, www.travel.state.gov
- **US Citizenship and Immigration Services (USCIS)**, 800-375-5283, www.uscis.gov
- **US Department of State, Visa Services**, http://travel.state.gov/visa_services
- **US Immigration Online—Green Cards, Visas, Government Forms**, www.usaimmigrationservice.org

LEGAL REFERRAL

- **AAA Attorney Referral Service of Georgia**, 404-252-8808
- **Atlanta Attorneys Online**, www.theattorneydirectory.com/georgia/atlanta.htm
- **Atlanta Bar Association**, 404-521-0777, www.atlantabar.org
- **Atlanta Legal Aid Society**, 404-524-5811, www.atlantalegalaid.org
- **Atlanta Volunteer Lawyers Foundation**, 404-521-0790, http://avlf.org
- **Legal Aid Georgia**, www.legalaid-ga.org/ga/index.cfm

LIBRARIES

See also **Libraries** in **Cultural Life**, and end-listings in the **Neighborhood Profiles**.
- **Cherokee County Central Library**, 770-345-7565, www.sequoyahregionallibrary.org
- **Cobb County Central Library**, 770-528-2320, www.cobbcat.org
- **DeKalb County Central Library**, 404-370-3070, www.dekalb.public.lib.ga.us
- **Fulton County Central Library**, 404-730-1700, www.af.public.lib.ga.us
- **Gwinnett County Central Library**, 770-822-4522, www.gwinnettpl.org
- **Smyrna Public Library**, 770-431-2860, www.smyrna-library.com

MARRIAGE LICENSES

- **Cherokee County Probate Court**, 678-493-6160, www.cherokeega.com
- **Cobb County Probate Court**, 770-528-1900, www.cobbcounty.org/judicial
- **DeKalb County Probate Court**, 404-371-2601, https://dklbweb.dekalbga.org/courts/probate
- **Fulton County Probate Court**, 404-730-4692, www.co.fulton.ga.us
- **Gwinnett County Probate Court**, 770-822-8250, www.gwinnettcourts.com

MUNICIPALITIES

CITY OF ATLANTA
- **Atlanta City Council**, 404-330-6030, www.atlantaga.gov
- **Atlanta City Hall**, 55 Trinity Avenue, Atlanta, 404-330-6000, www.atlantaga.gov
- **Atlanta Mayor's Office**, 404-330-6100, www.atlantaga.gov/mayor

METRO ATLANTA
- **City of Alpharetta**, 678-297-6000, www.alpharetta.ga.us
- **City of Austell**, 770-944-4300, www.austell.org
- **City of Avondale Estates**, 404-294-5400, http://avondaleestates.org
- **City of Canton**, 770-704-1500, www.canton-georgia.com
- **City of Chamblee**, 770-986-5010, www.chambleega.com
- **City of Decatur**, 404-370-4100, www.decatur-ga.com
- **City of Lawrenceville**, 770-963-2414, www.lawrencevillegaweb.org
- **City of Lithonia**, 770-482-8136, www.cityoflithonia.org
- **City of Marietta**, 770-794-5501, www.city.marietta.ga.us
- **City of Norcross**, 770-448-2122, www.norcrossga.net
- **City of Roswell**, 770-641-3727, www.ci.roswell.ga.us
- **City of Smyrna**, 770-434-6600, www.ci.smyrna.ga.us
- **City of Stone Mountain**, 770-498-8984, www.stonemountaincity.org
- **City of Woodstock**, 770-592-6007, www.ci.woodstock.ga.us

PARKS AND RECREATION DEPARTMENTS

COUNTY DEPARTMENTS
- **Cherokee County Parks and Recreation Department**, 770-924-7768, www.crpa.net
- **Cobb County Parks and Recreation Department**, 770-528-8800, www.cobbcounty.org
- **DeKalb County Parks and Recreation Department**, 404-371-2631, www.co.dekalb.ga.us/parks
- **Fulton County Parks and Recreation Department**, 404-730-6200, www.co.fulton.ga.us
- **Gwinnett County Parks and Recreation Department**, 770-822-8875, www.co.gwinnett.ga.us

CITY DEPARTMENTS
- **Alpharetta Parks and Recreation Department**, 678-297-6100, http://alpharetta.ga.us
- **Atlanta City Parks and Recreation Bureau**, 404-817-6788, www.atlantaga.gov
- **Chamblee Parks and Recreation Department**, 770-986-5016, www.chambleega.com
- **City of Decatur Parks and Recreation Department**, 404-377-0494, www.decatur-ga.com
- **Marietta Parks and Recreation Department**, 770-794-5601, www.city.marietta.ga.us
- **Roswell Parks and Recreation Department**, 770-641-3760, www.ci.roswell.ga.us

POLICE

- **Atlanta,** emergency, 911; non-emergency, 404-853-3434, www.atlantapd.org
- **Cherokee County**, emergency, 911; non-emergency, 678-493-4200, www.cherokeega-sheriff.org
- **Cobb County**, emergency, 911; non-emergency, 770-499-3900, www.cobbpolice.com
- **DeKalb County**, emergency within DeKalb County, 911; emergency outside DeKalb County, 404-294-2493; non-emergency, 404-294-2519, www.dekalbpolice.com
- **Fulton County**, emergency, 911; non-emergency, 404-730-5700, www.fultonpolice.org

- **Gwinnett County**, emergency, 911; non-emergency, 770-513-5000, www.gwinnettcounty.com
- **Georgia State Patrol**, 404-624-7000, http://dps.georgia.gov
- US Marshall's Service, Northern District of Georgia, **404-331-6833, www.usdoj.gov/marshals**

POST OFFICE

For information about the main post office, see **Mail Delivery** in the **Helpful Services** chapter. For addresses of neighborhood post offices, check the end-listings in the **Neighborhood Profiles**.
- **US Postal Service**, 800-275-8777, www.usps.com

ROADS

STREET MAINTENANCE
- **Atlanta**, www.atlantaga.gov/government/publicworks.aspx; days, 404-330-6654; nights, weekends, and holidays, 404-65-WORKS
- **Cherokee County**, 770-345-5842, www.cherokeega.com/ccweb/departments/public_works/rb
- **Cobb County**, www.cobbdot.org: days, 770-528-3666; nights, weekends, and holidays, 770-419-6201
- **DeKalb County**, www.co.dekalb.ga.us/publicwrks/index.htm: days, 404-297-3840; nights, weekends, and holidays, 404-294-2523
- **Fulton County**, 404-730-7400, www.co.fulton.ga.us/departments/public_works.html
- **Gwinnett County**, 770-822-7474, www.gwinnettcounty.com

ROAD CONDITION/TRAFFIC INFORMATION
- **AJC Metro Online**, www.ajc.com/metro/content/metro/traffic
- **Georgia DOT Road Condition Information**, 404-635-6800, www.georgia-navigator.com
- **Georgia DOT Traffic Information**, 404-624-1300, ext. 1000, www.georgia-navigator.com

SANITATION AND GARBAGE

- **Atlanta Public Works Department**, 404-659-6757, www.atlantaga.gov
- **City of Austell Sanitation Department**, 770-944-4300, www.austell.org

- **City of Decatur Sanitation Department**, 404-377-5571, www. decatur-ga.com
- **City of Marietta Sanitation Department**, 770-794-5581, www. city.marietta.ga.us
- **City of Smyrna Sanitation Department**, 770-319-5338, www. smyrnacity.com
- **Cobb County Garbage Pick Up**, 770-528-2500, www. cobbcounty.org
- **DeKalb County Sanitation Department**, 404-294-2900, www. co.dekalb.ga.us
- **Fulton County Garbage Pick Up**, 404-730-7400, www.co. fulton.ga.us
- **Gwinnett County Garbage Pick Up**, 770-822-5187, www. gwinnettcb.org

RECYCLING

- **City of Atlanta Recycling Hotline**, 404-792-1212, www. dreamsan.com/atlantarecycling.htm
- **Cobb County Recycling Information**, 770-528-1135, www. cobbcounty.org
- **DeKalb County Recycling Information**, 404-294-2900, www. co.dekalb.ga.us
- **Fulton County Recycling Information**, 404-730-8097, www.co.fulton.ga.us
- **Gwinnett County Recycling Information**, 770-822-5187, www.gwinnettcb.org

SCHOOLS

- **Georgia Department of Education**, 404-656-2800, www.doe.k12.ga.us
- **Atlanta City Schools**, 404-827-8599, www.atlanta.k12.ga.us
- **Cherokee County Schools**, 770-479-1871, www.cherokee.k12.ga.us
- **Cobb County Schools**, 770-426-3300, www.cobb.k12.ga.us
- **DeKalb County Schools**, 678-676-1200, www.dekalb.k12.ga.us
- **Fulton County Schools**, 404-768-3600, www.fulton.k12.ga.us
- **Gwinnett County Schools**, 770-963-8651, www.gwinnett. k12.ga.us

SENIORS

- **American Association of Retired Persons (AARP)**, **Georgia Office**, 404-881-0292, www.aarp.org/ga

- **The Center for Positive Aging**, 404-872-9191, http://center forpositiveaging.org
- **Cobb Senior Services**, 770-528-5364, www.cobbseniors.org
- **Fulton County Office of Aging**, 404-730-6000, www.co. fulton.ga.us
- **Georgia Association of Homes & Services for the Aging**, 404-872-9191, www.gahsa.org
- **Georgia Council on Aging**, 404-657-5343, www.gcoa.org
- **Georgia Nursing Home Association**, 678-289-6555, www.gnha. org
- **Georgia Senior Legal Hotline**, 404-657-9915, 888-257-9519, http://postscripts.tripod.com/id15.html
- **Gwinnett Coalition for Health and Human Services**, 770-995-3339, www.gwinnettcoalition.org
- **Medicare Fraud & Abuse Hotline**, 800-447-8477, www.medi care.gov
- **National Caucus & Center on Black Aged, Atlanta Office**, 404-892-6222, www.ncba-aged.org
- **Retired Senior Volunteer Program (RSVP) of Metro Atlanta**, 404-206-5005, www.seniorcorps.org
- **Seniors Enriched Living, Inc.**, 770-587-3750, www.sel-web.org
- **Social Security Administration**, 800-772-1213, www.ssa.gov

SHIPPING SERVICES

- **DHL**, 800-225-5345, www.dhl.com
- **Delta Dash**, 800-352-2746, www.delta.com/prog_serv/cargo/dash/index.jsp
- **FedEx**, 800-463-3339, www.fedex.com
- **Roadway Express**, 888-550-9800, www.roadway.com
- **UPS**, 800-742-5877, www.ups.com
- **US Postal Service Express Mail**, 800-222-1811, www.usps.com

SPORTS

- **Atlanta Braves**, 404-522-7630, www.atlantabraves.com
- **Atlanta Hawks**, 404-827-3865, www.nba.com/hawks
- **Atlanta Falcons**, 404-223-8000, www.nfl.com/falcons
- **Atlanta Thrashers**, 404-584-7825, www.atlantathrashers.com
- **The Masters Tournament**, 706-667-6000, www.masters.com
- **Clark Atlanta University Athletic Department**, 404-880-8126, www.cau.edu

- **Emory University Athletic Department**, 404-727-6547, www.emory.edu
- **Georgia State University Athletic Department**, 404-651-3166, www.gsu.edu
- **Georgia Tech Athletic Department**, 404-894-5447, http://ramblinwreck.collegesports.com
- **Morehouse College Athletic Department**, 404-215-2669, www.morehouse.edu
- **Morris Brown College Athletic Department**, 404-220-0270, www.morrisbrown.edu
- **Oglethorpe University Athletic Department**, 404-364-8422, www.oglethorpe.edu
- **University of Georgia Athletic Department**, 706-542-1231, http://georgiadogs.collegesports.com

TAXES

- **Federal**, www.irs.gov
  Income, 800-829-1040
  Forms, 800-829-3676
- **State**, www2.state.ga.us/departments/dor
  Income, 404-417-3210
  Forms, 404-417-6011
  Taxpayers Assistance, 404-417-2300
  Refunds, 404-656-6286
- **Cherokee County**, www.cherokeega.com
  Property Tax, 770-479-0439
  Tax Assessor, 770-479-0433
- **Cobb County**, www.cobbcounty.org/tax
  Property Tax, 770-528-8600
  Tax Assessor, 770-528-3100
- **DeKalb County**, www.co.dekalb.ga.us
  Property Tax, 404-298-4000
  Tax Assessor, 404-371-2471
- **Fulton County**, www.co.fulton.ga.us
  Property Tax, 404-730-6100
  Tax Assessor, 404-730-6400
- **Gwinnett County**, www.gwinnettcounty.com
  Property Tax, 770-822-8800
  Tax Assessor, 770-822-7200

TAXI SERVICE

- **Atlanta Yellow Cab Company**, 404-521-0200
- **Buckhead Safety Cab**, 404-875-3777
- **Checker Cab Company**, 404-351-1111
- **Norcross/Gwinnett Cab Company**, 770-458-1600
- **Style Taxi**, 404-522-8294, www.styletaxi.com

TELEPHONE

- **AT&T**, 800-222-0300, www.att.com
- **Alltel**, 800-501-1754, www.alltel.com
- **BellSouth**, 404-780-2355, 800-356-3094, www.bellsouth.com
- **MCI**, 800-444-3333, www.mci.com
- **Sprint**, 800-877-4646, www.sprint.com
- **Verizon**, 800-343-2092, www22.verizon.com

TOURISM AND TRAVEL

- **Atlanta Convention & Visitor's Bureau**, 404-521-6600, www.atlanta.net
- **Georgia Department of Tourism**, 800-VISIT GA, www.georgia.org
- **Georgia State Parks and Historic Sites**, 404-656-2770, 800-864-7275, www.gastateparks.org
- **National Park Service**, 800-365-2267, www.nps.gov
- **National Forest Service Reservation Line**, 877-444-6777, www.reserveusa.com

TRANSPORTATION

- **Amtrak**, 800-872-7245, www.amtrak.com
- **Atlanta Regional Commission's Ride Find**, 1-87-RIDEFIND, www.187ridefind.com
- **Cobb Community Transit**, 770-427-4444, www.cobbdot.org
- **DeKalb Peachtree Airport**, 770-936-5440, www.pdkairport.org
- **Greyhound Bus**, 800-231-2222, www.greyhound.com
- **Gwinnett County Transit**, 770-822-5010, www.gctransit.com
- **Hartsfield-Jackson International Airport**, 404-530-7300, www.atlanta-airport.com
- **MARTA**, 404-848-4711, www.itsmarta.com

UTILITY EMERGENCIES

ELECTRICITY
- **City of Acworth**, 770-974-5233
- **City of Buford**, 770-945-6761
- **City of Lawrenceville**, 770-963-2414
- **City of Norcross**, 770-448-2112
- **Cobb EMC**, 770-429-2100, 770-429-2110
- **Georgia Power Company**, 404-325-4001, 888-891-0938
- **Jackson EMC**, 770-963-6166
- **Sawnee EMC**, 770-887-2363
- **Snapping Shoals EMC**, 770-786-3484
- **Walton EMC**, 770-972-2917, 800-342-6582

GAS
- **Atlanta Gas Light 24-Hour Line**, 770-994-1946

LOCAL PHONE
- **BellSouth**, 404-780-2355, 800-356-3094

WATER
- **City of Atlanta Water Emergency**, 404-658-7220
- **City of Austell Water Emergency**, 770-944-4321
- **City of Marietta Water & Sewer Emergency**, 770-794-5230
- **City of Roswell Water Emergency**, 770-640-4100
- **Cobb County Water Emergency**, 770-419-6201
- **DeKalb County Water Emergency**, 770-270-6243
- **Fulton County Water Emergency**, 770-640-3040
- **Gwinnett County Water Emergency**, 678-376-7000

VOTING

For a list of voting stations, refer to **Voting** in the **Getting Settled** chapter. For Board of Elections officers, see above under **Elected Officials and Government**.
- **Cherokee County**, www.cherokeega.com
- **Cobb County**, www.cobbelections.org
- **DeKalb County**, https://dklbweb.dekalbga.org/voter
- **Fulton County**, www.co.fulton.ga.us

- **Georgia Secretary of State, Elections Division**, 404-656-2871, www.sos.state.ga.us/elections
- **Gwinnett County**, 770-822-8787, www.gwinnettcounty.com

WEATHER INFORMATION, 770-632-1837

ZIP CODE INFORMATION, 800-275-8777, www.usps.com

MARTA MAP

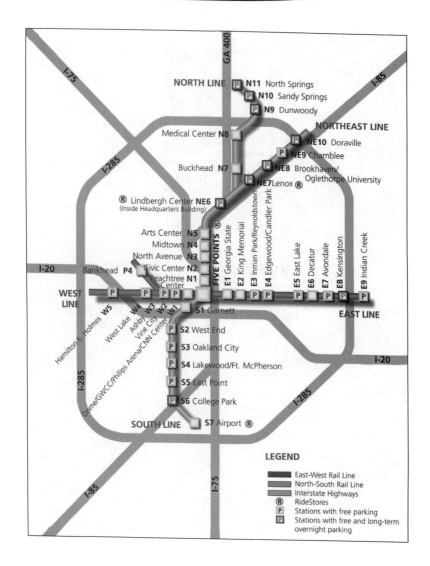

FIRST BOOKS®

Visit our web site at

www.firstbooks.com

for information on all our books.